Collaborative Enterprise Architecture

T0229200

Collaborative Enterprise Architecture
Enriching EA with Lean, Agile, and Enterprise 2.0 Practices

Stefan Bente

Dr. Uwe Bombosch

Shailendra Langade

AMSTERDAM • BOSTON • HEIDELBERG • LONDON
NEW YORK • OXFORD • PARIS • SAN DIEGO
SAN FRANCISCO • SINGAPORE • SYDNEY • TOKYO

Morgan Kaufmann is an imprint of Elsevier

Acquiring Editor: Andrea Dierna
Development Editor: Robyn Day
Project Manager: Jessica Vaughan
Designer: Greg Harris

Morgan Kaufmann is an imprint of Elsevier
225 Wyman Street, Waltham, MA 02451, USA

© 2012 Elsevier, Inc. All rights reserved.

No part of this publication may be reproduced or transmitted in any form or by any means, electronic
or mechanical, including photocopying, recording, or any information storage and retrieval system,
without permission in writing from the publisher. Details on how to seek permission, further information about the
Publisher's permissions policies and our arrangements with organizations such as the Copyright Clearance Center
and the Copyright Licensing Agency, can be found at our website: www.elsevier.com/permissions.

This book and the individual contributions contained in it are protected under copyright by the Publisher (other
than as may be noted herein).

Notices
Knowledge and best practice in this field are constantly changing. As new research and experience broaden
our understanding, changes in research methods or professional practices, may become necessary. Practitioners
and researchers must always rely on their own experience and knowledge in evaluating and using any
information or methods described herein. In using such information or methods they should be mindful of
their own safety and the safety of others, including parties for whom they have a professional responsibility.

To the fullest extent of the law, neither the Publisher nor the authors, contributors, or editors, assume any liability
for any injury and/or damage to persons or property as a matter of products liability, negligence or otherwise, or
from any use or operation of any methods, products, instructions, or ideas contained in the material herein.

Library of Congress Cataloging-in-Publication Data
Bente, Stefan.
  Collaborative enterprise architecture : enriching EA with lean, agile, and enterprise 2.0 practices /
Stefan Bente, Uwe Bombosch, Shailendra Langade.
      p. cm.
  Includes bibliographical references and index.
  ISBN 978-0-12-415934-1
  1. Management information systems. 2. Business enterprises–Computer networks. 3. Information technology–
Management. 4. Software architecture. I. Bombosch, Uwe. II. Langade, Shailendra. III. Title.
  HD30.213.B463 2013
  658.4'038011–dc23

                                                                                              2012014682

British Library Cataloguing-in-Publication Data
A catalogue record for this book is available from the British Library.

ISBN: 978-0-12-415934-1

Printed and bound by CPI Group (UK) Ltd, Croydon, CR0 4YY

Transferred to digital print 2012

Working together to grow
libraries in developing countries

www.elsevier.com | www.bookaid.org | www.sabre.org

ELSEVIER   BOOK AID
            International   Sabre Foundation

For information on all MK publications visit our website at www.mkp.com

To our families (Beate and Thomas; Christiane and Julian; Deepali, Pratik, and Tanishka), with many thanks for their support and patience.

Contents

Acknowledgments xi

CHAPTER 1 Why Collaborative Enterprise Architecture? 1
Reasons for This Book 1
Goals and Benefits of Enterprise Architecture 4
    Controlling IT Complexity 6
    Aligning Business and IT 9
The Gray Reality: Enterprise Architecture Failures 11
    Between Success and Disappointment 12
    Perspective: Between Bird's-Eye View and Nitty-Gritty on the Ground 14
    Governance: A Host of Directives, but No One Follows Them 19
    Strategy: Marathon or 100 m Run? 21
    Transformation: Between Standstill and Continuous Revolution 23
Enriching EA by Lean, Agile, and Enterprise 2.0 Practices 25
    How This Book Is Structured 28

CHAPTER 2 What Is Enterprise Architecture? 31
The Meaning of Architecture 31
Applying Architecture to an Enterprise 34
EA Applicability and Use 36

CHAPTER 3 What Enterprise Architects Do: Core Activities of EA 39
Defining the IT Strategy (EA-1) 41
    Defining the Goals 42
    Stipulating the Rules 43
    The Gartner Grid 46
    Identifying the Initiatives 48
    The Role of an Enterprise Architect 49
Modeling the Architectures (EA-2) 49
    Models and Views of Various Architectures 49
    Visualizing Cross-Relations and Transformations 51
    Modeling Standards 52
Evolving the IT Landscape (EA-3) 58
    Application Rationalization 58
    General IT Transformations 66
    SOA Transformations 67
Assessing and Building Capabilities (EA-4) 69
    Competence Development for Enterprise Architects 69

Formalizing Enterprise Architecture 74
EA Team Position in the Organization Structure 76
Developing and Enforcing Standards and Guidelines (EA-5) 78
Standardizing on Technology Usage 79
Enforcing Standards and Guidelines 83
Monitoring the Project Portfolio (EA-6) 86
Building the Project Portfolio 87
Auditing the Portfolio 93
Leading or Coaching Projects (EA-7) 98
Managing Risks Involved in IT (EA-8) 100

CHAPTER 4   EA Frameworks 105
What is an EA Framework? 106
The Zachman Framework for Enterprise Architecture 108
The Open Group Architecture Framework (TOGAF) 110
TOGAF Architecture Development Methodology (ADM) 111
TOGAF Architecture Content Framework 114
TOGAF Architecture Capability Framework 115
Gartner Methodology (Formerly META Framework) 118
The Role and Use of EA frameworks 121

CHAPTER 5   EA Maturity Models 123
Applying Maturity Model to EA 124
What is a Maturity Model? 124
Relevance of Maturity Models in EA 126
A Rule of Thumb for the Architectural Maturity of an Enterprise 126
OMB EA Assessment Framework 127
Architecture Capability Maturity Model of the US Department of Commerce ... 130
EA Maturity Model by MIT Center for Information System Research 132
Experiences with the Maturity Models 134

CHAPTER 6   Foundations of Collaborative EA 137
Reflections on Complexity 139
Beyond Threshing Machines 139
Structure and Behavior of Complex Phenomena 140
Principles of Managing Complexity 141
Management Capabilities of Hierarchies and Networks 146
The EA Dashboard as a Yardstick for EA Effectiveness 152

CHAPTER 7   Toward Pragmatism: Lean and Agila EA 159
The Architecture Factory: Applying Lean and Agile Methods to EA 160
Lean and Agile Principles as Facilitators for the Architecture Factory 162

Definition of a Lean and Agile EA 163
Lean and Agile Principles 165
   Team-driven and Flexible: Agile Software Development 165
   Learning from Mass Production: Lean Software Development 174
   Lean and Agile: Parallels and Differences 180
Building Block 1: Get Rid of Waste by Streamlining Architecture Processes 182
   The Seven Wastes of EA 183
   Value Stream Analysis Tools for EA 193
   Transition to a Lean and Agile EA Organization 203
   Summing It Up: Assessment by the EA Dashboard 205
Building Block 2: Involve all Stakeholders by Interlocking Architecture Scrums ..205
   An Agile EA Project 206
   Scrum Patterns for EA 209
   Summing It Up: Assessment by the EA Dashboard 215
Building Block 3: Practice Iterative Architecture Through EA Kanban 216
   Agile EA Requirements Management 217
   An EA Kanban Board Using TOGAF ADM 222
   Synchronization with Implementation Projects 230
   Summing It Up: Assessment by the EA Dashboard 233

CHAPTER 8   Inviting to Participation: EAM 2.0 235
A Primer on Enterprise 2.0 237
Building Block 4: Participation in Knowledge 246
   The Strategy Blog 247
   Collaborative Data Modeling: The ObjectPedia 249
   Weak Ties and a Self-Organizing Application Landscape 251
   Summing It Up: Assessment by the EA Dashboard 256
Building Block 5: Participation in Decisions 258
   The Diagnostic Process Landscape 259
   The Bazaar of IT Opportunities 261
   Summing It Up: Assessment by the EA Dashboard 264
Building Block 6: Participation in Transformation 265
   Mashing Up the Architecture Continuum 265
   The Change Management Microblog 270
   Summing It Up: Assessment by the EA Dashboard 277
The Bottom Line: Inviting to Explore 278

CHAPTER 9   The Next Steps: Taking Collaborative EA Forward 279
A Summary 279
Getting Started with Collaborative EA 283
   Interpreting the Organizational Attitude Toward Change 283

Motivate the Elephant 286
Direct the Rider 288
Shape the Path 290
Looking Ahead 293

Appendix: The Bank4Us Staff 295
References 297
Index 303

Acknowledgments

Writing a book is a strenuous journey. We are indebted to many people who helped us along the way.

Murali Padmanabhan, at the time coordinating the Tata Consultancy Services (TCS) learning and development initiative, established our early contact to Elsevier India. Without his efforts the book idea would never have taken off in the first place.

We are sincerely grateful to the TCS management, in particular to Krishnan Ramanujam and Santosh Mohanty, for their motivation, support, and friendly eye toward the book. Hermann Klein and Ingo Rosenstein, by their kind permission, made it possible for us to work on the book project.

Many thanks go to numerous colleagues at TCS, especially to Harish Iyer, Bernd Linowski, and Ameya Vanjari. They not only listened to our continuous rambles about architecture; they also provided many useful insights in return.

Ravindra Asundi, Beate Beering, Dirk Fiege, Bernd Linowski, and Gero Seifert took the trouble to struggle through 180 pages of the half-finished book to uncover the structural weaknesses, and they kindly and patiently pointed out how we could fix them. We are deeply grateful for the time they invested, and the gentle yet effective feedback they gave.

Bhadresh Vyasa, Sandeep Karkera, and Vinu Jade dedicated their time to the project by allowing us to interview them in depth about their experiences in various aspects of EA. Many thanks for that!

We are indebted to several eminent authors in our field, most notably John Zachman from Zachman International, Jeanne W. Ross from the Center for Information Systems Research at the Massachusetts Institute of Technology, and Steve Nunn and Andrew Josey from The Open Group for their kind permission, backed by active support, to reprint some of their intellectual property in this book.

Craig Mullins and Wayne Eckerson reviewed the final manuscript, providing many useful comments and improvement proposals. Our heartfelt thanks also go to the editors at Morgan Kaufmann: Rachel Roumeliotis, Andrea Dierna, and Robyn Day. You all effectively helped us through the tedious exercise of writing and finishing this book on time.

Last but not least, our sincere gratitude goes to our wives. They willingly accepted the sight of husbands brooding over their laptops on weekends. They agreed to family funds flowing into a writing workshop in India instead of into long-deserved family vacations. Furthermore, they actively supported our work in numerous ways, from discussions over proofreading to stepping in when we (again) neglected our household duties in favor of an authors' phone conference. Beate, Christiane, and Deepali, we definitely owe you one.

Why Collaborative Enterprise Architecture?

1

CONTENT

Reasons for This Book 1
Goals and Benefits of Enterprise Architecture 4
    Controlling IT Complexity 6
    Aligning Business and IT.. 9
The Gray Reality: Enterprise Architecture Failures 11
    Between Success and Disappointment 12
    Perspective: Between Bird's-Eye View and Nitty-Gritty on the Ground 14
    Governance: A Host of Directives, but No One Follows Them 19
    Strategy: Marathon or 100 m Run? 21
    Transformation: Between Standstill and Continuous Revolution 23
Enriching EA by Lean, Agile, and Enterprise 2.0 Practices..25
    How This Book Is Structured 28

Reasons for this book

Enterprise architecture (EA) is often projected as a multipurpose medicine that cures an enterprise of all pains and problems. EA comes in different flavors—sometimes a marketing gimmick in management talks, sometimes a means to boast about knowledge of some framework or other, and sometimes an academic research topic. As a consequence, there seems to be a mystical mist surrounding the field of EA. This mist obscures the meaning and purpose of this field—not only for the naïve observer but also for the mature architect.

In our professional lives, we (the authors of this book) have approached EA from the ground up, coming from the basic levels of IT and software architecture. When EA groups were established in our organizations, we experienced both the benefits and the shortcomings of EA. When eventually taking over enterprise architect roles ourselves, we had our own sets of successes and blunders. Over the years and across different roles in the IT organization, we have become convinced that something as vitally necessary as EA should be organized in a more effective mode. This reorganization should appropriately involve all stakeholders in the decisions, including business users and developers, instead of

1

acting out of an elite inner circle. It should adopt a more incremental mode of working and drop unnecessary bureaucracy in order to become more flexible.

The first time we came in touch with EA was about ten to fifteen years ago. We were, in separate companies, working as software architects at the project level. Shailendra was employed by an IT consulting company doing various projects for customers around the globe. At the same time, Stefan and Uwe were working in product development for a global network equipment provider. Still, our experiences with EA (both on the customer side and within our own organizations) were similar among all of us. There was often a mix of great expectations and disappointment in the actual result.

The need for an enterprise architecture was always plainly and painfully visible. In Stefan's and Uwe's company, the product lines behaved like independent principalities, each making its own technology platform decisions. A *Not Invented Here*[1] mentality prevailed. In the same way, each line was responsible for its own product management. Therefore, the alignment between customers' business needs and products' features was handled in a quite fragmented way. The different software applications in the overall product portfolio were hardly interoperable. They had overlapping and competing features that were jealously guarded by their respective product managers.

When we, as architects responsible for one of these products, met customers, we often felt as though we'd drawn the shortest straw. "Why do we have to export the data from product X and import it to product Y in order to use it there, instead of just opening Y from X's user interface?" asked the customer, and silently we had to agree with them. However, the situation on the customer side wasn't any better. Not only did the customers' different departments and business areas use different middleware (three different vendors, each in multiple versions, were nothing out of the ordinary); they also used separate sets of applications for the same tasks. This made system integration a challenging task for us when we had to build an integration platform, or deploy a business intelligence system that needed to draw data from virtually everywhere.

Given this evident lack of coordination amongst the software applications and between the application portfolio and the business needs, we often longed for a group of vigorous enterprise architects. They would ride in like the good guys in a Western movie and reinstitute order in a world of anarchy. And indeed, gradually we noticed the rise of an EA culture. EA groups were formed in the customer organizations as well as in Stefan's and Uwe's product development organization. But, alas, it was not the band of superheroes we had hoped for.

For each sensible move toward synergy and technology harmonization, there were also a few mindless decisions imposed on us from above. This, at least, was how we perceived the situation. In one of Shailendra's projects, the project architects had proposed Oracle for a data volume expected to be in the terabyte range. The customer's newly formed EA group, however, had just declared Microsoft the strategic vendor. They insisted on SQL Server for the project, which (in the version available at that time) Shailendra's team considered quite ill suited for such a large data volume. He had a very hard time talking the enterprise architects out of their decision.

In another project, where Uwe served as the lead architect, the EA group insisted on being the only design body for services deployed to the enterprise service bus (ESB). This meant a considerable risk of

---

[1]*Not Invented Here* describes the mindset of technical people to refuse reusing a solution from the market or neighboring department on the pretext that the minimal compromises needed for the reuse are unacceptable. The true and usually unspoken reasons might be the technophiles' wish to do it themselves, or they fear a loss of control.

delays for the project. First, one had to reserve time with an enterprise architect for doing the service design, and then one had to subordinate to the fixed three-month release cycle of the ESB. In addition, the quality of delivered service design was often debatable. No wonder that projects usually tried to avoid using the ESB at all and chose other—often less suitable—middleware options instead.

Over the years we started to take over responsibility in the enterprise architecture area ourselves—as platform architects, in consulting assignments, or, in Shailendra's case, as practice head for enterprise architecture within the company. Evidently we did a decent job, by and large, since each of us was granted more and more responsibility over time. However, we had ample opportunity to ourselves commit some of the blunders we had previously observed in EA groups. And we made full use of this opportunity:

- We steadfastly defended our own holy cows—insisting, for example, that everything should be modeled as a Java Enterprise Edition (JEE) entity bean and that stored procedures are impure. We tried to push the usage of our enterprise platforms by extensive micro-management and were surprised and embittered about the resistance from projects.
- Harmonization and integration of competing base platforms were activities we repeatedly, and with much heart, engaged in—often enough seeing in the end that integration projects were way too expensive to be realized or were no longer needed from a business perspective one year later.
- Designing a model-driven common middleware mediation layer, we yielded to the temptation of using highly complex meta- (and meta-meta-) models that were supposed to cover each and every foreseeable extension—only to fail with a simple side requirement coming in one month later.
- We repeatedly spent months on writing extensive IT strategy papers, only to discover in the formal review meetings that no one had read them. Those stakeholders whose opinion *really* counted hadn't even turned up.
- Often enough, we talked until we were blue in the face to convince different (and bitterly competing) business groups to come to an agreement on a shared application platform, shared data model, or shared infrastructure. Frequently such mediation was a wasted effort. None of the stakeholder groups was willing (or able) to compromise on its own unique requirements and service-level expectations.

The list could be continued further. On top of all that, we (of course) always believed ourselves to be right—at least at the time a decision was made. Assuming that we are not stupider than other architects, what could be the reason for such suboptimal outcomes? After exhaustive analysis and many discussions, we found that each of the previously described situations boiled down to *people issues*. These issues can be characterized by lack of interaction and communication, resistance to leaving the ivory tower, failure to involve the right stakeholders, specification as an end in itself, and so on.

Such behavior is human and occurs even among the most highly skilled individuals. The countermeasure is not attempting to change people. This will not work. The most effective remedy is to change the way of collaboration, the rules for interaction, and the organization structure.

We had seen techniques for making that work outside our architecture domain. As project architects, we had applied *lean and agile methods* for years. We had helped produce software in an incremental way, on time, and of good quality. The agile methodology involves all stakeholders on a regular basis and focuses on producing usable results within a fixed heartbeat. Lean practices avoid wasteful activities and help concentrate on the need at hand.

In addition, we had dealt with Web 2.0 and Enterprise 2.0[2] concepts in a couple of projects and had seen how well they, if properly used, can leverage the wisdom of crowds for decision making.

Couldn't these techniques also be applied to enterprise architecture? Are they appropriate for such a dignified, long-term oriented, and elitist discipline? Against a backdrop of the discussions, lectures, consulting assignments, and trials we have undertaken in recent years, we answer these questions with a clear *Yes*. In writing this book, we attempt to elaborate our view on the current best practices of enterprise architecture and how those practices can be enriched by lean, agile, and Enterprise 2.0 concepts.

Our effort in writing this book is a consequence of our desire to steer away from the mystical mist that surrounds EA, as we mentioned in the beginning of this chapter. We want clarity—as vivid and as realistic a picture of enterprise architecture as possible. We want to make *practical sense* of EA and make it more meaningful to use—for ourselves, for our fellow IT practitioners, and for managers. And we want to explore new, pragmatic ways of practicing EA that will work well in today's rapidly changing business world.

We will consider ourselves successful if you, the reader, can zealously and successfully translate our proposals outlined in this book into your own way of dealing with enterprise architecture. You are invited to follow us into EA as a realm of high-flying goals and humble reality—and then further toward pragmatic improvements.

Goals and benefits of enterprise architecture

We open this section with a little story. It illustrates in a nutshell, and in a somewhat idealized way, what targets EA should fulfill. It talks about enterprise architecture against the backdrop of a leading global bank, Bank4Us.

Bank4Us is a fictitious bank, yet its story reflects the realities of a typical large enterprise in today's global environment. We will meet various members of the Bank4Us staff—managers, enterprise architects, IT experts—in this and coming chapters. Bank4Us will serve as a common theme running throughout this book, illustrating how an IT organization can implement a collaborative EA. (We have listed the employees we will accompany in the Appendix, "The Bank4Us Staff," including a brief description of their roles, so in case you lose track of the players you can look them up there.)

The world of banking is changing rapidly: Customers are difficult to acquire and retain; competitor initiatives, coupled with economic recession, are eroding banks' market shares; technology-driven avenues for business growth are available but not yet tapped effectively. In response to this difficult market situation, the CEO of Bank4Us issues a vision statement that clearly underscores the bank's priority number one:

Best-in-Class Customer Experience: Anywhere, Anytime, Any Channel

---

[2]*Web 2.0* is a conglomerate of technologies, software principles, business models, and, most important, a different usage paradigm of the Internet as a social medium. The term *Enterprise 2.0* was coined by Andrew McAfee, describing the use of social software as a means of collaboration in an enterprise context. We will elaborate on both terms later in the book, in Chapter 8.

A new business transformation program named "Closer to Customer" is initiated. During the annual strategic planning sessions of the bank, Dave Callaghan, the bank's CIO, confirms his commitment to the CEO vision:

Our IT will act as a transformation engine to take the bank "Closer to Customer"—step by step. While we expect a business growth of 150% over the next five years, we will restrict the IT growth to 60% of our current investment level. We will adopt a "20/20" strategy, meaning 20% savings and 20% value addition. The savings will be attributed to legacy reduction/downsizing, reduction in number of system interactions, and reduction in IT operation/support cost. The value addition, on the other hand, will be achieved by customer empowerment, customer satisfaction, operational efficiency, and shorter time cycles.

Sarah Taylor, a program manager at Bank4Us, is unsure how Dave is going to fulfill these promises, given the current state of the bank's IT environment. Sarah has only recently joined the bank and is responsible for managing an application portfolio of 62 IT systems. These systems support the customer management platform for the retail line of business, one of a total of five business lines. At this point Sarah has only a rough idea about the bank's overall IT landscape.

To her knowledge, the total application portfolio consists of more than 3,000 applications, including around 600 aging legacy systems (systems with more than 10 years in a live environment). There is a significant functional overlap among these applications: For example, there are as many as 30 account-opening systems, more than 10 authentication systems, more than 20 credit decision engines, and almost 40 business intelligence tools.

The supporting technology infrastructure is equally complex. It includes more than 2,000 server machines hosting 20 versions of five operating systems. There are more than 10 database platforms and roughly 25 middleware platforms, with as many as 35 programming languages in use. The scale and complexity of the IT landscape is further aggravated by a large number of system interactions— some of them apparent, but most of them buried under the heap of heterogeneous technology platforms.

In this jungle of IT systems, Sarah already finds it difficult to control her portfolio of a mere 62 systems. She has the feeling that her knowledge about her own portfolio is quite limited and superficial at best, or grossly incorrect and outdated at worst. She does not dare deduce her own goals from the CIO's commitments. As impressed as Sarah is by Dave's confidence, all the more she is worried about the mandate set forth for the IT organization and its consequences for her own job. When Sarah discusses her concern with her supervisor, he advises her to speak to Ian Miller, an enterprise architect.

Ian is a member of the bank's EA group and will collaborate with Sarah on the architectural work related to the customer management area. The EA team at Bank4Us has existed for a couple of years now. Last year a new chief architect, Oscar Salgado, was appointed head of the team. Since then the EA team has been seeking to play a more proactive role in the business-IT interaction and is becoming more visible in the enterprise.

So, what is Ian expected to do? Ian was instrumental in crafting the CIO's mission and strategy based on the priorities of the business. He will be responsible for helping Sarah establish her project portfolio in alignment with the defined mission and strategy. He is supposed to sketch the complete picture of the IT landscape, show Sarah how the CIO's mission links to the IT landscape. Ian will also have to demonstrate how the planned projects will take the current IT landscape to the envisaged state over a period of time. He will explain to Sarah what that means for the business and, more specifically, how it influences her scope of work. After the project-planning phase, he is also committed to guiding her project teams so that the desired goals are met and expected benefits are realized.

In addition to Sarah, many more individuals and groups inside the bank organization need to be told the same story about the bank's IT landscape. Hence Ian and his team will consistently communicate with all the concerned parties in such a way that they can understand the information presented and act accordingly. In essence, Ian's task list and job description reflects what enterprise architecture is all about. It ensures that the enterprise IT landscape moves in the right direction to fulfill the strategic goals of the enterprise.

THE ENTERPRISE ARCHITECT

The Mandate of an Enterprise Architect

Information technology (IT) is a fairly young field compared to many other industry sectors. IT has been used in mainstream business for only 50-odd years. Over the last few decades, IT has made a startling impact on the way enterprises do business. As enterprises started relying more and more on IT to support their day-to-day business operations and to enable their long-term business strategies, the role and contribution of IT in the enterprise gained more and more importance. With a continuous addition of new applications, prolonged retention of legacy platforms, and a growing number of system interactions, the enterprise IT landscape has gradually reached a remarkable level of complexity. Apart from incurring heavy costs, this complexity impedes business changes and therefore causes frustration among business people. For business, IT is an asset and a liability at the same time. Broadbent and Kitzis (2003) characterize this reality as "IT has fallen victim of its own success."

So, what does this reality mean for an enterprise architect? In a very condensed form, it puts forth the following mandate for EA architects:

- *Controlling IT complexity.* Manage the IT landscape as an asset.
- *Aligning business and IT.* Ensure the business value of IT.

Controlling IT complexity

The answer to the most basic question, "What is it that enterprises want from IT?" is consistently the same across all industries. The answer is, "Enterprises want their IT to be stable, agile, adaptable, and efficient." Now, what does that mean?

- *Stable.* Reliable, resilient, available and fault-tolerant.
- *Agile.* Enable quick introduction of new products, services, and business processes; be responsive to market dynamics and customer needs.
- *Adaptable.* Adapt easily to different business contexts, regulations, mergers and acquisitions, and convergences.
- *Efficient.* Meet or exceed business and service-level expectations; minimize total cost of operations.

Unfortunately for IT, these noble goals are a far cry from reality today. IT invariably remains brittle, sluggish, inflexible, and expensive. This nuisance of IT is, in most enterprises, a compounding effect of the complexities originating from many sources:

- Complex business operations
- Technology changes
- Immaturity in software engineering
- An uncontrolled proliferation in the IT landscape (sometimes dressed as lack of organizational ownership in IT)

The prime reason for IT complexity is the inherent complexity of business itself. A typical global enterprise like Bank4Us in our example operates in a highly volatile market environment. Apart from supporting local customer demands and market regulations, enterprises must also respond to competitor challenges and market opportunities. In addition, they must keep pace with the emerging technology landscape and introduce innovation in performing their business tasks. To fulfill the myriad of such demands, an accelerating train of changes runs though the enterprise. These changes take place on different planes:

- *Business.* Changes in the business context (such as regulation, mergers and acquisitions, or the competitive landscape), new business models, new business products and processes, or new customer demands.
- *Technology.* Changes in the technology strategy (technology usage, vendor preference, new technology integration, legacy retirement, out-of-support software, server consolidation, license optimization, maintenance and upgrade), workload changes due to user and volume growth, or updated service-level expectations.

For Sarah's portfolio of customer management systems in Bank4Us, the business challenges mainly manifest themselves as new business models and new customer demands. They invariably require a high level of synchronization between the five business lines. With regard to technology, Sarah faces the inevitable pains when it comes to version upgrades of the middleware platforms her applications are based on. However, Bank4Us's EA team has in the past done a good job of keeping the technology strategy stable. So at least she doesn't yet have to go through the adventure of migrating between two different middleware implementations.

The immaturity of software engineering practices also contributes to IT complexity. In comparison to other engineering disciplines such as mechanical or civil engineering, the field of software engineering is quite young. The design, development, and operational processes are not yet as mature as those in traditional engineering disciplines. Despite the high-handed quality promises of software vendors, system integrators, and other players in the IT market, the reality on the ground often relies on improvisation rather than rigidly followed formal processes. Frequently, enhancements and quick fixes are introduced to operational systems in an ad hoc manner—sometimes to meet delivery commitments, sometimes in response to emergency situations.

In other disciplines, the engineering of a product comes to an end once it is shipped to the customer for use. From then on it is never redesigned or rebuilt. Once a compact family car has been manufactured, for example, it will not be upgraded to a convertible sports car. In contrast, IT systems are enhanced continuously while they are in use. Often something like the conversion from a family car to a sports car is actually attempted in IT—though not always successfully.

For Sarah, this inherent process immaturity is a constant challenge in every IT project. Her applications are customer-facing and are used across multiple time zones. Therefore, only a minimal downtime for redeployment is permissible. Furthermore, the testing procedures require a high amount of rigor. Sarah's worst nightmare is the proverbial call from the CIO's office in the middle of the night, enquiring why UK customers cannot access their account details. Fortunately, this situation has not happened yet.

To a great extent, IT complexity is also the result of an uncontrolled proliferation of redundant IT systems, caused by the IT organization's tendency to follow a stovepipe system integration style. In an enterprise with silo-based organizational partitions, each business unit typically has its own IT budget; therefore it will go its own way in procuring, building, and operating its IT systems.

In addition, IT departments are normally organized on a project (or a product) basis. The project teams decide everything locally. This is a trade-off: It allows for independence, agility, flexibility, and efficiency in the local environment, but it prevents leveraging enterprise-wide synergies. A large number of tactical and parallel IT systems mushroom up into different parts of the enterprise, often leading to a nearly unmanageable jungle of redundant applications and data stores.

System redundancy is, in our Bank4Us example, not much of a concern for Sarah. She sometimes regrets not having closer cooperation with her program management peers in other units, though, since that might be helpful in addressing common issues. For the enterprise architect Ian Miller, however, the redundancy causes more of a headache. For example, customer management systems are scattered across five different business units and therefore (because IT is organized mirroring the business) are spread over five different IT departments. If Ian needs to address issues with customer management systems, he also needs to talk to four other program managers besides Sarah and facilitate common ground among them.

The ever-expanding cosmos of enterprise IT is becoming more and more complex. An enterprise architect must safeguard IT as a corporate asset. The cost must be justified by what IT delivers. This means that every opportunity to eliminate needless complexity and costs in the IT landscape must be spotted and leveraged. In addition, the enterprise architect must make sure that every new addition or change to the IT landscape is justified by an agreed business purpose and that it has a committed business value.

EA provides guidance about what technologies are a strategic fit, which ones are deprecated, and which are emerging. The project managers on the ground need that input in order to take decisions on turning off legacy platforms, merging redundant applications, or introducing new systems—in effect, simplifying the IT landscape. The benefits may be realized in terms of:

- Reduced development effort
- Optimized integrations
- Decreased IT risks
- Lower IT costs
- Improved business confidence[3]

In essence, EA is a *hygiene factor* for the IT landscape.

Ian Miller, in our Bank4Us example, needs to facilitate the implementation of the CIO's mission statement. In his role as enterprise architect, he plans the first steps toward the cost-saving goal. First, he needs to get up-to-date information on the current costs of the applications in the IT landscape. The last survey conducted by Ian's predecessor is already more than two years old. It can serve as starting point, but Ian decides that it needs an update. In addition, he needs to understand which applications are used for what purpose. He would like to see a mapping of the business processes against the applications so that he can identify redundancies. Luckily enough, the business processes have been modeled only recently and can be assumed to be fairly up to date.

---

[3]Other than the remaining categories, *business confidence* is hard to measure. It manifests itself in the way the IT management is (or is not) involved in the crucial decision-making processes and what reputation IT has within the enterprise in terms of credibility and reliability.

Ian decides to make appointments with his main stakeholders before proceeding any further. One of his first meetings will be with Sarah. Since Ian has not only his CIO's cost-saving target to fulfill but also has the CEO's vision of a more customer-oriented focus in mind, Ian also needs Sarah's input on how well the current IT landscape supports customer orientation.

Aligning business and IT

The world of business is rapidly evolving; customers are demanding more sophisticated products and better services. The convergence of communication and computing is opening up avenues for new business models and revenue streams. The IT systems must support new ways of doing business collaboratively with partners and customers. The result is a "multi-entity" ecosystem that allows interaction at more touchpoints and a depth not previously attempted.

Today's business challenges are not going to be met by simply adding a few systems here and there nor by tidying up a few platforms in the enterprise IT landscape. The only solution may be to completely restructure the enterprise's operational and organizational regime in the new environment. It will be a transformational journey that has to start with EA.

The goal of enterprise architecture is to act as a guide, perhaps a pathfinder, who takes the enterprise on a transformational journey—from an incoherent and complex world with line-of-business separation, product-specific stovepipes, legacy systems estate, and costly operation to a more rationally organized and useful state with multiservice, revenue-generating platforms and an efficient operational regime. On the way, radical surgeries may be required to eliminate duplication, reduce costs, improve reliability, and increase agility in the business. EA acts as *a strategic foundation for business enablement*.

The transformational journey that begins with EA is long and hard. The effort may be cost-justified by identifying IT-centric benefits, but the real value of enterprise architecture can only be appreciated when it delivers *tangible business benefits*.

The enterprise architect must envision how EA will change the way the enterprise operates and how large the generated business benefits will be to outweigh the effort spent. The benefits must be realized in view of both long-term and short-term business priorities. For instance, when embarking on a multi-year plan for the deployment of a unified, strategic service-oriented architecture (SOA) platform for the enterprise, the business should be able to see the benefits of such a platform early enough (say, within the first six months) and then periodically thereafter (for instance, every three months).

In Bank4Us, the EA initiative "Closer to Customer" is geared toward delivering the following strategic business benefits:

- *Customer empowerment.* Customers should be enabled to manage their own banking environments (in buzzword lingo: "self-service, zero-touch, in real time").
- *Customer intimacy.* The IT systems should provide personalized customer service based on an intimate knowledge of the customer's needs, behavior, and lifestyle.
- *Customer satisfaction.* Operational synergies across the different lines of business should be leveraged to reduce the cycle time and failure rate in all customer interaction processes; that will help implement a true *single face to customer* concept.
- *Customer excitement.* Finally, the customers should be excited by innovative products and services. This allows the bank to respond to competitor initiatives and market opportunities in an agile fashion and to be the first in the market (or at least an early follower).

This list brings an interesting pile of activities for Ian. The starting point for any major activity in the bank is a business case; this has to be driven from the business side. Ian plans to participate in its creation process in order to understand the broader business perspective of the "Closer to Customer" initiative and to keep track of the big picture of the bank in his mind. Over a period of some weeks, he confers with various business stakeholders. One of them founds an informal working group with several other business managers and invites Ian to participate as a member of the EA team. The group begins with the preparation of the business case document for harmonizing the key customer-facing business processes across the five business lines of the bank.

The business case refers to the process maps for three customer-facing business processes:

- *Prospect to customer* (customer win)
- *Need to fulfillment* (customer servicing)
- *Trouble to resolution* (complaint resolution)

The case further highlights that the processes are, to an extent, similar across all business lines. There is about 30% commonality, but there's also a potential for much more standardization across the business lines. The business stakeholders estimate that the processes could even be unified to a degree of 80%.

As a next step, the business case also looks at the customer satisfaction goal that requires reducing the cycle times and failure rates in these customer-facing business processes. It explores the possibilities to measure the cycle time for the processes in an automated way. This would allow the business to effectively monitor and optimize the end-to-end process time in the future. It also identifies common failures and their effects in these processes. After many discussions, and by taking an active support role in compiling a business case and supporting documentation, Ian gains a decent understanding of the high-level business requirements.

Ian prepares an IT proposition in response to the business case documentation. The proposition highlights opportunities for process harmonization, data standardization, and capability reuse in the bank's operating IT environment. In addition, Ian gives a recommendation to the sponsors as to how they could monitor and optimize the customer-facing processes for minimum cycle time and straight-through processing with the help of available technologies. He gets his proposition vetted by Sarah and her peers and finalizes it for discussion with the sponsors and users on the business side.

Ian is wary from the litany of unsuccessful enterprise resource planning (ERP), customer relationship management (CRM), and similar IT-inspired programs. He has come to realize that IT alone is not enough to bring about a transformation. If the business leaders do not share ownership of both the implementation and the outcome, the path to IT transformation will be a disastrous journey. On the other hand, the business can neither simply rely on IT nor lead IT-enabled transformations. Hence the business expects IT to step up to the task.

For that purpose, Ian manages to involve CIO Dave Callaghan via his boss, the chief architect. Ian asks Dave to first generate a widespread agreement among business leaders as to the appropriateness of the CEO's vision and the IT-enabled transformation. Dave, in partnership with his counterparts on the business side, assures a joint ownership for the transformation. This step helps to get the program staffed adequately so that the necessary expertise is available on both the business side and the IT side. Dave now formally sets up a joint working group between IT and business and assigns Ian, Sarah, and others to that group.

As a next step, Ian participates in the brainstorming sessions with the subject matter experts from business and IT across the five business lines in order to review his proposition and resolve issues raised by the stakeholders. He applies some changes to his document to accommodate the stakeholder needs. This is the most challenging exercise that demands deep collaboration among all stakeholders, who come from different professional backgrounds and organizational cultures and may even have competing priorities. Luckily, the essence of Ian's ideas has survived this crucial process. He now expects Sarah and her peers to budget and plan further for this initiative.

Once the initiative has been approved, Ian takes this effort forward by working closely with Sarah and her peers. Jointly they identify those capabilities they can use from existing systems versus those they will need to buy or build anew. In the process, Ian looks at opportunities to maximize the reuse of applications, data, and infrastructure. He guides the project architects in defining the solution architecture and the deployment plan. Ian also identifies the initiatives that will enable change and bring in new technologies, if needed. Eventually Ian has to guide and govern the project implementation to make sure the intended outcome is achieved.

Whether EA is perceived as a hygiene factor for the IT landscape or as a strategic foundation for business enablement, it is obliged to deliver value. As a hygiene factor, benefits from EA can be valued in terms of reduction in management escalations, emergency occurrences, and year-on-year operational expenses. As a strategic foundation, EA facilitates the deployment of new capabilities. This way it helps IT gain more business trust—and hence more funding for new IT projects. Unfortunately, these benefits are difficult to quantify on a short-term base. Therefore they need to be tracked over a sufficient time period and then be normalized to a common baseline. Only then can they serve as a sensible benchmark for measuring the success of EA.

This is just a brief snapshot of EA activities. We will delve into the details in Chapters 2 through 5, where we present a more thorough definition of EA and give an overview of the practical activities, methods, and concepts it involves. For now, this overview should suffice to give you an impression of what the job of an enterprise architect comprises.

Bank4Us is not an enterprise architect's wonderland, but by and large EA is still able to perform its tasks. The practice on the ground is often more complex and less well organized than depicted in the story of Ian and Sarah, at least in many enterprises. Let's now look at this less glossy reality.

The gray reality: Enterprise architecture failures

Everyone is a moon, and has a dark side which he never shows to anybody.

—Mark Twain[4]

In the previous section, we outlined how EA is *supposed* to function. For many enterprises this is a somewhat idealized picture. The real Ians and Sarahs of this world often do *not* meet regularly, sometimes look down on each other, or in the worst case, rarely ever talk.

In our jobs as architects and consultants, we have seen quite a few enterprises from the inside over the past few years. We have seen a large firm, where the absence of an effective EA yielded shortcomings across all organizational units in touch with IT:

- Business managers who had no clear conception of how their business unit is utilizing IT
- Technical application owners who did not know which systems their application was interfacing with

---

[4]From "Pudd'nhead Wilson's New Calendar," in *Following the Equator*, 1897.

- Developers who felt uncertain about which framework to use (and consequentially downloaded whatever they felt suitable from the Internet)
- Operational staff who desperately experimented with restarting a bunch of information systems in production because they had no idea about their interdependencies

On the other hand, we encountered companies that, despite having a fully institutionalized EA in place, were in a state close to paralysis. The conglomerate of business, organizational, and technical dependencies had grown to a muddle that made reasonable changes impossible. As a consequence, these companies were still able to operate their existing IT assets for daily work, but they were unable to move in any direction toward the future. They had usually gone through several not-so-successful application rationalization attempts over the years.

In one such case, the only possible way to find out whether an application was not in use anymore and could therefore be actually ramped down was to literally place a red phone beneath the hosting server and then shut down the server. If no angry calls came through for a period of one month, the conclusion that no one needed the application anymore was considered safe. Everyone can draw his or her own conclusions on such an approach.

IT transformations being cancelled, a wrong portfolio of initiatives taken up, totally overambitious harmonization programs, anarchy due to ineffective governance—the list of possible IT blunders could easily be prolonged further. The reasons for such problems are usually manifold, of course, and cannot be pinned down to malfunctioning enterprise architecture alone. However, as we saw in the previous section, EA is supposed to prevent such failures—so why do they keep happening?

Let's take a closer look at the situations in which EA is not living up to its promises, then attempt an analysis of the reasons why not.

Between success and disappointment

Although EA has reached the mainstream, a skeptical undertone with regard to its effectiveness has always existed. In 2004, after completing many years of EA effort, the General Accounting Office (GAO)[5] reported a standstill in EA maturity within US government agencies: "Of the 93 agencies that we reported on in 2001 and 2003, 22 agencies (. . .) increased their maturity, 24 (. . .) decreased their maturity, and 47 (. . .) remained the same" (U.S. GAO, 2004, p. 27). In another account, an online survey revealed that the overwhelming majority of participants doubt the success of EA programs, at least within the first couple of years (Spacey, 2011).[6]

EA has not yet fully proven that it provides tangible business benefits in the same way that other enterprise functions do, compared to the effort and cost it accumulates. Although EA is all about business-IT alignment, it is historically an offshoot of the IT organization. Often enough it is a

---

[5]The GAO is a part of the legislative branch of the US government. It also functions as the audit, evaluation, and investigative arm of the US Congress.

[6]Eighty percent of the 300+ participants (status: November 2011) believe that less than half of all EA programs are successful in the first five years or are even a complete waste of time. It should be noted that the survey was published on a site (Simplicable.com) that specializes in EA topics. So it can be assumed that the participants deal with EA in one way or another and have per se open minds to it.

part of the IT organization and run by IT people, with only marginal participation from the business side.[7] Even if the real business problems are actually addressed, the cost-benefit justification is often IT-centric and fuzzy. It is based on the *perceived* value of architecture rather than using a viable proof point about the *actual* business value delivered in a real-life scenario. The business sponsors, however, want to know what EA actually delivers, not what it "could" deliver.

Does that mean that EA, in its current form, is too amateur to meet the needs of the time? Of course, our answer is *No*—otherwise we would not have written this book. But neither is it the shining white knight who renders all criticism obsolete. EA is needed and useful. But the way it is practiced today still has shortcomings that should be resolved in order to boost its universal acceptance.

Adopting a harsh critic's perspective, one could claim today that:

- EA does not scale to create any visible impact in a large enterprise setup.
- EA is not equipped with the right approach and toolset to cover the entire scope of work, from strategy through implementation.
- EA fails to keep pace with the speed of change in modern business.

Yet, according to literature and our own experience, spectacular failures happen only in a minority of EA programs. As a general rule, case studies documenting the *effect* of an EA program—whether success or failure—seem to be rare. Especially we have not found any documented cases where EA programs have actually been cancelled and the EA organization disbanded. More often, EA seems to slip into a gray mediocrity: Fulfilling some promises but failing others. An EA organization working in this mode is still too lively to be abandoned but does not have enough strength to effectively set the course for the whole IT organization.

We will take a closer look at the challenges and failures of EA in the coming sections. The four dimensions depicted in Figure 1-1 will serve as a structure for our analysis. We will come back to them

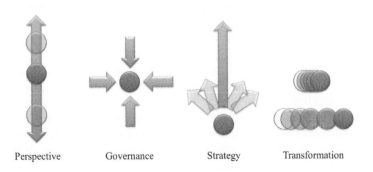

Perspective	Governance	Strategy	Transformation

FIGURE 1-1

Dimensions for analyzing EA challenges and failures.

---

[7]That this is a lively debated topic can be judged, for example, by the fact that the blog post "Six Reasons Why EA Should NOT Be Assigned to the IT Department" (Saha, 2011) quickly garnered 1,400 comments (status: November 13, 2011).

later, when describing *building blocks* for a collaborative EA, designed to tackle the identified EA problems:

- *Perspective.* What viewpoint does the EA group take? Does it prefer a "helicopter perspective" with little involvement in the hands-on IT business, or do its members involve themselves knee-deep in concrete architecture work in programs and projects?
- *Governance.* How strict is the adherence to, and enforcement of, rules set up by the EA group? Does the organization follow a laissez-faire approach, where each project has a high level of freedom, or is a rigorous control system in place to supervise compliance?
- *Strategy.* To what extent does the EA group focus on strategic planning, and what is the typical time horizon of the plans? Does EA follow the one "great vision," or—at the other extreme—is there no long-term planning at all?
- *Transformation.* What is the speed of change in the landscape of business models, processes, and IT systems? What kind of IT transformations are taken up?

We have condensed some of the more frequent practical EA anti-patterns (collected from own experience, some expert interviews, and material documented in literature[8]) into eight *EA caricatures* interspersed in the following text and summed up in Table 1-1. The caricatures match the extreme positions in each dimension. They exaggerate reality to bring out the essence of the problem more clearly.

In each dimension, the EA group should find its proper position between the extremes. This does not guarantee a catch-all solution as to how to do EA properly, but it provides a grid to classify the most common problems. No EA group will be a 100% version of a caricature—but so far, we have not encountered any organization that didn't show at least some of its traits.

Perspective: Between bird's-eye view and nitty-gritty on the ground

An Indian saying expresses that a bird flying high in the skies will always keep an eye on her babies in the nest down below. In comparison, what is the extent to which an enterprise architect looks at the concerns on the ground while flying high on the level of a corporate vision? A candid answer to this question reveals the degree to which the enterprise architect can succeed in translating a vision to a venture.

Enterprise architecture is predominantly approached through a top-down way of thinking: First articulate the corporate vision, then define key objectives and progressively drill down into the further details of implementation. The vision will help bring all stakeholders across all organizational silos of the enterprise under one common roof, and will motivate the entire workforce to reach for that vision. All the subsequent objectives, targets, projects, and activities can be derived from the vision and must lead toward the vision. At least in theory, this is how it EA is supposed to work.

We have encountered many examples whereby this process is less straightforward. An application rationalization project of a global logistics company was run under the maxim of considerably reducing

---

[8]Anti-patterns in EA and architecture in general can be found, for instance, in Kruchten (2008), Mar and Spacey (2011), Ambler, Nalbone, and Vizdos (2005), and Coplien and Harrison (2005).

Table 1-1 Caricatures of Enterprise Architecture

Dimension	Caricature	
Perspective	Too high: *Living in Cloud Cuckoo Land*	
	Too low: *In the Chief Mechanic's Workshop*	
Governance	Too rigid: *The Guardians of Wisdom*	
	Too weak: *The Overstrained Technical Advisors*	
Strategy	Too far-reaching: *A Deep Look into the Crystal Ball*	
	Too myopic: *Sweeping Up the Change Requests*	
Transformation	Too fast: *The Permanent Construction Site*	
	Too slow: *The Ever-Growing Backlog*	

the numbers of applications and application platforms in order to serve the corporate mandate: save costs. Among the concrete measures identified by the EA team was the global replacement of a parcel-tracking application by an already existing Web-based system. The planning had been finalized, and the budget was allocated.

Then a series of letters was sent to the country heads, announcing that the legacy tracking application was about to be replaced by the Web interface. You can imagine the surprise in the EA group when the Italian country head wrote a letter back, asking sarcastically if the IT department would also pay for a couple of thousand iPads. As it turned out, the handhelds that the logistics drivers in his region used were incapable of running a Web browser. No one on the EA team had known that.

This may be an isolated example, but it illustrates a general problem with regard to EA. On one side, an enterprise architect is expected to have a broad overview of both the IT and the business landscapes. On the other side, the enterprise architect needs to retain her grip on the details of business and technology to such an extent that she still understands the reality on the ground. This is a wide chasm that's not always easy to bridge.

PERSPECTIVE CARICATURES

Caricature #1: Living in Cloud Cuckoo Land

When an enterprise architect is too decoupled from the community of project architects and developers, she loses insight into the challenges of the IT projects on the ground. A similar gap can exist between the enterprise architect and the users of applications and processes on the business side. If the enterprise architect does not bother to ask the end users how well suited a process is, she is likely to evaluate the as-is process landscape in the wrong way. An EA organization in Cloud Cuckoo Land is ignored or circumvented by both the IT and business departments on the ground.

One possible symptom of Cloud Cuckoo Land is a tendency to focus on the *big picture*. The big picture is part of the standard mindset of EA, which everyone immediately associates with the activities of an enterprise architect. However, many of these big pictures you meet in practice have been over-abstracted to the point of insignificance and no longer address any relevant question.

In addition, the option for hierarchical search and semantic drill-in is often undermined by the loss of information between the abstraction layers. Semantic distortions are the rule rather than the exception. The main danger of such a kind of big picture is that it glosses over and obfuscates the gap of understanding between EA and IT management on one side and the IT reality on the ground on the other. This creates an atmosphere of false security at the corporate level and prevents triggering corrective actions.

EA entails making and following a set of policy decisions that steers the strategic direction for the evolution of IT. Often there is no one single "right" answer but a plethora of conflicting priorities and choices. The enterprise architect has to select those options that seem both most promising and least damaging at a given point in time. An example is the choice between the conflicting architectural priorities of performance, interoperability, and manageability. The right solution design for a certain type of application can look quite different for different enterprises. It can even vary at different points in time for the same business line of one enterprise.

If such policies are designed by an isolated group of experts with little bandwidth (and even less inclination to reach out to the people concerned by the consequences), EA is bound to run into a wide range of problems. Overlooking technical details can become far more costly than anticipated. "Architecture represents the significant design decisions that shape a system, where significant is measured by cost of change," writes Booch (2006). A high-handed focusing on the big picture is prone to overlook some of the significant (i.e., expensive, in the sense of Booch's definition) aspects of the solution.

The quoted example of not having Web-enabled handhelds for the logistics drivers would be, if it had not been detected in time, a good example of this risk. Another rich source of Cloud Cuckoo Land examples is the "naïve" way of implementing SOA, which was pretty common in the early days of this design pattern. The best example we found was the strict directive of the EA group of a logistics company to implement all data interchanges between systems as Web services—including a point-to-point connection that had previously been a nighttime batch job. It shovelled gigabytes of data through a web connection, including the transformation to and from XML.[9]

Another shortcoming of a top-down approach without sufficient grounding is that it may meet significant conscious or subconscious resistance in the people on whom such decisions are imposed. It is a trivial (yet surprisingly often disregarded) fact that the buy-in of co-workers can be neither taken for granted nor enforced by orders; it has to be earned by involving these people in the decision-making process.

So far, we have described the risks of a too detached and high-handed EA team. However, in the *Perspective* dimension the other extreme also exists and can be responsible for EA failures. An "old-school" type of CIO is firmly rooted in the IT department and focuses on maintaining the status quo: ensuring that the IT service-level agreements are kept and the costs are under control. An EA group operating in such an environment is prone to lack a quality that the Cloud Cuckoo Land variety has in abundance: broad vision. Decisions are taken from an IT-centric background, and there is little inclination to proactively approach the business and to position IT as an enabler for new business models and markets.

PERSPECTIVE CARICATURES

Caricature #2: In the Chief Mechanic's Workshop

If the enterprise architect focuses too much on purely technical issues or works merely as project architect, she runs the risk of neglecting the broad view and is not taken seriously by the business. This promotes the perception of IT as a cost-driving commodity instead of a business enabler. The role of an EA organization is then likely to be reduced to achieve cost reduction by managing standards and conducting IT rationalizations.

Often in such a setup, the EA group consists of *experts* instead of generalists. Each enterprise architect is a one-track specialist with a narrow focus on specific technologies or business requirements (such as security, performance, or user interface and stability), and no one in the team has a holistic view of the enterprise IT landscape.

Broadbent and Kitzis (2004) coined the term *chief technology mechanic* for the CIO running the shop in the preceding caricature. Apart from an organizational structure that places the EA team too close to the IT department, such a setup may also have other reasons. Insufficient

---

[9]The story dates back to 2007. By now, SOA has become so much a commodity that such a design is more unlikely today.

architectural skills can be one. Another possibility is that the IT landscape of an enterprise has grown to such complexity that no single person understands the whole of it or even the whole of one application. A chief architect of a car manufacturing company admitted that fact quite frankly—the enterprise was so large, so long in the market, and so riddled with poorly documented proprietary IT solutions that no single enterprise architect had the complete overview anymore. A holistic view of the enterprise's IT landscape appears hardly possible under such circumstances.

An EA group working in such fashion, with too much focus on the details and too little attention to the broad vision, tends to manage only singular aspects of the system. It basically abandons EA's claim to shape the IT landscape actively and capitulates in the face of complexity. EA effectively stops happening.

This situation drives IT into the passive role of a mere commodity. Commodities, however, are primarily perceived as cost drivers. Therefore the IT function will quickly find itself in an endless loop of cost reduction demands from the CEO. This leads to the "orange-squeezing effect," as Keller (2006) describes it: IT has managed to reduce its budget by 20% this year, and the applications are still operable. So why not ask for another 20% reduction next year? In the long run, this cycle leads to a degradation of IT within the enterprise. It also threatens the CIO's position. As Broadbent and Kitzis (2004) point out: Each enterprise needs electricity, but no one would think of establishing a chief officer of electricity on the board.

An EA group operating too much on the detail level will not be able to ensure the design of appropriate, business-aligned IT applications. We encountered a particularly good example of this at a global insurance company. Over the years, the company's IT department had developed a costly, proprietary content management system for their intra- and extranet, targeted at supporting the specific editorial process prevailing in this enterprise. In an assessment of the enterprise portal landscape it became evident that no one had ever bothered to precisely model the editorial process that had been the starting point of the development. The IT department had simply implemented a solution they thought would fit the business needs—with the effect that no one, neither on the business side nor on the IT side, was happy with the outcome. This situation is primarily the result of poor requirements engineering in the development project, of course, but an EA group with sufficiently broad vision would have insisted on doing the business architecture first.

Another phenomenon typically to be observed in a rather technology-savvy EA organization is a tendency to implement its own proprietary platforms instead of just reusing tried and tested industry standards. In the course of our careers we have seen several custom enterprise UI frameworks, each tailored to a special use case in the particular enterprise that was overrated at best, nonexistent at worst. (As a general rule, each enterprise considers its UIs to follow a unique paradigm, and almost always this is a case of self-delusion.) Such a *reinventing-the-wheel* mindset is a risk that leads to a hard-to-control jungle of technologies and solutions.

In summary, neither the big picture nor attention to detail alone will ensure successful EA work. The enterprise architect needs to be like a helicopter pilot who is fighting forest fires. Flying too high, she will no longer see the fires. Flying too low or even moving on the ground all the time, she will never get a complete picture of how much fire there is in the whole of the woods. She needs to fly at a middle level—sometimes higher to get an overview, sometimes lower to analyze a particular patch, and sometimes she will have to land in order to fix things on the ground.

This requires a practical framework for structuring the EA activities on a day-to-day basis, supporting the enterprise architect's workflow at all levels of operation and ensuring the participation of all stakeholders. The enterprise architect needs all the help she can get to master this tightrope walk.

Governance: A host of directives, but no one follows them

Any EA practice that has existed for some time has accumulated a vast amount of knowledge comprising a multitude of principles, policies, procedures, practices, techniques, lessons, and so forth. Depending on the organization's style, this knowledge is enforced with more or less vigor. That, however, does not guarantee the practical relevance of this knowledge. Often EA principles are perceived as a veritable nuisance by the practitioners on the ground.

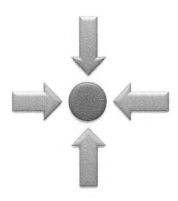

We were involved in the development of a Web-based workflow system for a reinsurance company. The project architect had proposed to use an industry-standard Web framework supporting page flow and transaction management in a very suitable way. The framework was in use in other systems within the company as well and was on the list of accepted technologies. Still, the EA group insisted on the proprietary standard user interface platform, which would have meant at least 50% more effort and a hefty project delay. Only after an escalation to C level was the project architect allowed to continue with the original choice.

Many EA-originated policies that appear obsolete today have not always been meaningless. Most probably they have emerged as the architecture group's overreactions to unlikely-to-recur situations that they experienced in their organization in the past. A frequent example is the uncontrolled proliferation of newly hyped technologies by the IT crowd, and the EA group's rigid attempt to reinstitute order. Once the technology has matured, the EA rules often appear overly strict and suppress a flexible use of the appropriate technology.

As time passes, policies tend to become stale. Given the unpredictable and rapid changes that happened over the last decade, it is obvious that many of them do not carry much prominence today. Nonetheless, they still continue to be part and parcel of enterprise architecture. EA should therefore also continuously check and revise its policies.

GOVERNANCE CARICATURES

Caricature #3: The Guardians of Wisdom

Sometimes the EA organization has an overly rigid approach to enforcing its own standards. Instead of discussing a sensible level of standardization with the IT crowd on the ground, enterprise architects invest their energy in political fights for IT standards that are irrelevant at best and that stall creativity at worst. Examples of standards with the risk of being applied in an overly strict manner are the exclusive use of SOAP-based Web services as a data exchange protocol for all kinds of internal and external interfaces, or a certain UI platform prescribed for all clients.

In addition, if enterprise architects claim to be the only decision-making body in technical matters, there is a huge risk that they create a bottleneck. If decisions take ages due to pending strategic issues, imminent changes in the business model, and so forth, IT projects can be seriously delayed. The practical consequence is that projects deliberately circumvent the enterprise architects—for example, by choosing less suitable technologies not managed by the EA group.

Simple Object Access Protocol (SOAP) is an XML-based information exchange protocol used in web service implementation.

An overly rigid EA governance is prone to producing a rampant bureaucracy of approvals and sign-offs. From experience we know that a sign-off rarely means that the matter is *really* closed. The approved document is usually not questioned or openly disregarded. Instead, the reality on the ground—in the IT department, in the projects implementing parts of an IT transformation—slowly creeps away from the documented status. The predominant effect reached by too much focus on formal governance is that the EA group and the executors on the ground just stop talking to each other. The EA group thinks everything is settled in their sense, and the practitioners are happy to have the EA guys off their back.

The preceding caricature, the Guardians of Wisdom, paints a picture of an EA group whose extensive controlling attitude borders on micro-managing the developers. The other extreme is an EA team that is notoriously understaffed, overstretched, and invisible. Here the governance is not rigid but nearly nonexistent. Strangely enough, the consequences of both extremes are so similar that they actually represent two sides of the same coin. A distorted governance—too strict or too weak—leads to a situation where the EA group is not taken seriously and is unable to reach out to its stakeholders and therefore ultimately fails to fulfill its mission.

GOVERNANCE CARICATURES

Caricature #4: The Overstrained Technical Advisors

If the enterprise architect is completely lost in an everlasting struggle against the entropy of business and technology change, no IT strategy worth its name will ever evolve. This is often the case in a hopelessly understaffed or under-empowered EA organization. The enterprise architect is taken hostage by a business that forever demands solutions right here, right now.

To catch up with the pace of business changes, the EA organization is permanently robbing Peter to pay Paul. In such a setup, the EA group does not manage to establish standards that are actually followed within the organization. The enterprise architect is in high demand by the business and the projects to act as the "useful idiot" who can help out in defending technical problems. He is a good-to-have advisor at best and a not-to-have auditor at worst.

The result of distorted governance is usually some kind of anarchy on the ground. Patterns like the *Not Invented Here* syndrome prevail. Under a weak EA governance, it can be found in all parts of the enterprise, from business over IT department to even the EA group itself. Business departments usually favor custom-tailored solutions over reusing a company-wide platform. IT projects often ignore enterprise standards for technologies and platforms, blaming them as unsuitable for their task at hand.[10]

Lack of governance can cause substantial risks, which are usually not recognized by the decision makers. In the case of a global insurance company, for instance, no book of standards was in place for the use of open source components. Every developer basically just downloaded the frameworks needed for his or her task at hand. No legal checks were conducted, not even a centralized systematic tracking

---

[10]Here, culprit and victim are often hard to differentiate. The example described at the beginning of this section—the EA group trying to enforce the use of the enterprise UI platform—could as well, from the enterprise architects' perspective, be taken as a symptom of a *Not Invented Here* mindset. This is another indicator of the ambiguous consequences of distorted governance: The consequences of too much and too little rigor are similar.

of the open source components in use. One simply needs to take a look at the great legal battles around Linux and Hibernate[11] to understand the possible financial implications of such a laissez-faire policy.

The decisions made by the overstretched and ineffective EA group painted in the *Overstrained Technical Advisors* are often neither well documented nor properly communicated. The business and IT stakeholders on the field rarely learn about those decisions in the first place. Even if they do get to know them, they hardly understand what analysis has gone into making those decisions.

In such a process, a talented team of architects leaves nothing behind but a pile of architectural models that cannot be adapted, used, or extended, simply because no one outside this expert group understands or appreciates why certain decisions have been made nor the models on which those decisions have been based. What remains is the document graveyard—an archeological evidence of their glorious architectural effort.

Strategy: Marathon or 100 m run?

Today's businesses face an unprecedented level of uncertainty and fast pace of change in their operating environments. Still, EA in general often favors the grand vision, the long-term-oriented strategy projected several years into the future.

Unfortunately, many EA initiatives tend to inherit the bureaucratic behaviors rooted in typical large enterprises. Therefore, today's EA, to a large extent, sticks to the work culture of the 1990s and shows many of the traits of a waterfall software development life cycle. This means long review and approval cycles for strategy programs, favoring a strategy that looks forward many years.

STRATEGY CARICATURES

Caricature #5: A Deep Look into the Crystal Ball
Enterprise architectures should not point too far into the future; otherwise they lose touch with reality. After a period of three years, both business situations and technology trends may change dramatically. Any strategy reaching beyond that time period therefore bears the risk of being based on speculation. The EA group may fall victim to tunnel vision, blinding out the creeping deviations of current reality from the projected future.

This situation is often accompanied by the *analysis paralysis* phenomenon: The enterprise architects are so entrenched in their strategic analysis activities that they do not have time for much else.

All stakeholders outside the EA group will perceive such types of planning as being executed from the ivory tower. This can decrease the appreciation of strategic planning as such—a dangerous path.

Against a backdrop of a volatile and fast-paced business environment, an overly long-term strategy bears many risks. If the milestone for a strategic vision points too far into the future, the impact on the

---

[11]The enterprise use of these very popular open source technologies had nearly been brought to a halt due to pending patent claims, with the risk of uncontrollable costs for license fees and compensations.

daily business is low. Here the pace of change is painstakingly slow.[12] This further widens the chasm between high-flying visions and the IT reality on the ground, often to a point of outright absurdity.

Frequently it does make sense for EA to be "deliberately myopic" about the long-term future. Gartner (2010) recommends that EA have a large portfolio of short-term strategies (around 3 to 12 months) instead of one grand vision. The expectation from the business side is to see incremental progress rather than hoping for a grand novelty far in the future.

Short-term strategies can be planned, executed, monitored, and adjusted incrementally within the context of prevailing dynamics of the external business and technology environment. Even if there still is a long-term vision in place, it is imperative for the enterprise architect to show some short-term benefits. Only that ensures that she can survive long enough to see the fulfillment of the long-term promise. This requires a certain paradigm shift for EA—from strategic to incremental, from meticulously planned to exploratory.

On the other end of the spectrum, very far away from the grand vision, the ultimate hands-on mentality rules. The rush to see quick wins can become so desperate that the enterprise architect ends up addressing tactical issues and plucking only low-hanging fruit. In that case, the EA team ends up not doing any strategic planning at all. Instead, the enterprise architects concentrate only on architecting minor changes to ensure day-to-day operability. Of course, this can no longer be called EA.

STRATEGY CARICATURES

Caricature #6: Sweeping Up the Change Requests[13]

If the enterprise architect applies too little strategic long-term thinking, the gap analysis between as-is and target states of the architecture is prone to deteriorate into a log of upcoming change requests. Talking to the business users is a very sensible activity for the enterprise architect. However, if she merely records the wish list without abstracting it into a future vision for the IT landscape, she reduces her role to that of a secretary.

Other indications of such a situation is that the EA tool is used as a software change management system and that the future state descriptions read like the solution architecture for the next upcoming software release.

Ultimately, the enterprise architect needs to determine at what point she should concentrate on the strategic intent of the enterprise and when it's time to turn to the tactical priorities on the ground—in other words, when she is running a marathon and when she's running a 100-meter run. These are seemingly different races, and the enterprise architect has to find the proper balance in between.

---

[12]In the case of a global insurance company, a large-scale vendor platform migration program had to content itself with migrating from a release *five* version steps out of date (and three years out of support) to a release *three* version steps out of date. The update to the current version was postponed to the next program, planned for another two years down the line.

[13]This caricature is based on the EA anti-pattern *Enterprise Architecture Is Not Change Management,* by Anna Mar (Mar and Spacey, 2011).

Transformation: Between standstill and continuous revolution

An IT landscape requires continuous evolution. Concentrating only on the operational aspects of IT will not be enough to meet future challenges. Both the innovations on the business side—new products, markets, and business models—and on the technology side, require a constant renewal. It is one of the core tasks of EA to plan and monitor this evolution. The change is either executed in smaller, incremental projects or as large-scale IT transformations. If the pace of change becomes too high, the operability of the whole IT system is at risk.

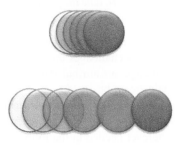

TRANSFORMATION CARICATURES

Caricature #7: The Permanent Construction Site

If the EA group drives the change in IT at such a pace that all stakeholders gasp for breath, the success of the IT transformations and the proper functioning of IT as a whole are at stake. This situation is often encountered at startups with lots of cash or in enterprises operating in innovative and booming markets.

Here the management is usually technophile and the EA organization dominated by innovation-hungry IT enthusiasts. This mix can lead to a mercurial strategy of radical changes toward the newest technologies without really understanding them in depth. The IT department has no time to develop a mature and consistent technology use; around the corner, the next technology hype is already attracting the focus of IT planners and decision makers.

On the other side of the spectrum, many ambitious IT-enabled business transformation programs come to a complete halt after encountering the harsh realities on the ground. Here is a fictitious example based on a real case. An initiative called *Global Spark* was undertaken in a manufacturing firm with the following mission statement:

> *Our strategic initiative Global Spark will deliver a single-instance Order-to-Cash (OTC) platform for worldwide operation that will vastly improve our customer satisfaction and operational efficiency. Thereby it will yield over $215 million in immediate quantifiable benefits and an additional $95 million in year-on-year ongoing benefits.*

The intent of the program was to leverage operational synergies among different business units spread across the globe and present a single face of the organization to customers around the world. However, two years down the line, the progress report of the Global Spark program read like this:

> *Global Spark is being implemented by a leading multinational systems integrator. The development of the technology platform has been under way for two years now. The functional requirements have changed three times, and current requirements are still considered to be in draft state by the major stakeholders. The program was scheduled for completion in an 18-month timeframe but has now been extended to 36 months. It was initially budgeted for $20 million, but we expect costs of $38 million as*

of now. To date the project has already spent $4 million in requirements gathering, business process analysis, and project planning.

In retrospect, when we look at why so many of these initiatives go wrong, we find that there are many challenges inherent to the complex nature of project management in IT. Quite a lot of these challenges are attributed to the risks involved in new technologies, new processes, and their adoption in mainstream business.

The popular blunders described in the list below are not caused by EA failure. However, a well-functioning EA is able to prevent the worst damage—for instance, by monitoring and timely escalation wherever needed in the following scenarios:

- *Pet programs.* Often enterprises take up wrong initiatives in the first place. Initiatives are merely shaped without charting a clear strategy or getting buy-in from all the stakeholders. "Pet programs," usually initiated at the behest of an individual sponsor without a roadmap of their long-term viability, become a problem. By definition, pet programs get a level of attention and investment that is not justified by their value. The problem becomes particularly visible if the sponsor moves on to a different job and her successor does not see the need for the program anymore. Once started, these programs acquire a life of their own and are rarely terminated, even after the sponsor's exit. Pet programs erode an organization's bottom line and are a severe drain in terms of costs and resources.

- *Poor program management.* Another obvious problem is poor project execution. This includes aspects such as inaccurate estimation of the work involved, poor reuse, extensive rework, redundant parallel effort, abrupt project termination, placing projects on the shelf, and production back-out. When inappropriate governance joins hands with poor project execution, the initiative loses momentum. Typically cases of inappropriate governance occur where the sponsors or other stakeholders, rather than the program manager alone, are also accountable for failure. The most common reasons for this situation would be lack of dialogue between business and IT stakeholders, complex cross-organizational engagements, poor accountability, and a major change in business direction partway through the program.

- *Over-ambition.* This is one of the most frequent causes of failure. It leads to cramping of too many requirements in a single release and, quite often, in the first release. The scope-creep does not leave any ground for priority management or schedule management during the project execution. Furthermore, scheduling too many programs for the available resources eventually leads to a setback in plans. The same applies to scheduling too many programs that focus only on a particular area of the organization, which then is unable to sustain the total pace of change. Every organizational group has only a limited capacity to absorb change. Exceeding that capacity creates a bottleneck and often makes a program fail.

- *Technology risks.* The risks in new technologies, and the ability of the enterprise to adopt new technologies, can endanger success. The immaturity of a technology platform or the inadequacy of a technology for the problem at hand are often overlooked under the pressure of releasing a solution in time. Technologies are volatile; they evolve continuously, or even worse, they come and go. Consequently technology platforms change in rapid succession. Although technology providers tend to ensure that their platforms have a support life of at least five years, in reality this is much less due to the lead times and delays within the enterprise while migrating to the newest version.

TRANSFORMATION CARICATURES

Caricature #8: The Ever-Growing Backlog

An EA organization that neglects change programs in the IT landscape—whether for lack of budget, planning capacity, strategic direction, or other reasons—just piles up a debt of necessary changes and adaptions.

If the enterprise architect is not driving change in the IT landscape but merely *documenting* it, he turns into a chief librarian rather than an architect of the IT landscape. The EA organization deteriorates into a documentation graveyard. The probability is low that someone will ever do anything useful with models and documents just stockpiled without an explicit purpose. And if these documents and models are indeed revisited at some point, chances are that they will be hopelessly outdated by then.

Of course, despite all risks in IT transformations, avoiding them altogether (as sketched in the caricature *The Ever-Growing Backlog*) just piles up a debt of necessary changes and adaptions. Reducing the system changes to only the most needed maintenance activities is only advisable for low-value-contributing support systems, which are run in the most cost-efficient way. Ultimately, change will always be required in some form or the other. Therefore, a well-working EA function is needed to deal with it.

Enriching EA by Lean, Agile, and Enterprise 2.0 Practices

"Action speaks louder than words but not nearly as often."

—Mark Twain

After this analysis of EA shortcomings, let's look forward again. We do not want to appear like a bunch of notorious bickerers: We also came across many enterprises in which a neat EA practice indeed showed its benefits. But there always was wide room for improvement, and tendencies to the one or other caricature described in the previous sections were always perceptible.

Our analysis of EA failures and shortcomings has revealed that EA needs to find its proper position in a complex and chaotic environment. The solution is not about eliminating chaos altogether. That would overstretch the meager powers of the EA or IT organization, or it could turn EA into an overly rigid control freak—just the other side of the coin.

As we will see, the real issue is *to balance chaos and order properly*. The question is how to leverage chaos to increase orderliness. "Chaos is created by people trying to solve immediate business problems, [and] you need to harness that energy even if it creates systems chaos," writes Eckerson (2011). The answer is given by a concept called the *Edge of Chaos*, originally introduced by Kauffman (1995) and Brown and Eisenhardt (1998). In brief, this concept states that any dynamic system *works most effectively when order and chaos are in balance*. Both too much order and too much chaos are counterproductive. We have incorporated the Edge of Chaos into an *EA Dashboard* that measures this order-chaos balance.

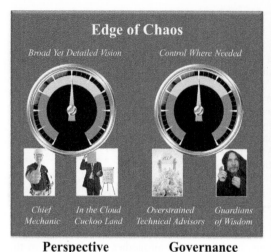
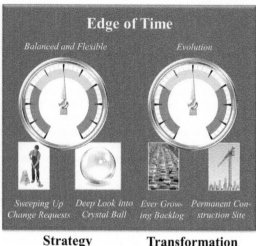

FIGURE 1-2

The EA Dashboard as a yardstick for effective EA.

The EA Dashboard, as depicted in Figure 1-2,[14] is a yardstick to measure any improvement proposals for EA. It is based on the dimensions of EA complexity introduced in the previous sections. We will introduce the classification criteria in detail in Chapter 6. As a general rule, based on our analysis of the EA failures in the previous section, it makes sense to seek a middle ground between the extremes on each gauge. We will measure the potency of our proposed EA improvements against this Dashboard.

But how can we achieve balancing EA between the extremes on the EA Dashboard? We do not believe we have the panacea for all grievances about EA. Nevertheless, something must be done to prevent EA from slipping into the gray mediocrity of yet another IT function that doesn't make an essential difference. This is basically what this book is about: proposals to take action. There is a lot to be done.

Opposed to a trend in recent publications to attack from the top down, from the more shining business and CxO perspective, our own professional roots are at the worm's-eye view of IT. This does have an effect on the approach of this book, too. Any optimization for EA needs to make sure that *all* stakeholders are on board and that they remain involved along the way—the business, the IT crowd on the ground, management, and the enterprise architects themselves. This idea can be summed up in two main challenges:

- How can we structure EA activities on a day-to-day basis in order to master a demand-driven workflow at all levels of operation and achieve a holistic result?

---

[14]The two structural EA dimensions *perspective* and *governance* are listed under *Edge of Chaos*, whereas the time-oriented dimensions *strategy* and *transformation* are subsumed under *Edge of Time*. This structure follows the terminology of Brown and Eisenhardt (1998). We will introduce this concept in more detail in Chapter 6.

- How can we elicit the participation of all, in particular the ground-level stakeholders, to balance the helicopter view and the ground-level perspective?

Our answer to these questions is to introduce lean, agile, and participation concepts into EA. We encapsulate our proposals for enriching the traditional way of doing EA in six building blocks. The first three are based on lean principles and agile practices from erstwhile software development, whereas the remaining three are drawn from Web 2.0 and Enterprise 2.0 concepts. These building blocks are the cornerstones of Collaborative Enterprise Architecture.

In software development, as project architects, we worked for years with lean and agile methods. Instead of the inflexible waterfall model, we could use a lightweight, efficient, and human-centric approach. It helped us move away from strict and error-prone up-front planning, which was only needed to avoid changes later on. With lean and agile methods, we could approach complex problems in an *iterative* fashion.

Another finding from the EA failures analysis is that EA is too often practiced in isolation. Sometimes this is deliberate, with an elitist mindset that considers only high-level decision makers, such as the CxO and the immediate next-level management, worth talking to. Sometimes it just happens—out of under-empowerment, from too much attention to detail or to concepts, and for other reasons. The countermeasure here is to introduce more participation of groups outside the "inner circle" into decision-making processes.

COLLABORATIVE ENTERPRISE ARCHITECTURE

The Three Guidelines of Collaborative EA

Altogether, our improvement approach for EA adheres to the following three guidelines:

- *Establish a lean set of processes and rules* instead of overloading the stakeholders with bureaucratic processes and unsolicited artifacts.
- *Adopt evolutionary problem solving* instead of blueprinting the whole future rigidly on a drawing board.
- *Foster and moderate open participation* instead of relying only on experts and top-down wisdom.

Practicing lean and agile methods means welcoming change, planning and executing incrementally, and focusing on structured human interaction instead of channeled reporting lines. These methods are an enabler for a reduced and efficient organization to deal with complexity—exactly what EA needs. By applying these methods to the creation of architecture instead of the creation of software, we follow the first two guidelines of collaborative EA in dealing with EA activities on a day-to-day basis.

- The focus on continuous deliveries avoids an EA that is simply dreaming of the future instead of realizing short- and mid-term benefits.
- Synchronization points (iterations, demos, frequent planning, and feedback workshops) ensure that EA is aware of the demands of the stakeholders and can easily adapt to changes in their requirements.
- Lean, as the second element our proposals, teaches us how to establish lightweight processes. Work items are pulled by demand instead of being pushed under (often false) assumptions.

Table 1-2 Collaborative EA Building Blocks 1 Through 3, Based on Lean and Agile Practices

No.	Building Block	Goal
1	Get Rid of Waste by Streamlining Architecture Processes	Values the sparse time of enterprise IT stakeholders by focusing on lean processes with as little management overhead as possible
2	Involve All Stakeholders by Interlocking Architecture Scrums	Makes sure that all stakeholders are involved by focusing on structured human interaction as a main channel of information flow
3	Practice Iterative Architecture Through EA Kanban	Welcomes change and favors iterative design over large-scale upfront planning and supports this approach with tools and methods

Table 1-3 Collaborative EA Building Blocks 4 Through 6, Based on Enterprise 2.0 Practices

No.	Building Block	Goal
4	Participation in Knowledge	Pursues new traits of sharing and combining knowledge by building self-organizing, company-wide information repositories
5	Participation in Decisions	Allows collaborative decision making by the relevant stakeholders on the ground
6	Participation in Transformation	Fosters transformation (that eventually changes the IT landscape) by participation

The practical implementation of these concepts has been condensed into three concrete building blocks, as outlined in Table 1-2. We will discuss them in more detail in Chapter 7, "Toward Pragmatism: Lean and Agile EA."

The implementation of the third guideline, *fostering participation*, is provided by three further building blocks, as shown in Table 1-3. They invite different user groups to contribute their knowledge, assessment, and opinion. They imply a paradigm shift from a one-sided reliance on subject matter experts to the *wisdom of crowds* being aroused by open-mined knowledge sharing.

Building Block 6, *Participation in Transformation*, for instance, shows a neat way to close the ubiquitous, awkward breach between enterprise architecture and implementation reality. The core tool is an architecture social software platform that is well integrated into other tools such as a configuration management database (CMDB) or dedicated EA tools. This platform can be a weapon against the divergence of high-level vision and ground-level facts. A detailed discussion can be found in Chapter 8, "Inviting to Participation: EA 2.0."

How this book is structured

Before delving into the details of our improvement building blocks, Part I of the book first explores in detail what EA is. This part comprises Chapters 2 through 5:

Chapter 2, "What Is Enterprise Architecture?" attempts a thorough definition of the term. Based on the generic meaning of the term *architecture*, we analyze the various facets of applying the term to an enterprise context.

In Chapter 3, "What Enterprise Architects Do: Core Activities of EA," we provide an overview of an enterprise architect's tasks, structured into eight main activities, EA-1 to EA-8. Grouped according to these tasks, we describe the best practices in EA, as they are practiced today. Later in the book we will refer back to these activities when discussing measures to make EA more efficient. In Chapter 4, "EA Frameworks," we describe the most well-known frameworks for structuring EA tasks and organizing an EA practice. Chapter 5, "EA Maturity Models," rounds out the picture with an overview of maturity models—frameworks that allow us to assess how well a company is running its EA practice.

Having examined the state of the art in EA, we come to our improvement proposals in Part II of the book, which consists of Chapters 6 through 8:

Chapter 6, "Foundations of Collaborative EA," comes back to the three guidelines for collaborative EA we stated earlier: the application of lean, agile, and Enterprise 2.0 concepts to EA. To begin with, we take a close look at *complexity*. What makes EA complex? And why can't that complexity be managed well by a traditional top-down, up-front planning approach? We establish a theoretical foundation to reason out these questions. With a brief reference to management, organization, and evolution theory, we arrive at the *Edge of Chaos* concept that we have already outlined briefly. This idea further leads us to introduce the *EA Dashboard* that combines the EA caricatures from the preceding section with the Edge of Chaos concept. The EA Dashboard serves as a yardstick against which to measure successful EA practices.

With the fundamentals of Collaborative EA laid in Chapter 6, we will turn back to concrete reasoning about corrective measures and practical steps to be taken. We have condensed them as six building blocks of collaborative EA and present them in Chapters 7 and 8. We measure the appropriateness and effectiveness of each building block against the EA Dashboard outlined in Chapter 6.

In Chapter 7, "Toward Pragmatism: Lean and Agile EA," we discuss how the application of lean and agile principles can render EA more pragmatic. We start off with a definition of lean and agile EA by transferring the main principles of Lean and Agile to the EA domain. In order to lay a solid foundation for our concept, we outline briefly the fundamentals of lean and agile software development, and compare both methodologies with each other. Finally, we describe our Building Blocks 1–3 (see Table 1-2 above) in detail. We will see how lean and agile thinking can be successfully incorporated into typical EA activities and processes, and how this will increase EA effectiveness, flexibility, and pragmatism.

In Chapter 8, "Inviting to Participation: EA 2.0," has a similar structure. First we describe the core concept of enriching the traditional EA methodology with collaborative Enterprise 2.0 mechanisms. As a foundation, we briefly outline the concepts behind Web 2.0 and Enterprise 2.0, with special hindsight to the use of these concepts in EA. Then we outline Building Blocks 4 through 6 (see Table 1-3) in detail. Each building block provides concepts that base EA on a more diverse, widespread judgment instead of restricting it to the wisdom of a few experts alone.

With Chapter 9, "The Next Steps: Taking Collaborative EA Forward," we conclude the book. After wrapping up the main ideas, we sketch the next steps for an enterprise architect who wants to implement some of these ideas in his or her daily work.

We encourage you to use this book as a toolbox. You can read it from beginning to end, but you can also pick only those chapters or sections that seem appropriate for your work or your immediate problem at hand.

We wish you as much pleasure reading it as we had writing it.

What Is Enterprise Architecture?

Our lives are frittered away by details; simplify, simplify.
—**Henry David Thoreau**

CONTENT

The Meaning of Architecture...31
Applying Architecture to an Enterprise 34
EA Applicability and Use 36

Enterprise architecture (EA) comes with a promise: *simplify IT*. The problem it is tackling here is about controlling the *complexity* and *cost* of IT while enabling the desired *change* and *competitiveness* for the business. The term *enterprise architecture*, in this context, appears to be self-explanatory: Apply *architectural thinking* to *simplify* the management of a complex enterprise IT landscape. There indeed are many experts who define EA along this line. Others take their own stance as to what EA means for their enterprises, given the business needs, the position of IT, and the political culture in their enterprises.

All these definitions are valid, since they provide a basis against which enterprises can scope and judge their own EA initiatives. Yet there is no consensus definition for EA today—even after 25 years of its existence. There are more fundamental truths about EA that cannot be encapsulated in a single definition. This chapter is our attempt to explore these truths.

We'll first look at the basic meaning of the term *architecture*. Then we will analyze what the term means when it's applied to describing or managing a complex system such as an *enterprise*.

The meaning of architecture

There is a widely used definition of architecture for software-intensive systems in the ANSI/IEEE standard 1471-2000 (IEEE Computer Society, 2000):

> *The fundamental organization of a system, embodied in its components, their relationships to each other and the environment, and the principles governing its design and evolution.*

Architecture is essentially meant to establish the structural foundation, behavioral characteristics, and principles that guide the creation, evolution, and operation of a system in the long run. In that way, architecture provides up-front knowledge about commonly accepted constraints and freedoms in the long-term design of the system and its constituent parts. It identifies:

- What in the system forms a stable foundation and hence is hard to change later on
- What else can remain dynamic and flexible in the long run

The architecture, or rather certain parts of the architecture documentation, is also meant to act as a basis to communicate the system knowledge to its stakeholders. The system stakeholders are the people who deal with creation, evolution, and operation of the system. There are many of them; for instance:

- The owner who pays for it
- The strategist who conceptualizes it
- The planner who plans its creation
- The designer who designs it
- The implementer who builds it
- The subcontractor who provides constituent parts for it
- The field support staff who maintains or operates it in the field

Each of these stakeholders looks at the system with her own viewpoint and cares only about her specific interests and concerns. For instance, the owner is interested in functional features and usage convenience, whereas the implementer mainly cares for technology environment, design specifications, and construction process. The stakeholders need to know about the system in the language they understand. The architecture serves this purpose by providing distinct views of the system, each view addressing the specific interest or concern of a specific stakeholder group. As a whole, the architecture may be used to view a broad outline or a detailed feature of the system, depending on who is looking at it and what is being looked at.

ARCHITECTURE

The Definition of Architecture

Architecture is the representation of the structure and behavior of a *system* and its constituent parts, plus a set of principles that guide the system's long-term evolution.

As the scale and complexity in a system grows, the need for proper planning in designing, building, and operating it becomes more and more important. Likewise, as stakeholder involvement in the system increases, the need for their shared understanding becomes crucial. *Architectural thinking* addresses these two key imperatives of managing complex systems. A small, simple, unilateral system, like the wooden birdhouse in Figure 2-1, does not require extensive architectural thinking, but larger and more complex structures do.

The following key characteristics of architectural thinking help us understand and manage a complex system:

- *Modeling.* Modeling provides an *abstraction* of a complex system for the purpose of understanding it before building or changing it. Abstraction reveals a small amount of important things that

Architectural Thinking is needed to build this...   *... and to build this...*

...but not to build this.

FIGURE 2-1

The relevance of architectural thinking.

can be dealt with at one time. This allows a selective examination of certain aspects of a system. Abstraction permits us to manage complexity and deal with essentials while ignoring inconsequential details.

- *Visualization.* Visualization is the depiction of the architecture model of a complex system, preferably using a formalized and precise notation. This serves the purpose of verifying that the model satisfies key requirements of the system. It also allows blocking out certain alternatives and making prerequisite decisions before creating or changing the actual system.
- *Communication.* The architecture models and viewpoints provide a mechanism via which to communicate knowledge about the system among system stakeholders, using a common vocabulary. The stakeholders can visualize the system in a way they can understand and act on. This enables them to mock up usage scenarios. Such scenarios imitate some or all of the external behaviors of the system in a consistent manner and in accordance with the interests and concerns of respective stakeholders.

This generic notion of architecture is applicable in many engineering practices, especially traditional civil, mechanical, and electrical engineering disciplines. It fits well for building and construction of houses or manufacturing cars. It has also been generally accepted in the world of computers. Hardware architecture, network architecture, and software architecture are predominantly used to define IT systems. But *enterprise architecture* goes beyond IT systems and pure technology.

Applying architecture to an enterprise

March and Simon (1958) define *enterprises* as complex systems comprising individuals or groups that coordinate actions in pursuit of common goals. During the late 1980s, John Zachman (1987) applied the notion of architecture to represent the functioning of an enterprise, specifically within the context of the enterprise IT landscape and the business environment. Therefore, the primary scope for the term *enterprise* in this book is reduced to the *enterprise IT landscape plus its relationship with the business environment*.

Enterprise architecture (EA), then, is loosely defined as *the architecture of a system where the system is the whole enterprise*. Figure 2-2, using an analogy with city planning, illustrates the core concept behind EA.

With Enterprise Architecture, *one can build this …*

With System Architecture, *one can build this…*

… and avoid this …

FIGURE 2-2

An illustration of enterprise architecture and its purpose.

ARCHITECTURE IN THE CONTEXT OF BUSINESS-IT MANAGEMENT IN AN ENTERPRISE

What Is Enterprise Architecture?

Enterprise architecture (EA) is the representation of the structure and behavior of an enterprise's IT landscape in relation to its business environment. It reflects the current and future use of IT in the enterprise and provides a roadmap to reach a future state. EA offers:

- An insight into the current utilization of IT in business operations,
- A vision for the future utilization of IT in business operations, and
- A roadmap for the evolution of the IT landscape from the current state to a future state, along with the transient states in between.

EA is documented using architecture artifacts such as model diagrams and principles. These are collectively referred to as the *architecture blueprint*.

ARCHITECTURE IN THE CONTEXT OF BUSINESS-IT MANAGEMENT IN AN ENTERPRISE

What Is Enterprise Architecture Management?

Enterprise architecture management (EAM) is a structured approach that an enterprise uses for creating, managing, and using enterprise architecture to align business and IT. EAM translates the enterprise vision into venture and takes the enterprise through the journey from its current state to the target state.

In this book, we use the term EA as a synonym for both EA and EAM, since in practice the two concepts are inseparable.

It must be noted that EA does not stand alone in its pursuit of managing the complexities of the enterprise IT landscape. Apart from pure EA, the role of an enterprise architect extends into the realms of other IT management practices as well, especially in strategic enterprise planning, IT investment management, IT project management, and IT infrastructure management.

Figure 2-3 shows that EA describes a clear *line of sight* from strategic goals through project investments to measurable business value and performance improvements—for the entire enterprise or for a part of the enterprise. EA helps organize and illuminate the relationships among the enterprise's strategic goals, investments, business solutions, and measurable performance indicators.

EA is however just one link in a lattice of integrated IT practice areas. Other practice areas, such as strategic planning, investment management, project management, and infrastructure management, must be equally strong and *fully integrated* with the EA practice. Only through such integration can EA provide a stable foundation for sound IT management practices, end-to-end governance of IT investments, and alignment of IT implementation with the enterprise's vision and strategic goals.

There is one more fundamental distinction of EA that should be noted here. In contrast to the traditional architecture practices, which primarily look at pure *technical* systems such as a bridge, a car, or a plane, EA deals with a *socio-technical* system. This difference is like the difference between a house and a home. A house is a mere structure that provides shelter; a home is a place where a family lives. The people element brings complex behavioral attributes into the functioning of an enterprise in the same way as it turns a house into a home. Hence, the term *architecture* does not literally apply to the enterprise in the same way as it has been traditionally applied to technical systems.

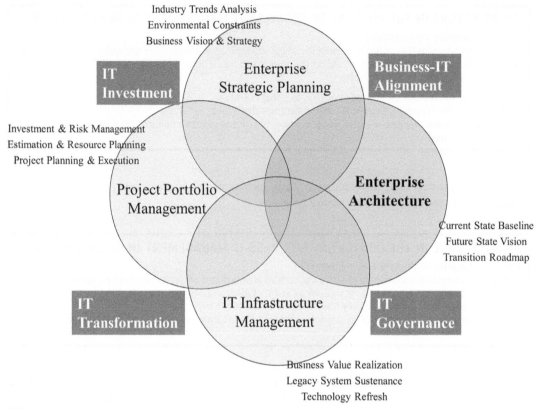

FIGURE 2-3

The position of enterprise architecture in IT management.

In this book, an enterprise is characterized as an organization of people who use (among other things) IT to do business. In that sense, enterprise architecture not only deals with technical aspects such as IT systems and infrastructure, but it also deals with social elements such as collaborative business processes, organizational leadership, political dynamics, and work culture in the enterprise. This fact carries great consequences for the way EA should be looked at and dealt with. We will elaborate this concept in greater detail in Chapter 6, in the section "Reflection on Complexity."

EA applicability and use

Today most large and midsize organizations across all industry sectors embrace EA as an authoritative entity having its own budget, headcount, processes, and organizational structure. EA is specifically predominant in companies with a decentralized organization and a distributed operational environment, where an enterprise-wide shared vision and an integrated strategic plan are the key imperatives for business success.

The way in which EA is approached is, however, specific to the context and scope within which the enterprise operates. A bank operates in a different fashion than a car manufacturer. Within the financial services industry, a retail bank does not work like an investment bank. Even within a retail bank there may be major differences between regions or market segments. In each case, EA is approached differently, but it always has a common purpose and theme: EA enables an understanding of the structure and behavior of the enterprise business and IT from a *holistic viewpoint*. It also provides a strategic approach to evolving the enterprise IT landscape. In that way, EA can deal with the complexity of its environment and manage the change in the enterprise's IT landscape and business environment.

EA can be applied to scopes other than the enterprise IT landscape alone. It has a valid use case in any of the following scenarios:

- Managing the business operation and the IT landscape of large and midsize enterprises
- Managing business and IT for a sufficiently complex subdomain of an enterprise
- Managing large-scale, IT-enabled business transformations in the enterprise
- Managing the product life cycle of a software product company

In many large companies, the term *EA* is applied to cases where the "enterprise" is not the entire company but just a sufficiently complex subdomain of the main enterprise. The business-IT ecosystem owned by a subdomain can already be complex enough to demand a dedicated EA focus for itself. Here are some examples:

- A line of business for a large bank—for instance, the retail-banking division with a country-wide network of 5,000 branches in a distributed operating environment
- Customer services of a telecom operator with more than 300 CRM applications across four business lines
- The regional operating unit of a manufacturer in Europe
- A unified web portal platform of an insurance firm that supports three business lines and five regional segments

To elaborate further, let's consider a global car manufacturing enterprise. The complexity of its information systems is enormous, ranging from human resources applications over marketing and finance up to supply chain management and computer-aided manufacturing systems. This complexity results from the multitude of business functions and operations at a global scale. Moreover, the enterprise typically is a merger of several companies producing different brands. This implies a great deal of diversity in business strategies, principles, and goals among different sub-domains of the enterprise.

Furthermore, the business is distributed all over the world and has to comply with the legal, cultural, and business stipulations in each country. Recently, many enterprises with distributed business operations and decentralized organizations have tried to leverage synergies across their business units, market segments, or geographic regions. These enterprises have engaged in large-scale, cross-organizational, IT-enabled business transformation initiatives. IT is placed at the core of business success by such initiatives. Their promise is to deliver tangible business benefits in terms of cost reduction, operational excellence, customer satisfaction, or product innovation. Such programs involve harmonization of significant parts of the business processes in different business units and system integration across data centers. Even if the scope is not the whole enterprise, EA is still required in such initiatives, since we need to instill a shared vision and a structured approach while managing the complexity involved.

Let's conclude by looking at software vendors such as Oracle, IBM, or Microsoft. From their perspective, EA usually does not involve dealing with their own supporting IT infrastructure but with the envisioning, roadmap creation, and release planning of their software products and platforms. EA in this context is employed to strategically manage the roadmaps and release plans for vendors' software products and platforms.

EA has a role to play whenever one plans to do anything that spans many applications, projects, business units, geographical regions, or market segments. It comprises methodology and taxonomy to deal with certain problems and demands in the strategic management of business and IT. In the next chapter, we will take a closer look at how an enterprise architect uses these tools to fulfill her mission.

What Enterprise Architects Do: Core Activities of EA

3

CONTENT

Defining the IT Strategy (EA-1) 41
    Defining the Goals... 42
    Stipulating the Rules 43
    The Gartner Grid 46
    Identifying the Initiatives 48
    The Role of an Enterprise Architect.. 49
Modeling the Architectures (EA-2) 49
    Models and Views of Various Architectures 49
    Visualizing Cross-Relations and Transformations 51
    Modeling Standards.. 52
Evolving the IT Landscape (EA-3)..58
    Application Rationalization.. 58
    General IT Transformations 66
    SOA Transformations 67
Assessing and Building Capabilities (EA-4) 69
    Competence Development for Enterprise Architects................................ 69
    Formalizing Enterprise Architecture 74
    EA Team Position in the Organization Structure 76
Developing and Enforcing Standards and Guidelines (EA-5) 78
    Standardizing on Technology Usage 79
    Enforcing Standards and Guidelines.. 83
Monitoring the Project Portfolio (EA-6)..86
    Building the Project Portfolio 87
    Auditing the Portfolio... 93
Leading or Coaching Projects (EA-7) 98
Managing Risks Involved in IT (EA-8)..100

In this chapter, we dig deeper into the question of what enterprise architects actually do to manage an enterprise's architecture. What duties belong to their role and make up their profession? What kinds of activities characterize their daily work, and what are the established best practices to perform those duties?

Because of the many facets of EA, any compilation of EA activities will probably be incomplete, but the selection we lay out in this chapter lists the situations we most frequently encounter in both practice and literature. The activities we find most characteristic and prevalent are shown in Table 3-1.

The emphasis on activities can be different in each firm; an activity that gets the most attention in one firm might be almost neglected in another. Therefore, we do not make an attempt to prioritize activities by importance or effort involved. Neither are we interested in putting them into a sequential order; this is achieved by frameworks such as the TOGAF™ Architecture Development Method, which we'll take a look at in the next chapter.

Table 3-1 Core Activities of Enterprise Architecture Management

Activity	Name	Description	Catchwords
EA-1	Defining the IT Strategy	EA-1 is about defining the rules for the future evolution of IT and identifying strategic initiatives to be pursued.	Mission statement, strategy, maxim process
EA-2	Modeling the Architectures	EA-2 is about making models for the current and the future states. There is a set of techniques, tools, and standards for modeling.	Modeling, EA tools, architecture blueprint, architecture repository
EA-3	Evolving the IT Landscape	EA-3 is about application rationalization and optimizing application landscapes with respect to certain predefined criteria. Evolving a service or process portfolio and modeling the next release of the various architectures (business, IS, technology) are part of this activity. SOA belongs to this activity as an architectural style aligning business and IT.	Roadmap, application rationalization, SOA, quantitative aspects, KPI, service portfolio, IT transformations
EA-4	Assessing and Developing Capabilities	EA-4 is about maturity assessment and competence development for the EA practice and for the IT department as a whole. This involves assessing the architecture practice and improving it. It also comprises the strategic planning of competences that must be there in the architecture team or IT department in order to work with the future set of products and standards.	Maturity assessment, architecture process improvements, competence development
EA-5	Developing and Enforcing Standards and Guidelines	EA-5 is about monitoring technology and standards, choosing the right ones, communicating them, and applying suitable means to check that standards and guidelines are followed accordingly. Examples of such means are reviews or automated tools (e.g., code sniffers in a build environment).	Technology radar, project governance, IT and architecture standards

Continued

		Table 3-1 Core Activities of Enterprise Architecture Management—Cont'd	
Activity	**Name**	**Description**	**Catchwords**
EA-6	Monitoring the Project Portfolio	EA-6 is about the enterprise architect's contribution to the project portfolio management. This comprises pushing through strategic EA projects as project owners, assessing projects with respect to strategic fit and standard compliance, and installing quality gates that projects have to pass. The quality gates also give an input to the backfilling of architecture models with the projects' deliverables.	Quality management, budget planning, strategic fit, architecture compliance review
EA-7	Leading or Coaching Projects	Enterprise architects are often engaged to lead or coach critical, high-value projects from a technical point of view. Their involvement in such projects goes beyond their usual high-level advise-and-monitor role.	Project architect, coaching
EA-8	Managing Risks Involved in IT	EA models allow answering questions about the risks involved in IT. What is the impact on business processes or organizational units of server X going down? Enterprise architects are often involved in planning issues, such as failover or 24/7 scenarios. They are also responsible for security guidelines and have a say on (or even control over) service-level agreements (SLAs).	Business continuity planning, security, SLA

Instead, the two major goals here are drawing a realistic picture of the kind of work that enterprise architects are entangled in and describing some of the established practices to succeed. But we'll constrain ourselves here to *contemporary* best practices, meaning approaches you can find out there in the field or in the relevant publications. They're not our invention, and in the following sections we describe those practices that are, in our own judgment, most well known and convincing.

In contrast, Part II of the book (Chapters 6 through 8) is dedicated to *improvements* of the state of the art. We will frequently refer to EA-1 to EA-8 (as shown in Table 3-1) to assess in which activities the improvements can do some good and how they change the current way of working.

But for now we'll stick to the current practice and hope that the newcomer to the subject gets a tangible view of EA, whereas the old hands may enjoy a quick recap, hopefully learning about one or two items they didn't know about before.

Defining the IT strategy (EA-1)

Half of the activities of EA are strategic by nature. Evolving the IT landscape, for example, entails drawing the future information system landscape, which certainly gives a strategic direction. But EA-1, as we shall see, sets up the principles guiding all subsequent strategic decisions and thus is the root and point of departure for strategy.

Defining the IT strategy positions IT in the enterprise environment and future direction and defines how IT can be better utilized to attain business goals. This process consists of three steps:

1. Defining the goals to be pursued over the time span covered by the strategy
2. Stipulating the rules that dictate how these goals are to be reached
3. Identifying the initiatives that move the enterprise's IT toward the goals

In this section, we'll walk through these steps one by one and explain the challenges and approaches involved in each of them.

Defining the goals

Let's first take a look at an example of a typical business goal: The automotive industry has become highly volatile in the past few years. Manufacturing plants are shooting up like mushrooms in emerging markets, and the car companies force their suppliers to keep up with this rapid pace. As a manufacturer of shock absorbers, for instance, you must be able to build up a new supply plant sufficiently fast wherever in the world your major customer decides to build cars; otherwise, you're out. The ambitious goal your business management derives from this challenge is:

> *We must be able to ramp up a plant in half a year in any geographic region, and we want to reach this capability in one year.*

This is a business goal, and quite a good one. It scores quite high when benchmarked against the acronym *SMART*. This quality seal gathers the features a useful goal should have: *Specific, Measurable, Actionable, Relevant, and Time-bound.* The previously stated business goal could be a trifle more specific about the geographic regions and under what conditions a plant is considered "ramped up." But it at least states a metric and the ramp-up time and nails down the time horizon of one year (it is time-bound). The addressees probably recognize it as relevant and roughly know the first steps to act on it (it is actionable).

But in practice, one often finds that goals lack some or all of the SMART qualities. Mack and Frey (2002) list some caricatures of goals that are, for instance, absurdly unspecific: "Increase our market share," "Make our products more attractive," "Keep existing customers and acquire new ones." It indeed is close to impossible to derive guidance from such goals—in particular if they just are a small excerpt of a long CEO Christmas list. Platitudes like this don't pass the "Dilbert Test" illustrated in Figure 3-1: *State the opposite, and watch whether something absurd takes form.*

FIGURE 3-1

The "Dilbert Test" for platitude goals.

The Christmas list, meaning the obstacle of an unfocused or even contradictory set of goals, can only be mitigated by urging the board of business managers to decide for a handful of them. If the business leaders decide to drop "Make our products more attractive" but not "Keep existing customers and acquire new ones," we at least have a clue where the business is heading. Strategic initiatives consequentially should invest in marketing and CRM rather than in improving the product development or manufacturing chain. In most cases, however, the issue won't be an "either/or." Instead, prioritization of goals will be required, a step that inherently belongs to defining goals. A choice or ranking implies a mandate to act on, and the maxim process we shall describe a little later can help in pushing a business board to make it.

Several flavors of the term *goal* are in use. Some talk about objectives, some about requirements, and others swear by formulating visions. These flavors have their point, but in terms of the bottom line it is all about agreeing on *what* is wanted, *how eagerly* it is wanted, and maybe *who* wants it. There's no need to be overly subtle about it.

Stipulating the rules

There's a broad consensus that *defining the IT strategy* is an exercise that cannot be achieved without an intense collaboration between business and IT. Broadbent and Kitzis (2005) regard the involvement of senior business executives in the definition of the IT strategy as *the* crucial factor in turning IT from a cost-generating infrastructure to a business enabler. Nevertheless, in practice it is difficult to get business executives on board.

A proven approach to tackling this obstacle is the so-called *management by maxims* process conceptualized by Broadbent and Weill (1997). The process is far from being rocket science: It boils down to gathering the senior business and IT representatives for an intense one-day brainstorming workshop. The pain of business executives to devote some time to IT is thereby kept at a minimum. To make the most of such a day, there must be three topics on the agenda:

* Definition of the business maxims
* Derivation of IT maxims out of the business maxims
* Agreement on the extent of shared services and infrastructure support

For the day to be a success, the topics must previously be prepared by some assistants; the enterprise architects typically belong to this group. On the day itself, it might be just the chief enterprise architect who is invited to the illustrious workshop.

The first two agenda items are about maxims. Broadbent and Kitzis (2005) define a *maxim* as a "statement that specifies a practical course of conduct." They recommend formulating not more than six business maxims that "[...] need to be concise, compelling, concrete, easily communicated, and readily understood as statements that people throughout the entire organization can use as guidelines for making decisions and taking actions." Here are two examples of good business maxims taken from their book (2005, pp. 84, 91):

* All sales employees are decision makers about taking new policies and cross-selling.
* Maximize independence in local operations with a minimum of mandates.

Deducing IT maxims from such business maxims is the second topic on the agenda. There can be more IT maxims than business maxims, but the catalogue should still be crisp enough to be remembered

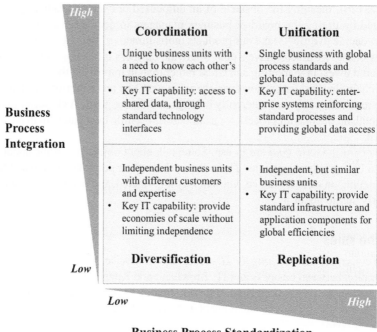

Business Process Integration — High / Low

Coordination
- Unique business units with a need to know each other's transactions
- Key IT capability: access to shared data, through standard technology interfaces

Unification
- Single business with global process standards and global data access
- Key IT capability: enterprise systems reinforcing standard processes and providing global data access

Diversification
- Independent business units with different customers and expertise
- Key IT capability: provide economies of scale without limiting independence

Replication
- Independent, but similar business units
- Key IT capability: provide standard infrastructure and application components for global efficiencies

Business Process Standardization — Low / High

FIGURE 3-2

Four operating models (Ross, 2005, used with kind permission)

by members of the organization in their daily decisions. The two examples stated previously, for example, could give rise to the following IT maxims:

- All sales employees, wherever they are, must have access to contract and customer data.
- Business units can determine the most suitable applications for their business, provided they comply with a minimum set of standards set throughout the enterprise.

The last item on the agenda is to get an idea of the enterprise's need for shared services and infrastructure. The deeper rationale for this exercise is to position the firm (or maybe even individual business units) in what Jeanne W. Ross from the MIT Center for Information System Research calls an *operating model*. Ross (2005) distinguishes four main categories of operating models, as shown in Figure 3-2.

Technical people, especially technology-focused architects, have a bias for standardization and integration and tend to believe that these most naturally belong to the canonical goals of each enterprise. But it is not a matter of maturity in which of the quadrants of the Ross model an enterprise ends up; it depends on the business outlook, the competitive strategy, and the enterprise governance. Let's take a brief look at each of these parameters.

Broadbent and Kitzis (2005) distinguish three fundamental *business outlooks*, namely:

- *Fighting for survival.* Budget cuts, layoffs, and cancellation of initiatives characterize this outlook. The emphasis is on cost reduction.

- *Maintaining competitiveness.* The enterprise is parsimoniously balanced between cost savings and investments in initiatives. Budgets are flat, and new initiatives must be thoroughly justified.
- *Breaking away.* These are the happy days for new initiatives. Budgets are generous, and the challenge for IT is in keeping up with the growth, or even better, driving it.

The second parameter following the *business outlook* that influences the need for standardization and integration is the *competitive strategy.* The economist Michael Porter (1998) describes three generic strategies that, on a rough scale, classify all approaches to competition. These are:

- *Cost efficiency.* Offering a better price is the main competitive advantage. The emphasis is on operational excellence to keep costs low.
- *Differentiation.* The enterprise tries to combat competitors by better products, quality, or customer care. The emphasis is on product leadership or customer intimacy.
- *Focus strategies.* The enterprise gains advantages from occupying market niches.

Even in the generic terms sketched here, it becomes evident that an enterprise architect who is much in favor of standardization and integration can do harm to an enterprise that is breaking away and strives for differentiation by developing the most innovative products on the market. While business is demanding a rapid positioning of new IT applications and services, the EA hits the breaks by imposing standardization and integration compliancy on the development teams.

Enterprise governance is of equal importance as the previous two parameters. Weill and Ross (2004) define *governance* as a body of meta-regulations for management, stipulating the following issues:

1. What kind of decisions must be taken
2. Who is accountable for making these decisions
3. How decisions are made and eventually monitored

One core question decided by governance is how much autonomy is granted to business units or geographical regions. In case this autonomy is high, would a quest for high IT integration and standardization not be like fighting windmills?

Therefore, the enterprise architect must be aware of the business outlook, the competitive strategy, and the enterprise governance and must use them as landmarks in decision making. The maxim process provides a useful opportunity to call for information about these parameters.

A remarkable feature of the maxim process is that it is about abstract rules only. Broadbent and Weill (1997) coined the term *management by maxims* for a kind of strategy definition founded on abstract decision rules. This approach actually does away with a popular misunderstanding of what a strategy actually is. Elementary game theory defines a player's strategy as a "complete plan of action for whatever situation might arise; a plan that fully determines the player's behavior at any stage of the game, for every possible history of play up to that stage" (Wikipedia "Strategy," 2011). The player becomes an executor of an algorithm in this conception, as visualized in Figure 3-3.

But for complex games like chess, there is no algorithmic strategy that *guarantees* a win. Who would expect that there is an algorithmic plan of action that guarantees a successful transformation of the enterprise's IT, a plan ensuring that all business goals are met? This algorithmic concept of a strategy has its limitations.

FIGURE 3-3

Strategy as algorithm: A popular misconception.

Complex systems cannot be managed at an object level, only at a *meta level*. This will be one of our insights we discuss in Chapter 6, "Foundation of Collaborative EA," where we reflect on the key implications of complexity. Management at a meta level basically means *management by maxims*.

Existing frameworks for defining an IT strategy widely acknowledge this constraint. The TOGAF framework, for example, uses the term *principle* instead of *maxim*. But principles are defined as "general rules and guidelines [...] that inform and support the way in which an organization sets about fulfilling its mission" (The Open Group, 2009, p. 265). Thus, *principle* can in practice be regarded as a synonym for *maxim*. Principles are identified in the Preliminary and Architecture Vision phases of the TOGAF™ ADM, and they form a foundation for the subsequent architecture definition endeavor.

It is a good practice to accompany the bare statement of a principle by a rationale, a set of implications the principle might have, and possibly further auxiliaries such as metrics or the application context. This helps the decider and is recommended by TOGAF as well as by Weill and Ross (2004).

The Gartner Grid

Gartner Research has elaborated another methodology for formulating IT strategies in a series of papers published during the years 2002 and 2003. The definition of *strategy* in these papers is very concise (Mack and Frey, 2002):

A strategy takes a vision or objective and bounds the options for attaining it.

The approach to "bounding the options" actually is spelling out abstract decision rules and therefore is yet another instance of management by maxims. The most often cited concept from Gartner's papers is the two-dimensional grid shown in Table 3-2. This grid can be used to check the completeness of IT strategies.

On one hand, this grid ensures that all aspects of the IT strategy that may require a decision further down the road are guided by rules. On the other, it lists all inputs from the business strategy that can have an impact on IT and therefore must not be neglected.

The seven inputs from the business strategy are spelled out as follows:

- *Geographic*. This is about the expansion and national/international distribution of the enterprise.

Table 3-2 Business Strategy Elements Mapped to IT Strategy

| | | IT Strategy | | | |
	Infrastructure	Service	Applications	Integration	Sourcing
Geographic					
Governance					
Future					
Legacy IT					
Virtual					
Customer					
Funding					

(Row labels under "Inputs from Business Strategy")

- *Governance.* Who makes decisions, and how are they made? Are the business units or geographic regions relatively autonomous, or is there a strong central authority?
- *Future.* This concerns how far the time horizon of business plans is. They can be long-term, midterm, or even bound only to what has to be done next.
- *Legacy IT.* Is there a will to make drastic changes, or is the attitude conservative and committed to the current way of operation?
- *Virtual.* This is about the involvement and integration of service providers and other partners. What capabilities and processes are kept in-house, and which are handed over to partners?
- *Customer.* How strongly does the enterprise want to engage its customers?
- *Funding.* Who is paying and how much? How are projects funded, and what are the criteria for granting budgets?

These inputs must be taken into account, according to Gartner. If they are not available right away, the enterprise architect must seek answers and hold the business side accountable for giving them.

The business imperatives are then mapped to five components of the IT strategy, which can briefly be explained as follows:

- *Infrastructure.* This is the technology component, comprised of hardware, software, and network elements.
- *Service.* This concerns the services provided by the IT department to the enterprise, to partners, and to customers.
- *Applications.* This is about the portfolio of applications, their business functions, and the processes and organizations it supports.
- *Integration.* All means making the enterprise act as a single unit are subsumed under this component.
- *Sourcing.* This component addresses the source of all the people who perform the IT-related strategic work. In particular it sets rules for selecting internal employees or external service providers.

Now, how can we use the Gartner grid in practice? Let's take the example of an automotive supplier and the goal we discussed earlier:

We must be able to ramp up a plant in half a year in any geographic region, and we want to reach this capability in one year.

This requirement can be seen as one of the inputs in Gartner's Geographic row. But what does it imply for the different columns of the IT strategy? Here is a walk-through that should sketch the idea:

- *Infrastructure*. The IT organization decides to go for highly standardized technology stacks that can rapidly be replicated to new sites. The rule is to prefer out-of-the-box solutions over custom implementations.
- *Service*. The guideline is to rely as much as possible on onsite services but to work according to the standards established in other parts of the world. Services are to be provided in the local language.
- *Applications*. The principle is to utilize the standard applications and global templates of business processes. Customization must be justified by strong reasons—for instance, country-specific legal constraints.
- *Integration*. The integration is to be kept to a minimum. Integration costs grow over-proportionally with the number of sites, and a tight integration can slow the implementation.
- *Sourcing*. The work is done by onsite forces. External suppliers are preferred in order to keep latencies for training and education at a minimum.

In practice, the mapping rarely is straightforward and without logical conflicts. A good governance of strategic planning should not leave the IT side alone with business requirements that are impossible to accomplish. Instead, there must be feedback loops allowing for a reconsideration or reprioritization of business maxims.

Identifying the initiatives

Just envisioning the goals and stating the rules does not get things going. One also has to identify the strategic initiatives people should start working on. We intentionally use the term *initiative* because the plan of action is usually yet too coarse to speak of well-scoped projects. At this granularity, it is not about a proper project portfolio management: The *how* is widely unclear, there's no target architecture in place, and all we have is intentions to start with. A typical scenario would be an imaginary car manufacturer, Cars4Us, which has committed to the goal of keeping existing customers.[1] A high-level business maxim aiming at this goal could be:

We make the customer perceive us as a helpful companion, and we maximize the number of services and contact points accordingly.

The different business units of Cars4Us examine this maxim and come up with initiatives as to how to put this into practice. Customer care concludes they should point the customer to all service incidents and technical checkups in advance. Therefore, they take up a business initiative that models the whole life cycle of a car, with all probable events and corresponding interactions (car care, repairs, new purchase, etc.) with the customer. The IT initiative derived from it implements this process in the customer relationship management (CRM) system and automates such things as sending notification mailings about upcoming technical checkups.

---

[1]This scenario is derived from a real case example the authors encountered in one of their client projects.

Marketing, on the other hand, intends to extend the services beyond the narrow scope of car care-taking. They kick off an IT initiative centered on mobile applications in order to explore what kind of helpful gadgets could be offered on a smartphone. The range is wide: racing games with Cars4Us models, augmented reality manuals for the car, or apps alerting the user to events such as concerts or football games close by. The initiative is complemented by an investment into customer analytics. Cars4Us wants to learn about the customer and her wishes from the mobile interactions.

This example illustrates that there's no way to systematically deduce the right initiatives. There's not even a framework for guidance. One is left to one's own creativity and a thorough understanding of the enterprise and the way the business is run.

The initiatives usually do not directly lead to implementation projects. The latter are rather pursued by pre-projects detailing the requirements and target architecture to a level that allows for proper project planning of effort, business value, and risks involved.

The role of an enterprise architect

Enterprise architects are typically not accountable for the enterprise's IT strategy. It is the CIO who signs off on it and has to answer for it. Nevertheless, enterprise architects usually participate in strategic boards and meetings, prepare decisions, or elaborate drafts coming out of such meetings. There can be parts of the IT strategy on which enterprise architects have little to say—for instance, in defining service-desk policies. But even if they are not primary speakers in these parts, they are at least informed or consulted. Hence EA is deeply involved in shaping the enterprise's IT strategy.

Defining the IT strategy is a hot spot with regard to interpersonal issues, since it is on the borderline between business and IT and critically depends on the collaboration between the two. In a sense it is the stage for a culture clash, a meeting point of businesspeople on one side and IT folks with roots in programming on the other. On university campuses these two species looked at each other with suspicion, sometimes even with deprecation. If the atmosphere between business and IT is poisoned anyway, which is not a rare constellation, it is embarrassing how such meetings can easily distort into recriminations. The enterprise architect sits on the borderline between these two camps, and the best thing for him to do is to take on the role of moderator. This requires a good dose of political aplomb.

Modeling the architectures (EA-2)
Models and views of various architectures

Making architecture models probably is what most people primarily associate with the profession of an architect. Software developers expect the architect to come along with a blueprint for implementation. Managers expect they have to gaze at annoyingly complex diagrams when an enterprise architect starts explaining why a cable fire affected so many business processes.

Models are abstractions of some part of reality. They suppress irrelevant details but strive for being accurate with respect to the points of interests. Models are always bound to a certain purpose; otherwise there is no way to tell what is relevant and what is not. An enterprise architect, for instance, models the way IT is currently used in the enterprise as well as the roadmap to future use. But she typically does not model the air conditioning in the server rooms or the cabling for employee workplaces. What goes into the model and what is left out depends on the model's use cases, and there is a wide range of things that can be done with an enterprise architecture model, namely:

- *Design and planning*. The model is a tool for designing the future evolution of the enterprise's IT. It is a means to identify the gaps between *as is* and *to be* and the corresponding needs for action.
- *Analysis and assessment*. The model helps analyze the impact of incidents or changes. It allows assessing issues such as strategic fit, compliance with laws and regulations, or risks.
- *Implementation and operation*. The model is a framework of orientation for detailed design. It is a knowledge base for operating and maintaining information systems.
- *Communication and enforcement*. The model is a foundation for explaining and motivating changes. It is a means to assure that the intended architecture is actually implemented in the intended way.

There are probably more use cases than the ones we've listed, but this selection suffices to characterize the model as an important asset of enterprise architecture management. On the other hand, making and maintaining a model is laborious and expensive. Therefore, one should not ride a hobbyhorse when doing so but instead stick to what the actual use cases require. Striving for completeness, true-to-detail reproduction of reality, compliance to some architecture standard as an end in itself, or gold-plating the model is a waste of effort.

Communication is a use case deserving special attention. The enterprise architect uses the model to answer specific questions of stakeholders. Take, for example, the country head of an enterprise's Mexican branch. He wants to learn about a new global business process that is planned to replace a local mode of operation. Concerns like this are not directly addressed by the model itself, and the enterprise architect is well advised not to present raw model material such as business process modeling notation (BPMN) diagrams to senior managers. Stakeholders have a specific viewpoint on a subject, and their perspective must be addressed by a corresponding view on the model.

The country head, in our example, wants to know whether the business process replacement changes the roles and responsibilities of his personnel, whether there are any investments needed, and how the IT total cost of ownership is affected. Other aspects such as strategic fit with the global IT strategy are of little interest to him. It is the enterprise architect's job to draw a tangible view, custom-tailored for this specific stakeholder.

The distinction between model and view is sensible and commonly made.[2] There actually are technically oriented people who believe that the model is the sheer truth, whereas views are what you "tell the kids." But the enterprise architect who seriously takes the role of mediator between the various parties who have stakes in IT should abandon this somewhat nerdish attitude.

A holistic view of the enterprise's IT requires more than one architecture to cover all aspects. On the business side, we have the business architecture that is concerned about the business goals, key performance indicators, organizational units, geographical locations, processes, business capabilities, and even more entities of the business realm. On the technology side there is the infrastructure architecture, consisting of servers, networks, data stores, software products, standards, frameworks, and further miscellaneous hardware and software thingies of which a runtime environment is composed. The TOGAF framework we are going to take a closer look at in Chapter 4, "EA Frameworks," distinguishes as many as four different architectures that are layered from the business architecture down to the technology components: business architecture, data architecture, application architecture, and technology architecture.

---

[2]See, for instance, the IEEE 1471 standard that defines a meta-model for architecture descriptions (IEEE 2000).

Visualizing cross-relations and transformations

Enterprise architects are in charge of making the entanglement of business and IT comprehensible. The models they create must therefore capture relations between all architecture layers, from business down to technology. Likewise, the views on top of these models should visualize how the entities of the layers, which in a first approach appear rather isolated, are in fact interwoven. Figure 3-4 depicts a highly simplified but typical example from a fictitious logistics company.

This *process map* draws a relationship among business processes, the organizational units in charge of them, and the applications supporting these units in their duties. It highlights, for example, that the organizational Unit B uses a rather old 2.3 release of the CRM system, whereas Unit E is already equipped with the more modern release 3.0. As a consequence, Unit B has to work with the legacy applications GDA and DES to manage the whole pickup and delivery processes.

Another kind of view that is widely used to visualize relations is the *cluster diagram*. Figure 3-5 is, again, a highly simplified example of a more technically oriented cluster diagram that draws a relationship between technology platforms and applications based on those platforms. The applications are sorted into clusters according to the technology they are built on; the reader can learn from it, for example, that release 7.1 of the Settlement application is built on an exceptional technology mix (MS SQL Server and JBoss) that might not accord with an enterprise's technology standards.

We can choose from among a large variety of process maps and cluster diagrams. The process map can, for instance, also be used to visualize relationships between processes, supporting application functions, and business objects involved in these functions. But the two examples shown should suffice to illustrate how they address relationships, dependencies, and cross-concerns. The reader interested in a broader treatment of best-practice EA views may refer, for instance, to Hanschke (2010).

Another peculiarity of enterprise architecture models is that they have a time dimension. The models do not merely present a snapshot of the architecture(s) at a particular point in time; they capture

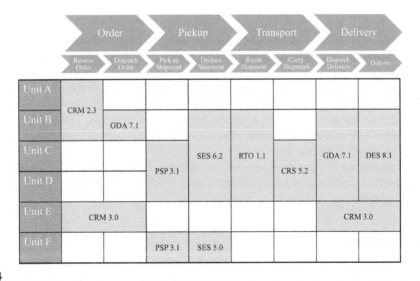

FIGURE 3-4

Process map.

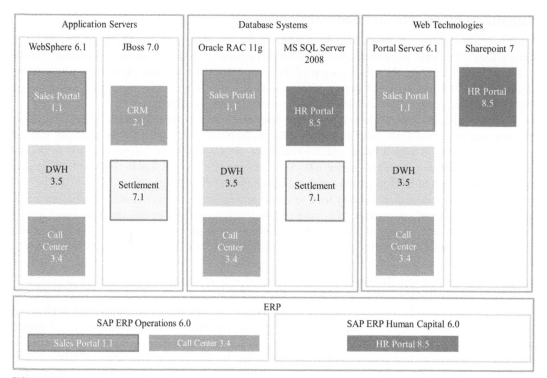

FIGURE 3-5

Cluster diagram.

the current state, the future desired state, and possibly a roadmap of transition states along the way. Figure 3-6 is a simplified example of an *application roadmap* addressing the evolution of the application landscape.

Another frequently used means of eliciting "Aha!" effects of how things will evolve is a *flip-book of consecutive states*, like the one in Figure 3-7. The two consecutive states show the simplified application landscape of a logistics company, clustered by functional domains. The arrows mark the data flow with regard to a central business object. The flip-book now clearly demonstrates the effect of an application rationalization on this flow.

There is an abundance of variants of such landscape maps. You may use them to relate applications with technology stacks, business objects with application functions, or whatever results in a better understanding of how the bits and pieces fit together.

Modeling standards

The notation, terminology, and conceptual meta-model of enterprise architecture models are not standardized in practice. Unlike software design, where most practitioners nowadays agree that the Unified Modeling Language (UML) is *the* language in which to express software architectures, there is no such convention about enterprise architecture. Some core concepts such as business process can be found

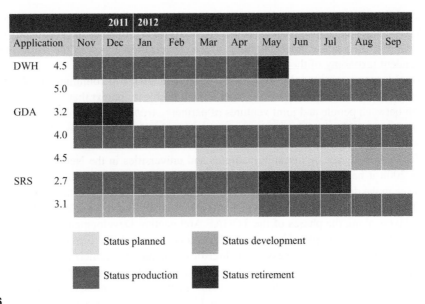

		2011	2012									
Application		Nov	Dec	Jan	Feb	Mar	Apr	May	Jun	Jul	Aug	Sep
DWH	4.5											
	5.0											
GDA	3.2											
	4.0											
	4.5											
SRS	2.7											
	3.1											

☐ Status planned   ☐ Status development

☐ Status production   ☐ Status retirement

FIGURE 3-6

Application roadmap.

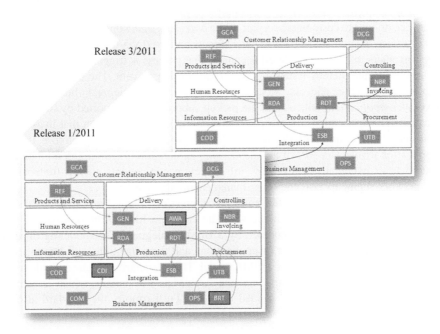

FIGURE 3-7

Flip-book visualization of an application rationalization.

in most models; even there the notation and maybe also the definition are not unanimous among enterprises. The modeling language being used in an enterprise is formed by the vocabulary of concepts that has grown over the years, condensing much of the organization's view of the world as well as the vendor-dependent taxonomy of the modeling tools that are in place.

The nonexistence of a universally understood, reliable language to communicate about enterprise architecture has become an obstacle—even more so in a business context that increasingly counts on collaboration between people and joint ventures of partners. *ArchiMate* is a modeling standard that is supposed to overcome this obstacle and that up to now remains the only serious attempt to standardize EA notations.

ArchiMate was designed by research institutes and universities in the Netherlands from 2002 to 2004. Since 2008 it has been under the stewardship of and published at The Open Group (2008). As we shall see in the description of the TOGAF framework in Chapter 4, the taxonomy of ArchiMate resembles TOGAF's own content meta-model. ArchiMate therefore is a perfect fit for modeling the architecture layers along the phases of the TOGAF Architecture Development Method.

Figure 3-8 shows an example of how ArchiMate models a simplified *pickup and delivery* process that belongs to the core express business of any logistics company: Customers can ring up a call center and request the pickup of a parcel from some place in order to get it transported to a destination address.

The standard distinguishes three modeling layers—namely the business, application, and technology layers; they are depicted by different shadings in Figure 3-8. Let's briefly traverse these layers from top to bottom to get to know the most important concepts of the ArchiMate taxonomy.

First we learn from the business layer that the pickup and delivery process consists of three subprocesses: *pickup*, *transport*, and *delivery*. Furthermore, the process implements the *pickup* service, a business service offered to customers as a part of the *parcel shipment* product governed by an *express* contract. The service is supported by *call center agents* and used via the *order acceptance* business interface by customers that have registered accounts. The process is triggered when a customer calls up the pickup service and thereby issues a *pickup order* business event. The customer submits information such as the consignee address, which is comprised in a new *shipment* business object.

The next layer, *application*, tells us that the pickup subprocess is supported by the *order management* application. The application offers a *process order* application function that is used by the call center agents via the *order entry* API, the user interface of the application. Furthermore, the order management application invokes an API of the *dispatching* application to assign orders to pickup routes.

The bottom layer eventually shows how infrastructure components such as database systems, servers, and network segments host the order management application.

Though rather simplified, the example conveys an impression of how ArchiMate models entities, in particular of the granularity of detail it addresses. The decomposition of the process, for instance, is much coarser than the detailed flow modeled by a BPMN[3] diagram. The modeling of applications does not go deeper than the delineation of applications and their functions and interfaces, which is much less than what is usually captured in a UML model. This granularity is quite suitable for modeling larger parts of an enterprise IT-landscape, and the ArchiMate vocabulary, which is summed up in Table 3-3,[4] indeed offers the concepts needed to do so. Furthermore, the standard also addresses

---

[3]BPMN stands for *business process modeling notation* and is an OMG modeling standard for capturing business processes.
[4]Adapted from Lankhorst (2009).

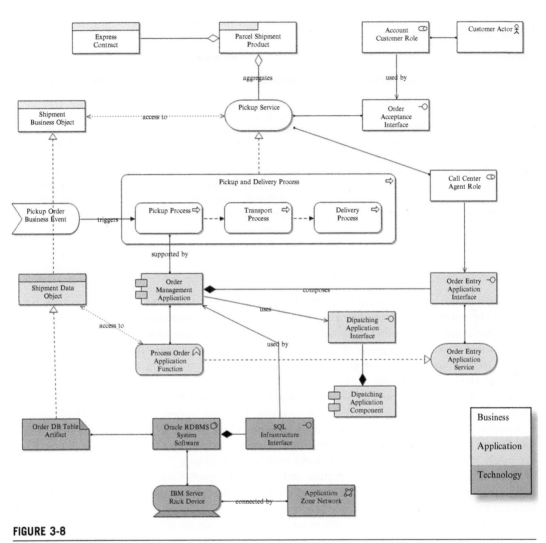

FIGURE 3-8

ArchiMate model example.

the requisite cross-relations from business down to technology, which is a major concern of EA modeling.

But ArchiMate also has some shortcomings.[5] The concepts are ambiguous and not as straightforward to apply as intended. In practical work, you often start wondering whether, for instance, this portal page now offers a business service, a business function, or an application interface.

---

[5]We are referring to the version available at the time of writing, which is version 1.0. Version 2.0 is scheduled for approval by the Board of the Open Group in February 2012.

Table 3-3 The ArchiMate Taxonomy

Layers	Aspects		
	Information	**Behavior**	**Structure**
Business	Business object Value Product Contract Role	Business service Business function Business process Business event Business interaction	Business actor Business interface Business role Business collaboration
Applications	Data object	Application service Application function Application interaction	Application interface Application component Application collaboration
Technology	Artifact	Infrastructure service System software	Node Device Network Infrastructure interface Communication path

When it comes to communication, models like Figure 3-7 also tend to be a trifle bulky; such drawings must be interpreted and simplified by views to convey a message to stakeholders. ArchiMate proposes some standard views that leave out model elements or use simplified relationships to come to drawings that are simpler to grasp. (For more details, refer to the chapter "Architecture Viewpoints" in The Open Group [2008].) But in practice the architect needs to expend some creativity to create additional views in PowerPoint so she can get her ideas across.

Although ArchiMate is not that old as a standard, there are already remarkably many EA tool vendors claiming support of the standard—for example, Rational System Architect by IBM, BizzdesignArchitect by Bizzdesign, or Abacus by Avolution. There is also an Eclipse-based open source tool for drawing ArchiMate models, called *Archi*[6]; maintained by the University of Bolton (UK), it accurately implements the standard and works well in practical use.

But managing the enterprise architecture with Archi, Microsoft Visio, or any other plain drawing tool is an impossible undertaking. The costs of keeping the data up to date are prohibitive, and the rift between model and reality will soon be insurmountable. Such drawing tools fall short of the major requirements an EA toolset should fulfill beyond capturing plain models, namely:

1. The tool has a timeline for planning and simulating future states of the architectures.
2. It supports quantitative assessments and optimizations of the IT landscape; in other words, it supports *application rationalization.*
3. It has rich facilities to visualize models and craft views addressing specific stakeholder viewpoints as well as publishing functions for sharing knowledge.
4. It is integrated with other tools, as depicted in Figure 3-9.
5. It facilitates communication by feedback, collaborative authoring, and other means of participation.

Dedicated EA tools such as Rational System Architect or Abacus more or less fulfill requirements 1 through 3. But there are no tools on the market yet for making the enterprise architect's dream of

---

[6]http://archi.cetis.ac.uk/index.html.

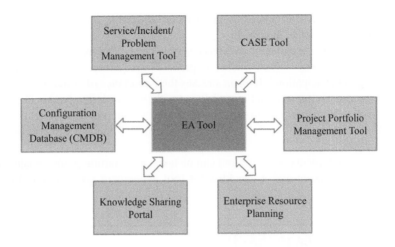

FIGURE 3-9

An EA dream: The integrated EA tool.

integration with all related sources of information come true. Such an unobstructed synchronization of data would be a powerful weapon in defeating the drifting apart of EA models and reality, a safeguard "that which must not, cannot be."[7]

Wide-ranging IT-management tools such as alfabet's planningIT offer EA and some of the neighboring functionality in one product offering, but they come with a price tag that is hard to sell to the chief information officer (CIO) "just for architecture." In addition, this approach does not help if there already are other CASE[8], CMDB[9], or what-have-you tools installed. But even if the CIO is in a spending mood, the price tag restricts such tools to a small circle of authors since they mostly are desktop applications licensed per user.

Some creativity is required to balance the need for up-to-date EA models with the integration costs of the vision expressed in Figure 3-9. Since there are no standard integration interfaces, the realization of any synchronization arrow of the diagram in most cases means investing in custom implementation. The maxim here is to make the best of an existing blend of tools for EA purposes.

On the other hand, a manual refresh of the models is strenuous and has a slight *ex post* skew: just documenting what *has been* implemented. Manual refresh usually is a dead end because it only allows for modeling an isolated core of high-level entities. The result therefore misses an important requirement of architecture models: They should be *continuous* and ideally should support a seamless drill-in

---

[7]Cited from Christian Morgenstern's poem "The Impossible Fact":

And he comes to the conclusion:
His mishap was an illusion,
for, he reasons pointedly,
that which must not, cannot be

Palmström, the protagonist of Morgenstern's poem, was run over in traffic. After recovering, he brooded over how this could happen to him and started studying legal texts. But since law forbade the accident to which he fell victim, he came to the harebrained conclusion stated and continued his life as a happy bunny.

[8]Computer-aided software engineering, a tool supporting complex software design tasks.

[9]Configuration management database, an information repository for the components of an information system.

from high-level application landscapes to fine-grained class diagrams, project schedules, configuration parameters, operational incidents, and so on.

Finally, stale and unfertile architecture models can only be avoided by inviting a wider audience to take part in architecture concerns. This demand is expressed by requirement 5, and we'll embark on it in Chapter 8, "Inviting to Participation." It again stresses the importance of collaboration—this time not with adjacent information systems, as in Figure 3-9, but with the *people* involved in IT. Today most EA tools are pretty weak with respect to participation. They mostly support a one-directional publication by architects to the world but don't implement feedback channels. Chapter 8 will give us an idea of how to overcome this obstacle.

The short list of requirements we've set out can be taken as a starting point for educated selection of an EA tool. More guidance and a checklist for tool assessment are available in, for instance, Schekkermann (2011).

Evolving the IT landscape (EA-3)
Application rationalization

> *When you can measure what you are speaking about and express it in numbers, you know something about it.*
>
> **—Lord Kelvin (1824–1907)**

In Chapter 1, we learned that Dave Callaghan, the CIO of our fictitious Bank4Us, mandated 20% savings over the next planning period in a strategic statement and explained further that:

> *The savings will be attributed to legacy reduction/downsizing, reduction in number of system interactions, and reduction in IT operation/support cost.*

Now, Bank4Us is running more than 3,000 applications in its data centers. Such a number of applications of different generations tends to proliferate to an entanglement that resembles a rampant jungle. Ian Miller and his group of enterprise architects take the CIO's statement as an imperative to boldly thin out this jungle. But how can they accomplish this kind of cultivation?

Identifying applications and key performance indicators

The first major step in such an initiative of *application rationalization* is, evidently, to get an overview of the current set of applications. As a prerequisite, there must be some guidelines that nail down what counts as an application.

APPLICATIONS

What Is an Application?

Though the term *application* is a central notion of IT, there is no commonly accepted or precise definition of this term. The Open Group (2011) defines the term in its TOGAF standard as:

> *A deployed and operational IT system that supports business functions and services; for example, a payroll. Applications use data and are supported by multiple technology components but are distinct from the technology components that support the application.*

Continued

This explanation leaves room for interpretation and certainly is not a sufficiently sharp delineation to come to a catalogue of enterprise applications in a straightforward manner. Further discussions are to be expected. Keller (2007) even claims that the struggle for an explicit definition of *application* is somewhat pointless because the domain experts working in a business unit already know their usual suspects. There's some truth in this view, since the term *application* will always remain fuzzy to a degree. The identification of applications therefore needs to be backed up by the intuitions of domain experts. Nevertheless, there must be in place some guidelines that are sufficiently sharp to ensure that one doesn't end up comparing apples with oranges across the business units. If one business unit counts single Java EARs[10] as applications, a moderately complex three-tier IT system with database, business logic, and presentation tier can easily consist of 100 applications. If another unit counts such a system as a single application, the enterprise-wide comparison is out of balance.

   The guidelines for identifying applications probably differ from enterprise to enterprise and certainly depend on the granularity of the enterprise's architecture management. But as a starting point we suggest the following common traits of applications:

- They provide *end-user functionality* (as opposed to mere system software).
- They provide *cohesive* functionality having a common purpose.
- They are somewhat *self-contained deployment units.*
- They are *logical entities* in the sense that they are to some extent independent from the implementation technology.
- They have an *owner* who is responsible for development and maintenance.

The enterprise architects at Bank4Us are well prepared with a sufficiently up-to-date catalogue of applications at hand. In companies without an enterprise architecture practice, the composition of such a catalogue can be the first painful, laborious obstacle.

Given such a catalogue, the next step is to quantify what should be improved. This implies the agreement on some key performance indicators[11] (KPIs) that one wants to optimize—numeric values that should be increased or decreased. Ian Miller and his team decide that the CIO's directive is best measured by the following KPIs:

- *Total cost of ownership (TCO) of an application.* This entails all costs related to the application: Development of new features, maintenance, trouble-ticket resolution, server costs, license fees, and whatever else is on the bill for changing or running the application.
- *Strategic fit (SF) of an application.* This KPI tells to what extent an application is considered "legacy" on a scale from 1 to 10. It captures both technology and business aspects. An application scores high if it fits well with the envisioned business architecture, is built on standards and products that are considered future proof, and is in its prime with regard to the software life cycle.
- *Value contribution (VC) of an application.* This measure reflects the business value generated by the application. There are only few cases where a definite amount of money can directly be associated with an application; in most cases, the VC will be a unitless value, like strategic fit. VC summarizes the importance of the application for the business processes it supports, how well it supports them, and what revenue streams are involved in these processes. This KPI reflects the business criticality of the application as well as the impact of replacing or retiring it on the organization.

---

[10]EAR stands for *enterprise archive* and is the deployment unit to an application server in the Java world.

[11]The notion of a key *performance* indicator is much wider than application performance in the sense of response times or throughput. It is a general notion for a measure of how well a certain entity performs a task and is used in many areas, such as economics or manufacturing.

- *Fan-in and fan-out of an application.* The *fan-in* of an application *A* counts the different data flows entering *A* in the course of processes directly or indirectly supported by *A*. These data flows can be interface invocations by other applications, messages consumed by *A*, or global data structures—for instance, database tables read by *A*. The *fan-out*, on the other hand, counts how many data flows leave *A*. These can be interface invocations by *A* on other applications, messages sent out by *A*, or global data structures modified by *A*. Henry and Kafura (1981) have proposed these KPIs as measures of procedural complexity.

Ian and his team conclude that these four KPIs should suffice. Further measures just make the comparison of applications less comprehensive. They also agree on the weight each KPI should get in a comparison, and they play for a while with the idea of an all-comprising KPI-formula, such as:

$$Weight_1 \cdot TOC + Weight_2 \cdot SF + Weight_3 \cdot VC + Weight_4 \cdot (Fan - In + Fan - Out)$$

But then they drop this "world formula" idea because it gives the simplistic impression that decisions could be based solely on a quantitative assessment of this variable.

The slightly complicated *fan-in* and *fan-out* KPIs are there to capture the CIO's statement that the number of system interactions should be reduced. They raise some discussions about why the CIO included this reduction in a strategic initiative that primarily is about cost savings. Ian explains that this is because the total costs of an application landscape are a mix of *application costs* and *interface costs*, as schematically shown in Figure 3-10.[12]

The distribution of functionality to many applications results in a highly modular landscape with increased interface costs. Take, for instance, the costs to keep several versions of an application interface concurrently alive in order to serve both new and old clients—these costs do not occur, if the same functionality is integrated into a single application. But integrating widely unrelated functionality into a single application, on the other hand, also generates surplus application costs. The hardware costs, for example, are higher with each installation, and the synchronization overhead of development projects also adds to the bill. To find the proper cohesion and compromise between modularity and integration is a U-curve optimization, and the Fan-In/Fan-Out KPI's can help quantifying it. As a general rule, only a

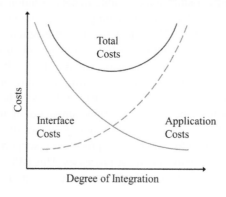

FIGURE 3-10

Application and interface costs.

[12]Adapted from Winter (2006)... and used with Robert Winter's kind permission.

medium Fan-In/Fan-Out value allows for a minimal Total Cost of Ownership (TCO)—both minimizing and maximizing the Fan-In/Fan-Out will at some point increase the TCO.

This exemplifies an important point about application rationalization: The KPIs to be optimized seldom are independent variables. The expectation to freely lift them all to an optimum is misleading. As Garajedaghi (2011) puts it, there is a certain slack between the variables: One variable can be modified as if it were independent in some range of tolerance, but there is an excision where it starts affecting the others.

The best thing to hope for is, therefore, some equilibrium representing a local optimum. A more practical consequence for now is that it is crucial to agree on the weight of each KPI and consider the effect of changes on the whole tuple of KPI values.

Assessing applications

The agreement on the KPIs prepares the groundwork for assessing the applications in the application catalogue. The goal is to come up with a table like the one shown in Table 3-4.

Ian picks a common scheme invented by Ward and Peppard (2003) to visualize the score of applications in four different quadrants, as shown in Figure 3-11. This scheme classifies applications into four main categories:

- The *Stars* ensure the current and future business of the enterprise. They are already used in important business processes and primarily support innovative products or services the company backs on as key differentiators in comparison to their competitors. Their importance for the future business is expected to grow. Furthermore, they fit well into the technology roadmap.
- The *Wild Cats*, sometimes also called *Question Marks*, have a certain potential for future business but do not contribute much to the current business operations. In a sense, these are prototypes that still have to prove their usefulness. They typically explore how new technologies can help seize new business opportunities.
- The *Cash Cows* form the operational backbone of the current business. They ensure today's core operations and generate the largest share of business from IT. Any outage of such a system is a pain and is likely to end up on the CIO's desk. But a cash cow does not fit nicely into the envisioned future operations and is technology-wise considered "legacy."
- The *Poor Dogs* are not important, neither today nor in the future. In some cases they are just residues, the quick wins for an application rationalization initiative. In other cases they are support systems that are somehow needed but do not make a crucial difference to the enterprise. A typical example is an application for tracking working hours.

Table 3-4 Excerpt from an Application Assessment

ID	Application	TCO	SF	VC	Fan-In	Fan-Out
RLD	Large debit reporting	240	4	4	2	8
RCD	Corporate debit reporting	430	6	7	3	12
ROE	Own equity reporting	390	3	9	5	3
RB2	Basel II reporting	1,210	10	3	1	23

TCO Total cost of ownership (K $/year)
SF Strategic fit (rating 1–10)
VC Value contribution (rating 1–10)

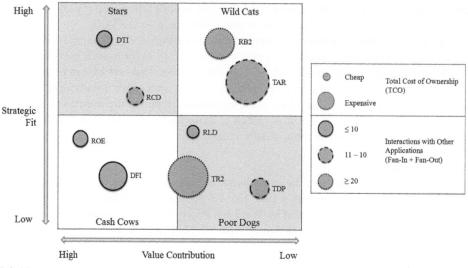

FIGURE 3-11

Ward-Peppard classification of applications.

These four categories have different key quality requirements and therefore must be treated in different ways, as Figure 3-12[13] indicates.

It is worth highlighting that EA must show different attitudes to the four quadrants as well: Enterprise architects should not impede the capturing of crucial new ground for Stars and Wild Cats by restrictive quality gates or standardization and integration requirements. Viable applications typically run through a transition from Wild Cats over Stars to Cash Cows, and EA should foster their maturing with smoothly increasing quality constraints.

Another aspect worth noting is that the different categories of applications might claim for different approaches in software development, too. Wild Cats and Stars benefit most from *agile software development* because of its focus on bringing new features to life.

Cash Cows, on the other hand, are merely maintained and therefore offer no compelling reasons to switch to agile (assuming that this is not the approach the company is most acquainted and proficient with). Furthermore, the upgrade of a central Cash Cow needs extensive nonfunctional tests, requires that users and administrators are trained beforehand, and usually implies the physical rearranging of some core business processes. All this needs planning in advance, which does not fit easily into agile software development, with its functionality scoping on a three-week basis.

Stipulating how the four categories of information systems are to be treated is typically also something achieved in EA-1, "Defining the IT Strategy." Figure 3-12 is just one typical example of such a stipulation.

---

[13]Adapted from Ward and Peppard (2003).

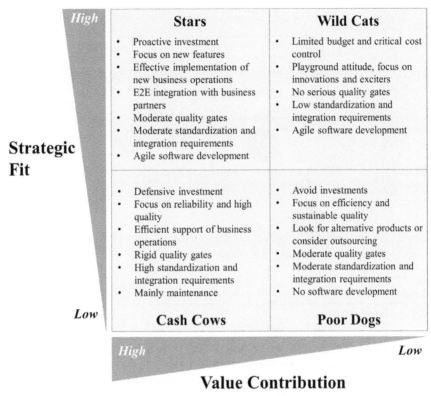

FIGURE 3-12

Strategies for treating various applications

Assessing alternatives

Let's turn back to Ian's application rationalization journey at Bank4Us. The KPI assessment of the application catalogue gave him hindsight into the applications with a high potential for optimization. The application TR2 in Figure 3-11, for example (a trading application developed in the 1990s, as far as Ian knows), is close to a Poor Dog but causes tremendous costs. Nevertheless, simply ramping it down will be an intricate matter since it shows a lot of interactions with other applications, and presumably it is deeply interwoven into the data- and workflows of the enterprise. But maybe there are other options?

Consequentially Ian's next step is to deep dive into the refactoring options of each optimization candidate. Can a candidate be ramped down by rearranging some business processes or shifting functionality to some other applications? Can the application be refactored so that it is less interwoven with other systems? Can at least a couple of business functions be taken over by some star applications? Ian and his team discover that a small extension of the Wild Cat trading application *TAR* (see Figure 3-11) would make a larger part of the *TR2* functionality superfluous, with only minor changes to the business processes and one additional system interaction (fan-in) added to TAR.

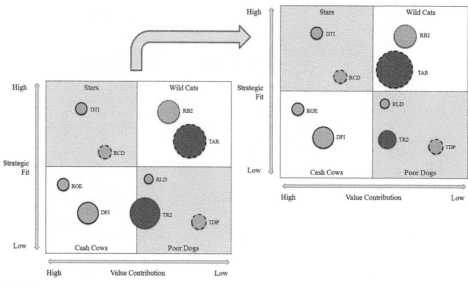

FIGURE 3-13

Reassessment of a transformation.

This appears to Ian and his team as the healthiest thing to do in comparison to other options. Hence, they redraw the architecture models, accommodate this change into the target architecture, and reassess the modified overall landscape once again, as shown in Figure 3-13.

Application rationalization is an optimization with constraints, as you can see from Ian's reasoning. One essential constraint is that the rationalization measures must neither disrupt daily operations nor cause critical changes to the business processes or organization. Therefore, the impact of these measures must be assessed, and this will be the easier the better you have accomplished activity EA-2, *Modeling the Architectures*. An up-to-date EA model highlighting the relations between business processes, organizational units, services, applications, and so forth makes such an assessment a piece of cake. (Well, this statement needs to be taken with a grain of salt; it still remains a challenge, of course.)

But many enterprises are far from having such a model in place, so the assessment can really become a desperate endeavor. According to our experience, a high percentage of application rationalization initiatives fail, and they fail because of the inability to assess the impact of even humble changes. When you are consulting a company in an application rationalization and you touch the ground for the first time, you're likely to meet ironic people telling you things like: "We have tried to ramp down application SIS in 2005 and 2007 already, and now you with your supernatural powers come to the rescue?"

The dose of sarcasm depends on the personality, but the reason for the failure of earlier attempts usually is that they unraveled so many unknown ramifications and configurations that people eventually decided they'd better not touch anything. Chapter 1 already reported on highly respected enterprises that lost track of their IT to such an extent that the lunatic "hotline approach" becomes an acceptable reengineering method: Install an emergency phone right beneath the application server, shut the server down, and wait to see who calls.

The Bank4Us example also illustrates that application rationalization is a recursive process. Options that seem promising and feasible are applied to the architecture model, and the resulting target landscape is reassessed using the same KPIs as in the first round. Since the target landscape is just a vision and not operational, one is relying on guesswork here more than usual. But the effect of an improvement must be quantified somehow.

The guesswork character of this projection into the future brings us to an important question: How are the KPI values actually calculated? How did Ian and his team come to the conclusion that the return on equity (ROE) application has a TCO of $390,000 per year but a poor strategic fit of three?

The answer in brief is: *Facts and opinions.* A concrete indicator such as TCO can mostly be calculated on the basis of facts—by gathering the bills and contracts pertinent to the application under inspection or by collecting maintenance efforts from incident management systems and similar sources. But the evaluation of an imaginary measure such as strategic fit (SF) mostly relies on opinions. To gather them, Ian and his team have conducted a series of interviews with subject matter experts with different responsibilities: business and IT strategists, application owners, software developers, and operating personnel.

But the question "How well do you think the application fits to the strategy?" is too abstract for a non-erratic answer. Most people will shrug their shoulders. Ian therefore decomposes the SF-KPI into about two dozen base indicators and places them on a scorecard, as shown in Table 3-5.

The scores of the individual base indicators are then aggregated according to some weighted formula to the KPI value of SF.

In collecting opinions, it is crucial whom you decide to ask. The prevalent approach is to nominate subject matter experts and conduct interviews with them. This narrows the circle to a small, illustrious group of adepts whose judgments are hopefully full to the brim with insight. But if the majority of users say that a certain application is cumbersome, the experts' praise of it is to be taken with care. Chapter 8, "Inviting to Participate," therefore suggests complementary means of Enterprise 2.0 to come to a broader, balanced assessment.

Summary

Application rationalization is one special but prevalent example of EA-3, Evolving the IT Landscape. It also is an example of a transformation that is not driven by tangible functional requirements but by non-functional strategic concerns such as reducing costs or complexity. We have seen how KPIs are the pivotal tool to drive such transformations, right in the spirit of the often-cited tenet by Peter F. Drucker[14] that "If you can't measure it, you can't manage it." They are the key to a precise understanding of the goals,

Table 3-5 Excerpt of a Scorecard to Estimate the KPI Strategic Fit

ID	Base Indicator	Score (1–10)
BI1	The application fits into the technology road map	5
BI2	The application supports the strategic goal of customer empowerment	3
BI3	The application supports multichanneling and mobile devices	3
BI4	The application resolves an existing business impediment	7

---

[14]Peter F. Drucker (1909–2005) was an influental US economist and one of the intellectual giants in management theory.

crucial for identifying areas of improvement, and simulating the effect of changes. We also saw how deep dives into areas of improvement depend on how well an enterprise maintains its knowledge about its IT. Only if a sufficiently accurate and up-to-date model of the enterprise architecture is available, one can assess the impact of changes and simulate their costs and benefits.

General IT transformations

The evolution of the IT landscape is not only driven by strategic initiatives—that's a pivotal thing to note when we're looking at IT transformations in general. What we mean by *strategic initiative* is something like Ian's rationalization project at Bank4Us: The CIO issues a strategic goal, the enterprise architects work out a target architecture matching this goal, identify what has to be done, and mandate the vassals in the development and operational departments to put things into practice.

In most enterprises we have seen so far, these strategic initiatives are not even the main force having an effect on the IT landscape. The decision of an automotive company to intensify marketing by adopting mobile devices or the plan of an ocean carrier to open a wide range of B2B services to logistics partners do not typically stem from the strategic board. In companies with good strategic governance, such initiatives are in line with the strategic direction, but they are nevertheless brought to the table and owned by business units. They also can bypass the desk of enterprise architects: The initiatives are run as business projects, and the target architecture consequentially is in the hands of project architects, who by majority do not belong to the EA group.

The IT metamorphoses that enterprise architects encounter in practice are therefore a mix: In a few initiatives they are the masterminds; in a lot of others, planning and design is out of their hands. In those cases not owned by EA, the role of enterprise architects is limited to taking care that the evolution stays within strategic boundaries (see EA-5, *Developing and Enforcing Standards and Guidelines*) and to "backfilling" the architecture by integrating the solutions designed by others into the overall picture (see EA-6, Monitoring the Project Portfolio). The development of an IT landscape resembles more of a true evolution, where different actors and purposes try to push their business through, rather than a transformation planned by some mastermind.

Another peculiarity of Ian's rationalization project is that it takes applications as a focal point. Applications traditionally are the units of ownership, deployment, and maintenance; they also are things that are internally well known and distinguishable as icons on the company desktops. But they are not the only possible focal point, maybe not even the best one in a modern architecture.

Dave Callaghan, the CIO of Bank4Us, also mandated customer empowerment as a strategic goal. But the customer view comprises products, contracts, services, business user interfaces, or customer processes. The enterprise's applications are aliens from this viewpoint.

Wouldn't it therefore be more natural to take the *business architecture* as a point of departure, instead of immediately gazing at applications? Then, the paramount step toward customer empowerment would be to draw a picture of the as-is landscape of services, business interfaces, and products and to design an improved to-be landscape offering more functions, processes, and a lighter access. Only the second step would then jump to applications and explore the options to support the envisioned business architecture by application functions and collaborations.

This is roughly the order prescribed by the TOGAF Architecture Development Method (ADM), which we take a closer look at in Chapter 4, "Architecture Frameworks." The last step in ADM, leading to a full blueprint of the CIO's customer empowerment mission, is mapping the application architecture to technologies—the software components, third-party products, standards, servers, routers, and what else there is when getting down to the nitty-gritty. This priority order—from business architecture over applications to technology—shifts the focus from a *technology-centric* to a *business-centric* design. It better fits initiatives that have a business momentum instead of an IT momentum, such as bringing down application costs.

The strong use of KPIs is the last peculiarity of application rationalization that needs to be differentiated when we're looking at IT transformations in general. Many strategic goals are qualitative by nature, as we can see from the Bank4Us goal of customer empowerment, and their translation into quantitative values seems rather artificial.

Often the assessment of target landscapes simply compares the different alternatives against a checklist of requirements. Compliance is noted by a checkmark, and the pros and cons of exceptions are discussed with regard to contents but without referring to numeric values. Nevertheless, it is worth striving for a KPI representation of qualitative goals, even if they are just unitless score values, as shown in Table 3-7. Three primary reasons count in favor of quantification:

- The compliance with a generic goal, such as customer empowerment, usually is not a matter of "either/or" but of "more or less." There are many shades of gray between "black" solutions that do not empower customers at all and "white" ones that make customers crowned regents. These shadings can only be captured by numbers.
- The assessment of alternative target architectures in EA covers a large area of the IT landscape. The cases in which one alternative outplays the others in all dimensions are rare and do not cause much headache. It becomes interesting if an alternative offers more customer empowerment in some applications but scores lower in others. In such a case, some aggregation algorithm is needed to come to a holistic comparison.
- The formulation of KPIs sharpens the understanding of a goal. This is in line with Lord Kelvin's tenet that the ability to express something in numbers signals a deeper understanding of the subject. *Qualitative* is sometimes just a euphemism for *fuzzy*.

SOA transformations

Transformations toward a *service-oriented architecture (SOA)* belong to the more technically driven changeovers of the IT landscape one frequently encounters today. Some time ago there was a debate about the slogan "SOA is dead," put into the world by the Burton Group (Manes, 2009). Still, the larger firms we've seen over the past few years have kept SOA on their strategic agendas.

For good reason, SOA is a very suitable architecture paradigm for designing large software systems. The proposed next-generation replacements, such as Sam Ruby's Resource Oriented Architecture (ROA) (Richardson and Ruby, 2007), did not make it to the enterprise IT agenda. Maybe this is because they are not true replacements of SOA but instead are necessary extensions of a too narrow understanding of "services." The term *service* had found a rather one-sided interpretation by the WS-*[15]

---

[15]*WS-** stands for the body of standards defined by the Organization for the Advancement of Structured Information Standards (OASIS). This is a broad set of standards defining various aspects of Web services such as protocol binding, security, or routing. The implementation of such Web services mostly uses SOAP and either http/https or asynchronous messages. WS-* nowadays is a label for the heavyweight Web services that best fit the internal line-of-business applications because of their standardization and coverage of nonfunctional aspects.

Web services and the extension to REST[16] and other implementation styles of "service," which is the core of ROA, WOA, MOA[17] (and so on) just correct this narrow-mindedness.

But a truth behind the provocative "SOA is dead" is that SOA certainly is past its peak of inflated expectations. Today it will be difficult to find sponsors and followers for an initiative that turns the whole enterprise IT upside down just for the sake of SOA. If SOA is still on the agenda, it is an architecture standard for changes that are needed for other reasons, but not an end in its own right. For example, the ocean carrier striving for a B2B integration with its logistics partners will probably build a solution in the SOA way. As a side effect, the IT landscape moves closer to SOA in that case.

Nevertheless, there are considerable advantages of SOA, regardless of any hype cycles:

- *Business-centric design.* A good SOA design sets the priority on business capabilities and processes.
- *Reuse of functionality.* SOA services expose functionality with a potential for wider cross-organizational use. The SOA paradigms of encapsulation, statelessness, and service-level agreements help in utilizing existing assets in many contexts. Furthermore, SOA services have a coarse granularity and thereby avoid the felt-like weave of distributed interactions that made earlier attempts with distributed objects (e.g., CORBA[18]) fail.
- *Flexibility.* SOA clearly separates control logic from business logic and data: The control logic is incorporated in processes, whereas business logic and data are made available by services. This allows for a flexible mapping between the two parts of the game; ideally, processes can be rearranged without much impact on the services, and vice versa.
- *Multichanneling.* SOA also separates the presentation logic from control logic, business logic, and data. This implies that the business processes, functionality, and data are no longer bound to a particular end-user application. You can start a process from your desktop, take the next step with your smartphone, and receive progress reports via Short Message Service (SMS).
- *Decoupling of functionality and technology.* Business architecture and technologies have different life cycles. The technology-agnostic concepts of SOA introduce a level of abstraction that protects the business functionality from heterogeneity and change in the underlying technical infrastructure.
- *Stability.* The SOA concept of loose coupling and the corresponding techniques stabilize the IT landscape. Outages and performance fall-offs become locally isolated and no longer drag along contiguous applications.

The business-centric design aligning business processes and services with underlying application functionality makes SOA an ideal ally for EA. Both have business-IT alignment on their primary agenda. "SOA provides a unique chance for the first time in IT history to create artifacts that have enduring value for both, the business as well as the technology side," write Krafzig, Banke, and Slama

---

[16]*REST* abbreviates *Representational State Transfer* and is a more lightweight counterproposal to WS-*. It relies on the capabilities of http/https and intends to offer a simple-to-use, wide-ranging communication API to Web applications.
[17]The acronyms *WOA* and *MOA* abbreviate Web-Oriented Architecture and Message-Oriented Architecture, respectively.
[18]*CORBA* stands for Common Object Request Broker Architecture and is the most elaborate platform- and programming language-independent standard for distributed objects.

(2006). They see SOA as an approach for renovating the IT landscape and SOA governance as a means of enterprise architecture management. But given that the IT landscape consists of vast areas with good old mainframes and other assets far off from service orientation, it should be clear that EA must have a much wider scope.

Assessing and building capabilities (EA-4)

Draupadi,[19] the heroine of the Indian epic *Mahabharat*, emerged as a full-grown woman from the sacrificial fire (*Yagnya*), and proclaimed to the whole world that she was immaculate. Unfortunately, we do not have any such mechanism to produce fully equipped enterprise architects "just like that." The scarcity of enterprise architects (or the right IT resources in the right positions, in general) is quite evident in the IT industry. Despite attractive offers, many IT positions remain open, waiting long for "true love's kiss." In some cases, they are inappropriately filled, and in some others their tasks are silently stapled to the job descriptions of the enterprise architects.

The face of IT is changing continuously and rapidly. On the one hand, it is becoming more commoditized, centralized, and outsourced. On the other hand, IT is venturing into providing value-added services to the business, like business process design, product design, business transformation and innovation. As a consequence, the portfolio of IT service offerings is expanding, and IT leadership is becoming more and more crucial. Ross (2011) states:

> If, despite the emergence of a digital or information economy, the business leaders are not positioned to lead IT-enabled business transformations (...), the need for IT to do so becomes acute (...). Ensuring the right talent to realize the IT organization's ambitions is a critical challenge, many CIOs told us.

The question on the CIO's table is: Is the current workforce equipped to adjust quickly and effectively to the challenges ahead? The activities in the IT unit are gearing toward business process engineering, architecture realization, and program management. This goes far beyond mere application development, system implementation, and project management, which were sufficient only a few years ago.

As a consequence, enterprises are realizing the importance of strategic competency management—an antithesis to the reactive demand fulfillment of the past. In the ideal case, they actively look at the future possibilities, demands, and constraints in the organization. This means developing long-term workforce plans, defining multiple career paths, investing heavily in their people, facilitating internal and external training programs, and offering rotations between business and IT roles.

Competence development for enterprise architects

In the first century BC, Marcus Vitruvius Pollio[20] described an ideal architect as follows:

> A man of letters, a skilled draftsman, a mathematician, familiar with historical studies, a diligent of philosophy, acquainted with music, not ignorant of medicine, earned in the responses of juris consultis, familiar with astronomy and astronomical calculations.

---

[19]In Indian mythology, Draupadi is the guardian deity of noble education and supreme knowledge. She was born all-knowing and possessed 32 auspicious qualities (*rujus*) at her birth. Draupadi symbolizes the knowledge accrued when noble deeds are performed with an attitude of surrendering everything to God (Lord Krishna in Hindu philosophy).

[20]Marcus Vitruvius Pollio was a Roman writer, architect, and engineer who was active in the first century BC. He is best known as the author of the multivolume work *De Architectura* (*On Architecture*).

Today the image of an enterprise architect in IT continues to be loyal to this 2,000-year-old definition—in the sense that an enterprise architect in today's information age is perceived as a multidimensional personality. She knows a lot of things and can do many things. The role of enterprise architect entails:

- Making important and (quite often) difficult decisions single-mindedly, to ensure the conceptual integrity of the enterprise's business and IT; moreover, she needs to take those decisions *early enough* so that a plan is in place for everyone else to follow (see Activities EA-1, EA-2, and EA-3).
- Being cognizant to what is going on in the projects, watching out for important issues, and addressing them before they get out of control; at the same time, she has to work in intense collaboration across the projects (see Activities EA-5, EA-6, EA-7, and EA-8).
- Communicating at technical and nontechnical levels with conviction and restraint; quite often this requires us to stand up in a meeting and convey bad news to the sponsors or stakeholders in the most sensible manner (relates to all Activities EA-1 through EA-8).
- Keeping the organization on-ramp and on par with technology advancement in the industry (see Activities EA-1, EA-3, EA-5, and EA-6).

In a nutshell, the role of enterprise architect demands a plethora of multidisciplinary skills. This includes hard skills such as business acumen, technology expertise, and project management. Even more important are soft skills such as executive communication, collaborative influence, and organizational leadership.

Competency tree for an enterprise architect

The first step in profiling an enterprise architect is to build a competency tree. This means identifying the *competency areas* relevant to the enterprise architecture, organizing them in a structure, and defining associated *proficiency levels*.

A competency area entails the body of knowledge pertaining to a subject or a field of study. These can be areas as different as customer relationship management, enterprise data management, integration patterns, Web 2.0, agile methodology, or project management. The proficiency levels help measure an individual's depth of knowledge and level of experience in a given competency area. The competency areas for an architect can typically be grouped under four main *capability streams*:

- *Business acumen.* This pertains to an individual's knowledge, skills, and experience in the specific business domain under consideration. For instance, the IT organization in Bank4Us needs broad and deep insight into the banking domain, ranging from the basic account-opening process in retail banking up to risk analysis and hedging of exotic derivative products in investment banking.
- *Technical expertise.* This of course is the core competence required for any IT organization. It depends on the technology environment of the enterprise as to what expertise is required there. In Bank4Us, deep know-how in mainframe, Java/JEE, packaged CRM, Unix/C, and relational database management systems (RDBMS) such as Oracle, DB2, and MS SQL Server are valued.
- *Process excellence.* This deals with the knowledge about main IT processes, comprising software engineering (for example, agile and waterfall), quality management, operational management

(e.g., ITIL), program management, investment and risk management, procurement, and vendor relationship management.

- *Organizational leadership.* This area primarily comprises people and behavioral skills pertaining to team leadership, intense collaboration, communication, and negotiation.

A balanced competence framework should list about 10 relevant competency areas for each of the preceding capabilities. If needed, this structure can be further enhanced—for instance, by decomposing a competency area into a three-level tree showing a *subject area* (root), *topics* (branches), and *learning modules* (leaves). Such a tree is specific to the skills and experience requirements in a given enterprise and needs to be set up with hindsight into the context of market opportunities, organizational needs, and environmental constraints of that enterprise.

Having defined the competency tree, the proficiency of an individual in a given competency area can be ranked using a set of evaluation criteria. Here is a suitable scale of five levels:

- *Level 1.* Limited knowledge, basic awareness.
- *Level 2.* Trained, conceptual knowledge, some educational background.
- *Level 3.* Applied knowledge; is able to design and optimize a solution approach under supervision.
- *Level 4.* In-depth knowledge; masters the current state of art and is able to design and optimize a solution approach independently; can guide project teams; acts as an advisor to others.
- *Level 5.* Expert; advances the state of the art; industry recognition; international publications; speaker at conferences (maybe even delivering keynotes); panel member in standards bodies.

Table 3-6 shows an illustrative enterprise architect skill profile for Ian Miller, enterprise architect at Bank4Us.

Table 3-6 Ian Miller's Bank4Us Enterprise Architect Skill Profile (As an Illustration of the Concept)

Name	Ian Miller	Reports to	Chief Architect
Position	Enterprise architect	Interfaces with	Program managers
			Project managers
			Project architects
			Business architects
			Business experts
			IT management
			IT infrastructure team
			IT platform vendors
Education	PhD (mathematics)	IT experience	24 years
Mission	To provide the best possible IT solution for a business problem within the enterprise context		

Skill Area	L1	L2	L3	L4	L5
Business Acumen					
Business domain knowledge				X	
Business process modeling			X		
Business and IT trend analysis				X	
Business solution envisioning and opportunity creation				X	
Value articulation and cost/benefit analysis				X	

Continued

Table 3-6 Ian Miller's Bank4Us Enterprise Architect Skill Profile (As an Illustration of the Concept)—Cont'd

Skill Area	L1	L2	L3	L4	L5
Technology Expertise					
System analysis and modeling				X	
Data analysis and modeling					X
Software effort and cost estimation model				X	
Technology assessment and prototyping			X		
Software and hardware sizing and capacity planning				X	
Performance Assurance, Testing, and Usability					
Reuse and automation				X	
Software industry standards and best practices				X	
Emerging software trends and technologies					X
Architecture frameworks, tools, and techniques				X	
Process Excellence					
Software development life-cycle process				X	
Software maintenance and support process			X		
Software infrastructure management process		X			
IT program and portfolio management process				X	
Architecture validation and conformance process				X	
Organizational Leadership and Behavioral Qualities					
Broad vision and deep sense for the big picture					X
Innovation and thought leadership				X	
Analytical reasoning and problem solving				X	
Learnability: Proactive and fast learner				X	
Multitasking and time management				X	
Face-to-face, verbal, and written two-way communication				X	
Communicate at technical/nontechnical levels				X	
Conflict resolution and negotiation				X	
Fluent; convincing rather than argumentative					X
Flexible in mind; staying calm under pressure				X	
Collaborative influence; multicultural workforce				X	
Full life-cycle project team leadership			X		

One practical question remains: How should one measure and assess an individual's proficiencies in each of the stated skill areas? A proprietary profile definition, as shown in Table 3-6, can be replaced or extended by adopting the *Open Certified Architect (Open CA)* program as a standard mechanism to benchmark an individual for her architectural competencies. Open CA is an architect certification offered by The Open Group. It qualifies an individual to be a practitioner architect based on a stringent evaluation of that person's skills and experience in the role of an architect. The certification is offered at three role levels or positions:

- *Level 1. Technical architect*, typically architects working at project level.
- *Level 2. Master architect*, for architects normally working at program level.
- *Level 3. Distinguished architect*, usually architects focusing at enterprise level.

In essence, the Open CA certification program offers a yardstick to qualify an architect using fairly precise and measurable criteria. It is certainly not 100% foolproof, yet it is worth a serious attempt.

Building the competence

When organizations take a strategic view on the career progression of their IT staff, they tend to spend more money training them. The training may be facilitated through external training institutes or channelized through online media. However, beyond a certain point, only experience (and not knowledge) counts. You can acquire the tacit knowledge needed for higher proficiency levels only through your own experience and, to some extent, by learning from the lessons of experienced people in the field. *Job rotation* is a good tool to get adequate exposure and experience in the field of aspiration. In addition, the enterprise architect should join a *community of practice* in her interest area.

A rather easy way of job rotation is for architects to spot business analysts and technical developers who would make good architects. These professionals' intrinsic talent can be sensed by looking at the kind of questions they ask about their projects. For instance, are they curious to know how their solution is going to be used by the business? What benefit it is going to deliver? How is their project linked to other projects? This constant analysis helps elevate or change their roles to make the best use of available (and rather scarce) talent as well as to offer them better exposure to be a good architect.

Another way of job rotation, especially for practicing architects, is to switch position between strategic activities to operational activities at regular intervals (maybe quarterly or semiannually). The balance of strategic and operational experience must be a prerequisite for promotion to the next level.

It is also a best practice, if it is possible, to recruit or depute people from the business side to the IT side, and vice versa. This applies especially to businesspeople with project or program management backgrounds. They can be more easily groomed to acquire technology management expertise. In addition, they bring their business acumen and experience to the IT crowd.

In a similar manner, IT personnel with reasonable business understanding can be deputed into business—as apprentices and ambassadors, especially engaging them in the activities related to process modeling, process analysis, data analysis, business executive training, and so forth. Enterprise architects need to have complete and rounded personalities to be successful. This can only happen if their career progression spans strategy and operation and across business and IT.

Although learning by experience is the best way, it is a rather long process. Learning from others is a reasonable approach, too. There are many ways to facilitate this type of learning. A *community of practice* consists of a group of people bound together by shared expertise and a passion for a joint mission, working together to foster and develop knowledge. It provides a sense of belonging to the individuals working on different projects and a platform for sharing and developing common competencies.

Evidently, a community of practice requires an economy of scale in terms of opportunities and demands for it in order to become a viable, sustainable, and successful venture. In essence, it is meant to fulfill needs in a specific competency area by proactive provisioning of:

- A skilled and trained workforce
- Strong partner relations
- Tested and proven technical solutions and development methodologies

We will look into new avenues of fostering a community culture in the organization in Chapter 8, "Inviting to Participation."

Formalizing enterprise architecture

One of the top concerns while setting up a new enterprise architecture practice is to figure out who in the organization should do what. There are many questions to answer:

- How should the enterprise architecture team be organized?
- What skills does it have to possess?
- Where does it report to?
- How does it engage with other stakeholder groups?
- How is funding organized?
- What decision authority does it have?

The list is certainly not exhaustive. There are many options to consider, and there is no *one* right way to implement and operate an enterprise architecture practice. It depends on many organizational factors such as business imperatives, operational model, and governance structure of the enterprise.

TOGAF, the Open Group EA framework that we will cover in detail in Chapter 4, does provide a few hints in this direction. The preliminary phase of the TOGAF Architecture Development Method (ADM) describes a typical approach for initiating EA for an organization. In addition, consulting firms like Gartner also help the organizations set up an enterprise architecture practice.

Team organization

Normally, the scope of EA is larger than what enterprise architects can handle. It is too much work for one person to manage and too much work for one centralized group of people to deal with. On one hand, it requires a lot of breadth and depth of knowledge and experience. On the other hand, it needs quite some coordination and collaboration. Moreover, the enterprise will not stand still until the EA team has plotted its course of action; it will continue to operate in its "business as usual" way while the enterprise architects are preparing the course of corrective actions.

In view of such organizational constraints, the best positioning of EA is probably as a community of practice that operates at three levels:

- *Core team.* Owns and operates enterprise architecture; small in size.
- *Extended team.* Subject matter experts, key contributors, working committees, governing bodies.
- *Community.* Interested parties, project team participants and contributors, users.

The *core team* comprises full-time resources dedicated to the EA practice. Profiles of core team members should reflect a broad coverage of skills and a diversity of experience and soft skills rather than a deep specialization in specific technologies. Generalists are typically preferred over specialists. A deep familiarity with the business domain and processes is of equal or even higher importance than IT technology mastership. Typically, members of the EA core team should originate, in roughly equal parts, from business and IT departments.

The *extended team* consists of well-respected experts in their respective field of expertise—business or IT. They are typically specialists who are invited into the EA fold by solicitation. The extended team comes into action on an as-needed basis. The members normally engage as part of working committees or governing bodies that are geared toward a specific focus area currently under incubation or investigation by the EA team. This can be, for instance, a working group for digital marketing strategy, customer analytics, information security, anti-money-laundering vigilance, or cloud sourcing, to name just a few examples.

In addition, the CIO (or chief architect) may also appoint an *architecture review board* (ARB) to manage the review of projects and assess project alignment with the enterprise architecture. In a way, the ARB is an extended team that assesses each proposed project or investment for compliance with EA.

The *community members* are the users and stakeholders of enterprise architecture. The community includes corporate leadership, business leaders, business relationship managers, senior IT executives, and, more important, project teams and business users.

With respect to the structure described here, an enterprise architecture practice can be viewed as a core team plus a dynamic virtual team, functioning simultaneously at any given point in time.

Team composition

To begin with, the core team must have at least one full-time person who is fully responsible for the enterprise architecture. This is ideally the chief architect, appointed by the CIO. The chief architect is an executive position that serves a dual role:

- *Architect in charge* for the enterprise's IT landscape
- *Chief program manager* for enterprise architecture initiatives

The chief architect is supported by the core team of architects, as described. The core team is typically a pool of enterprise architects that in turn is supported by an extended team of business, application, data, and infrastructure architects. Table 3-7 provides a typical listing of functional roles and associated responsibilities assigned to the core team members. Often some of these roles and responsibilities are shared, paired up, or contracted out.

An architect usually operates at a particular level in the organization (enterprise, program, or project level). The position depends on her proficiency, experience, and seniority.

If needed (typically in large organizational setup), the enterprise architecture effort may be treated as a formal *program*. In that case, the chief architect is equipped with a dedicated *program management office* (EA-PMO) for enterprise architecture. The EA-PMO is established specifically to manage and control the development, use, and maintenance of the enterprise architecture. The PMO is tasked with ensuring the success of enterprise architecture as per the stated performance measures while managing the finances and risks involved.

Having formalized an EA organization in the enterprise, the health of EA should be checked periodically. This is essential to assess EA's progress, effectiveness, and value contribution within the enterprise. The standard means of performing an assessment is to use an EA maturity model. We will cover this topic in Chapter 5, "EA Maturity Models."

Table 3-7 Enterprise Architecture Core Team: Functional Roles and Responsibilities

Role	Responsibilities
Chief architect	Heads the enterprise architecture practice; organizes and manages the core team; directs development of the baseline and target architecture.
Enterprise architect	Provides architecture strategy and planning consultation for the enterprise, business units, and project teams.
Business architect	Models and describes business processes, scenarios, and information flows.
Information architect	Analyzes and documents business information needs, logical and physical data models, and associated relationships.
Application architect	Specifies application interfaces, control logic, and data flows.
Infrastructure architect	Analyzes and describes system environments, including hardware, operating systems, application software configuration, network and communication infrastructure.
Security architect	Focuses on IT security aspects in the enterprise architecture, including design, operations, encryption, vulnerability, access authentication, and authorization processes.
Integration architect	Specializes in enterprise integration aspects, including integration paradigms such as service-oriented architecture, event-driven architecture, messaging, publish-and-subscribe, and the underlying middleware technologies.
Configuration control	Ensures that all changes to enterprise architecture are identified, tracked, monitored, and appropriately documented.
Quality assurance	Makes sure that all established project standards, processes, and practices are followed.
Risk management	Identifies, monitors, and controls risks in enterprise architecture in light of environmental factors and constraints.
Technical editor	Ensures that architecture policies, models, and other documentation within the enterprise architecture repository are clear, concise, usable, and consistent with the configuration management standards.

EA team position in the organization structure

In a typical large organization, an enterprise architecture group or even many enterprise architecture groups may be functioning at different places. Figure 3-14 shows potential places where the enterprise architecture group can possibly reside within the corporate structure of such an organization.

Many industry analysts and academic researchers indicate that the most appropriate place for an EA team is under the *corporate strategy* or any such senior business leadership team (for example, CFO or COO). In that setup, the EA function is intentionally moved outside the IT organization to ensure its independence from IT and to align it better to the business. This position (shown as *position 1* in Figure 3-14) gives EA the clout to raise enterprise architecture issues to the highest levels and make decisions based on the best interests of the entire enterprise. However, in practice EA is rarely positioned this way today.

In practice, we predominantly meet the EA group in the direct reporting line to the CIO of corporate IT, as shown by *position 2* in Figure 3-14. Corporate IT is typically *the* IT organization at the highest level, with its own budget and management control. For our subsequent discussions, especially in our Bank4Us example, we presume the positioning of enterprise architecture group to be this way.

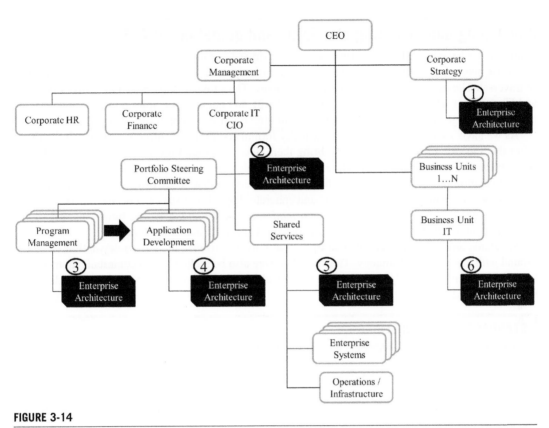

FIGURE 3-14

Typical places for the EA team in an enterprise organization.

It also makes sense to establish an EA group while executing a large, multiyear business transformation program that potentially cuts across multiple business units, product lines, customer segments, or geographic regions of the enterprise. In that case, EA can reside at *position 3* in the figure and stays within the purview of that program, with direct reporting to the program director or program management office (PMO).

When the enterprise IT landscape is transformed by a number of ongoing programs and projects, the EA group may be located in the realm of the application development organization (shown as *position 4* in Figure 3-14). In this case, it tends to become quite IT development-centric.

When the enterprise requires extensive focus on the *run-the-business* scenario and an efficient day-to-day business operation, especially in a shared service mode and with a large IT landscape, enterprise architecture is often found at *position 5*. In this case, the risk for the EA team is to focus too much on IT implementation issues.

Finally, if a business unit of the enterprise carries a large IT estate, it may have its own enterprise architecture, as shown by *position 6*.

In summary, there is no such thing as *the* single right place for the EA team in the organization structure. In general, the right placement for EA is the position where it can seek a balanced view on business-IT alignment that is neither too strategic nor too tactical, neither too broad nor too deep.

Developing and enforcing standards and guidelines (EA-5)

Until now we have looked at EA activities that are primarily strategic in nature. They identify *why* an enterprise needs to change, *what* it aims to achieve in a stipulated time horizon, and the possible paths of traversal. The outcome of these activities is *strategy*. The strategy is expressed in terms of business and IT maxims (see EA-1), architecture models (EA-2), and guiding principles plus a roadmap for the envisaged change (EA-3). It provides a long-term direction for the enterprise change.

As we have seen, strategic issues are basically formulated in the boardroom and the CIO's office. After that the enterprise architect has to bring them down to ground-level execution on the IT shop floor. He has to tell *how* the architecture should be implemented and *by what technologies*.

The creation of standards and guidelines helps the EA do that. They offer a crystallization point where vision and strategy take a solid state and concrete shape. For instance, a business maxim stating that *The security and privacy of customer information is non-negotiable* can be turned into a series of security standards that the enterprise can impose on its projects and IT systems.

Standards and guidelines are also an opportunity to *synchronize* the day-to-day activities on the ground with the vision and strategy. They can therefore also be looked at as a communication conduit between the boardroom and the staff on the ground, allowing them to communicate strategic decisions and receive feedback.

STANDARDS AND GUIDELINES

Standards and Guidelines: Shifting the EA Focus to Implementation

The standards are essentially the *choices and constraints* that are directly imposed on the design, development, and deployment of business solutions. The enforcement of standards is intended to meet strategic architectural goals—for instance:

- Addressing enterprise-wide common concerns such as security, integration, and manageability in a consistent manner
- Meeting the service-level expectations such as availability, fault tolerance, performance, and scalability in a cost-effective manner
- Improving productivity in the solution development by encouraging reusability, repeatability, and rationalization
- Ensuring long-term viability of the solution implementation by promoting accessibility, interoperability, supportability, configurability, and extensibility

---

Taking a top-down approach, the enterprise architect should derive the standards from the upstream business and IT maxims, architecture principles, and industry standards.[21] But the standards can also evolve bottom-up, as the corollary of the best practices and lessons learned during the projects.

For instance, projects may develop a few common software components during their solution development, supporting common needs such as logging, single sign-on, online payment, connection pooling, and so forth. These components may then be formalized into a set of reusable libraries and frameworks that improve consistency, reliability, and productivity in future projects.

---

[21] Industry standards are widely accepted by software vendors, implementers, and systems integrators. Their specifications are in some cases controlled by neutral forums such as W3C (Worldwide Web Consortium), OASIS (Organization for the Advancement of Structured Information Standards), or OMG (Object Management Group). There also are *de facto* standards not controlled by any such forum but still so stable that they are generally accepted. Examples are JEE; .Net technologies; the JBoss Application Server; Java frameworks like Seam, Struts, or Hibernate; or Adobe's Portable Document Format (PDF).

An enterprise architect is a key player here. Being well positioned to have a holistic view of the enterprise, she must be a driving force in identifying common IT needs of the enterprise, formalizing common ways of addressing them, and imposing them as standards for enterprise-wide usage.

Both the top-down and bottom-up approaches carry certain benefits and risks. A top-down approach maintains the big picture but may be plagued with an "ivory tower syndrome" that might result in a blind and futile enforcement of standards. The bottom-up approach, on the other hand, is concrete and pragmatic by nature but may end up in unnecessarily proprietary solutions.

As a consequence, the formalization of standards is a continuous process, combining top-down and bottom-up approaches. The enterprise architect tracks emerging trends, conducts industry research, assesses technologies, and then standardizes the use of such technologies for an enterprise. At the same time, she assimilates experiences from the past projects to establish standards and guidelines for the future projects.

During that process, the enterprise architect always seeks to minimize the number of in-use technologies in order to enhance the manageability of the environment and to deliver a consistent set of IT services. It is a tight rope walk for the architects because it involves balancing the need for *consistency* in a large-scale system implementation with the need for *diversity* of solutions demanded by the business. This means in detail:

- *Consistency*. In a large-scale system environment, consistency in solution implementation is critical. It enables predictability, fosters repeatability, encourages reuse, increases productivity, and improves manageability.
- *Diversity*. In a dynamic market environment, openness for a diverse set of solution implementations is equally important. It promotes innovation, enables business growth, and offers a competitive edge in the marketplace.

Standards are essentially meant to offer guidance to the project teams in selection and usage of technology while building their business solutions. Likewise, they are also meant to aid the architects in the governance of solution design and implementation in accordance with the target architecture.

Standardizing on technology usage

Technologies emerge and continuously evolve over time. Many technologies come and go, but only a few of them succeed and sustain. One of the fundamental considerations in determining the strategic fit of an application is to look at its underlying technologies. This base needs to be rated in relation to the strategic importance and supportability of those technologies in the overall schema of the enterprise. The overall schema of the enterprise's technology usage can broadly be classified as shown in Figure 3-15.

This classification plots an enterprise's *ability to execute* the projects in a given technology on the X-axis and plots the *strategic importance* of the given technology on the Y-axis. This classification closely relates to the Ward and Peppard scheme, described earlier in the "Evolving the IT Landscape (EA-3)" section. The Ward and Peppard scheme is better suited for application classification, whereas this scheme focuses on the technology layer. Comparing the two schemes leads to the following findings:

- *Star* and *Cash Cow* applications will be scattered across the *Core* and *Declining* technology areas.
- *Wild Cats* will be spotted in the *Emerging* square.
- *Poor Dogs* can be found anywhere.

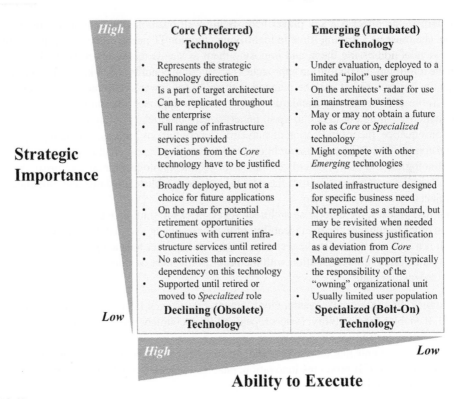

FIGURE 3-15

Technology classification in an enterprise

Having categorized the technology usage in the enterprise based on the aforementioned classification, one of the primary responsibilities of the enterprise architect is to inform the project teams of acceptable technology usage. This comprises the *technology products* they can use and the *technology standards* they must follow while building business solutions:

- *Technology products.* This comprises any software that is acquired to support an enterprise's business or IT needs. It includes commercial products, open source, libraries, frameworks, and any other code that the project teams did not create internally.
- *Technology standards.* This refers to one or more related specifications that have been approved externally by standards development forums, have been widely used and accepted by the industry, have been enforced by the government, or have been internally mandated for use within the enterprise. Standards come in the form of policies, guidelines, constraints, or conformance criteria.

The enterprise architect thus provides guidance on the permissible range of technologies that a project team may select to meet their business requirements. However, the approved technologies are not necessarily equal in terms of their supportability and quality of service. Each technology is subject to certain constraints. It is apparent from Figure 3-15 that supportability depends on the categorization (Core, Declining, Emerging, and Specialized). Opposed to that, the service level depends on business demand and cost structure and can, for instance, be classified as *platinum*, *gold*, or *silver*.

The technology guidance primarily comprises a list of *technology products* and *technology standards* that have been assessed and rated to be either compliant or noncompliant with the enterprise's strategic technology direction. It should therefore cover each and every technology that is relevant to the enterprise—from web browser to data storage; from coding standards to UI guidelines; and from modeling tools to security guidelines. A mature technical architecture is one that fulfills all the following criteria:

- Identifying the key technologies
- Describing the enterprise strategy for technology provision
- Containing a list of vendors, products, and standards associated with the technology
- Including a model for technology implementation

In the best possible case, such standards enable project teams to *assemble* a significant portion of their solution using the guidance contained in the technical architecture and the list of approved products and standards. The teams should not use forbidden technologies but at the same time should minimize the portion of their own development.

In reference to the technology classification in Figure 3-15, the EA group at Bank4Us does not have dedicated specialists for many Core and Declining technologies within the EA group itself. In general, the competency in some of these technologies—for instance, mainframe or CRM—often resides within the IT delivery units owning those environments. Oscar Salgado, the chief architect leading the EA group of Bank4Us, finds it therefore appropriate that the IT delivery units should be responsible for maintaining the approved product list and standards specifications for their own technology environment.

In addition, Oscar ensures that a single point of contact (SPOC) for the architecture group is appointed from every delivery unit. The SPOC makes sure that appropriate communication between the IT delivery unit and the architecture group is established and ensures a continuous information flow between the two. Oscar does not want his team to be too deeply involved in the Core technology domains belonging to those units. He wants his team to focus only on the *edge* of those technology islands—on the interaction of the IT delivery units with the rest of the enterprise.

Nevertheless, Oscar also looks for the opportunities for short-term job rotation for his architects. That way, they can participate in ongoing project activities within such independent IT delivery units. The primary role of Oscar's enterprise architects there is coaching and reviewing projects. This helps them to keep an eye on the end-to-end solution delivery that runs across many of these units.

Oscar takes a similar stance for the Specialized technology space simply because its footprint is too small to attract enterprise-wide attention. It is always the owning organizations who should care for these technologies.

On the other side of the spectrum, generalized technologies such as .Net, JEE, and similar development platforms have widespread proliferation across the bank. Oscar therefore takes over the ownership of them under his EA regime. The EA team offers a crystallization point for these technologies to which the project teams can refer and contribute.

Irrespective of whether a technology is centrally controlled by the EA group or not, Oscar ensures that the approved lists of technology standards and product specifications are maintained by the respective owners and that they are accessible to the EA group and the wider IT community over the bank's intranet. That way, Oscar's team has an up-to-date, consolidated list of all the products and standards employed within each technology environment at the bank. Table 3-8 presents a partial view of this list. Such a view is available on the EA Website accessible to all project teams over the Bank4Us intranet.

Table 3-8 Bank4Us Technology Products and Standards List (Partial, to Illustrate the Concept)

Area	Description	Owner
Security Standards	**http://intra.bank4us.com/EA/standards/security**	**IT Management and Security**
Password policy	Password creation, use, and protection Password reset, storage, and format	
Authentication	Identity: user, role, single sign-on	
Authorization	Access: functional entitlement, data entitlement	
Information classification	Public, internal, confidential, and secret	
Crypto standards	Encryption: cryptographic control policy	
Legal Standards	**http://intra.bank4us.com/legal**	**Compliance**
Sarbanes-Oxley Act	Sarbanes-Oxley Act (SOX) Internal Control over Financial Reporting (ICFR) SOX and ICFR Relevance in System Design	
Data Protection Act	How to handle user-based personal data	
Country-Specific Crypto	Compliance to country-specific cryptographic laws	
Open Source	JBoss Application Server 7 Apache Tomcat 7 Subject to legal and architecture approvals	
Operations Standards	**http://intra.bank4us.com/operations**	**IT Operations**
User desktop (PC global)	Base install, extended install, and optional install	
Log file format	Common Log File Format	
Naming standards	Database, message queues, files, variables	
Java and J2EE Standards	**http://intra.bank4us.com/EA/standards/jee**	**IT Management and J2EE**
J2EE platform road map	Strategic use: technologies, tools, and products list	
Java/J2EE	J2EE specifications with versions	
Proactive J2EE infrastructure (PJI: Bank4Us proprietary)	http://intra.bank4us.com/EA/standards/jee/PJI/ PJI J2EE Reference Architecture J2EE Development Framework and Infrastructure	
Development standards	Java Coding Style Guide PJI Application Development Guide Standard J2EE design patterns	
Web technologies	Rich Internet application: CSS, AJAX libraries Microsoft Internet Explorer 7.0 Mozilla Firefox 9 Google Chrome 16.0 Safari 5	
UI design guidelines	http://intra.bank4us.com/EA/channels/web-browser/Styleguide_g.pdf (look and feel)	**Corporate branding**
System Documentation	**http://intra.bank4us.com/EA/standards/modeling**	**IT Management and EA**
Modeling	Unified Modeling Language (UML) 1.3 or later	
Tools	Modeling and documentation tools	

As far as the Core, Declining, or Specialized technologies are concerned, the respective IT units in the bank possess a sustainable delivery capability. They are fully equipped with mature product implementations, established standards, and an experienced staff. However, this is not the case with the Emerging technologies and there are large numbers of new technologies shooting up like mushrooms. The bank does not have expertise on these new technologies. It is the EA group's task to lead the way and harness the bank's new technologies.

Introducing new architectural paradigms

Looking at the CEO vision, "Best-in- Class Customer Experience: Anywhere, Anytime, Any Channel," CIO Dave Callaghan has recognized the pressing need for a comprehensive approach for integration within and beyond the bank. Dave has therefore translated the CEO vision into an IT maxim that says:

> *Our systems must support new ways of doing business collaboratively with our partners and customers—an architecture that allows electronic bonding at more touchpoints and at a depth not previously attempted. The styles of electronic bonding should now include multidevice, service orientation, white labeling as well as the more traditional web portals and B2B gateways.*

For Oscar, this need for better integration is further fueled as a consequence of his decision to manage the technology areas in the bank at their edges rather than in their entirety. Since he intends to offer more local autonomy to individual technology owners (the IT delivery units themselves), he needs to ensure stringent control at their edges: their integration and interaction with the rest of the enterprise.

On the ground, Ian Miller, the enterprise architect working on Oscar Salgado's team, supervises all business projects around *Closer to Customer* for architectural conformance. It is a regular governance activity that he conducts in addition to his application rationalization mandate. He has recently observed a growing demand from the business side for enabling mobile channels, accessing mainframe data over the Internet, synchronizing customer data across disparate systems, and so forth.

He has briefed the EA group about the need for a mobile platform, integrating to a host of heterogeneous back-end systems in the bank, and using a common integration layer. The EA team has opted for an SOA approach for the proposed integration platform, including the introduction of an enterprise service bus (ESB). However, no one in the current EA group has much insight into SOA. Oscar therefore recruits Shashi Malhotra, an SOA expert, into his team. Shashi joins the team with a mandate for ESB use at the bank. His task lists contains the following activities:

- Provide a base to bed the ESB technology at Bank4Us
- Confirm the approach and understanding of ESB use and implementation
- Establish standards and guidelines for service development and integration
- Act as evangelist for future SOA opportunities at the bank

We will accompany Shashi in rolling out a pilot project on ESB use in the next subsection, "Monitoring the Project Portfolio (EA-6)."

Enforcing standards and guidelines

Skim through any document published by an EA group anywhere in the world and somewhere you will see a *notice-cum-guidance-cum-threat* that typically says something along these lines:

> *All projects will be evaluated based on their consistency with the direction, products, and standards specified by the enterprise architecture. The project teams must adhere to the policies and standards*

stated in the enterprise architecture. Only the use of the listed tools, products, and technologies is permissible. The rare deviations need to be justified.[22]

The architects and developers on the ground react to such guidance with a mixed-emotions mindset. Widespread acceptance, subsurface resistance, and outright denial are the predominant reactions.

Let's look at the *widespread acceptance* scenario first. This is the best-case scenario, reflecting a positive attitude of project teams toward the standards. They follow the standards not because an authority like EA says they should but because they themselves have come to realize that it is the right thing to do. They have nurtured the standards from the ground up. It has helped them do their job better in the past and will continue to help them in the future. Without doubt there will be pros and cons to any stipulated standards, but there is an overall agreement that they are the right thing. These standards have now seeped into their habit and culture.

For instance, at Bank4Us, the Proactive JEE Infrastructure (PJI) listed in Table 3-11 is widely used. At the time of its introduction, it substantially improved the productivity of project teams in JEE development. This sounds like a dream come true for the enterprise architects.

Unfortunately, developers and architects in the project teams don't often really feel this way. More often, they show *subsurface resistance* toward the standards. They are typically frustrated with the constraints that such standards impose on them. Reasons are manifold: The standards and products are outdated, the newest library versions are not available (or approved by EA), the best possible solution for the project turns out to be nonstandard-complaint, and so forth.

At Bank4Us, the aforementioned PJI standard has by now grown into a massive proprietary code base. It costs too much in maintenance, and over the years has lost its significance. It locks the project teams into an outdated version of underlying JEE application server. Many enthusiastic developers and architects complain that they are notoriously late in leveraging the newer standards and rich feature sets, which are readily available in the latest version of JEE platform. They also complain that they cannot reduce the project costs by moving their noncritical applications to an open source platform.

At the extreme end, some project teams show *outright denial* for standards adoption. This is especially true for the standards enforced on them. Quite often it is not the developers but the project managers who are wary of immature industry standards. Although compliance with industry standards is essential for long-term sustenance, they might not necessarily be ready for primetime use. Sometimes they have been stipulated in the hope of anticipated benefits but without knowing their practicality.

Such decisions may stem from sheer enthusiasm fueled by market hype or the innovativeness of an idea. However, in the absence of concrete proof points, it is a challenge for enterprise architects to convincingly adopt such standards to the mainstream development. Amid tight delivery schedules, inflating project scope, and unanticipated technical glitches, a mandate for such standards is prone to move down to the bottom of a project team's agenda and then drop off the list.

Such a mixed-emotions mindset—which includes widespread acceptance, subsurface resistance, and outright denial—characterizes the organizational dynamics of the enterprise. If the emotions

---

[22]This is a complied, condensed version of concrete examples of EA mandates we have come across in various projects and in many companies.

are leaning more toward the latter two, one could call it *organizational inertia*. There are two extreme kinds of standards adoption strategy to deal with organizational dynamics:

- *Eager adoption.* Incubate the emerging industry standards and the cutting-edge technologies right away, and then proactively enforce them in order to become the first mover in the market. This is expensive in terms of development costs simply because it adds to the project effort and risks. It also neglects the opportunity to skip immature versions and reduce the number of upgrades. On the positive side, this strategy might offer a competitive edge and hence be suitable for applications belonging to the *Wild Cats* categories and for *Emerging* technologies.
- *Reluctant adoption.* Defer adoption until as late as possible. This is expensive in the long run if the enterprise has to catch up with the industry at a later point in time. In that case, technology debt will accumulate and a wide software installation base will be in use when the need for adoption arises. This will demand a massive and dedicated migration project later on. However, this adoption strategy generally minimizes the immediate software development costs. This applies especially to the applications belonging to the *Poor Dogs* category and the technologies in the *Core* and *Declining* quadrants.

In practice, the most rational approach will be a tightrope walk between these two extremes. In mature EA organizations, interim *project reviews* provide a mechanism whereby a formal dialogue between the enterprise architects and project teams is established. In that case, a golden mean between the two extremes—*eagerness* and *reluctance*—is reached by consensus.

The first interim review, called an *architectural conformance review (ACR),* is conducted during the design phase of the project. It must be concluded before the development phase can begin. The ACR allows project teams to consult with enterprise architects and validate the conformance of their solution design against the prescribed standards.

The second interim review is called a *post-implementation review (PIR).* It takes place after each production deployment and allows enterprise architects, along with other project stakeholders, to reflect on the performance of the project in regard to their specific interests and concerns. We will outline both ACR and PIR processes in the next section, "Monitoring the Project Portfolio (EA-6)."

STANDARDS ENFORCEMENT STYLES
Extreme Enforcement of Standards
At Amazon, SOA standards are known to be nonnegotiable. Google engineer Steve Yegge tells the story of Amazon's rather ruthless style of enforcing SOA standards (2011).[23] In around 2002, Jeff Bezos (Amazon's CEO) issued his mandate for SOA:

> *The project teams must expose their data and functionality through service interfaces only and they must communicate with each other through these interfaces only.*

Bezos then mentioned:

> *Anyone who doesn't do this will be fired.*

Continued

---

[23]Steve Yegge posted an internal memo on Google+, which by mistake was leaked into the public domain. The narration quoted here is from this memo posting, known as *Stevey's Google Platforms Rant*.

STANDARDS ENFORCEMENT STYLES—CONT'D

What Bezos said was meant that way; it expressed his conviction for the SOA in no-nonsense terms. Amazon has made lots of progress since the SOA mandate was given in 2002, and it will have learned a lot of new lessons on the way. The infrastructure they had built for selling books has now transformed into an externally accessible, extensible computing platform.

However, this is an exceptional case. It is not apt to follow this style of enforcement in typical large enterprises. The statement is meant to set the long-term direction. In Chapter 9, where we discuss strategies of how to change the direction of EA in an enterprise, we will refer back to this story as an example for style called *Black and White Goals*.

One needs to be aware that this is a double-edged sword. If enforced strictly, such a statement will take away an open, creative, and risk-taking culture. If not enforced strictly, it becomes a mockery. Nevertheless, the morale of this story is: A mandate for standardization has a chance to succeed when it comes from the highest *authority* and it comes with a strong sense of *urgency* and *conviction*.

At Bank4Us Oscar Salgado, the chief architect, takes a balanced view and has established the following architectural principle: "Standardize wherever possible, deviate wherever necessary." His rationale behind this principle is that 100% standardization is not possible and not needed. The effort of his team, however, must be focused on improving the level of standardization, progressively and definitively.

Monitoring the project portfolio (EA-6)

Project portfolio management begins with *portfolio planning*—normally a yearly exercise spinning off from activity EA-1, "Defining the IT Strategy." Portfolio planning takes up the input from the IT strategy—business and IT demands, current gaps, maxims, and high-level strategic initiatives—and translates it into work packages for projects. The program managers, under the stewardship of the CIO, fiercely engage in defining, prioritizing, and estimating IT projects.

What is a portfolio? A *portfolio* refers to an abstract collection of programs and projects gathered for management convenience. The constituents do not necessarily have a common business theme. The main purpose of the portfolio is creating value and maximizing return on investment.

A *program*, on the other hand, is a collection of projects sharing a common business case or objective. It is meant to realize business benefits defined by the business case. In both cases, a *project* is a temporary endeavor to accomplish a prescribed unit of work, usually constrained by timeframe, budget, and deliverables. For the sake of brevity, key elements of portfolio, program, and project are summarized in Table 3-9.

It may be noted that the management attention and approach in portfolio management starkly differ from the traditional way of running projects. Without portfolio management, once a project has been funded its business value is normally not reexamined again. The monitoring focus is only on key metrics, such as quality, schedule, and scope. With portfolio management, however, you review the portfolio periodically—typically quarterly—and you question each project: "Does this project still make sense?"

If it does not, you take corrective action. The projects are viewed in relation to one another, not as a stand-alone venture in isolation. This approach allows balancing the projects in the portfolio: High-risk projects are complemented by safe projects, short-term by long-term ones. One should continuously rebalance the portfolio to maximize the value and optimize the return on investment. The principles and approaches employed here are essentially those applied to managing a financial portfolio.

Table 3-9 IT Project Portfolio Management: A Summarized View

	Portfolio	Program	Project
Scope of work	• Portfolio scope definition • Business-IT alignment • Investment management and risk analysis • Benefit realization Management • Knowledge management	• Comprehensive program Planning • Change and risk management • Infrastructure and release management • Coordination of project deliveries • Program communications–internal and external • Business-IT collaboration • Measurement of results	• Project planning • Scope • Budget • Schedule • Resources • Deliverables • Risks • Metrics
Manager role	• Portfolio manager	• Program manager	• Portfolio manager
Manager is accountable for	• Investment and risk management— optimize on value delivered	• Business case implementation— milestones, quality, scope	• Business solution implementation— milestones, quality, scope
Sponsor	• Portfolio sponsor (CIO)	• Business sponsor	• Business sponsor
Sponsor is accountable for	• Total cost of ownership • Return on investment • Value creation	• Business benefit valuation	• Business solution enablement
Management control	• Portfolio steering committee	• Program committee; program management office	• Project management

IT portfolio management indeed stems from the concepts in financial portfolio management, whereas EA has its roots in architecture and technology. The two are separate disciplines and carry different genes. Yet they must be fully integrated with each other, as both have a common goal: Evolve the enterprise IT landscape in a strategic direction to *maximize benefit realization in the long run*. In the process, both practice areas attempt to take organizational politics out of IT investment decisions.

Building the project portfolio

Let's chalk out a rough sketch of the strategic planning process in an enterprise. It begins with the strategy formulation, wherein business units within the enterprise engage in preparing their *business plans*. They derive their business strategy based on the CEO's mandate and the implied business maxims. Then they identify the business initiatives they will undertake and prepare a *time-bound* business plan to implement their strategy. Earlier in EA-1, "Defining IT Strategy", we had a cursory look at how this happens in a car manufacturer example, Car4Us.

Figure 3-16 depicts an illustrative portfolio planning process. One of the primary inputs to this process is the collection of business plans coming from all business units. Each business plan identifies the *gaps* in the enterprise's IT landscape that need to be bridged for the respective business unit so that it can meet its business objectives. These gaps can broadly be classified as *functional gaps* and

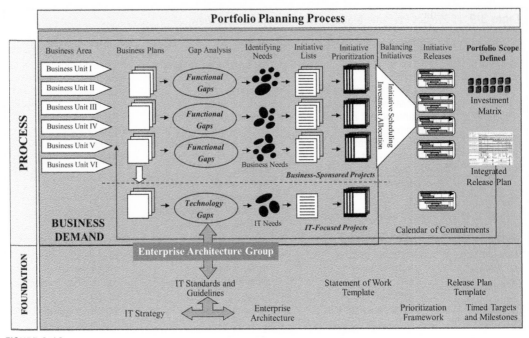

FIGURE 3-16

An example to illustrate the concept of a portfolio-planning process.

technology gaps. The functional gaps are translated into *business needs*. The technology gaps are translated into *IT needs*. These business and IT needs form the basis for identifying and defining *IT initiatives* or *projects*.[24]

At this stage, the needs are stated at high level only, sufficient enough to scope the IT initiatives and gauge the order of magnitude for each initiative. This helps arrive at a ballpark cost estimate for each initiative. Evidently this exercise calls for deep insight into the enterprise that only the experienced program managers and seasoned architects there can bring to the table. For that reason, the Portfolio Steering Committee at Bank4Us is composed of Dave Callaghan, the CIO as the chairperson, and senior program managers. Chief architect Oscar Salgado is invited along as a member as well.

In general, enterprise architects are not accountable for portfolio planning. It is the business units that drive the CIO's agenda. Nevertheless, enterprise architects play an important part in it. Acting as an assessor or an advisor, enterprise architects are well positioned and fully equipped to perform the following activities:

- Identifying and consolidating *common* IT needs across the business units
- Seeking opportunities to introduce IT-focused initiatives into the portfolio
- Prioritizing projects based on benefit potential, architectural fit, and implementation risks

---

[24]*Initiatives* are expressed as intentions and work streams. They are coarsely defined at a high level with work packages and ballpark estimates. In contrast, *projects* are more concrete. They are defined in a formal way using a statement of work, a project charter, or a project proposal.

With day-to-day exposure to the activities in EA-1 through EA-8, enterprise architects know what the enterprise does, how it works, and how it behaves. This insight can make them influential personalities in the portfolio planning process. In Bank4Us, Oscar, the chief architect, is a member of the Portfolio Steering Committee for the very same role—as an advisor and as an assessor.

Pushing IT-focused effort into the portfolio

IT-focused effort comprises any activities that do not stem from a qualified business case or do not enjoy business sponsorship. Yet this effort is needed, if only to ensure better IT management. It comes in different flavors: *migration, consolidation, decomposition, reengineering, replacement,* or *retirement* of existing applications (or technologies, or infrastructure). It may as well be for *incubation* of new technologies in the enterprise: concept creation, technology research, prototyping, and piloting.

The goal of an IT-focused effort is to help the evolution of the IT landscape toward the target state architecture. Hence, as depicted in Figure 3-16, it usually falls under the premise of EA. In the absence of direct business sponsorship, enterprise architects have to find some way to add such IT-focused effort to the project portfolio. There are two ways this can happen:

- *Dedicated approach.* The venture is executed as a separately funded project, often referred to as an *infrastructural project.* Normally the investments come from the CIO's own IT budget.
- *Opportunistic approach.* In this case, the initiative is included in the business-sponsored projects that are required as a result of new business requirements or major enhancements.

Let's again turn back to Bank4Us to see how this can happen there.

Ian Miller, the enterprise architect in charge of an application rationalization program, is looking at downsizing the legacy environment, for which he takes a deep dive into the bank's current IT landscape and identifies rationalization opportunities. He uses the practices and techniques outlined in EA-3, Evolving the IT Landscape, to do that. He and his team have defined a series of work packages for the rationalization effort and now prepare the rationalization roadmap along with supporting cost/benefit analysis.

Oscar Salgado, the chief architect, is convinced that there are tangible rationalization targets that they must chase in the near future. However, the rationalization effort involves many, many stakeholders. It demands explicit and impartial funding—essentially to avoid any bias toward a particular business unit. Therefore, Oscar has taken the *dedicated approach* and seeks centralized funding from the CIO's budget. He therefore catalogues all rationalization proposals in the current year for CIO sponsorship.

In parallel, Oscar has observed that many business units, in their business plans, consistently express a need for mobile applications. These applications would help them interact more closely with their customers. Oscar has recognized a need for a *common mobility platform* and a need for better integration capabilities that can seamlessly integrate the mobility platform into the bank's IT backbone. The top two priorities for the business are ease of integration and real-time access to information.

Oscar acknowledges that the current IT landscape lacks these critical capabilities in a big way. Hence, *mobility* and *integration* are on his radar during this year. As described in the previous section, "Developing and Enforcing Standards and Guidelines (EA-5)," he plans to pilot an enterprise service bus (ESB) as part of a more complete approach to integration at the bank. For that reason, he has recruited the SOA expert Shashi Malhotra onto his EA team to start working on the ESB mandate.

The stories of disillusionment with earlier attempts at enterprise application integration (EAI) are not yet forgotten at the bank. Oscar is cautious about the widespread skepticism toward and lack of experience in SOA. He prefers an *opportunistic approach* for the ESB deployment. Therefore, he instructs Shashi to set up an ESB infrastructure that can implement *real-life* integration scenarios at the bank. This infrastructure must demonstrate the applicability of SOA to the bank's needs and address the integration needs and pain points of the business. This is a better way of getting the funding, and it will also keep the pilot effort relevant to the business.

Shashi consults with the program managers and their business counterparts. They work closely to come up with a list of integration scenarios in their projects that can be potential candidates for piloting. There are 14 of them. Shashi now needs to evaluate them and shortlist the most appropriate ones for his pilot project. To that effect, he prepares a questionnaire and seeks information about these integration scenarios from concerned business and IT experts. Shashi's weighted scoring of the integration scenarios yields the scorecard depicted in Table 3-10. This scorecard helps him shortlist 4 out of 14 scenarios for his pilot project.

The pilot project has now been scoped; it covers typical integration requirements for the bank. As the next step, Shashi needs to come up with two things: ballpark cost estimates (how much product vendors and implementers will charge) and a fallback strategy (how to back out without risking the project if the ESB does not perform its job).

Oscar finds Shashi's approach sensible, practical, and safe. They now need to convince the respective program managers to apportion the ESB cost into their project estimates and be the *first movers* for ESB technologies at the bank.

Prioritizing the projects

Looking back at Figure 3-13, you find many IT initiatives being identified to fulfill the IT needs of business units. These initiatives need to be prioritized, shortlisted, and then budgeted as projects for execution. To prioritize them, three things are needed: a list of initiatives, the criteria for prioritization, and most important, the right set of people to participate in the prioritization process.

The first step in the prioritization process is to define what constitutes a project and to enforce this definition so that the projects can be compared on equal footing. This can be done easily by mandating a standardized *statement of work* or *project charter* template.

The next step is to provide *a consistent framework for prioritization*. It must allow assessing all projects with an impartial eye. It should be based on predefined criteria, such as value contribution, strategic fit, implementation risks, cost, and so forth. The criteria depend on the enterprise and its market outlook, business priorities, and organizational constraints. Yet generic prioritization criteria are worth mentioning: They may act as a springboard to establish a tailor-made prioritization scheme for a specific enterprise. The parameters are as follows:

- *Value contribution.* This parameter expresses the business value the project aims to deliver. Is it meant to reduce expenses, increase revenue, contribute to competitiveness of the company, or serve regulatory compliance? Is the benefit quantifiable?
- *Strategic fit.* This parameter recognizes if the project is taking the enterprise in the strategic direction. Is this project serving the strategic intent of the enterprise, whatever that may be—for instance, be a first mover, be an early follower, enhance brand value, or improve market penetration?

Table 3-10 Defining and Scoping an IT-Focused Pilot Project (ESB Deployment)

ESB Pilot Project Scoping	Integration -1	Integration -2	Integration -3	Integration -4	Integration -5	Integration -6	Integration -7	Integration -8	Integration -9	Integration -10	Integration -11	Integration -12	Integration -13	Integration -14
The pilot project key criteria:														
Has demonstrable IT and business benefit if implemented now	1	0	0	0	1	1	0	0	0	1	1	0	1	1
Has the "right" level of business visibility (visible but not critical if fails)	0	0	1	1	1	0	0	1	1	1	0	0	0	0
Will be used in a B2B role immediately or in the short term	0	0	1	0	1	0	0	0	0	1	1	0	0	0
Has business potential for workflow and process management	1	1	1	1	1	0	1	1	1	1	1	1	0	0
Will address data quality issues	1	1	1	1	0	0	1	1	1	1	1	0	0	0
Will address delays in getting/sending critical data	1	1	1	1	0	1	0	1	1	0	1	0	0	0
Will reduce high operational costs	0	0	1	1	0	1	0	1	1	1	1	0	0	0
Sum-1:	4	3	6	5	4	3	2	5	5	6	6	1	1	1
Load by weight factor (*Sum-1* x 1.5)	6	4.5	9	7.5	6	4.5	3	7.5	7.5	9	9	1.5	1.5	1.5
The pilot should also (secondary) :														
Have low impact to project timeframe	0	0	0	0	0	0	0	0	0	1	0	1	0	0
Have short implementation timeframe	0	0	0	0	0	0	0	0	0	1	0	1	0	0
Involve a limited number of users	0	0	1	1	0	0	1	1	1	1	1	1	1	1
Be capable of backing out easily (on failure)	0	0	0	0	1	1	1	0	0	1	0	1	0	0
Sum-2:	0	0	1	1	1	1	2	1	1	4	1	4	1	1
Final score (Sum-1 x 1.5 + Sum-2)	6	4.5	**10**	**8.5**	7	5.5	5	8.5	8.5	**13**	**10**	5.5	2.5	2.5

- *Cross-LOB[25] ranking.* This criterion looks at the cross-organizational impact of the project. Who is the sponsoring business unit, and how relevant is this project for other business units and to the enterprise as a whole?
- *Implementation risks.* This value measures the deployment feasibility, ease of implementation, or probability of success. Is the enterprise really capable of executing this project?
- *Integration complexity.* This parameter assesses the level of interdependencies and integration requirements stemming from this project. How well are the upstream and downstream dependencies in the project managed? How easy it is to seamlessly integrate the project implementation into the enterprise's IT landscape?
- *Cost.* This criterion gauges whether the cost estimates are in the permissible range for business acceptance and in line with the anticipated value contribution of the project. Are the costs justifiable and within sound limits?

These criteria are to some extent interrelated. For instance, high-value projects are normally big; they bear high costs and high risks. As a consequence, the entry barrier for high-value projects is also quite high. One such big project causes more damage when it fails than 10 small ones.

The criteria we've outlined are generic and can be further extended or drilled down as needed. However, most of the criteria are not really quantifiable and cannot be objectively assessed. At best, one can do the rating on a scale of 1 to 10. As a result, the prioritization process requires tacit knowledge of the enterprise. The steering committee, comprising program managers and chaired by the CIO, typically brings that knowledge to the table. The same steering committee also serves as the decision authority.

The third step is the prioritization process itself. The steering committee prioritizes the projects under the known organizational constraints such as available funds, sourcing capacity, project interdependencies, and so forth. The process involves a what-if analysis on multiple portfolio scenarios, adjustment to parameters and constraints in the portfolio, and simulating and assessing alternatives. The goal is to determine the optimal allocation of investments to initiatives and projects. It follows pretty much the same approach that is employed in financial portfolio analysis.

The output of the prioritization process, among other things, comprises:

- An *investment matrix* that shows which programs get investments (along the rows) and from which source (along the columns)
- An *integrated release plan* that shows broad timelines for the IT initiatives, with critical interdependencies and constraints highlighted
- A *feedback loop* into the business units

The project prioritization does not have a closed-form solution. It is a constrained optimization process that involves many parameters and is fairly complex. As the size of a portfolio grows, prioritization gets overwhelmingly complex, and a simple spreadsheet-based assessment becomes futile. Beyond this point, the use of a more sophisticated portfolio management tool does make sense. Taking a deep dive into the portfolio analysis process is beyond the scope of this book. Interested readers can refer to the literature available on the subject of IT portfolio management.[26]

---

[25]LOB stands for line of business.

[26]We can recommend the book *IT Portfolio Management Step-by-Step: Unlocking the Business Value of Technology,* by Bryan Maizlish and Robert Handler (2005), or the MIT Center for Information Systems Research Website at http://cisr.mit.edu/research/research-overview/classic-topics/it-portfolio-management/.

Auditing the portfolio

Once the projects have been planned and funded, they move into delivery mode. The project teams are formed and the work begins. The focus is to deliver software features in accordance with the defined scope, specifications, and timeline. Formal management control is in place to ensure that the project delivers what has been committed to.

While the short-term goals of the business are being met by the projects, enterprise architects need to guard the enterprise IT landscape. They have to ensure that solutions are designed and implemented in view of the long-term goals of the enterprise and in alignment with the envisaged target state. Although enterprise architects should not be involved too deeply in the day-to-day project execution, they need to keep an eye on the projects, especially during design, acceptance, and deployment phases.

In more mature EA organization, this is done by a formalized *portfolio governance*. The role of portfolio governance is to provide a decision-making framework that is logical, robust, and repeatable to govern project investments. Figure 3-17 depicts an enterprise architect's viewpoint on portfolio governance. It typically comprises two formal review processes: an *architecture conformance review* and a *post-implementation review*.

These processes act as tollgates for every project delivery that enters the enterprise's IT landscape. Ross (2005) identifies the post-implementation review as one of the essential management practices for mature EA organizations. In the next section we will go through the architecture conformance and post-implementation reviews.

Patrolling for architecture conformance

The earliest entry of enterprise architects into a project may happen at the time of the project kickoff. It is the time to gain a first-cut understanding of the business requirements and to recommend the technology prerogatives for solution implementation. This involvement is, however, restricted to an advisory role.

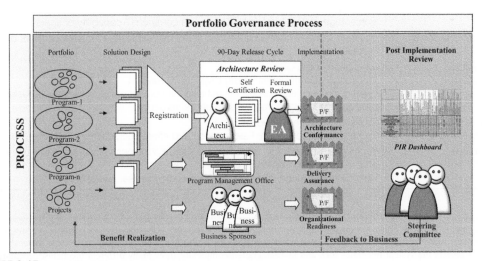

FIGURE 3-17

An example to illustrate the concept of a portfolio governance process.

A more formal engagement of enterprise architects in the projects usually begins during the design phase, primarily for review of the proposed solution design for conformance against the stipulated architectural principles and standards. This engagement instills a governance mechanism. This mechanism enables project teams, in consultation with the enterprise architect, to confirm the alignment of their solution design with the enterprise architecture, its policies, its technology roadmap, and its technology portfolio.

What does an enterprise architect need to review the solution designs for? There is no standard list of parameters on which such a review can be based. Again, it pretty much depends on the priorities and constraints of the enterprise. Nevertheless, the criteria listed in Table 3-11 give an idea of an enterprise architect's possible architectural concerns during the design reviews.

As shown in Figure 3-17,[27] the architecture conformance review begins with a *registration*. The project team registers its solution design for architecture review to a governing body. TOGAF (The Open Group, 2011) identifies such a governance body as *Architecture Review Board (ARB)*. The registration is needed to plan ahead the engagement of the project teams with the ARB during the upcoming delivery cycle. It helps them identify the design artifacts they want to put through the review process. It also chalks out the plan as to who, when, how, and on what criteria the reviews will be conducted.

Table 3-11 Architecture Conformance Criteria (An Example to Illustrate the Concept)

Criteria	Metrics
Technology usage	• Standards compliance, justification for deviation • Infrastructure reuse, shared services—productivity gain, effort, and cost savings
Capability completeness	• Business scope completeness—count and/or percentage of: customer types supported, product types supported, processes supported • Technical implementation completeness—count and/or percentage of: correct implementations, correct interface exposures, operations supported
Capability reuse	• Percentage of installed base (migrated to use common IT capability or shared services) • Percentage of user base (migrated to use common IT capability or shared services)
System shutdown	• Systems shutdown variance—actual vs. target (expressed in terms of count or percentage)
Integration complexity	• Integration complexity • Integration maturity index: Using CMM for integration • Level of process standardization achieved in percentage (across lines of business/product-portfolio/geographies): Actual vs. target
Process harmonization	• Process cycle-time reduction • Process failure reduction: Failure mode and effect analysis (right-first-time)
Data quality	• Timeliness, accessibility, completeness, and correctness (accuracy and integrity) of data in given business context • Data ownership, consolidation, synchronization, reuse, and sharing

---

[27]Integration complexity may be expressed as a function: Integration Complexity $= f$ (i1, i2, i3), where i1 = relation complexity (how many systems or instances a system has a relationship with), i2 = interface complexity (how many different business objects the system integrates for), and i3 = integration complexity (how many different mechanisms/techniques/methods are used to implement the integrations).

It is expected that all the project teams register their solution designs for review by enterprise architects. It is, however, at the discretion of enterprise architects to determine which solution designs demand a *formal review* and which ones do not. Usually the enterprise architects need to focus their efforts on architecturally challenging areas in the enterprise.

Wherever practicable, the enterprise architect may recommend that the project architects themselves perform the review of their solution design and claim the *self-certification* for conformance. The enterprise architect can then determine whether such self-certification is justified, depending on the evidence produced by the project architect plus any other background factors such as the strategic importance of the solution and the track record of the project team. This minimizes the overhead for everyone.

We will explore new and effective ways of achieving this goal using the *architecture scrum* in Chapter 7, "Building Block 2: Involve All Stakeholders by Interlocking Architecture Scrums." These scrums enforce strong rules for timeliness and quality and facilitate regular interaction and communication.

In essence there are two routes to certification for architecture conformance: *self-assessment* or a formal *architecture conformance review*. In either case, conformance certification must be sought by the project team before the solution design is finalized and the development begins. In some cases, the enterprise architect may grant a conditional certification, requiring the project teams to take corrective action to close the identified nonconformities prior to solution deployment.

After certification, if the project team makes any *material change* to the solution design, it must pass through the review process again. A material change is any change that invalidates the basis on which earlier conformance certification was granted. The enterprise architect comes back into the picture again during the acceptance testing phase. There the enterprise architect has to revalidate whether the solution being deployed is indeed architecturally conformant at that stage.

This is an idealistic sketch for an architectural governance process. In practice, we find project teams invariably fail to comply in many different ways and request exceptions. The most commonly encountered reasons are:

- Tight project timelines
- "Scope creep"
- Inadequacy of architecture
- Specificity of business requirements that cannot be fulfilled with the standard architecture as stipulated by the enterprise architects
- Open issues in the stipulated architecture itself

Some reasons are genuine, whereas some are mere excuses. What do enterprise architects do then?

1. Grant a *conditional certification,* telling the project team to close the nonconformity at the earliest possible project milestone in the future, or
2. Place a red mark on its status report to the steering committee, essentially escalating the nonconformance of the project higher up

In the first case, the project team may agree to take all possible corrective actions and the enterprise architect may also take a softer stand. They compromise and make a deal. But later the project team either gets dismantled due to the project closure or it demands additional funds or time for making *post facto* changes in design and deployment. It is quite unlikely that additional funds will simply be granted for the sake of architectural compliance.

In the second case, the enterprise architect is bound to meet resistance in escalating nonconformance to the steering committee. However, she rarely has a really strong case to make the steering committee act in her favor. This is especially true when the solution has already been implemented by the project team and is working as intended in the production environment.

So, neither compromise nor confrontation works well. It is therefore of utmost importance for an enterprise architect to convincingly negotiate. He needs to create a win-win situation for both parties rather than falling into the trap of argumentative discussions. It is a real test to measure the enterprise architect's interpersonal skills.

In Bank4Us, the enterprise architects assess solution designs by conducting formal architecture reviews. Oscar Salgado, the chief architect, reports a consolidated *architecture conformance report* to the steering committee at the end of each 90-day delivery cycle. The report is a dashboard, as shown in Table 3-12, intended to be discussed during the post-implementation review.

Taking a collective view of portfolio performance

The *post-implementation review* is a process (see Figure 3-17) by which the steering committee takes a collective view of the portfolio performance at the end of each delivery cycle—typically a 90-day release cycle. In addition to the steering committee, this review may seek participation from other stakeholders, such as business sponsors, program managers, and enterprise architects. Each stakeholder has different concerns and motives to judge the success or failure of a project.

Apart from the *architecture conformance* discussed earlier, *delivery assurance* and *organizational readiness* are the other two predominant management concerns in the post-implementation review (Table 3-13).

The essence of post-implementation reviews is that the performance and outcome of all the projects are viewed in comparison with each other, not in isolation. This allows to assess the overall portfolio performance more often (for instance, once every quarter). A consolidated performance dashboard reported at the portfolio level on a quarterly basis is a powerful management tool. It offers a number of strategic levers to the CIO, supporting the following activities:

- Adjusting the priorities and investments rapidly in response to the business flux
- Balancing the project pressure and change impact among different departments
- Assessing the strategic value of projects that have a seemingly low ROI
- Providing feedback on strategic decisions back to the business more frequently

Making it a two-way dialogue

Both architecture conformance and post-implementation reviews are opportunities for an enterprise architect to engage closely with project teams. On one hand, they allow the enterprise architect to guide the development effort and ensure that project teams conform to the strategic direction. On the other hand, they help her backfill the enterprise architecture by consciously gathering and assimilating the best practices and lessons learned in real-life projects.

EA begins with conceptualization, idea generation, and philosophical preaching, but it gains substance only after gathering practical revelations from the projects on the ground. Hence these review processes can well be seen as mechanisms to backfill the enterprise architecture. They should enable two-way communication between the enterprise architecture and the project teams—guiding but also learning,

Table 3-12 Architecture Conformance Success Scorecard (An Example to Illustrate the Concept)

Title: **Architecture Conformance Scorecard**
As on: **15-Apr-2012**
Contact: **Oscar Salgado**

Owner	Program Name	Cycle Start	Cycle End	PIR Date	Criteria			
					Technology Usage	Integration Complexity	System Shutdown	Capability Reuse
C2C Program Office	C2C–Customer Win	01-Jan-12	31-Mar-12	15-Apr-12	G	R	G	G
C2C Program Office	C2C–Customer Servicing	01-Jan-12	31-Mar-12	15-Apr-12	G	G	R	G
C2C Program Office	C2C–Complaint Resolution	01-Jan-12	31-Mar-12	15-Apr-12	G	G	G	R
Customer Relations	Customer Data Integration	01-Apr-11	31-Dec-11	15-Jan-12	G	R	G	G
Risk and Compliance	Anti-Money Laundering	01-Jan-12	31-Mar-12	15-Apr-12	G	G	R	R
IT Innovation Lab	Enterprise Service Bus: Pilot	01-Jan-12	31-Mar-12	15-Apr-12	G	G		
Marketing	Digital Marketing Platform	01-Oct-11	31-Jun-12	15-Jul-12	G			
Mainframe Operations	Mainframe Revitalization	01-Jun-11	31-Dec-12	15-Jan-12	G	G	G	G
Treasury Front-Office	Derivative Product Research	01-Oct-11	31-Mar-11	15-Apr-12	G	G	R	R
Treasury Back-Office	Centralized Rate Server	01-Jan-12	31-Mar-12	15-Apr-12	G	G	G	G
Conventions	G, Green: Compliant							
	R, Red: Noncompliant							
	Blank: Not applicable							

Table 3-13 Post-Implementation Review Criteria (For Illustration Only)

Criteria	Metrics
Delivery Assurance (Accountable Roles: Program Manager, Project Manager)	
On-schedule	• Schedule variance: actual vs. baseline
Within budget	• Cost variance: actual vs. baseline
	• Effort variance: actual vs. baseline
With quality	• Open defects: count by severity
Requirement stability	• Change requests: count and effort estimates
	• Unsolicited change request: effort estimates
Scope change impact	• Change request effort: actual vs. baseline
Rework impact	• Unsolicited effort: actual vs. estimated
Open requirements	• Deferred requirements: count and criticality
Open issues	• Unresolved escalations: count and criticality
Organizational Readiness (Accountable Roles: Business Sponsor, Business Liaison)	
User acceptability	• User feedback: exceeds expectations, meets expectations, not satisfied
	• User on-boarding: time taken by an average new user to learn and use the new features (learning curve)
Workforce alignment	• Learning: number of user training (hands-on) sessions conducted: actual vs. target
	• Knowledge base: online user guide, help, tutorials
Vendor performance	• Service-level compliance
	• Goal-based reward vs. penalty
Direct business benefits (if tangible)	• Agility: time to implement, time to market (product launch time), time to respond
	• Efficiency: reduction in cycle time, reduction in effort, reduction in failure rate, reduction in cost

governing but also getting feedback. We will discuss additional, innovative ways to do that in both Chapter 7, "Toward Pragmatism: Lean and Agile EA," and Chapter 8, "Inviting to Participation."

Leading or coaching projects (EA-7)

A computer is a stupid machine with the ability to do incredibly smart things, while computer programmers are smart people with the ability to do incredibly stupid things. They are, in short, a dangerously perfect match.

—Bill Bryson[28]

A software architect who is not in touch with the evolving source code of the product is out of touch with reality.

—Craig Larman and Bas Vodde[29]

---

[28]Bill Bryson, *I'm a Stranger Here Myself* (1999, p. 168).
[29]See Larman and Vodde (2009, p. 285).

Sometimes the enterprise architect needs to leave her large-scale drawing board and become involved in a project or program in a technical leadership role. There are several possible reasons for such an assignment:

- A project has been identified as carrying high risk from an EA perspective (a new and unfamiliar technology, a critical business process, a new implementation partner, a project reaching across several business lines, and so forth).
- Higher management has issued a request for a high-profile "technical watchdog" to supervise a strategically important project with board-level attention.
- A project has been triggered by the EA organization itself (like the ESB pilot project in our Bank4Us example in activity EA-6); in that case, the EA team will want to micro-manage the solution architecture.
- An enterprise architect adopts a mentoring role for a junior architect as a personal development measure.

The standard books on EA do not cover this particular aspect of an enterprise architect's work. Malicious tongues could assume that this is due to EA's elitist self-conception; however, the more likely explanation is that an enterprise architect in a project or program faces the same challenges as a "normal" project architect. This is certainly true to an extent.

As a software architect, one frequently encounters the notion that a good specification or model speaks for itself—just like a religious icon that gives its blessing to the developers all by itself, by the sheer force of wisdom. This, of course, is nonsense. During a project's development phase, the architect proactively needs to make sure that her design is actually implemented.

The two quotes at the beginning of this section describe the tightrope walk for the architect in this situation. On one hand, she needs to keep a certain mental distance from the development team. As a technical leader, the architect needs to look carefully at what the developers make of his specification; she must prevent the developers being carried away by technology enthusiasm or "gold-plating" tendencies.

On the other hand, the architect has to be deeply involved in the development work herself. Otherwise, she does not know what is going on and, even worse, how suitable her design is. She needs to get his hands dirty; the lean and agile community calls this an *all-hands-on-deck* mindset (Coplien and Bjørnvig, 2010, p. 2). Without this mindset, the developers will mock the architect as a mere PowerPoint jockey who excels in drawing pictures with no relation to reality.

Any project architect needs to master this balance of proximity and distance to the developers. On top of that, an enterprise architect has to meet special challenges, when she assumes a technical leadership position in a project or program.

Depending on the project context, the enterprise architect can be perceived as savior, intruder, or wisenheimer from the top floor. She cannot completely avoid that perception, but she can influence it. Her best weapons for overcoming preconceptions are a hands-on mindset, as described, and an open communication style without a know-it-all attitude. "If 'Communication Is King,' then clarity and leadership are its humble servants," writes Mark King (Monson-Haefel, 2009, p. 9).

Another challenge might be harder to handle. There is a natural conflict of interest between a project architect and a member of the EA team. The best and easiest solutions for the project do not always match the "big picture" pursued by EA. This makes the enterprise architect a servant of two masters. Typical conflicts include:

- Use of nonstandard frameworks or libraries, which might save the project a lot of effort but is an unwelcome standard violation from EA point of view
- Extension of the project scope to accommodate a general EA target—for instance, the provision of service interfaces, which increases the project effort and risk
- Different time horizons in technical planning—short-term, milestone-oriented project planning versus a long-term strategic EA vision

The enterprise architect must not overemphasize the global perspective and attempt to build the enterprise's universal IT solution with a single project. On the other hand, she cannot ignore the big picture, either, and turn a blind eye to development of the larger IT landscape.

There is no patent answer to these challenges. The enterprise architect must make do with professional experience and common sense. As part of a project architecture group, the enterprise architect is the key person to ensure proper judgment on a number of difficult and subtle design decisions. This ability can be expressed by a number of "distinguish X from Y" issues in the design process. Each of them carries the aforementioned dilemma (project versus EA focus) in its genes.

- *Distinguish* nonstandard solutions justified by project needs *from* sheer technology enthusiasm and flippant design decisions
- *Distinguish* investing justified effort into the design phase (for instance, on careful interface design, taking up requirements of surrounding systems such as connectivity and performance), *from* modeling as an end in itself and death by analysis paralysis
- *Distinguish* unavoidable domain complexity (which can only be attenuated by skillful requirements engineering) *from* solution complexity as an indicator of design soundness (as simple as possible, as complex as needed)

Leading other architects in these decisions and coaching them to judge for themselves are essential parts of the enterprise architect's activity in such a project. In turn, the enterprise architect can benefit from the deep technical expertise in specific technology areas that project architects and developers will bring to the table. Usually more of a technical generalist herself, the enterprise architect should actively involve herself in technical project issues, such as a performance problem due to thread contention somewhere in the server-side Java code. It is a chance for her to gain new insight into common problems as well as to better understand the risks of certain technologies and design patterns.

"There is no 'I' in architecture," says Dave Quick (Monson-Haefel, 2009, p. 54). Architects—enterprise architects in particular—need to be team players, share their knowledge, constantly check the quality of their own work, and distinguish factual from personal criticism. A good enterprise architect is not a solo artist—maybe the first violinist but always an orchestra musician.

Managing risks involved in IT (EA-8)

Enterprises are exposed to a wide range of risks. Bank4Us, for instance, has subdivided the whole range of risks it can fall victim to into several categories, as shown in Figure 3-18.

The palette of threats ranges from strategic risks (for example, outsourcing a business unit that turns out to be a competitive differentiator) over environmental risks (political changes or natural disasters) to regulatory risks—the peril of accidentally violating laws or regulations.

FIGURE 3-18

Typical risk categories of a financial institution.

Since IT is involved in almost all enterprise activities, it also has its share in all risk categories. On one hand, existing risk scenarios affect IT. A fire, for example, might destroy not only office documents and furniture but also a mail server handling the messages of a wider region. On the other hand, IT also adds new risk scenarios, such as the threat of a denial-of-service (DoS) attack on an online brokerage portal.

Nevertheless, IT risks must not be considered as a new, separate risk category. "IT risk is business risk" write the authors of the ISACA[30] *Risk IT – framework for risk management* (2009). The bad thing about the denial of service attack obviously is not that some web server goes down, but the financial loss and the damage of reputation caused by the outage of the trading site.

Yet from a chief IT mechanics perspective, damages of the IT landscape sometimes look different from the business point of view. What appears as an IT catastrophe—for instance, the irreparable crash of a complete server cluster—sometimes has only a negligible impact on the business figures. Unfortunately this statement also applies in the other direction: Tiny IT bugs can trap the regulatory reporting of a financial institute and cause a penalty in the double-digit million-dollar range. One of the major principles of *Risk IT* is, therefore, to bind IT risks to business objectives and to evaluate risks in *business* currency, not in *IT* currency.

Enterprise architecture is a key to a business-oriented management of IT risks that adheres to this principle. A well-maintained EA model captures the linkage between business and IT and hence facilitates the tracking of IT effects on the business. Figure 3-19 provides an example of how an EA model helps bind IT risks to business objectives.

Bank4Us offers a product called *raw material trading access*. Customers who subscribe to this offering can trade raw materials such as coal, silver, or cotton with the help of an agent in the local branch office. The local agent places orders to the NYMEX[31] trading place by using the branch office trading portal application.

The outage of the order placement process initiated by this portal has a clear price tag assigned to it: Given the average daily trading volume, an outage of one hour causes a loss of US$160,000, not counting compensations for lost trading opportunities and the somewhat intangible loss of trust and reputation.

---

[30]ISACA is an independent, nonprofit, global association engaging in IT governance practices and standards. The group's bestseller is the IT governance standard CoBiT (Control Objectives for Information and Related Technology). It is complemented by *Value IT* and *Risk IT*, frameworks for investment and risk management.

[31]New York Mercantile Exchange, the largest trading place for raw material and commodities.

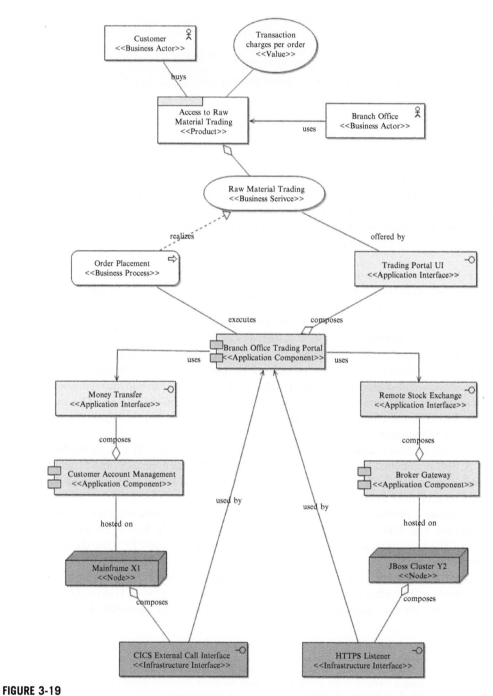

FIGURE 3-19

Tracking a business objective down to IT infrastructure.

Given these considerable costs, the risk managers at Bank4Us are interested in tracking down what failures in IT can actually cause such an outage. The ArchiMate EA model shown in Figure 3-19 helps solve this puzzle. By following the dependencies, the risk hunters find that the availability of the order process depends, for example, on the functioning of the CICS External Call Interface (ECI) hosted on a particular mainframe computer.

Although this is a simplified example, it makes clear the key role of EA in risk management. It bridges the layers and provides the knowledge base for a business-oriented impact assessment. Typical questions EA helps answer are:

- What business processes are affected if the JBoss server cluster Y2 goes down, and in what state?
- Which organizational units will be cut off from messaging if mail server DUCLONM01 goes down?
- Can damage of router 192.8.56.287 cause an outage on some business service, and if so, what is the expected financial loss?

Enterprise architects are not accountable for IT risk management. This usually is in the hands of the CIO or some senior management board. Yet, according to CoBiT, they are at least partly responsible for identifying risk scenarios, assessing their impact, and defining suitable risk responses (ISACA, 2007, p.65).

While participating in activity EA-1, Defining the IT Strategy, enterprise architects also are at least informed about the risk management policy. This policy sets out how big the risk appetite and tolerance of the enterprise is. Is it a risk-averse, conservative firm investing heavily in avoiding bad surprises and mitigating their impact? Or is it an opportunity-seeking organization with a relaxed attitude toward losses and deviations?

Since the protection against risk doesn't come free, this question needs a well-considered answer. The policy also defines the responsibilities and communication channels with regard to managing risks and thereby forms what the risk IT framework calls *risk governance* (ISACA, 2009). According to ISACA, IT risks can occur in three subdomains (ISACA, 2009, p. 11):

- *IT benefit/value enablement risks.* These are risks causing a suboptimal exploitation of IT assets or missed opportunities in business enablement.
- *IT program and project delivery risks.* These are the usual project risks involved in the prosecution of IT initiatives.
- *IT operations and service delivery risks.* These are the risks involved in running the IT infrastructure and delivering IT services to the enterprise.

EA has its share in all subdomains. With its focus on business-IT alignment, EA can be regarded as a general antidote against benefit/value enablement risks. Enterprise architects are also consulted in managing the risks of IT projects. In some cases, they even take the driver's seat in such initiatives, as described in the section "Monitoring the Project Portfolio (EA-6)." Finally, they are at least partly in charge of identifying risks hidden in the current IT landscape—as outlined in the examples—and to accommodate suitable risk responses in the future target landscape.

There are four general types of possible risk responses:

- *Avoidance of risks.* This means erecting a protective barrier that makes the occurrence of the risk event impossible. But waterproof barriers in most cases are quite expensive or even technically impossible.

- *Reduction and mitigation of risks*. This entails lowering the frequency of risk events, absorbing the impact of these events, or installing an early warning system.
- *Sharing or transferring risks*. Insurance policies, partnering, or outsourcing are typical means to get rid of the full burden of a risk.
- *Accepting risks*. This means to consciously accept the risk and take no action to decrease its probability or impact.

The mindset of an IT mechanic sometimes is inclined to the reduction and mitigation of risks and neglects the other risk responses as viable alternatives.

When dealing with risks, one needs to clearly differentiate between risks and uncertainty. The Factor Analysis for Information Risk (FAIR) framework gives the following formal definition of a risk (Jones, 2005):

> *[Risk is] the probable frequency and magnitude of a future loss.*

According to FAIR's taxonomy, a risk basically consists of two constituents, namely:

- *Loss event frequency (LEF)*. This measures how often a threat agent (for instance, a hacker, but also a thunderstorm) comes across the asset, how probable it is that the agent attacks the asset in such a case and how vulnerable the asset actually is (how well it resists the attack).
- *Probable loss magnitude (PLM)*. A measure for different kinds of losses, ranging from costs for replacing a damaged asset or diminished competitive advantages to legal fines and judgments.

According to this definition, a risk is always bound to a well-defined event and has known consequences. The probabilities in LEF and PLM can have a wide or narrow confidence interval, but otherwise they are well-known factors of the risk estimation.

Risk responses therefore can be planned. *Uncertainty* prevails, on the other hand, in case there is an overall lack of knowledge about the constituents or factors involved in a situation. There is no use in planning responses, because it is widely unclear what to respond to. The only reasonable plan of action is to approach the land of the unknown in an iterative trial-and-error approach. Many of the so-called "risks" in IT actually are uncertainties, and the approaches to tackle them are different from those in risk management. Agile software development, for instance, is an example of such an approach.

EA Frameworks

CONTENT

What Is an EA Framework? 106
The Zachman Framework for Enterprise Architecture 108
The Open Group Architecture Framework (TOGAF) 110
    TOGAF Architecture Development Methodology (ADM) 111
    TOGAF Architecture Content Framework 114
    TOGAF Architecture Capability Framework 115
Gartner Methodology (Formerly META Framework) 118
The Role and Use of EA Frameworks 121

There have been many misconceptions about EA in the minds of IT practitioners, IT managers, and even seasoned IT architects themselves. For instance:

- *EA = Zachman Framework?* You attend a one-day seminar on Zachman Framework and join the elite club of enterprise architects.
- *EA = TOGAF?* You attend a five-day training and certification course on TOGAF and then roll up your sleeves to "do enterprise architecture" the very next day.
- *EA = Gartner?* You consult an expert from Gartner or Forrester, then do what they tell you to do in EA. If you do this well, all sins, misdoings, and agonies related to your IT will disappear.

These statements may sound a little exaggerated. Nonetheless, we have heard undertones of them on several occasions—sometimes in our formal business meetings with customers, sometimes while listening to presentations in conferences, and sometimes even in informal chat with our peers walking down our office corridors. Moreover, such misconceptions seem to be more prevalent where non-IT people have ended up managing IT. EA has always been cursed with gross generalization and oversimplification. Perhaps it's due to the widespread ignorance about this field that such myths become popular.

    Zachman, TOGAF, and Gartner (amongst many others) are undoubtedly good resources on the subject of enterprise architecture. They are early explorers and trendsetters that have survived the test of time. These frameworks are meant to help you bring order to your chaotic enterprise IT landscape. To that effect, they give a direction for your thinking about enterprise architecture. They also provide best practices, tips, and techniques for doing EA in your business. But that is as far as they will go. They do not guarantee success. Using these frameworks ultimately boils down to what you can actually do (or need to do) in EA for your enterprise and how well you can relate your EA effort to what the frameworks have to offer.

It thus becomes necessary to understand what Zachman, TOGAF, and Gartner imply from a practical standpoint: what they are, what they are expected to do, and what they are *not* expected to do. At the onset, we want to clarify that none of them can be a silver bullet for your enterprise architecture initiative. They are no all-in-one cure for the miseries and pains of your business-IT environment, either.

The following sections give a brief overview of these frameworks and their relevance for practical use. To begin with, let's first look at what the term *EA framework* really means.

What is an EA framework?

An *EA framework* is a set of assumptions, concepts, values, and practices that constitutes a way of looking at enterprise reality via views on (architectural) models. It offers a fundamental structure, serving as a scaffold for developing, maintaining, and using EA.

Over the last 25 years, a number of enterprise architecture frameworks have come and gone. These frameworks have originated from different sources and have been applied in different contexts. Philip Allega, research analyst at Gartner, highlights an overwhelming proliferation of EA frameworks with a bit of frustration. In a blog entry titled "My Mother has an EA Definition, too," he commented on the introduction of a new EA definition by the Enterprise Architecture Research Forum (EARF), South Africa, in August 2010[1]:

> If they'd only add a framework/approach to this definition I could notch my list of EA frameworks/approaches I'm tracking up by one *(note: if you're curious, I'm at 77 right now and if you've got one, please let me know).* For those of you who aren't used to reading with a sarcastic voice, **please try using sarcasm when you say (out loud):**
> *The world really needs yet another definition of enterprise architecture*
> *<large, tired, shoulder shrugging sigh>*

The true number of EA frameworks depends on what you count as a "framework", but there is definitely an abundance of them. Moreover, they are quite different from each other. For instance, the *Zachman Framework for Enterprise Architectures* and *The Open Group Architecture Framework (TOGAF)* have hardly anything common between them except two words: *architecture* and *framework*. TOGAF, in fact, acknowledges Zachman as a complementing framework, which implies that TOGAF and Zachman indeed have only minimal overlap.

We cannot cover all the frameworks (or approaches, or methods—whatever you call them) that are out there.[2] We will not assess, compare, nor endorse any of them, either. For the sake of brevity, we will simply have a quick glance at the methods we listed in the introduction:

- Zachman Framework for Enterprise Architectures
- The Open Group Architecture Framework (TOGAF)
- Gartner Methodology (formerly META Framework)

---

[1]Bold and italics highlighting of the text by the original blog writer, Philip Allega.
[2]Readers interested in a broader treatment of EA practices may refer to online resources such as https://www.globalaea.org, www.enterprise-architecture.info, or http://eai.ittoolbox.com/.

We have selected each of them intentionally:

- *Zachman*, because it is one of the first explorations in EA;
- *TOGAF*, since it is an open EA framework; in our context, "open" means industry-agnostic, vendor-neutral, and community-based;
- *Gartner*, because it is one of the many recognized consulting firms for EA in the corporate world.

Of course, these frameworks are not the only ones that constitute the EA body of knowledge, as pointed out earlier. We do *not* intend to endorse these three frameworks as the best ones. However, these three are de facto among the most widely known approaches today. This is perhaps due to their versatility, visibility, and market impact so far.

EA has also received significant attention from academia, consulting firms, and governments. A number of academic institutions offer research briefings and learning programs regarding EA approaches and practices. They have been quite active and visible with their research on various EA topics in the last five years. Just to name a few prominent examples:

- *Center for Information Systems Research, Massachusetts Institute of Technology (CISR–MIT), United States.* The focus of CISR–MIT is on developing enterprise architecture as a strategy based on their extensive industry research.
- *Software Engineering for Business Information Systems (sebis), TU München, Germany.* Sebis concentrates on developing EA patterns (as opposed to frameworks) and evaluating EA management tools.
- *Center for Enterprise Architecture, Pennsylvania State University, United States.* The focus of the college is on curriculum formalization, competency development, and advanced research in the EA area.

In addition, many established IT consulting firms, such as Accenture, Boston Consulting, Cap Gemini, Deloitte, Forrester, Gartner, HP, IBM, McKinsey & Company, and others, usually have their own EA approaches or methods (proprietary frameworks, so to speak) that they use while performing EA activities for their clients.

Finally, we should mention the Federal Enterprise Architecture (FEA). It is the enterprise architecture for the largest and most complex enterprise on Earth: the US federal government. Although FEA has been available only since 2006, its history dates back to 1996, when the US Congress passed a bill known as the Clinger Cohen Act.[3] This bill mandates that all government agencies take steps to improve the effectiveness of their IT investments. FEA enables them to do that. The US government is one of the most serious adopters of enterprise architecture. The claim can be made that no enterprise has spent more money in EA than what has gone into FEA to date.

Is there hope that this zoo of frameworks will disappears in the future and give room to only a few best-in-class frameworks? The answer to this question is tricky—maybe or maybe not. The main reasons for this state of affairs are as follows:

- *EA is perceived as an enterprise-specific initiative.* It has a strong dependency on the way the enterprise operates. A number of enterprise-specific factors, such as business imperatives, organizational structure, work culture, and political dynamics, may have significant influence on

---

[3]See http://dodcio.defense.gov/docs/ciodesrefvolone.pdf.

the modus operandi of an EA organization. This makes it difficult to define a *one-size-fits-all* framework.

- *EA research is not proceeding as fast as one could wish*. The field of EA is still young and immature. It may traverse different paths before it will ultimately stabilize as a mature discipline. The rapid changes in the business and IT world, coupled with difficulties in recognizing the value of EA (in terms of cost/benefit and return on investment), might be the key reasons for EA not being able to progress faster.
- *EA frameworks fail to strike a balance*. Some EA frameworks are *too generic*. They tend to become too abstract and academic to deliver any tangible outcome. Other frameworks are *overly specific*. They tend to become too exhaustive and complex to be put into practice in a meaningful way. For instance, the Zachman Framework shows a tendency to fall into the first category (too generic), whereas the FEA leans toward the second category (overly specific). What is really needed is a way to strike a difficult balance between too much and not enough detail. In this respect, there is a wide chasm between the current ways of performing EA.

The Zachman framework for enterprise architecture

The beauty of the Zachman Framework[4] is that it visualizes the entire enterprise at one glance, just the way the periodic table of elements visualizes all 118 known chemical elements by selected properties of their atomic structure. By providing a classification schema, the Zachman Framework attempts to bring order to the complex world of business and IT, as the periodic table does for chemistry and chemical reactions.

Zachman is a framework of *elements*—a total set of descriptive representations to fully describe a complex object (the enterprise). It has 6×6 (some say 6×5) cells, as depicted in Figure 4-1 (Zachman, 2008). The columns are called *Abstractions*. They answer key questions about the enterprise: *What* (data), *How* (function), *Where* (network), *Who* (people), *When* (time), and *Why* (motivation). The rows are called *Perspectives*. Each row represents a viewpoint of a single group of stakeholders.

Zachman has a somewhat conservative view of enterprise architecture. Each cell in the Zachman grid defines primitive element and contains an elementary architectural model. Each cell must represent *one and only one aspect* of an enterprise. The architecture is "pure" only if you are able to extract different architectural aspects, as per the Zachman classification schema, and represent each of those aspects with a stand-alone model.

In that case, a cell contains a single-variable primitive model—only one architectural aspect, just like a basic chemical element in the periodic table. For instance, Cell [3,1] (*System Model (Logical) – Data*) must contain only the Logical Data Model and nothing else. It will not provide any information about ownership, usage, or location of the data that is being described. If you add that, then you are not doing architecture, you are doing the implementation—so says Zachman.

---

[4]For exhaustive information on the Zachman Framework, refer to www.zachman.com.

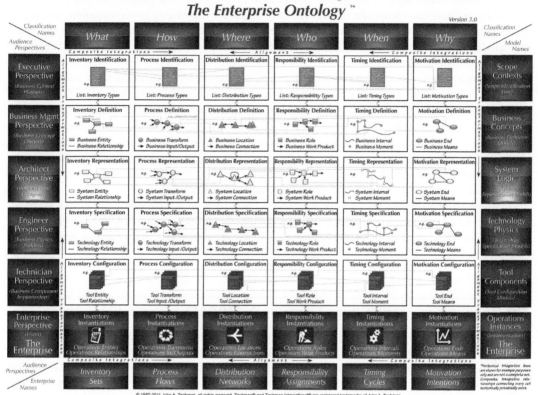

FIGURE 4-1

Zachman Framework 3.0 (Zachman, 2008, used with kind permission).

Accordingly, EA has to obey certain ground rules imposed by the Zachman Grid:

- *Rule 1: The columns have no order.* Each column (aspect) is equally important.
- *Rule 2: Each column has a simple, basic model.* Each column describes one complete aspect of the enterprise using primitive models only.
- *Rule 3: The basic model of each column is unique.* Each model in a column is related to the others. They are abstractions of the same enterprise aspect, yet each model represents a distinct and unique concept.
- *Rule 4: Each row represents a distinct view.* The rows describe stakeholder perspectives (*Executive, Business Management, Architect, Engineer,* and *Technician*).
- *Rule 5: Each cell is unique.* Each model representation or cell differs from the others in essence and not merely in level of detail.
- *Rule 6: Combining the cells in one row forms a complete view.* Each row provides a comprehensive view of the enterprise from the perspective of a group of stakeholders.

If a model covers more than one cell from the Zachman Grid, it becomes a composite model, just like a chemical compound. A composite model is very useful for the purpose of implementation. According to Zachman, composite models are only meant for the *ease of implementation*, not as part of the architecture. It is up to the architect to define the composite models by combining several primitive models. The composite models form architectural work products, which can then be taken to facilitate the implementation.

Again, referring to the periodic table analogy, a composite model is just like a chemical compound that can be produced by a chemical reaction between two or more elements. A *Logical Data Model*, when combined with a *People Model*, describes ownership and usage of entities. In the same way, data models that also include the physical location of data entities become composite models.

Zachman's classification schema for architecture models does make sense, at least theoretically. However, it does not really provide any insight into the dependencies and relationships among the primitive architectural models. The practical viability of building the primitive and composite models is pretty much left to the enterprise architect to explore and determine.

In essence, the Zachman Framework is simply a framework of *EA elements*. It does not stand for itself but can be used (as a whole or in parts) as a complement to other major EA frameworks, such as TOGAF and FEA, or even in any custom frameworks or approaches that you may have in your enterprise.

The open group architecture framework (TOGAF)

If Zachman is a framework of elements providing the *constituents* of enterprise architecture, TOGAF is a *recipe* that tells how to build up those constituents—the work products of EA.

TOGAF is a generic yet comprehensive methodological framework for developing enterprise architectures. It is owned by The Open Group consortium and free for your own use within the enterprise. As The Open Group states, TOGAF is the codified common sense for enterprise architecture management. It has been developed based on the experience of EA experts and practitioners for a decade or more. TOGAF can be applied across industries. It is agnostic to the technology in use. Moreover, it is equipped with a vast knowledge base - both in terms of online literature and community support.

TOGAF 9.1, the current version at the time of this writing[5] (The Open Group, 2011), has five basic parts:

- Architecture Development Methodology (ADM)
- Architecture Content Framework
- Architecture Capability Framework
- Enterprise Continuum and Tools
- Reference Models

For the sake of brevity, we will look at only the first three parts of TOGAF. They are most relevant to the scope of this book.

---

[5]January 2012.

TOGAF architecture development methodology (ADM)

The most significant component of TOGAF is the *Architecture Development Methodology (ADM)*. It essentially defines a full life-cycle process for planning, designing, realizing, and governing enterprise architecture. TOGAF ADM has a genetic resemblance to the traditional waterfall software development model. This model typically consists of phases such as planning, analysis, design, development, testing, and deployment, organized in sequential order (Figure 4-2). Each phase in the waterfall software development life cycle (SDLC) can be fully described by entry criteria, tasks, verification, and exit criteria. TOGAF ADM adopts a similar approach.

ADM consists of eight phases A to H, and a *Preliminary* one at the start (Figure 4-3). Each phase is fully described using an *objectives–approach–inputs–steps–outputs* pattern, akin to the waterfall model. The phases will be executed from A to H, normally in sequential order.

However, there are fundamental differences between the waterfall SDLC and TOGAF ADM. In general, software development projects are short-lived. They are scheduled for a fixed time and have a budget for a limited effort. They have a clear beginning (project funding) and end (system deployment and maintenance transition).

In contrast, EA is a continuous journey for the enterprise in a search for a better tomorrow. So, what TOGAF does is to simply tie the last phase (H) of an ADM cycle to the first phase (A) of the next cycle. This way ADM becomes an iterative, repeatable, and continuous process for the enterprises to follow. As a consequence, the funding model and the engagement model for TOGAF (the EA group in the enterprise) must be apportioned accordingly.

As another difference, in waterfall SDLC the requirement analysis phase is typically executed during the early part of the project life cycle. In contrast, TOGAF ADM has a *Requirements Management* part that always stays at the heart of the process. All ADM phases (A–H) are closely tied to this part. Focus and effort during all phases are derived from, and lead to, the core Requirements Management process.

There are also a few practical aspects that TOGAF ADM has to tackle. For instance, for most enterprises it is unrealistic to assume that the architectural initiative starts on a green field and that the ADM Phase A (*Architecture Vision*) will be the first step. The enterprises would typically have many ongoing or past initiatives that involve architectural development efforts.

Moreover, architectural activities in the enterprise cannot follow a strictly linear, sequential, and step-by-step procedure the way that TOGAF ADM advocates. More likely, these activities take place in a random and chaotic manner. Sometimes they even happen parallel to each other, depending on the organizational, operational, or implementational priorities.

TOGAF recognizes this situation and flexes its muscles to adapt to it, at least to some extent. First, it allows you to begin with *any* of the ADM phases in between. Furthermore, it is permitted to iterate over

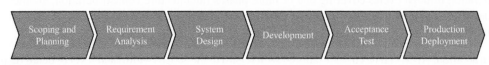

FIGURE 4-2

Waterfall software development life cycle.

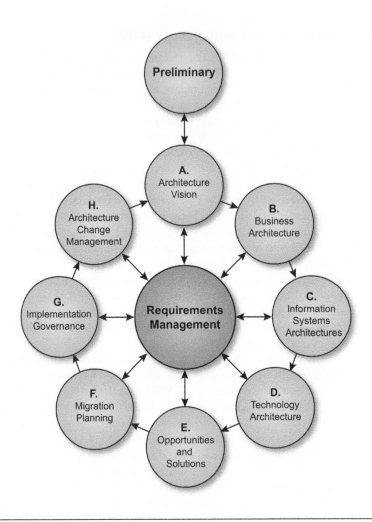

FIGURE 4-3

TOGAF Architecture Development Methodology (The Open Group, 2011, used with kind permission).

a part of the ADM cycle that can be logically demarcated, as indicated in Figure 4-4. ADM supports iterations in many ways, the two most important ones being:

- Iteration through the entire ADM cycle (phases A–H)
- Iteration through cycles covering one or more phases (architecture context iteration, architecture definition iteration, transition planning iteration, architecture governance iteration), as shown in Figure 4-4

In addition, ADM can be custom-tailored with regard to the scope (width) and level of detail (depth) of work to be taken up in one iteration, to suit the given circumstances and constraints in your organization. In essence, although it appears at first sight to adhere to a strict waterfall pattern, TOGAF

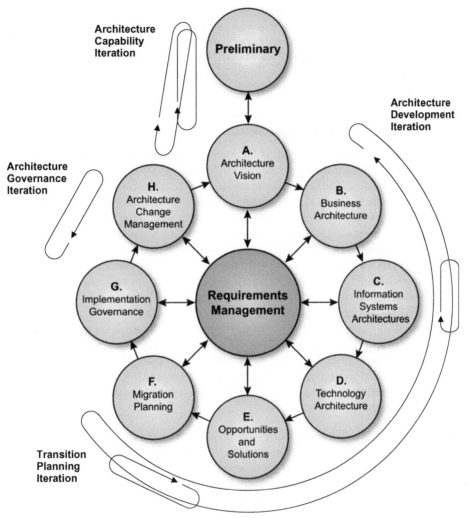

FIGURE 4-4

TOGAF ADM iterations (The Open Group, 2011, used with kind permission).

ADM is surprisingly flexible. It allows phases to be reorganized, reordered, combined, or performed partially, if that fits the need of the enterprise. It is also possible to jump back from any point to any other point within an iteration. The only constraint is that all intermediate steps between the two points must be carried out again.

TOGAF, from version 9 onward, has a new module called *ADM Guidelines and Techniques*. It provides specific guidelines about the adaptation of the ADM process in your particular enterprise environment. It also offers certain techniques for formalizing your architecture development and management.

To sum up, TOGAF ADM brings discipline to the architecture development process. It promotes a sense of consistency and repeatability while offering amazing flexibility. We have seen these qualities as being critical in practice when dealing with the management of any large-scale endeavor like EA. We will return to these aspects of TOGAF ADM in Chapter 7, "Towards Pragmatism: Lean and Agile EA." As we will see there, TOGAF can be reconciled in a quite natural way with the flexibility of a lean and agile EA approach.

TOGAF architecture content framework

ADM provides a description of what needs to be done—the *process* to create an architecture. In contrast, the *Architecture Content Framework*, introduced in TOGAF 9, describes what it should look like in the end—the *work product*. The Content Framework offers a consistent and structured way to present architectural work products. It acts as a companion to ADM as it standardizes the inputs and outputs of ADM processes. There is a clear map from the content framework to the TOGAF ADM processes. In addition, it also makes it easy to reference and classify architectural work products. This way, it makes the complementary use of the Zachman Framework obsolete.[6]

The Content Framework is a significant addition to TOGAF 9. It provides a *Content META Model* (an information model for the actual architectural models and views) as well as a *classification schema* to categorize and organize your architectural work products.

The Content META Model defines the elements that constitute the enterprise architecture. It further differentiates the elements as *core* (the ones that are mandatory for architectural description) and *extensions* (which may be used optionally). This gives room to adapt or extend your own content META model as the situation may demand. Figure 4-5 shows an overview of the entities in the framework; Figure 4-6 depicts the entity-relationship diagram for the Content META Model.

The content framework uses three categories to describe a *work product* (i.e., the output or input of an architectural activity):

- *Deliverables*. These are the formal work products created by the projects and are contractually binding. Deliverables can contain many artifacts.
- *Artifacts*. Artifacts are fine-grained work products that describe architecture from a specific viewpoint. These include architectural requirements, use-case specifications, class diagrams, network diagrams, or any sort of architecture models. Artifacts are further classified into *catalogues* (lists of things), *matrices* (relationships and dependencies between things), and *diagrams* (visual depiction of things). The collection of all artifacts makes up your *architecture repository*.
- *Building blocks*. These are the packages of functionality defined to meet certain business needs, published through a standard interface and available for enterprise-wide consumption. They are interoperable, reusable, and replaceable across the organization. In a way, building blocks are nothing but the connotation of well-established architectural concepts such as *services* (as in SOA) and *capabilities*. Building blocks are further classified into *architectural building blocks* (ABB, the ones that are technology-aware) and *solution building blocks* (SBB, those that are product- or vendor-aware). The building blocks can be combined to deliver architectures and solutions.

---

[6]It is an individual choice if one wants to use the TOGAF 9 Content Framework, or any other external frameworks such as Zachman or ArchiMate, together with TOGAF ADM.

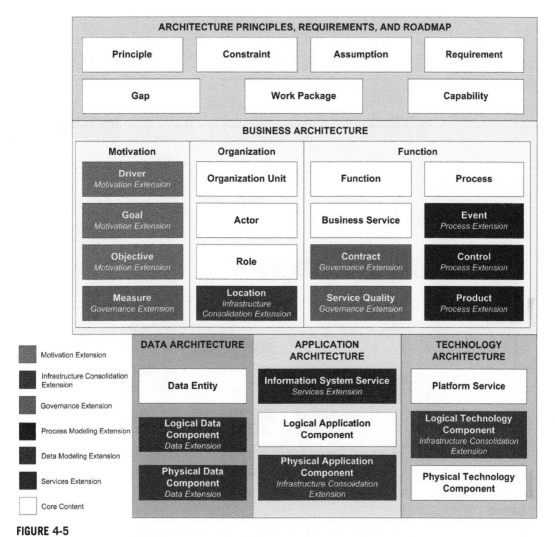

FIGURE 4-5

TOGAF Content META Model (The Open Group, 2011, used with kind permission).

The work products, such as catalogues, matrices, and diagrams, are nothing but different viewpoints derived from the architectural elements in the META model. These viewpoints are shown in Figure 4-7.

TOGAF architecture capability framework

TOGAF ADM shows the *way* (the processes) to do EA, and the Content Framework defines the *artifacts* that EA should produce. Yet setting up an EA practice is difficult and expensive. It has to deal with a variety of organizational and operational intricacies. The TOGAF 9 *Architecture Capability*

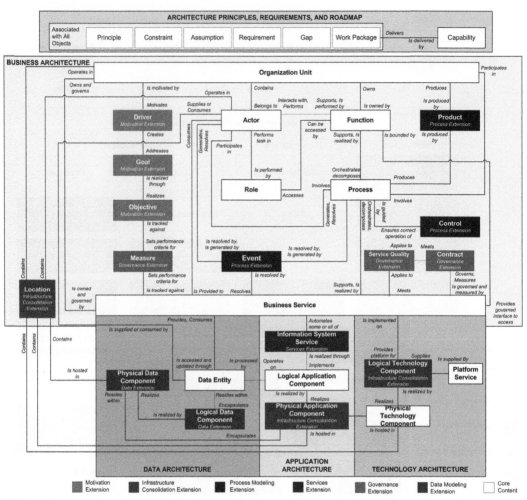

FIGURE 4-6

TOGAF: Entities and Relationships in the Content META Model (The Open Group, 2011, used with kind permission).

Framework attempts to address this need by providing a set of concepts—from institutions to rule sets and models—for a successful implementation of EA governance. The framework defines the following main concepts:

- *Architecture board.* The board governs the implementation of the IT strategy. It comprises stakeholders owning the review and maintenance of architecture at two levels. The first one is the *global* level (organization-wide), and the other is a *local* one (domain-specific). The board is responsible for reviewing and maintaining architecture with identifiable and stated accountability,

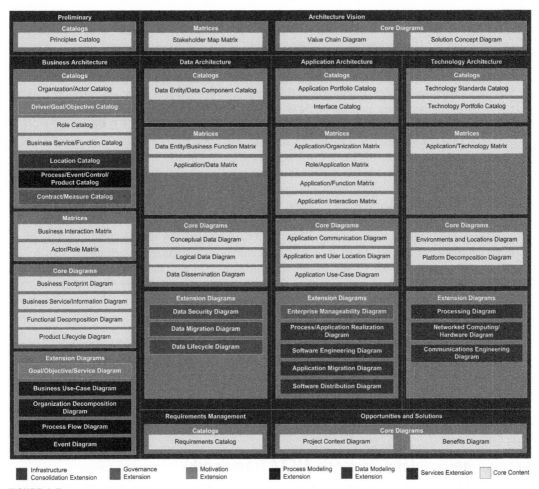

Preliminary		Architecture Vision	
Catalogs	Matrices	Core Diagrams	
Principles Catalog	Stakeholder Map Matrix	Value Chain Diagram	Solution Concept Diagram

Business Architecture	Data Architecture	Application Architecture	Technology Architecture
Catalogs	**Catalogs**	**Catalogs**	**Catalogs**
Organization/Actor Catalog	Data Entity/Data Component Catalog	Application Portfolio Catalog	Technology Standards Catalog
Driver/Goal/Objective Catalog		Interface Catalog	Technology Portfolio Catalog
Role Catalog			
Business Service/Function Catalog	**Matrices**	**Matrices**	**Matrices**
	Data Entity/Business Function Matrix	Application/Organization Matrix	Application/Technology Matrix
Location Catalog	Application/Data Matrix	Role/Application Matrix	
Process/Event/Control/ Product Catalog		Application/Function Matrix	
Contract/Measure Catalog		Application Interaction Matrix	
Matrices			
Business Interaction Matrix	**Core Diagrams**	**Core Diagrams**	**Core Diagrams**
Actor/Role Matrix	Conceptual Data Diagram	Application Communication Diagram	Environments and Locations Diagram
Core Diagrams	Logical Data Diagram	Application and User Location Diagram	Platform Decomposition Diagram
Business Footprint Diagram	Data Dissemination Diagram	Application Use-Case Diagram	
Business Service/Information Diagram	**Extension Diagrams**	**Extension Diagrams**	**Extension Diagrams**
Functional Decomposition Diagram	Data Security Diagram	Enterprise Manageability Diagram	Processing Diagram
Product Lifecycle Diagram	Data Migration Diagram	Process/Application Realization Diagram	Networked Computing/ Hardware Diagram
Extension Diagrams	Data Lifecycle Diagram	Software Engineering Diagram	Communications Engineering Diagram
Goal/Objective/Service Diagram		Application Migration Diagram	
Business Use-Case Diagram		Software Distribution Diagram	
Organization Decomposition Diagram			
Process Flow Diagram	**Requirements Management**	**Opportunities and Solutions**	
Event Diagram	**Catalogs**	**Core Diagrams**	
	Requirements Catalog	Project Context Diagram	Benefits Diagram

■ Infrastructure Consolidation Extension ■ Governance Extension ■ Motivation Extension ■ Process Modeling Extension ■ Data Modeling Extension ■ Services Extension □ Core Content

FIGURE 4-7

TOGAF Content META Model viewpoints (The Open Group, 2011, used with kind permission).

and has decision-making authority. The cost for such an architecture board can be justified by preventing ad hoc and unconstrained IT implementations, which, if ignored, would essentially end up in high costs, high risks, lower quality, and difficulty in reuse and replication.

- architecture contract. The contract is a joint agreement between implementation partners and sponsors regarding the deliverables in terms of quality and fit-for-purpose of the architecture chosen for the implementation. The contract helps to monitor architectural integrity, standards adherence, and risk avoidance in the solution implementation.
- *Architecture compliance.* The compliance of the solution implementation against the stated architecture contract is vetted through a formal compliance review and decision-making processes. The compliance of projects and implementations is evaluated by two key processes, a *project*

impact assessment at the project start-up, and an *architecture compliance review* at each key milestone of the project life cycle. The compliance process assesses the adherence[7] of a project implementation to the architecture contract or specification, to aid the "go/no-go" decisions for the project execution.

- *Architecture Maturity Model.* TOGAF 9 proposes an Architecture Maturity Model (ACMM) that tracks the progress and penetration of EA in the enterprise. It was originally developed by the US Department of Commerce. The ACMM is meant to assess the enterprise based on nine EA elements (EA capabilities)[8] and then grades the enterprise on a scale of six EA maturity levels.[9] The scorecard derived from a periodic EA maturity assessment process is to be reported to the sponsors and stakeholders of EA. We will discuss maturity models at a little more length in Chapter 5, "EA Maturity Models."

- *Architecture Skills Framework.* Both *enterprise architecture* and *enterprise architect* are widely used but poorly defined terms in the industry. Moreover, an EA organization would typically need a variety of skills and many different roles. To address this need, TOGAF 9 proposes that the enterprise must set up an *EA practice*. This is a formal competency management initiative of skills development and certification by which an enterprise recognizes its architects. That is necessary in order to align the skills available in the enterprise with the architectural activities that the enterprise plans to do. In addition, *The Open Group Certified Architect (Open CA) Program* devised by The Open Group offers a yardstick to evaluate (and certify) an architect in terms of architectural skills and experience.

The aspects of enterprise architecture management described in the Architecture Capability Framework are interwoven into TOGAF ADM processes as well. For instance, the ADM Phase G is all about *Implementation Governance.* Phase G includes *Architecture Compliance* review processes. Another example is that the *Statement of Architecture Work* created in ADM Phase A is essentially an architecture contract between the architecting organization and the EA sponsor. Likewise, assessment of EA maturity may be a key activity in the *Preliminary Phase* of ADM.

Gartner methodology (formerly META framework)

Suppose you are following a perfect diet. You also exercise regularly to keep yourself fit. But still you happen to feel that you are no longer healthy, energetic, enthusiastic, and at ease. What do you do? You will perhaps visit a doctor—a medical practitioner who knows about health matters and whom you would trust the most for her knowledge and expertise in that area. Depending on your income and the graveness of the problem, you will go and see the family doctor next door, or the expensive private specialist in the city.

---

[7]The adherence of a project implementation to the architecture specification is stated by terms such as *compliant* and *conformant*. However, the terminology usage may differ between enterprises, and many fine-grained terms may be needed to formulate the IT compliance strategy (for example: *fully conformant, conformant, compliant, consistent, nonconformant,* and *irrelevant*). TOGAF provides blueprint definitions for all these terms.

[8]The architecture elements for maturity assessment are as follows: Architecture Process, Architecture Development and Progression, Business Linkage, Senior Management Involvement, Operating Unit Participation, Architecture Communication, IT Security, Architecture Governance, IT Investment, and Acquisition Strategy.

[9]Maturity Level: 0–None, 1–Initial, 2–Under Development, 3–Defined, 4–Managed, 5–Measured, 6–Optimized.

Similarly, despite rigorous adaptation of a comprehensive framework such as TOGAF and significant investment in skill development, enterprises might not see any visible business impact from the effort that has gone into EA. "Are we doing the right things?" they might ask themselves. The benefits are far in the future at best, nonexistent at worst (or so it seems to the enterprises). What do the enterprises do then? They call a "doctor" with vast knowledge and experience. This expert on EA is supposed to be well acquainted with emerging industry trends and competitor initiatives in this field and hence might have better insight into state-of-the-art EA.

The established consulting companies (Gartner, Forrester, Accenture, Boston Consulting, Cap Gemini, Deloitte, HP, IBM, McKinsey & Company, and many others) provide such EA experts. Usually they bring their own proprietary approach. This book is not the place to provide a complete overview of all the consulting providers. Instead, we have picked Gartner as one of the more distinguished EA consulting companies and describe their EA framework as a showcase for the complete consulting market.

Gartner is one of the leading industry research firms in IT. It offers consulting services to corporate customers, especially for their strategic IT management. Enterprise architecture, being strategic in nature, is one of its core research areas. Although Gartner has been actively pursuing enterprise architecture for more than a decade, what it has to offer in this field today essentially stems from the META Group, a consulting firm that Gartner acquired in 2005. The META Group was the market leader by then and a competitor to Gartner.

Today one would go to Gartner (like any other consulting company) to seek professional advice on enterprise architecture because the firm is recognized as an expert in the field. Gartner helps enterprises embark on their enterprise architecture journey. It does not create enterprise architecture for its customers. Instead, Gartner consultants guide enterprises in setting up a process by which EA can emerge from their business strategy—in other words, Gartner helps to set up an EA practice. In Gartner's view, enterprise architecture is a *verb*, not a noun; it is an ongoing process, not an artifact. Gartner defines enterprise architecture as follows (Allega, 2010):

> [. . .] the process of translating business vision and strategy into effective enterprise change by creating, communicating, and improving the key requirements, principles and models that describe the enterprise's future state and enable its evolution. The scope of the EA includes the people, processes, information and technology of the enterprise, and their relationships to one another and to the external environment. Enterprise architects compose holistic solutions that address the business challenges of the enterprise and support the governance needed to implement them.

Gartner does not publish a formal framework or a process to do EA. Gartner analysts often quote: "Just enough enterprise architecture, just in time." Questions such as what framework or methodology to follow, what taxonomy to use, or what standards to conform to are of least concern and perhaps irrelevant. Nonetheless, what makes Gartner a trusted advisor is perhaps its group of research analysts. The analysts group specializes in EA and operates in close collaboration within Gartner. It carries out applied research and establishes a common knowledge base on varied enterprise architecture topics. Over the years Gartner has been authoritative in analyzing emerging trends, observing adoption patterns, and recommending best practices to its customers in the EA area.

Gartner will approach enterprise architecture with a top-down approach that is highly tailor-made for the business context of its customers. It will further insist that the enterprise architecture must be driven by the enterprise's top management and with a complete picture of the enterprise in mind. The prime focus for Gartner is always the CEO's vision and priorities.

In Gartner's view, enterprise architecture is about establishing a shared business vision and strategy for the enterprise. Gartner says that enterprise architecture starts with a *vision* as to *where an organization is going* and a *strategy* as to *how to reach there*. Any activity that does not address these questions is inconsequential for Gartner. Gartner will typically advise not for delve into the current state architecture for the enterprise. Where the enterprise is today is not important for deciding where it wants to reach in the future.

Gartner probably assumes that you can sell off all your old problematic IT stuff in a garage sale and purchase new IT things for a better tomorrow. The effort in enterprise architecture must be focused on strategic concerns rather than the nitty-gritty of today's operational problems on the ground. They will vanish, or at least become irrelevant in the longer run, if you address them as part of the strategic concerns.

Gartner gives overarching importance to two things: *establishing a shared vision and bringing all stakeholder groups behind the shared vision* with clear, continuous, and consistent communication. To this end, Gartner will first look at the business context of the enterprise, beginning with the CEO's priorities for the enterprise. It will then help the CEO and CIO to specify the vision for the target state, based on the CEO's priorities. The contact will be at CxO level, and the dialogue will always be in business language. Gartner will articulate the CEO's ideas into a *common requirements vision* (CRV) in such a way that all stakeholder groups will be able to understand exactly what it means for them. The CRV identifies and states the key changes needed to drive CEO vision in the enterprise.

Next, Gartner will start telling the story to stakeholders about where the enterprise is heading and what business drivers it is responding to. This will be a plain story without any prescribed documentation standards, acronyms, or techno-jargon. The only goal is to ensure that the stakeholders understand—and share—a common vision. The Gartner philosophy is as follows: If an organization has a single shared vision for the future and all stakeholders are behind that vision, the organization is already fully equipped to consider the ramifications of the vision into the business, technical, information, and solutions architectures for the enterprise.

The shared vision dictates changes in all these architectures, assigns priorities to those changes, and relates them to the business value. EA is about bringing together all the stakeholders: the business owners, the information specialists, and the technology implementers. If these three groups can be unified towards a shared vision that drives business value, enterprise architecture will be a success; otherwise, it will be doomed.

Based on the shared vision, the Gartner consultants review the business changes with the business sponsor, and the technical or information changes with the CIO or IT owners. At the same time, they make sure to bring everybody together as one team. The success metrics are always expressed in business terms, such as operational profitability, business growth, and customer satisfaction, so that everyone can understand that, too—clearly and precisely.

As the last step, Gartner will work with business owners to develop a target business architecture supporting the CEO vision. Subsequently, its consultants will work with the CIO to develop a target information architecture that realizes salient features outlined in the CRV and supports the new business architecture.

In essence, Gartner, as a strategist or as an advisor, offers thought leadership in the enterprise architecture arena. But to what extent that thought leadership travels from the CEO and CIO office down to the shop floors of business and IT is entirely contingent on the organizational leadership of the enterprise.

The role and use of EA frameworks

At Bank4Us, *Dave Callaghan*, the CIO, had asked one of the expensive, exclusive consulting companies to advise him on the appropriate EA strategy for his company. That was two years ago. As a result of this engagement, the EA team was reorganized and enlarged. In addition, Dave—in need of someone driving EA further—managed to entice the head consultant away from this company, and appointed him as head of the EA team. This is how *Oscar Salgado*, now the chief architect, joined Bank4Us.

Due to his background in management and strategy consulting, Oscar is a firm believer in corporate visions and full-scale EA frameworks that allow translating the board's business maxims into practical action. Before he took over the EA team, the enterprise architects had not seriously used any formal methodology. Oscar introduced TOGAF, in combination with the Zachman framework, for classifying the architecture artifacts. He sent his architects to a one-week top-notch training, and stubbornly insisted on his team sticking to this new methodology.

Since then, Oscar has seen some benefits of adhering to the TOGAF framework. Undoubtedly, it has given the less capable architects within his team a sense of direction, like a railing protecting them from straying too far from the target. But he has also heard complaints from others—often the top performers in his team—that since the introduction of TOGAF the number of documents to be written has increased even more, and the target readership has less and less time to read them. Oscar Salgado is realist enough to recognize some truth in this.

Ian Miller, in charge of the *Closer to Customer* IT transformation and reporting to Oscar, was one of the early TOGAF adopters in the team. Ian is skeptical by nature, which makes him a bit wary of high-flying methodologies in general. Being a well-known enterprise architect at Bank4Us, Ian is often asked for his opinion about using Zachman or TOGAF in his work. If he is honest, he does not have any shining success stories, and might even not see them in future. His main criticism is that it is difficult to show a step-by-step use of a framework in a real-life scenario.

But besides a skeptic, Ian is also a pragmatist. This is why he regards EA frameworks as a set of practices suggested by the experts and practitioners in this field. It is an orderly collection of codified common sense, best practices, and lessons learnt from the past experiences. For Ian, TOGAF is like a toolkit containing many tools and the techniques to use those tools. He has decided for himself that he will use only the tools that are fit for his purpose at hand. He uses them by having learned the right techniques to use them. For Ian, it is the same thing as when he is at home, building a bookshelf for his son. If he needs to use a screwdriver, he takes the screwdriver from this toolkit. If he does not need the hammer, he will not even take it out. Nevertheless, he has to know *all* tools in his box, so that he can use the appropriate one to do right things at the right time for the right purpose.

How can you apply Ian's pragmatic toolbox approach to your own EA work? We will look at some new ways of doing this effectively in "Chapter 7 Making EA Pragmatic: Lean and Agile EA". We will introduce the notion of *Architecture Factory* and introduce lean and agile ways of doing enterprise architecture. By innovatively incorporating the principles and practices from the Lean (as in manufacturing and software engineering) and the Agile methodology (as in software engineering) to the world of EA, we will sketch as to how a comprehensive EA framework like TOGAF can be leveraged in your own EA—selectively, flexibly, and pragmatically.

EA Maturity Models

CONTENT

Applying Maturity Model to EA..124
    What Is a Maturity Model?..124
    Relevance of Maturity Models in EA 126
    A Rule of Thumb for the Architectural Maturity of an Enterprise 126
OMB EA Assessment Framework..127
Architecture Capability Maturity Model of the US Department of Commerce...............130
EA Maturity Model by MIT Center for Information System Research 132
Experiences with the Maturity Models 134

In the previous chapter, we saw that the EA frameworks are meant for effective management of enterprise architecture—just like what a diet-and-exercise plan does for healthy living. Both are prescriptive in nature, yet both need to be custom tailored for individual use. If so, EA maturity assessments come as diagnostic medical tests that help detect the deficiencies in EA against some recognized benchmark and accordingly take corrective actions for the desired improvement. EA frameworks aim to bring an *order* to EA management, and maturity models *measure that orderliness* and give the direction for improving it as needed.

The notion of maturity models is not new to IT organizations. There has been a continuous urge to improve IT practices and make them increasingly effective. In the early 1990s, the Software Engineering Institute (SEI)[1] established the first Capability Maturity Model (CMM) for software development. It was meant to provide a consistent basis by which software development practices can be objectively measured, benchmarked, and improved. In subsequent years, it was realized that CMM can be applied as a general model to aid in improving many other organizational practices.

---

[1]SEI is a research and development center sponsored by the US Department of Defense and operated by Carnegie Mellon University.

Applying maturity model to EA

In this section we look at the general notion of a maturity model and how that can be leveraged in effective management of enterprise architecture.

What is a maturity model?

A *maturity model* can be best described with the *Maturity Grid* shown in Table 5-1. This grid is made up of three parts:

- *Maturity level.* A model typically identifies a number of maturity levels, organized in ascending order. The *columns* in Table 5-1 represent maturity levels.
- *Capability area.* To assess the maturity of an organization in a particular field, the model identifies certain capability areas that are critical for the effectiveness and success in practicing that field. The *rows* in Table 5-1 represent capability areas.
- *Assessment criteria.* The model identifies a set of criteria in each capability area at each maturity level. These criteria are nothing but the descriptions of a practice or condition that is of importance in the respective field. The *cells* in Table 5-1 represent the assessment criteria.

A formal maturity assessment process should be followed to objectively evaluate an enterprise against the assessment criteria. The enterprise must fulfill the criteria by demonstrating relevant characteristics and supporting the same with appropriate evidence.

Generally, maturity levels in any capability area are cumulative. The attainment of a particular maturity level in a capability area requires fulfillment of the criteria at that level plus fulfillment of the criteria at all previous, less mature levels. The outcome of the assessment process is the *maturity scorecard*. It tells which criteria the enterprise satisfies and which ones it does not. It gives an indication of where the enterprise currently stands with regard to practicing the concerned field. It also identifies the gaps the enterprise must address in order to achieve desired improvements and results.

Let's assume that a qualified assessor performs the assessment of an enterprise in a field of practice by validating the policies, processes, artifacts, and other supporting evidences against the assessment criteria. Let's also assume that the underlying maturity model defines five maturity levels and identifies six capability areas for evaluation. The results of the assessments can then be represented as shown in Table 5-2.

Table 5-1 A Maturity Grid

Capability Area		Maturity Level				
		Level 1	Level 2	Level 3	Level 4	Level 5
	Area 1	Criteria (1, 1)	Criteria (1, 2)	Criteria (1, 3)	Criteria (1, 4)	Criteria (1, 5)
	Area 2	Criteria (2, 1)	Criteria (2, 2)	Criteria (2, 3)	Criteria (2, 4)	Criteria (2, 5)
	Area 3	Criteria (3, 1)	Criteria (3, 2)	Criteria (3, 3)	Criteria (3, 4)	Criteria (3, 5)
	....	Criteria (*, 1)	Criteria (*, 2)	Criteria (*, 3)	Criteria (*, 4)	Criteria (*, 5)
	Area n	Criteria (n, 1)	Criteria (n, 2)	Criteria (n, 3)	Criteria (n, 4)	Criteria (n, 5)

Table 5-2 A Maturity Assessment Result

Capability Area	Maturity Level				
	Level 1	Level 2	Level 3	Level 4	Level 5
Area 1	✓	✓	✓	✓	✓
Area 2	✓	✓	✗	✗	✗
Area 3	✓	✓	✓	✗	✗
Area 4	✓	✓	✓	✓	✗
Area 5	✓	✓	✗	✗	✗
Area 6	✓	✓	✓	✗	✗

The maturity score for this enterprise can be viewed in a number of ways. In the classical *staged maturity approach*, an enterprise is certified at a maturity level only if it satisfies *all* the criteria for that maturity level plus *all* the criteria for all preceding maturity levels in *all* capability areas (entire columns). With the assessment result in Table 5-2, the enterprise will simply be certified at maturity level 2. It will then be advised to take corrective action in capability areas 2 and 5 if it subsequently wants to reach maturity level 3. This approach creates an impression that the enterprises can be placed at a single maturity level, whereas in reality enterprises may have different maturity levels in different capability areas.

In contrast, a *continuous maturity approach* provides a more realistic view of maturity. Here the maturity score for the enterprise is calculated using the simple average method. For the example in Table 5.2, the maturity score of the enterprise is calculated as follows:

$$\text{Maturity score} = (\text{Sum of maturity levels reached in each capability area})/$$
$$(\text{Number of capability areas})$$
$$= (5 + 2 + 3 + 4 + 2 + 3)/6$$
$$= 2.83$$

Or alternatively,

$$\text{Maturity score} = (\text{Number of criteria fulfilled})/(\text{Number of capability areas})$$
$$= (6 + 6 + 4 + 2 + 1)/6$$
$$= 2.83$$

Yet another way of looking at maturity is the extent to which an enterprise has attained a maturity in each capability area. With the same example in Table 5-2, it is expressed in percentages as:

- Level 1: 6/6 = 100%
- Level 2: 6/6 = 100%
- Level 3: 4/6 = 66.66%
- Level 4: 2/6 = 33.33%
- Level 5: 1/6 = 16.66%

Thus in a continuous maturity approach it is not necessary to fulfill all the criteria at a particular maturity level and all its predecessors in order to attain that maturity level. It offers the flexibility to prioritize and focus only on specific improvements that are beneficial and cost-justified. It also allows planning and implementing the improvements in different areas at different rates, as the situation may demand.

When the enterprise advances in its maturity level over a period of time, it gradually gains control over and improves on its practices pertaining to the concerned field. The maturity model provides a formal, effective, and proven way to do that. In essence, a maturity model can be used as:

- A catalogue of practices that an enterprise must follow to mature in a field
- A yardstick against which to periodically measure the improvement in practices
- A framework within which to manage the improvement plan

Relevance of maturity models in EA

Like many other IT practices, EA is a *process-rich* and *contemporary* field. It involves many processes; you can easily do them in the wrong way. The enterprise and its employees need to learn the processes right in the first place. In addition, EA is a nontraditional field of practice. Many of the paths are still less traveled.

EA maturity models show the possible milestones and landmarks for the EA journey. By employing a maturity model, enterprises gradually learn to introduce right policies, processes, and practices while venturing into this new unknown field. The maturity model helps them do so by periodically measuring, benchmarking, and tracking the effectiveness of the steps they have taken in their EA effort. Because the maturity model defines ascending levels of maturity for management of EA, it can be used to determine the following parameters:

- *Where EA stands today.* The model can be used to provide a set of benchmarks against which to determine where the enterprise stands in its progress toward the ultimate goal: having EA capabilities that effectively facilitate organizational change.
- *How to proceed on EA.* A maturity model can serve as a high-level basis for developing specific EA improvement plans, as well as for measuring, reporting, and overseeing progress in implementing these plans to attain the next level, if needed.

The scope of a typical EA maturity assessment entails the evaluation of the following criteria:

- The state of EA itself (work products)
- The state of EA-related activities, processes, and practices
- The state of EA capabilities (people skills, organizational construct)
- The buy-in to EA (management commitment, stakeholder participation)

At the lower maturity level, the focus of enterprise architecture is typically on creating awareness, formalizing processes, and developing architectures. At the higher maturity level, the focus shifts to the use of architectures and value measurement.

EA maturity models are available in abundance. But before we look at a few of them, let's first have a glance at a *rule of thumb* for EA maturity.

A rule of thumb for the architectural maturity of an enterprise

To get a first-hand impression about the architectural maturity of an enterprise, we can look at the two ratios pertaining to IT investment patterns:

- Run-the-business IT cost / Business revenue
- Run-the-business IT cost / Change-the-business IT cost

The ratio *(Run-the-business IT cost / Business revenue)*, expressed in percentage, can be benchmarked with the industry standards or compared with the closest competitors of the enterprise. If this is lower than either industry standards or competitors, it is an indication to believe that the enterprise's IT is at least working in a cost-effective mode.

The second ratio *(Run-the-business IT cost / Change-the-business IT cost)*, expressed in percentage, helps identify the *role* that IT plays in the business. Ross et al. (2010, pp. 2, 7) suggest that the lower this ratio is, the better it is. According to their survey, a ratio of 60:40 or less tells that IT is being perceived as a *business change driver*. A larger chunk of IT budget is apportioned to the new IT initiatives because IT has been optimized for its day-to-day operational support. IT also seems to enjoy a trust relationship with the business for new development.

In contrast, a ratio of 70:30 or more indicates that IT plays the role of an *order taker*. The business looks at IT as a support function, not as an enabler. With regard to this performance indicator, you can face pretty grim situations involving enterprise IT out in the field. In one of our projects, an insurance company struggled for three years to bring down this ratio marginally, from 87:13 to 84:16.

It must also be noted that EA is not the only contributor to these ratios. Many other downstream IT practices, such as project management, service management, software development, and so forth, play an equally influential role. Nonetheless, since EA is an upstream practice in IT management, we consider these ratios indicators for the *notional state* of EA. They help in determining how to proceed with an elaborate EA maturity assessment for the enterprise: where the focus should be and where the expected targets can reside.

OMB EA assessment framework

The US Office of Management and Budget (OMB)[2] mandates that all government agencies must *effectively* adopt the Federal Enterprise Architecture (FEA) in their IT management. In that context, OMB (2009) has established an EA maturity model called the *OMB Enterprise Architecture Assessment Framework (OMB EAAF)*. It is supposed to provide government agencies with a common benchmarking tool for planning and measuring their efforts to improve enterprise architecture management as well as to provide the OMB with a means for performing the same activity government-wide. OMB EAAF is perhaps the most comprehensive, robust, and practically enforced EA maturity model.

OMB audits the government agencies for their EA maturity and then uses the scorecard as a decision tool to fund their IT initiatives. Linking IT investment to EA maturity is a smart move. It is like granting scholarships to students only if they continue to score well in their exams, year on year. With EA maturity playing a key role in the budgetary approval process, OMB signifies and enforces the strategic importance of enterprise architecture (FEA) in and across the government agencies.

OMB EAAF identifies five maturity ratings (levels 1–5) without qualifying them with names or descriptions. It then groups the capability areas in three categories: *completion* of enterprise architecture; *use* of EA to drive improved decision making; and *results* achieved in advancing program effectiveness.

---

[2]The Office of Management and Budget is a part of the Executive Office of the President of the United States. It serves the function of presidential oversight on federal agencies.

The *Completion Capability Area* looks at the extent to which the architecture development is complete at the enterprise and segment[3] levels.

- *Target enterprise architecture and enterprise transition plan.* The baseline and target architectures must be well defined, showing traceability through all architectural layers. The enterprise transition plan,[4] including major IT investments, must be submitted.
- *Architectural prioritization.* A formal and documented process to prioritize and plan the architectural work must be in place.
- *Scope of completion.* The extent to which enterprise IT portfolio funding is supported by the completed segment architectures needs to be measured.
- *Internet Protocol Version 6 (IPv6).* The EA (including enterprise transition plan) must incorporate Internet protocol version 6 (IPv6) into the IT infrastructure's segment architecture and IT investment portfolio. (This is an enterprise-specific mandate by the US government, so to speak.)

The *Use Capability Area* measures the extent to which the necessary EA management practices, processes, and policies are established and integrated with strategic planning, information resources management, IT management, and capital planning and investment control processes.

- *Performance improvement integration.* The extent to which the enterprise has aligned its performance improvement plans[5] (on the business side) with its enterprise transition plan (on the IT side) in terms of process and outcomes.
- *CPIC integration.* This parameter measures the alignment between the enterprise transition plan and capital planning and investment control (CPIC).
- *FEA Reference Model and Exhibit 53 data quality.* This assesses the completeness and accuracy of mapping the IT investments in the IT portfolio with the base FEA reference architecture model. *Exhibit 53* is the business case for the IT investments demanded, or made, in the projects.
- *Collaboration and reuse.* The progress in migrating to target applications and shared services portfolio and creating a services environment within the enterprise. It also measures the progress in information sharing, with a focus on reuse.
- *EA governance, program management, change management, and deployment.* This parameter benchmarks the degree to which the enterprise governs and manages the implementation and use

---

[3]Segment architecture is the next layer of EA for a government agency (which is seen as an enterprise). The segment architecture describes a portion of the enterprise. There are three types of segment architectures: *enterprise services* (e.g., knowledge management, security management, geospatial mapping, reporting), *business services* (human resource, financial management, direct loans, and so forth), and *core mission area* (e.g., health, homeland security, pollution prevention and control, energy supply, education grants). The term *services* here is not to be confused with service as in *service-oriented architecture (SOA)*. The two terms have entirely different connotations.

[4]The enterprise transition plan identifies a desired set of business and IT capabilities along the path to achieve the target enterprise architecture. It also identifies the logical dependencies and priorities among major activities related to project or program and investment. The enterprise transition plan supports an IT-enabled performance improvement plan to fulfill the overall mission of the government agency.

[5]The performance improvement plan captures enterprise-wide improvement opportunities linked to the government agency's mission performance and strategic goals.

of EA policies and processes. We will take a brief look at corresponding assessment criteria later in this section.

The *Results Capability Area* validates whether the enterprise is measuring the effectiveness and value of its EA activities by assigning performance measures to its EA and related processes and then reporting on actual results to demonstrate EA success.

- *Mission performance.* This figure measures the extent to which the enterprise is using EA and IT to drive program performance improvement (that is, the business results).
- *Cost savings and cost avoidance.* Values the extent to which the enterprise is using EA and IT to control costs. The cost savings are best reflected in steady-state spending (*run-the-business* IT costs), which should go down over time as legacy systems are consolidated and retired.
- *IT infrastructure portfolio quality.* This parameter assesses the progress toward developing a high-quality portfolio of infrastructure investments, in terms of end user performance, security, reliability, availability, extensibility, and efficiency of operations and maintenance. (This also includes innovation and new technology induction.)
- *Measuring EA program value.* Measures the direct benefits of EA value to the decision makers. EA value measurement tracks architecture development and use, and monitors the impact of EA products and services on IT and business investment decisions, collaboration and reuse, standards compliance, stakeholder satisfaction, and other related measurement areas and indicators.

Let's take a further glance at an example of how the assessment criteria are specified in this model. Table 5-3 is a reprint of the assessment criteria for maturity *level 1* and *level 5* of *EA governance, program management, change management, and deployment* in the *Use Capability Area*. Here read *Agency* as a synonym of *Enterprise*. It must be noted that each criterion is specified in a standard format. It identifies the *activities* that must be performed and the artifacts that are produced or used to attain that level.

Looking at the structure and the content of OMB EA Assessment Framework, one can convincingly conclude that it is a *complete* EA maturity model. The only drawback, however, is that it is very specific and tightly aligned with OMB, FEA, and the US federal government and their terminologies.

Table 5-3 OMB EA Assessment Framework: Example Criteria

Use Capability Area: **EA Governance, Program Management, Change Management, and Deployment**
Level 1   **Activities**   The agency has developed a vision and strategy for EA.   The agency has begun to identify EA tasks and resource requirements.   The agency has appointed a chief architect, has senior level sponsorship of its EA program, and has funded an EA program.   The agency has developed an EA policy to ensure agency-wide commitment to EA.   The policy clearly assigns responsibility to develop, implement, and maintain the EA.   **Artifacts**   EA program plan, EA policy

Continued

Table 5-3 OMB EA Assessment Framework: Example Criteria—Cont'd

Use Capability Area:
EA Governance, Program Management, Change Management, and Deployment

Level 2	...
Level 3	...
Level 4	...
Level 5	**Activities**

The EA governance committee ensures EA compliance throughout the agency. If noncompliance is identified, the committee is responsible for developing a plan to resolve the issue.

Alignment to the EA standards is a common practice throughout the agency.

The compliance process is reviewed and updated when deficiencies or enhancements to the process are identified.

The agency's head or a designated operations executive has approved the EA governance plan in writing.

The EA repository and its interfaces are used by participants or support staff for the CPIC, SDLC, and strategic planning processes.

Current EA information is readily available to participants in these processes as well as the broader agency user community.

Users are informed of changes, as necessary.

Artifacts

EA governance plan, EA governance committee meeting minutes, governance plan approval, EA communications plan, and training plan and materials

Architecture capability maturity model of the US department of commerce

The US Department of Commerce published the *Architecture Capability Maturity Model (ACMM)* Version 1.2 in December 2007. We list it here because it is endorsed by the TOGAF 9.1 standard (The Open Group, 2011, p. 51). Compared to the other maturity models introduced in this chapter, however, ACMM is sketchy and less precise in documentation.

ACMM is inherited from the original SEI-CMM (see the introduction of this chapter). It determines whether appropriate EA practices are in place and are being effectively managed and used. To this effect, ACMM identifies five maturity levels that are based on the original SEI-CMM definitions:

- Level 0: *None.* An organization does not have an explicit architecture. (We do not really count this as a level.)
- Level 1: *Initial.* Limited architecture processes, documentation, and standards exist, but in a mostly ad hoc and localized form. There is a limited management awareness but no explicit governance in place.
- Level 2: *Under Development.* The essential architecture processes have been identified and defined. The basic current architecture and target architecture have been described. The management is aware and basic governance is in place.
- Level 3: *Defined.* The architecture processes are largely followed. The current and target architectures are well defined and communicated. The senior management and the other stakeholders are aware and supportive.

- Level 4: *Managed.* The architecture processes are part of the organizational culture. The architectures and processes are periodically assessed and revised. The senior management and the other stakeholders participate in the architecture evolution.
- Level 5: *Optimizing.* There is a concentrated effort to optimize and continuously improve the architecture processes, with direct contribution from senior management and key stakeholders.

ACMM broadly considers nine capability areas[6] for maturity assessment:

1. *Architecture Process.* To what extent are the architecture processes established?
2. *Architecture Development.* To what degree are the development and progression of the architectures documented?
3. *Business Linkage.* To what extent are the architectures linked to the business strategies or drivers?
4. *Senior Management Involvement.* How much are the senior managers involved in the establishment and ongoing development of architecture?
5. *Stakeholder (Operating Units) Participation*:
   - To what degree has the architecture process been accepted by the stakeholders?
   - To what extent is the architecture process an effort backed by the whole organization?
6. *Architecture Communication.*
   - To what degree are the decisions of architecture practice documented?
   - What share of the architecture content is made available electronically to everybody in the organization?
   - How much education is done across the business on the architecture process and contents?
7. *IT Security.* To what extent is IT security integrated with the architecture?
8. *Governance.* To what degree is an architecture governance (governing body) process in place and accepted by senior management?
9. *IT Investment and Acquisition Strategy.* How does the architecture influence the IT investment and acquisition strategy?

ACMM lists the criteria for each maturity level in each capability area. For example, Table 5-4 is a reprint of *Maturity Level 4* criteria for all the capability areas. Here, read *operating unit* as a synonym for *stakeholder* (or *business line*).

Table 5-4 ACMM: Example Criteria at Maturity Level 4

		Maturity Level
Capability Area		**Level 4: Defined** Managed and measured enterprise architecture process.
	Architecture process	The enterprise architecture process is part of the culture, with strong linkages to other core IT and business processes. Quality metrics associated with the architecture process are captured. These metrics include the cycle times necessary to generate EA revisions, technical environment stability, and time to implement a new or upgraded application or system.

Continued

---

[6]In ACMM, capability areas are termed *architecture elements.*

Table 5-4 ACMM: Example Criteria at Maturity Level 4—Cont'd

		Maturity Level
	Architecture development	EA documentation is updated on a regular cycle to reflect the updated enterprise architecture. Business, information, application and technical architectures defined by appropriate *de jure* and *de facto* standards. The architecture continues alignment with the Department of Commerce and Federal Enterprise Architectures. An automated tool is used to improve the architecture's usability.
	Business linkage	Capital planning and investment control are adjusted based on the feedback received and lessons learned from updated enterprise architecture. Periodic re-examination of business drivers occurs.
	Senior management involvement	Senior management team is directly involved in the architecture review process.
	Operating unit participation	The entire operating unit accepts and actively participates in the EA process.
	Architecture communication	Architecture documents are updated regularly and frequently reviewed for the latest architecture developments and standards. There are regular presentations to IT staff on architecture content. Organizational personnel understand the architecture and its uses.
	IT security	Performance metrics associated with IT security architecture are captured.
	Governance	Explicit governance of all IT investments. Formal processes for managing variances feed back into enterprise architecture.
	IT investment and acquisition	All planned IT acquisitions are guided and governed by the enterprise architecture. RFI and RFP evaluations are integrated into the EA planning activities.

EA maturity model by MIT center for information system research

Jeanne W. Ross, from the MIT Center for Information System Research, has suggested an EA maturity model. In this model, Ross (2006) identifies four stages of architectural maturity. They are characterized by their IT investment patterns and by the management practices they are required to have. The IT investment patterns for these maturity stages are described as follows:

- *Level 1: Business Silos*. At this level, IT investments are put into local applications, predominantly driven by the business cases addressing local business needs of individual business units (or departments). The cost savings derived at this stage are primarily derived from the local business unit level optimization.
- *Level 2: Standardized Technology*. Here the enterprises begin to pull economies of scale by standardizing technology platforms and developing shared infrastructure services across their business units. The cost savings at this stage come from *IT* efficiencies (cost and risk reduction at the enterprise level).
- *Level 3: Optimized Core*. At this stage, the enterprises begin to leverage organizational synergies by sharing data and standardizing the business processes across its business units. The business benefits received at this stage come from *operational* efficiencies (process harmonization, data availability, and data quality at the enterprise level).

- *Level 4: Business Modularity.* On this last level, enterprises are focused on smaller, reusable application and process components to support a more modular and flexible operating model. The business value generated at this stage can be measured in terms of the enterprises' strategic agility and responsiveness to market dynamics. IT enables the enterprise to respond rapidly to competitor initiatives and market opportunities. It is thereby directly contributing to business growth.

The IT investment patterns in the enterprises change as they move from one stage to the next.

The model further outlines how enterprises can progressively learn and formalize practices at each stage. This way they can benefit from the current stage and, if appropriate, move toward the next stage. It was statistically observed that at each level specific management practices contribute significant value to the enterprise. The enterprises must therefore enable new management practices as they progress from one stage to the next. These management practices need to support the investment patterns at respective maturity stages. The key management practices for each stage are summarized in Table 5-5 (Ross, 2006, p. 3).

Table 5-5 EA Maturity Model by MIT–CISR (Ross, 2006, used with kind permission)

Capability Area		Maturity Level			
		Level 1: Business Silo	Level 2: Standardized Technology	Level 3: Optimized Core	Level 4: Business Modularity
	IT management	Well-designed business case Standardized project methodology			
	Centralized IT funding		An IT steering committee An infrastructure renewal process Centralized funding for enterprise applications		
	Standardized technology environment		Architects on project teams An architecture exception process Formal architecture compliance process A centralized standards team		
	Senior management involvement			Enterprise-wide process owners A statement of enterprise architecture guiding principles Business leadership in project teams Senior executive oversight of architecture initiatives IT program managers	
	Communication and assessment				One-page architecture graphic to communicate enterprise vision Post-implementation assessment A formal research and adoption process A full-time enterprise architecture team

The final word of advice by Jeanne Ross (2006, p. 3) is worth repeating:

The firms embarking on an enterprise architecture journey should plan for steady increases in IT value through gradual enhancements in IT management (architectural maturity progression from stage 1 to stage 4, step by step). We have found no shortcuts to business value from IT.

Experiences with the maturity models

The best-documented case of broad usage of the EA maturity model is the OMB EA Assessment Framework. Despite a robust EA maturity model and stringent management control by the OMB, many government agencies have not progressed well on EA. In 2005 (after eight years of the federal EA initiative), the General Accountability Office (GAO)[7] criticized a number of government agencies for their failures in EA adoption. The defaulter list includes the Federal Bureau of Investigation (FBI), National Aeronautics and Space Administration (NASA), and the Departments of Defense and Homeland Security (Sessions, 2006). This probably sheds a bad light on the maturity of some US agencies in terms of their EA culture; however, the application of an EA maturity model has at least uncovered this state.

In our own experience, we have seen that the maturity models have their limitations. For instance, a telecom company in Europe that we dealt with in our work does convincingly rate itself at the highest level (Level 4) on the MIT–CISR EA Maturity Model. It has every practice in place and satisfies every condition that the maturity model demands. However, the company is still struggling to get any closer to its vision of business modularity, even after putting significant effort and investment in its EA program for the last seven years (since 2004).

Quite often, a maturity assessment has a tendency to show some (or all) of the following traits:

- *Subjective.* The maturity assessment is highly subjective and is influenced by assessors' bias of perception. Although a number of measures are taken to remove subjectivity in the assessment process, it still lingers and shows.
- *Academic.* Often a maturity assessment is performed for the sake of compliance in accordance with the imposed letter of the law. It rarely reflects the true intent and spirit of the enterprise for excellence in the respective field.
- *Manipulative.* As people get acquainted with the assessment process, they learn how to create the perception of compliance without practicing it in real life. It then becomes an oversimplified, superfluous farce for the sake of certification only—an act of pseudo-certification. The maturity scorecard looks impressive on paper, but it rarely shows the true picture of the extent to which EA has actually been ingrained in the spirit and culture of the organization.
- *Bureaucratic.* As the maturity assessment process becomes an all-encompassing audit, it tends to be an overly complicated, strenuous, and bureaucratic process. It can lead to considerable administrative overhead and costs. Many organizations take up the assessment process as a formal project and bring a dedicated team on board (a *project management office,* or *PMO*) to pass through it smoothly.

---

[7]The General Accountability Office (GAO) is responsible for monitoring the effectiveness of different organizations within the US federal government.

- *Superfluous.* Two or more organizations might not be equal, even if they are rated at the same maturity level. In reality, they might have totally different agendas, scopes, and ways of performing EA. The abstraction of the maturity score to a single number does not necessarily give a real benchmark for comparison of the spirit, character, or personalities of two organizations, even though from the outside they seem to be akin.
- *Misleading.* The maturity model generally suggests a linear and unilateral path of progression toward a higher maturity. At the very least, it leaves the impression that the more you do, the better it will be. As a result, you can overdo things while chasing a desired maturity level. However, higher maturity is not a goal in itself. Not all enterprises are ambitious to reach the highest maturity level, and not all of them need to. The benefits of a higher maturity level might not justify the costs of attaining it. In addition, the formality and rigor at a higher maturity level may in fact conflict with a culture of innovation and creativity in the organization.

To overcome some of these limitations in the maturity models, we propose the *EA Dashboard,* as introduced in Chapter 1 as a supplement to the EA maturity models. Unlike an EA maturity model that demands a unilateral maturity progression for an EA effort, irrespective of the contextual priorities and constraints of the enterprise, the EA Dashboard helps us take a balanced view that measures the effectiveness of an EA effort in light of the ground realities in the enterprise. With a more pragmatic and broader look at EA, the EA Dashboard offers a realistic and convincing approach to govern an EA effort. This is its sole goal: We will not attempt to offer an objective list of criteria to create an industry benchmark by it. We will discuss the EA Dashboard at further length in Chapter 6.

Foundations of Collaborative EA

CONTENT

Reflections on Complexity 139
    Beyond Threshing Machines 139
    Structure and Behavior of Complex Phenomena 140
    Principles of Managing Complexity.. 141
    Management Capabilities of Hierarchies and Networks 146
The EA Dashboard as a Yardstick for EA Effectiveness 152

Despite the well-thought-out repertoire of frameworks and best practices set out in the previous two chapters, enterprise architecture in many organizations is far from having the sustainable and sweeping effect that it promises. Our caricatures way back in Chapter 1 outlined the extremes to which the idea of managing EA often deteriorates. But how can we do better and avoid these extremes?

The key success factor is to what extent a *collaboration on EA* between all stakeholders comes alive. The often-recited mantra—that the executive board's commitment to an EA initiative is the deciding momentum—falls short of the mark. If an EA initiative is running into a dead end, it is mostly the breach between strategic vision and ground-level reality that makes it go astray.

The commitment of the CEO is a necessity, but it's not a sufficient condition for closing this breach. It fails to be a substitute for a living, self-dependent collaboration. With commanded EA, people *must* collaborate, because the chief is saying so. But as soon as high-level management attention goes away, EA again becomes stale unless it is valued and supported by the ground-level personnel involved in designing, developing, operating, or simply using IT. Hence collaboration is the leitmotif for a better way to practice EA.

But how can we elicit collaboration and apply it as an antidote to a stale EA? Our antidote has three guiding principles as ingredients, as listed in Figure 6-1.

These three guidelines can be mapped to the toolkits set out in the subtitle of this book: lean, agile, and Enterprise 2.0, respectively.

- *Lean* opens our eyes to all kinds of waste, such as piles of unread specifications or extra processing due to following bureaucratic governance. This gives us a systematic way to eliminate waste to

137

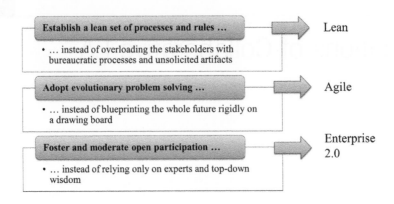

FIGURE 6-1

The three guidelines of collaborative EA.

come to a streamlined, demand-driven delivery process. Pragmatism, reduction of bureaucracy, and lightweight processes are what lean techniques subscribe to.

- *Agile* teaches us how to approach a problem in an iterative manner. It allows us to learn with a managed trial-and-error approach that has short-term feedback cycles, which is characteristic of an evolutionary problem-solving strategy. The feedback cycles bring all stakeholders together with a constant heartbeat, thereby guaranteeing collaboration.
- From *Enterprise 2.0*, we import insights and practices that help give birth to a living community of knowledge workers. This in particular avoids the notorious breach between high-level vision and ground-level reality.

But what makes us believe that the three guidelines will do the job? The rationale comes from both foundational and hands-on arguments. One foundational argument is that any enterprise architecture is beyond doubt a complex being and must not be managed as though it were simple. Applying management practices that rely on predictability, up-front construction, or detailed plans of action is bound to fail when they're applied to complex systems.

Furthermore, we'll discover that a *network of peers* under suitable circumstances has a higher capability to shape and control a complex system than a *command-based hierarchy* (we will come back to both terms and discuss them in greater detail). This is the abstract root reason that a well-organized collaboration on EA matters in a network of stakeholders, has a deeper impact on the enterprise architecture, and can shape it more purposefully than a hierarchical top-down approach.

The hands-on argument rests on our practical building blocks introduced in Chapter 1. They are subsumed under the headlines of the three guiding principles in respective chapters. Chapter 7, "Toward Pragmatism: Lean and Agile EA," for example, proposes a systematic sieve that is inspired by lean methods and filters out typical waste in an architecture work stream. The gains of our building blocks are demonstrated by an EA Dashboard that indicates the key traits of success or failure.

We have repeatedly stressed that EA is about managing a *complex* system without explaining what the trail of complexity actually entails. Let's leave the path of practical reasoning for a moment and consider complexity from a general perspective. We invite the impatient practitioner to lean back, and remember a statement by the economist Friedrich August von Hayek: "To prefer something practically applicable means to relinquish the power our thinking provides us with."[1]

Reflections on complexity
Beyond threshing machines

Complex systems have characteristic properties. Their structure and behavior are fundamentally different from simple systems such as the threshing machine depicted in Figure 6-2.

The threshing machine has a firm composition consisting of a steam engine transforming heat into mechanical force and a coach that is driven by this force via a belt. The coach takes cereal ears as input to the chute on the roof, threshes the corn off the ears, and throws the straw out at the left end. Though the apparatus comprises quite a few components, it is not complex in the proper sense. There's just one rather limited thing it is capable of doing when put into a suitable environment, and managing it simply means operating a few levers at the steam engine. Pushing the lever makes the wheels and belts run faster so that more corn and straw is produced.

Now compare this to the landscape of information systems in today's enterprises! Envision the incredible zoo of information systems, applications, and interfaces: Even when we limit the level of detail to the elephants in this zoo, a printout of the landscape map would easily fill a wall. The map would show a snapshot of an expanding cosmos of systems where messages are echoing in a network that gets denser all the time. And mark this: Each single information system is already a highly compound being in itself, with its numerous hardware components, drivers, and the deeply layered software stack it operates.

FIGURE 6-2

Model of a threshing machine.

German Historical Museum, used with permission

---

[1] See Hayek (1969, p. 49); translation by the authors.

The transparent causality and predictability of a threshing machine are lost in this picture. The number of components and interdependencies has grown to an extent that puts the IT landscape into a different category from the threshing machine. We are not making an ontological statement here: A Laplace demon[2] with the intellectual capability of predicting the movement of all atoms in the universe would probably see no difference between the information systems compared to the threshing machine. But with our more modest intellectual powers, humans cannot *understand* IT in the same way as the threshing machine, and likewise we should not attempt to *manage* it along the same lines, which is the important point.

In Miyazaki's *Sen and Chihiro Spirited Away*,[3] the six-armed mechanical Kamaji is steering a giant bathhouse by swiftly operating an entanglement of wheels, levers, and triggers. It looks fascinating, but it is certainly not a role model for operating an enterprise's IT. Managing a landscape of information systems feels a lot more like keeping a garden at equilibrium and cultivating its shape than handling a giant threshing machine with hundreds of gauges and levers.

But we haven't reached the peak yet. Enterprise architecture management is not simply concerned with a landscape of information systems. It primarily looks at how *people* utilize information technology, how daily routines and work processes are or should be interwoven with information systems, how human capabilities and automated functions interoperate, and so forth. We are not looking at a technical system but at a sociotechnical one. But with humans entering the scene, we beyond doubt have the first "system components" in our scope, for which the behavior and interactions must not be regarded as "simple." This is true in particular because today's workplaces are no longer cutting down human degrees of freedom in the way Henry Ford's production lines did.

Hence we are better off at this point with accepting that the system EA is dealing with in fact is complex, to understand what this entails, and to decide which management approaches are appropriate and which are not.

Structure and behavior of complex phenomena

Let's move on from an "Uh-oh, this might be complex" gut feeling to a clearer understanding of complex phenomena. There is no general definition of complexity; different branches of science have created their own stipulations. Some jesters mock that the definition of complexity is best exemplified by the definition of complexity. But fortunately we do not depend on a sharp delineation of complexity. What we're after is an overall understanding of the phenomenon and a derivation of what it means for

---

[2]The French mathematician and astronomer Pierre-Simon de Laplace (1749–1827) invented the thought-experiment of an intellect with unlimited computational capability to illustrate his deterministic view of the world. He believed that if such an intellect "would know all forces that set nature in motion, and all positions of all items of which nature is composed," it would be able to compute the whole future and past out of the laws of nature. "For such an intellect nothing would be uncertain and the future just like the past would be present before its eyes" (Laplace, 1814). Though this view of the world is somewhat outdated today, the "Laplace demon" is still a concept used in many "what if we weren't limited by our intellectual powers?" thought experiments.

[3]*Sen and Chihiro Spirited Away* is the famous animated fantasy adventure by the Japanese artist Hayao Miyazaki. It won the Academy Award for Best Animated Feature in 2001. Kamaji is one of the fantastic creatures helping Chihiro in her struggle against the witch Yubaba. He is the chief technology mechanic of Yubaba's bathhouse and looks like a cross between a human and a spider.

management. A first step toward understanding is the following list of structural characteristics of complex systems:

- A complex system is composed of many components.
- The behavior of one component influences the behavior of many other components.
- The system has an internal state, and its behavior does not depend solely on input but also on the state.
- The variety of the system, that is, the number of states it can have, and the differences these states show are high.
- The system has many channels of interaction with the environment, and the variety of inputs and outputs is high.

This list remains a fuzzy characterization. One may ask what the quantifiers *many* or *high* mean, and you could argue whether any of these bullet points can be dropped in one or the other case. But since there's no doubt that the sociotechnical system EA is concerned with satisfies all these criteria, it would be a pointless discussion. That's why we claimed that we don't depend on a sharp delineation.

Next, what differences in the behavior can we expect from complex systems in comparison to simple ones?

Table 6-1 gives some hints at the differences.

Table 6-1 Simple and Complex Behavior

Simple System	Complex System
Shows the same behavior under the same external conditions (strong causality).	Behaves differently even if the external conditions are exactly the same. Has its "own will."
Shows similar behavior under similar external conditions (weak causality).	Small deviations in the external conditions can sometimes lead to a completely different behavior.
Variations in the external conditions lead to proportional variations in behavior (linearity).	The relationship between conditions and behavior is nonlinear, sometimes discontinuous.
Works as anticipated along its preconstructed lines. Shows no life of its own.	Shows emergent structures and generates spontaneous order and regularities.
Is accurately fitting into a certain environment but likely to become unstable in case of changes.	Is sufficiently well integrated into the current environment but capable of absorbing vast changes (viability).
Is essentially bound to a particular environment and must be reconstructed if this ceases to exist.	Is able to learn and adapt to new environments (adaptability).
Has a delimited interface with the environment and can be isolated from observers.	Has permeable boundaries and tends to alter the behavior when being observed (second-order cybernetics).

Principles of managing complexity

Now, what have we learned from this brief comparison with regard to mastering the complex sociotechnical system EA is concerned with? From general considerations like this we certainly cannot deduce hands-on recipes that will make enterprise architects roll up their sleeves to give them a try tomorrow morning. It is more a set of principles guiding our expectations and attitudes with respect to the EA game that comes out of our reflections.

Principle 1. Stay at coarse granularity in analyzing complex systems (such as enterprise architectures) and predicting their future.

The large number of influential factors and the inevitable discontinuities in the behavior of complex systems limit our ability to explain and predict things to coarse grains. Detailed descriptions and explanations of their causality as well as single-point predictions are exceptional cases. In the words of an IT saying, coarseness of grains is not a bug but rather a feature of managing complexity. Finer granularities cause an exponentially increasing effort and are likely to end up in a quixotic project. What is achievable in the domain of complex phenomena is[4]:

- A general understanding of how things work *in principle*
- A more or less fuzzy prediction *of a range* of future states

Furthermore, our scientific education elicits a certain bias for positive propositions. But in complex areas, negative explanations of what has *not* happened or predictions of what will definitely *not* be the case can sometimes be as useful as positive ones.

As an enterprise architect, your CIO might ask you what the target application landscape will be three years from now. The most appropriate response might be: "No clue, but I can list fifteen percent of the current applications that will definitely be discontinued in this timeframe." It might not be recommended to answer this way, though, because you immediately have a nasty political problem on your plate. But it is important to treat this as a political problem and not a problem of how you do application landscaping.

Principle 2. Strengthening a complex system's ability to change wins over optimizing the status quo.

A complex system shows a certain "life of its own" or has its "own will." It shows a notorious recalcitrance to stay close to the drawn lines and generates emergent, not anticipated, structures. Constructing such a system *ex ante* is, therefore, a thankless if not useless task.

Architects who have led large software development programs know how it feels when "the best blueprint and architecture principles ever" very soon are subject to "creative interpretation" by the implementers on the ground. The initial architecture is transformed (the planner might say distorted) by the thought process of the hundred brains involved in the program. Architects sometimes feel like pulling their hair out and shouting for stronger governance.

But it is more insightful to acknowledge that such change is not only inevitable but is in fact a necessary ingredient of success. The constructed information system is interwoven with the people developing, maintaining, and using it, and this conglomerate certainly is a complex system in the sense characterized previously. Such a system is viable to the extent that it can preserve its identity under changing conditions; a necessary prerequisite of this ability is to form variations responding to changes or late insights. A rigid corset, on the contrary, is likely to break down on the bumpy road of a two-year program.

What holds true for the initial state of a system also applies to later phases of the life cycle. We have a certain tendency to dream of optimal states. Take, for example, a sermon like this:

> *When we have eventually transformed our legacy applications into a SOA landscape, our IT problems will be easy to solve. We shall eventually be able to adapt our IT landscape to the pressing business demands in an agile fashion.*

Most professionals would hesitate to explicitly subscribe to such a naïve vision, but it is embarrassing how such "happy salvation" beliefs hover as tacit assumptions over so many endeavors.

---

[4]*Cf.* Malik (2008, p. 182 *ff*).

With regard to the nature of complex systems, it is not advisable to search for the "optimal enterprise architecture." Optimality is always relative to an environment, and the frame conditions are likely to change. Hence it is better to accept certain ugly spots of the IT landscape and strengthen the viability of the whole, which means developing and using capabilities such as being able to learn, solve problems, adapt, or absorb disruptions.

There is also another argument in favor of this principle. An enterprise resembles a self-transforming, adaptive organism rather than an extremely complex (but ultimately static) machine. It is a sociotechnical system captured in permanent evolution. More precisely, it coevolves alongside the other enterprises in its market segment in an everlasting struggle against displacement and extinction.

"Now here, you see, it takes all the running you can do, to keep in the same place," says the Red Queen in Lewis Carroll's *Through the Looking Glass*.[5] In a competitive world, some constant amount of improvement is required to merely defend your own position. All players in the market operate in a "fitness landscape," where enterprises (similar to biological species) constantly perform minor or major transformations in the pursuit of fitness peaks in that landscape.

The principle behind this phenomenon is called *coevolution*; by transforming itself and its business processes, the enterprise changes the survival game not only for itself but also, through changing the market conditions, for its competitors. This makes the fitness landscape dynamic, and the peaks of optimal fitness are changing at each evolution step. An EA that tries global optimization for an enterprise is, in terms of the coevolution process, searching for the global fitness peak (or peaks)—for the global optimum in competitiveness. By a relatively simple thought experiment[6] it can be shown that the complexity of this search is in exponential order of the enterprise's complexity itself. "Therefore, finding the global peak or one of a few excellent peaks is a completely intractable problem," writes Kauffman (1995). Such a search is an NP hard task, which basically means that there is no simpler search algorithm than to test all combinations—resulting in a combinatorial explosion of the number of options.

Opposed to the futile search for global optima, strengthening the ability to change enables the enterprise to flexibly adapt itself to an ever-changing fitness landscape. Principle 2, "Strengthening a complex system's ability to change wins over optimizing the status quo," expresses that this strategy yields better results—eventually. We will see a bit later, in the section "Benchmarking Hierarchies versus Networks of Managers," what a suitable organizational structure valuing this principle can look like.

Principles 1 and 2 can be directly derived from Table 6-1. To get further advice, we now turn to a theorem about systems in general, not only complex ones. It is the *Law of Requisite*

---

[5]The biologist Leigh van Valen used this quote in postulating his *Red Queen Hypothesis* (van Valen, 1973), which sees the evolutionary ecosystem as a kind of zero-sum game whereby the gain of one species equals the loss (or even extinction) of another one. This leads to an "arms race" in which each species must constantly improve its fitness to keep pace with the newly developed competitive advantages of others.

[6]Kauffman (1995) chose a very simplified model for a participant in a coevolution process. Kauffman's reasoning deals with biological species, but his argumentation applies to enterprises as well. An abstracted genome defining system traits is modeled as a set of N Boolean variables, each representing a gene. For every gene, a *fitness function* is defined that delivers a value between 0 and 1. The function value depends on the state of that gene plus contributing inputs from K other genes (with $K < N$). The overall fitness is then defined as the mean value of all fitness functions. Even with such a very simple model, the number of local optima in a fitness landscape explodes when K approaches N. The search for a global optimum is an NP hard problem under these conditions. (*NP hard* is a term from computation complexity theory.)

Variety, formulated and proven by William Ross Ashby, one of the fathers of cybernetics in (Ashby, 1958)[7]:

> *The larger the variety of actions available to a control system, the larger the variety of perturbations it is able to compensate.*

Ashby himself shortened this statement to a more memorable slogan:

> *Only variety can absorb variety.*

The general scenery of this law is sketched in Figure 6-3: A controller is managing a system by acting on some control variables based on observations taken from the system. These adjustments are necessary to cope with perturbations stemming from somewhere inside or outside the system and to keep the system in line with the goals that are also pre-given from somewhere. One usually has gauge values such as temperature and thermostat position in mind when thinking about observed and control variables, respectively.

With regard to sociotechnical systems, however, there are more options. Take, for example, the traffic system of a country. Some ordinary gauge values are available, such as the number of traffic injuries per year. But control variables, for instance, include *rules* the drivers and pedestrians must obey. It is important for the applicability of the model that the actions of the controller are not confined to such simple things as turning a thermostat, because enterprise architects typically exercise their control more by designing blueprints or setting rules than by turning some gauge value up or down.

One further term needs explanation before we can draw some conclusions—namely, the term *variety*. The variety of a system denotes the number and variance of states it can attain and is a measure of the system's complexity. In short we could say that the essence of control or management is reducing the variety of the system and stabilizing it in the boundaries of the states that are admissible according to the goals.

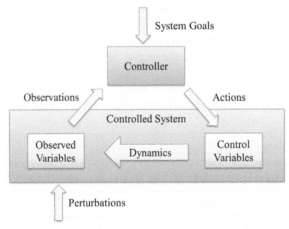

FIGURE 6-3

A cybernetic control system.

---

[7]We recommend Heylighen (2001) as a more readable source of information.

Now, what does Ashby's law tell us? It claims that there is a certain relationship among the following factors:

- The complexity of the environment (measured by the variety of the perturbations or influential factors)
- The complexity of the controller (measured by the variety of the repertoire of actions available to the controller)
- Finally, the variety of the system itself

If we denote the varieties in this order by $V(E)$, $V(C)$, and $V(S)$, respectively, the relationship can be expressed by a proportional equation as follows:

$$V(S) \approx V(E) - V(C)$$

Assume that it is our task to design the system's control C. What are the variables in this equation that can be influenced? $V(E)$ must be regarded as fixed; the environment won't do us a favor and morph into something simpler. $V(S)$, on the contrary, is not altogether pre-given. It has two ingredients: On one hand, it is an inherent construction property of the system, something we cannot alter right away. But on the other hand it reflects the *accuracy of control* required by our management ambitions, and depends on how rigidly and precisely we want to determine what is going on.

Therefore, how simple the management of a system can be depends on:

- How complex the system is in itself
- How widespread the environmental factors are
- How fine-grained the goal settings are

These background considerations pave the way for further guiding principles.

Principle 3. Management, in particular EA, has about the same complexity as the system it manages.

This principle should be regarded as a caveat against "EA made easy as a pie" promises. Newcomers to EA frameworks such as TOGAF are sometimes daunted by the complexity of such frameworks and start grumbling about the difficulties in grasping it. But with an eye on the complexity of the system EA is managing, our principle sets the expectations right. Neither the newcomer nor stakeholders like the CIO should expect that EA is simple as 1-2-3.

Principle 4. Complex systems (such as enterprises) cannot be managed at an object level but only at a meta level (management by rules).

Managing a system at the object level means intentionally positioning its elements, planning and constraining their interactions, and giving detailed instructions as to how they must behave and interact in each instance. We learned already from Table 6-1 that complex systems show a certain reluctance to stay faithful to their blueprints and generate emergent structures. Influence at the object level therefore tends to be similar to herding cats.

Ashby's law also gives us a hint as to how complex such a managing instance would have to be. An EA office acting as a direct controller to the IT and enterprise architecture of an organization is far beyond these capabilities, even if it employed the most brilliant brains that money can buy.

Certain levels of indirection and abstraction are inevitable. A viable EA therefore confines itself to cultivating emergent structures by means of abstract rules and relies on the local knowledge of autonomous subunits. Concretizing the rules down to code, server configurations, and other interventions at the object level is left to subunits. The use of abstract rules does not render simpler the overall management of a system—Principle 4 still applies—but it is the only reasonable approach from the top down. In a sense, it leverages the self-management capabilities of subordinated levels to do the job.

Following P. Weill and J. W. Ross (2004), who promote a similar management approach, we call Principle 4 the *Management by Rules* principle.

The final principle we want to set out is based on research by Kauffmann (1993, 1995):

Principle 5. Complex systems (such as enterprises) are best managed at the edge of chaos.

The term *edge of chaos* was coined by Kauffmann and is, simply speaking, the fine line between too little and too much control over a system. Kauffman's work indicates that systems show a sudden transition from a rigid, "frozen" state to chaotic behavior when certain control parameters are increased. Only in between, along the edge-of-chaos line, the systems show an efficient, structured behavior.

Brown and Eisenhardt (1998) have conducted a couple of empirical studies, which indicate that the same principle applies to the way enterprises structure their internal processes. The most efficient EA, it seems, exercises just so much control that the organization operates at the edge of chaos—structured enough not to let the IT slip into anarchy but not so rigid that it is locked into bureaucratic permafrost.

Management capabilities of hierarchies and networks

Ashby's *Law of Requisite Variety* states that "only variety can absorb variety" and thus gives us a lower bound for the complexity of a management organization in relation to the complexity of the managed system and the required accuracy of control. But this management organization can of course be much more complex than needed; it can be an exuberant entanglement of roles, communication channels, and so forth on top of an innocent tiny system.

Furthermore, Ashby's law gives no indication which organizational form of the management apparatus deals *most economically* with complexity. To fill this gap, we end our reflections on complexity with a comparison of the two most prevalent organizational forms: *hierarchical organizations* that rely on a top-down information flow, and *network organizations* that exchange information in a network. The latter structure is based on an exchange of information between peers on equal terms.

How can we estimate their respective capabilities, their parameters of influence, and how they compare? These considerations give a hint of how to position and organize an EA office and are the foundation for our building blocks described in Chapters 7 and 8.

Since we are asking about the *capability* to manage complexity, we will benchmark our organizational forms against a system with *unlimited complexity*: Only then can we examine how far they can go. In a system with limited complexity, the capability of one manager to shape and control things sometimes appears as a threat to other managers, since it diminishes their piece of the cake, their degrees of freedom to shape and control things.

Let's put this managerial jealousy aside by envisioning a system with an unlimited need for management, where the capability of one manager is welcomed by other managers as an opportunity to even shape and control more things. Enterprise architects with a notoriously understaffed team will not find it difficult to envision such a system. In this happy situation, the IT landscape anyway seems

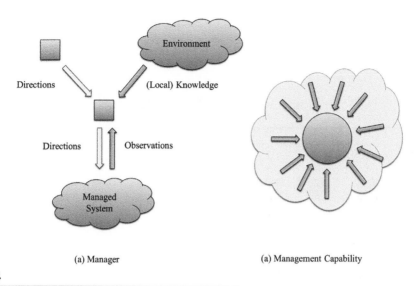

(a) Manager   (a) Management Capability

FIGURE 6-4

Illustrations of the concepts *manager* and *management capability.*

like a Hydra[8]: If you get one part nicely in shape and under control, immediately two other parts pop up that need taming. There's no end to the management capability you need.

What we mean by *manager* here is explained in Figure 6-4. It is an entity that gives design and control directions while taking into account observations from the managed system, local or global knowledge about the environment, and directions from other managers. In this general sense, an enterprise architect must certainly be considered a manager.

The capability of a manager is her ability to constrain the current and future state of affairs. It is her power to shape the system and keep it in certain bounds, as depicted in drawing (b) of Figure 6-4. A manager's capability is proportional to the *variety* of her design and control activities—namely their breadth and effectiveness.

With these definitions in mind, we now take a look at the first prevalent organizational form, the *hierarchy.* Figure 6-5 shows a simple balanced hierarchy with its major construction parameters, the height and branching.

A characteristic feature of a hierarchical management organization is that the management capability depends on the level in the hierarchy—it is a function $C(l)$ of the level. For simplicity let's assume that the capability drops proportionally from one level to the next. In formulas, this can be expressed as:

$$C(l+1) = a \cdot C(l); \text{ where } 0 \leq a \leq 1$$

This implies that $C(l) = a^l \cdot C$, where C denotes the capability of the top manager. We interpret the parameter a as the *degree of autonomy* in the hierarchy. In autocratic hierarchies, this parameter will be close to zero. For example, you might think of an old-fashioned, patriarchic handicraft business

---

[8]*Hydra* is a monster from Greek mythology. It possesses many heads; for each head that is cut off, the beast is able to grow two new ones.

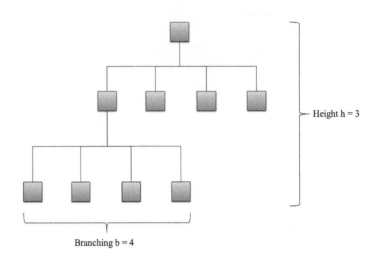

Height h = 3

Branching b = 4

FIGURE 6-5

A simple balanced hierarchy.

where all decisions must eventually be made by the grand old craftsman and owner of the establishment. If you address someone at the journeyman (apprentice) level with a question, he shrugs his shoulders and replies that he first has to ask the master. The subordinates might add a pinch of local knowledge and interpretation to the master's commands, but that's about all of their autonomy.

In modern organizations and more complex enterprises, however, the parameter a will be considerably higher than zero. An abstract reason for giving more autonomy to the subordinated levels is hidden in the formula that adds up the overall management capability of the whole organization:

$$C(H) = C + b \cdot a \cdot C + b^2 \cdot a^2 \cdot C + \ldots + b^h \cdot a^h \cdot C = C \cdot \Sigma_{l=0}^{h} b^l a^l$$

This sum is the best that can be expected from a hierarchy. It makes certain idealistic assumptions, namely that the capability of level l is not diminished by the lower-level $l+1$ and that the different branches of the hierarchy do not issue contradictory directions.

But we learn from this formula that *autonomy pays off*; moreover, it pays off *exponentially*. Figure 6-6 illustrates this concept nicely for seven hierarchy levels and a top capability $C=1$.

As we can see, the capability of an autocratic organization to manage complexity is almost reduced to the mastermind's capability to do so. More local autonomy, on the other hand, soon greatly increases this capability.

But what happens if we make a shift in paradigm from hierarchies to *networks of managers*? It is a popular bias that networks somehow excel at hierarchies. Professionals are, for instance, stunned by the success of loosely organized open-source projects in managing and shaping highly complex software architectures. In these projects—so the argument continues—the design and control are in the hands of the crowd, the network of contributors. Still, they manage a complexity that easily overcharges many rigidly organized companies. Isn't this the magic of the mysterious *network effect*?

Even if we concede that open-source projects are not as loosely organized as people tend to believe, this is a question worth looking at. But an appeal to gut feelings about the omnipotence of social networks, which often is the basis of such discussions, certainly is not sufficient for our purpose. In what

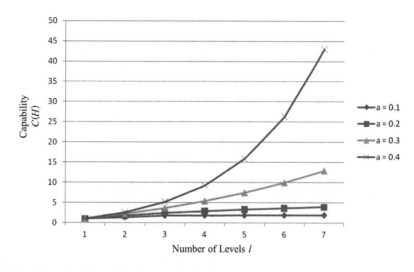

FIGURE 6-6

Exponential growth of the management capability.

follows, we strive for an abstract model of the network effect with regard to management capabilities and identify the parameters it depends on.

What is the management capability of, for instance, a simple network of managers like the one shown in Figure 6-7?

We can only give an abstract answer to this question if we make idealistic assumptions as we did in the case of hierarchies. We assume a well-designed, working network, where none of the

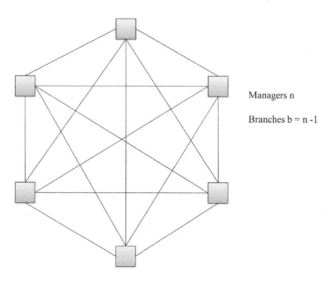

Managers n

Branches b = n -1

FIGURE 6-7

A simple network.

participating managers is messing up the other manager's business, for example, by issuing contradictory directions.

If there is no network at all and the managers work independently without overlapping responsibilities and without insight into what others are doing, the overall capability simply adds up to $C(N) = n \cdot C$. But on the basis of well-functioning communication channels, managers can synchronize their own directions with what they know about the other's intentions.

On this ground, it is conclusive that a manager's capability to design and control a system is increased by the awareness of what the other managers aim at and plan. Furthermore, it is not altogether unrealistic to assume that this increase is proportional to the number of peers a manager is able to synch up with. There might be an upper limit for how much information about others' intentions any one manager can absorb, but let's set this aside for a moment.

The capability of a single manager can therefore plausibly be quantified by a term $C + (n-1) \cdot a \cdot C$, where the parameter a this time does not reflect the local autonomy, as in the case of hierarchies, but how well aligned are the different nodes of the network. The total capability of the network would then add up to:

$$C(N) = n \cdot (C + (n - 1) \cdot a \cdot C) = n \cdot C + n \cdot (n - 1) \cdot C \cdot a$$

The second term of the formula, $n \cdot (n-1) \cdot C \cdot a$, quantifies the network effect and is just a variant of *Metcalfe's law*. This law, named after the inventor of the Ethernet protocol, Robert Metcalfe, states that the value of a network increases by $n2 \approx n \cdot (n - 1)$ with the number n of members. With these two formulas at hand, we can conclude:

The capability of a hierarchy of managers to cope with complexity is significantly lower than that of a corresponding network.

The argument can be given in a single line, keeping in mind that $n = \sum_{l=0}^{h} b^l$:

$$C(H) = C \cdot \Sigma_{l=0}^{h} b^l a^l < C \cdot n < n \cdot C + n \cdot (n - 1) \cdot C \cdot a = C(N)$$

Metcalfe's law was a hot topic during the Internet bubble because investment gamblers misinterpreted it as a "natural law" predicting quadratic revenue growth from linearly increasing investments. Recent criticism points out that the value of a network grows more modestly by $n \cdot log(n)$ (Briscoe, Odlyzko, and Tilly, 2006).

The argument is based on yet another law, *Zipf's law*. The linguist George Kingsley Zipf sorted English language words by frequency of occurrence and discovered that frequency approximately decreases in a harmonic sequence *1, 1/2, 1/3, 1/4, 1/5,* and so forth. This observation turned out to be transferrable to many other statistical phenomena: Whenever we sort a collection by size or value, the distribution is stunningly close to some variant of the harmonic sequence.

This transfer might work for the contact list of a networker, too: It is indeed plausible that not all partners on this list provide equal value to the networker, and Briscoe and his coauthors claim that sorting the list from very important persons (VIPs) to marginal random contacts resembles the harmonic distribution. Hence, if we accept this hypothesis, the network effect is no longer measured by the quadratic term $n \cdot (n - 1) \cdot C \cdot a$ but by a more moderately growing, logarithmic formula, namely:[9]

---

[9]This is because the harmonic series $\Sigma_{k=1}^{\infty} \frac{1}{k}$ converges to $log(n) + E$, where $E = 0.5772\ldots$ is the Euler constant.

$$n \cdot \Sigma_{k=1}^{n-1} \frac{c \cdot a}{k} \approx n \cdot (\log(n) + 0.5) \cdot C \cdot a$$

But even this damped growth outperforms the hierarchical capability $C(H)$, and the same argument works for all kinds of *positive* network effects. The comparison theorem therefore holds true unless we assume that networking diminishes a manager's capability C to influence the state of affairs or that a hierarchy in fact increases this capability.

There are other indications still that networks might be more efficient than hierarchies. Let's go back to the notion of an enterprise as a participant in a coevolution process, competing for market share (just as species compete for habitats to ensure their survival).

The long-term survival of an enterprise is determined by its ability to continuously search for peaks in the volatile fitness landscape formed by itself and its competitors. This search means nothing else but a constant adaptation of business portfolio, organization structure, and strategy in the coevolution process. The enterprise's survival in the market follows the same basic laws that govern the survival or extinction of a species.

One of the key factors determining a system's adaptability seems to be the "connectivity" within the system's internal structure (Kauffman, 1995; Bak, 1996; Lucas, 2005). If the agents within the system are insufficiently connected, the system is too cool and static. At the other end of the spectrum, with too much connectivity the system overheats and slips into chaos.

The agents within an enterprise are essentially its employees. A network structure between them allows for a flexible tweaking of the connectivity, depending on the problem at hand. In comparison, in a strictly hierarchical organizational structure the connectivity cannot be varied and adapted so easily.

There is yet another, although related, angle to this idea. Hierarchical organizations are efficient at implementing a centrally devised strategy. In evolutionary terms, where adaptation by self-transformation is paramount, this is often only the second best option. Kauffman (1995) has shown that an internal organizational structure in "patches," each independently optimizing its fitness, usually works better for the whole system when the fitness landscape is rugged and volatile. A network structure is a more natural implementation of such patches than a strict hierarchy. We will deal more closely with concepts for such "local independence" in Chapter 7, "Toward Pragmatism: Lean and Agile EA."

It is time to draw a bottom line to this notable dose of theory and formula work. Did we say that an organization of architects should have a network structure rather than a hierarchy? Not quite, since a network has considerable downsides in comparison to a hierarchy. A hierarchy, for instance, has the advantage that management directions reliably reach the ground after passing all hierarchical levels. In a network, directions can oscillate between managers for an undetermined time. That's the reason that systems in which reaction times are paramount are better off with hierarchies.

Furthermore, working networks are apparently more difficult to build. With a hierarchy, it seems to be a lot easier to reach a noncontradictory, nonoverlapping set of roles and responsibilities; at least the track record of organizing firms hierarchical is longer and has more proven practices at hand.

This list of downsides can probably be continued, and you may find good reasons in this list to decide for a hierarchical EA office. But eventually we have to concede that there indisputably remains one important advantage of a network: It is more capable of managing complexity. Lots of people share a gut feeling that if it gets really complex, we have to employ networks to do the magic. This is more than a gut feeling, as we have seen in the above mathematical deduction.

The EA dashboard as a yardstick for EA effectiveness

"Everything exists": That is one extreme. "Everything doesn't exist": That is a second extreme. Avoiding these two extremes, the Buddha teaches the Dhamma via the middle path.

—Buddha

In the following two chapters, we will lay out our set of building blocks to strengthen collaborative elements in EA. In preparation, let's consider how to gauge the applicability of our measures. We have no case studies available to prove their effectiveness, but we can offer a simple yardstick against which each proposal can be valued.

Reducing a long list of potential EA problems to merely a handful of criteria will make it easier to judge if and how a specific measure might have an effect. For this purpose, we go back to the four dimensions of EA complexity introduced in Chapter 1. To recap, the four dimensions are *Perspective*, *Governance*, *Strategy*, and *Transformation*.

In each of these dimensions, there is an interplay between chaos and order. The most effective mode of operation is to strike a balance between the two extremes and to move along the *edge of chaos* (see Figure 6-8) that separates them. The underlying assumption is that EA will work best if the enterprise architects find the optimal middle ground. This is the best compromise between a top-down, long-term-oriented EA style and a collaborative bottom-up, evolutionary mode.

This assumption is backed up by research results from management theory. The advent of the first Internet boom, around the millennium, has triggered a lot of research in this area. Markets and competition in the IT area changed more quickly than ever before. Companies rose from startups to multibillion-dollar operations within a decade, or virtually disappeared in the same period, or underwent dramatic transitions to survive. Strategy had evolved into a deciding asset.

Our concept is primarily based on the ideas of Brown and Eisenhardt (1998).[10] They took up the *edge of chaos* notion introduced by the evolutionary biologist Kauffman (1995) and applied it

Chaos   *The Edge of Chaos*   **Order**

FIGURE 6-8

Maneuvering at the edge of chaos.

---

[10]Many authors express similar concepts—for instance, Schwartz (1996) or Freedman (2000). The guiding theme of these books is that successful strategies in a complex, volatile, and unforeseeable environment should allow for a certain amount of chaos in favor of increased flexibility.

to the business world. Brown and Eisenhardt's basic message, derived from their research on selected industry case studies, is (somewhat pointedly) that an organization fares best when it accepts a certain amount of—but not too much—disorder in various dimensions of business activities.

The EA Dashboard as depicted in Figure 6-9 has been inspired by their taxonomy, with the original categories adapted to the more specialized terms of EA. The structural dimensions *Perspective* and *Governance* are summed up under *Edge of Chaos*, whereas the more time-oriented dimensions *Strategy* and *Transformation* are subsumed under *Edge of Time*. This is a related term introduced by Brown and Eisenhardt to describe an organization's take on *change processes* such as modernization and future visions. Otherwise, there is no semantic difference between edge of chaos and edge of time. In both cases, the extreme positions in the Dashboard's gauges are exactly the EA caricatures introduced in Chapter 1.

Being at the edge of chaos involves staying clear of the extremes. Structure and processes are strong enough to provide guidance, whereas on the other hand they are still slight enough to have flexibility and not to consume too much management attention. In a similar fashion, navigating at the edge of time involves having the right pace of change for transformations and the right amount of foresight. EA reaches a state of optimal efficiency when it operates in the unstable equilibrium of the "edge of X" middle-ground position.

In the subsequent Tables 6.2 through 6.5, the criteria for judging an EA organization in each dimension are listed in detail. Taking these criteria, the individual position of the gauge hand can be determined.

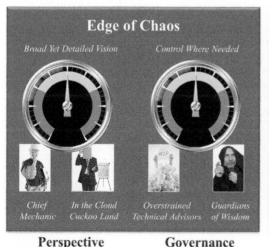

FIGURE 6-9

The EA Dashboard.

Table 6-2 EA Dashboard: Criteria in the Perspective Dimension

	Perspective		
	Too Low	**About Right**	**Too High**
	In the Chief Mechanic's Workshop	*Broad Yet Detailed View*	*Living in Cloud Cuckoo Land*
Focus	Technology focused, no broad vision	Right balance between big picture and technical reality on the ground	Ivory tower of concepts and strategy
Organizational setup	Directly part of the IT organization, or at least strongly connected with it	Independent organizational unit, short reporting line to CIO	Anywhere
Network	Primarily among IT crowd, few network ties with business	Equally well connected with the business, IT, and higher management	Main connections to higher-level management
Team composition	Technical experts	Mix of experienced business experts, IT architects, and go-betweens at home in both worlds	Management consultants

Table 6-3 EA Dashboard: Criteria in the Governance Dimension

	Governance		
	Too Weak	**About Right**	**Too Rigid**
	The Overstrained Technical Advisors	*Control Where Needed*	*The Guardians of Wisdom*
Rules	"Break rules" culture in architecture, standards are ignored	Concentration on a few guiding architecture principles that are kept at all times	Many standards, blindly followed
Processes	Very few or no EA processes in place	A few core EA processes that are universally accepted and continuously revised and updated	Comprehensive and rigid EA process framework
Communication	Random communication—everybody talking to everybody	Continuous communication, formal and informal, between stakeholders (business to EA, EA to projects, etc.)	Communication only along narrow and strictly defined channels
Role of the enterprise architect	Mere advisor, only formal but little de-facto authority, ownership, or accountability	Guide, mentor, auditor, with healthy amount of formal authority	Intimidating enforcer of rules

Table 6-4 EA Dashboard: Criteria in the Strategy Dimension

	Strategy		
	Too Myopic	**About Right**	**Too Far-Reaching**
	Sweeping Up the Change Requests	*Balanced and Flexible*	*A Deep Look into the Crystal Ball*
Vision	No vision at all	Multiple parallel scenarios to remain flexible, with many inexpensive pilots as part of the strategy	One single and firm vision for the future, based on belief and speculation rather than research
Planning	No planning for application portfolio and strategic initiatives at all	Planning for foreseeable time horizon only, continuously revised	Meticulous planning over a long time horizon, with little deviation from plan
Focus	Reactive mode, focus entirely on today's problems	Balancing attention between present and future	Proactive mode, intense focus on future, ignoring the present

Table 6-5 EA Dashboard: Criteria in the Transformation Dimension

	Transformation		
	Too Slow	**About Right**	**Too Fast**
	The Ever-Growing Backlog	*Steady Evolution*	*The Permanent Construction Site*
Renewal	Mainly maintenance of existing systems	Applications are replaced according to consistent criteria, but without haste	Applications thrown out in rapid succession
Enhancements	Functional enhancements mainly by layering existing applications	Design of new capabilities decided case by case, either by new applications or by enhancement of existing ones	Functional enhancements mainly by creating new systems
Outsourcing	New systems are developed and run externally, own IT staff concentrates on existing systems	Outsourcing is spread across old and new applications	Own IT staff does only "fancy" new development, existing systems are outsourced
Readiness to take risks	Conservative, focus on ensuring operability	Moderate, cautiously taking risks when needed	High, aggressively taking risks

The EA Dashboard uses findings from management theory to provide a measuring instrument for EA groups and the building blocks of collaborative EA. In subsequent chapters we will indicate by the Dashboard in which dimension of EA complexity the respective proposal can have an effect. This way we will provide an easy-to-use application guide for our building blocks.

Toward Pragmatism: Lean and Agile EA

CONTENT

The Architecture Factory: Applying Lean and Agile Methods to EA 160
    Lean and Agile Principles as Facilitators for the Architecture Factory 162
    Definition of a Lean and Agile EA 163
Lean and Agile Principles 165
    Team-Driven and Flexible: Agile Software Development 165
    Learning from Mass Production: Lean Software Development 174
    Lean and Agile: Parallels and Differences 180
Building Block 1: Get Rid of Waste by Streamlining Architecture Processes 182
    The Seven Wastes of EA 183
    Value Stream Analysis Tools for EA 193
    Transition to a Lean and Agile EA Organization 203
    Summing It Up: Assessment by the EA Dashboard 205
Building Block 2: Involve All Stakeholders by Interlocking Architecture Scrums 205
    An Agile EA Project 206
    Scrum Patterns for EA 209
    Summing It Up: Assessment by the EA Dashboard 215
Building Block 3: Practice Iterative Architecture Through EA Kanban 216
    Agile EA Requirements Management 217
    An EA Kanban Board Using TOGAF ADM 222
    Synchronization with Implementation Projects 230
    Summing It Up: Assessment by the EA Dashboard 233

So far we have taken a good look at the state of EA today. We have analyzed both the benefits and the shortcomings of contemporary patterns in EA. Enterprise architecture is a sound, sensible, and necessary step for a large company to stay competitive and make best use of its IT investments. However, the current way of actually creating an EA, enterprise architecture management, is somehow trapped between the Scylla of over-formalization and the Charybdis of under-empowerment.[1]

---

[1]Scylla and Charybdis are a pair of monsters guarding a narrow strait in Greek methodology. Sailors passing the strait would inevitably come within reach of one of the two. It should be noted that Scylla is described as a sea monster with four eyes and six heads, with three rows of sharp teeth each, which makes it a suitable image for over-formalization. Charybdis, on the other hand, is an all-mouth creature swallowing and belching water, creating vicious whirlpools able to suck in whole ships—and certainly also enterprise architects with no real influence in the organization.

So, what can help in this dilemma? The goal of a well-functioning EA is worth pursuing, but the path is riddled with obstacles and ambiguities. *Pragmatism* is one way out this dilemma. The word pragmatism is derived from the Greek word *pragma*, meaning act or deed. Pragmatism is "a practical approach to problems and affairs" (Merriam-Webster, 2011). Being pragmatic means stripping intellectual concepts down to their core so that they become mere tools for achieving simple, concrete goals.

PRAGMATISM

The Meaning of Pragmatism

The online dictionary Merriam-Webster lists *pragmatic* as the second most frequently looked-up word.[2] Evidently, pragmatism is both a popular and a confusing notion in our time. It is an appealing concept in a world of increasing complexity, a shortcut with both opportunities and risks.

A prominent example for brutally pragmatic behavior can be found in ancient Greek history. According to mythology, reign over Asia was promised to the man who could untie a sacred knot in the ancient town of Gordium. Alexander the Great (356–323 BC), conqueror of Persia, didn't even attempt to unbind the knot, but just cut it with his sword.

On a meta level, one could say that Alexander disposed of the concept of "untying knots" since it was irrelevant to his agenda (giving a demonstration of his willingness and ability to rule over Asia) and concentrated on the core idea of having the knot loose to fulfill the ancient promise. In general, *cutting Gordian knots* relates a violent act that may be justified in some cases and less so in others.

A caveat for pragmatism in EA, with its inherent long-term orientation, is the trade-off between agility on one hand and stable planning on the other. How pragmatic can EA actually be without losing the important qualities of any kind of enterprise-level processes: repeatability and measurability? This chapter will attempt to find a satisfactory answer to this question.

A natural approach to unloading some ballast from EA and cutting through knots not worth untying by hand can be found in the principles of lean and agile software development. Cornerstones of these methodologies are reduced process overhead, people empowerment, and a strong focus on deliverables. Lean and agile methods can help make EA more down-to-earth, efficient, lightweight, and flexible, without neglecting the traditional qualities, processes, and tasks of EA work. Basically, this approach puts the first two of our three central maxims from the previous chapter into practice:

- *Establish a lean set of processes and rules* instead of overloading the stakeholders with bureaucratic processes and unsolicited artifacts
- *Adopt evolutionary problem solving* instead of blueprinting the whole future rigidly on a drawing board

---

The architecture factory: Applying lean and agile methods to EA

To avoid one misunderstanding right from the start: We do *not* assume that all IT development projects are executed according to the lean or agile methodology. Our approach to enterprise architecture works with waterfall projects just as well as with agile or lean projects. The proposal we are making here is to *apply lean and agile principles to the EA processes themselves*, irrespective of the methodology used in the downstream software development projects.

---

[2]Looked up June 29, 2011. The list ranks retrieval counts during a period of four months.

EA as practiced today has all the traits of a well-developed IT profession—methodologies, frameworks, tools—but it lacks an effective implementation and integration into the enterprise context. EA should make sure that architecture is not an art practiced in the seclusion of the enterprise architect's study room. It should also ensure that the enterprise architect doesn't turn into the IT handyman, fixing the odd problem here and there. The vision for a well-positioned EA group is a scalable and cost-efficient delivery organization for architectural services that operates in a fast and flexible way. In other words, it should work like an *architecture factory*.

The concept of a "software factory" came up at the end of 1960, when frustration about the error-prone and painstakingly slow ways of software programming was on the rise. The idea was to introduce to software creation a semi-automated assembly process and techniques from modern mass production (Bemer, 1968). The original vision of a fully automated software production process has not come true. However, the factory notion, maximizing effectiveness while minimizing time and costs, has diffused into mainstream thinking in the IT community. Characteristic properties of a factory include reliability, reproducibility of results, a sensible division of labor, defined supplier and delivery channels, the use of standardized tools, and so forth.

What kind of factory is meant here? It should be clear that architecture creation should not and cannot be turned into a fully automated process. It is nonsense to strive for a full-fledged factory model where human architects are reduced to performing a limited set of standard activities in a standardized environment. In fact, such a goal might have brought EA into its poor shape in some enterprises.

The most appropriate vision for an EA factory is a semi-industrialized shop, dedicated to craft manufacturing. If we were talking about car manufacturing, the architecture factory would resemble the small, highly specialized shop for producing high-end sports cars rather than the huge plant producing 500,000 compact cars per year.

In German, there is a subtle but clear difference between *Fabrik* (factory) and *Manufaktur* (manufactory), whereas in English the two terms are synonyms. A *Fabrik* is a shop for fully automated mass production; a *Manufaktur* is a small and customized shop where high-end products are created using a high amount of craftsmanship. The Volkswagen Phaeton, their top-of-the-line model, is built in a so-called *Gläserne Manufaktur* in Dresden, Germany. This is a brand-new showcase plant with wooden floors and huge windows, where skilled workers apply a lot of manual customization. Since the word *factory* sometimes has a negative connotation, our architecture factory should be understood here in the sense of a German *Manufaktur*.

In the ideal architecture factory, the enterprise architects and other stakeholders in EA are highly skilled individuals who work in a custom-tailored environment. The factory supports their effectiveness and creativity via lean processes, guidelines, and tools. Most major consulting firms operate with a comparable model in the EA consulting domain. EA is run as a dedicated practice with experienced consultants and analysts, a carefully nurtured knowledge base, and a formal engagement model and delivery process.[3]

The production tools of the EA factory are EA frameworks, maturity models, processes, governance models, and so forth. They just need to be organized in a "sufficiently factory-like" manner. This means again avoiding the extremes. There should be neither too much nor too little of a "factory

---

[3]Whether in-house EA groups should be organized in a similar way, too, or just be a regular division of the IT department is a frequently debated topic (see, e.g., Saha, 2011). The consensus seems to be that EA is better positioned as a dedicated entity, with some independence from IT management.

notion" within EA. Too much of it leads to the bureaucracy trap of overregulation, overdecomposition of workflows, and overstandardization of tools and activities. An EA organization with too few factory characteristics, on the other hand, neglects the overall organization structure. It tends to be unstructured, poorly organized, and unpredictable and leaves each enterprise architect in his own private silo, coping with an overwhelmingly complex enterprise and IT environment around them.

Lean and agile principles as facilitators for the architecture factory

How can EA accomplish the tightrope walk between too much and too little factory affinity? Here we can learn from software engineering in general. The lean and agile methodologies have introduced certain new principles to traditional software development. They have replaced the inflexible, ponderous waterfall model with a more lightweight, efficient, and human-centric approach: lean and agile software development methods.

Talking of factory models again: The waterfall model is like a Taylorian factory—many processes, strict division of labor, strong decomposition of tasks, organization of the software creation process in a sequential assembly line. Above all: The waterfall approach requires strict up-front planning to avoid changes in the complex production machinery later on.

Lean and agile methodologies have formulated their antithesis: welcoming change, creating and planning incrementally, and focusing on structured human interaction instead of channeled reporting lines. At the same time, lean and agile methods fully subscribe to the factory notion, too. They do not strive to abolish organizational structures and revert to the software-developing "noble savage"[4] working on her own. Lean and agile methods introduce a reduced and efficient organization to produce large and complex software systems. As they focus on the highly skilled individual interacting with her peers, their factory notion is very close to the craft manufacturing shop we formulated previously as an ideal model for EA.

So, let lean and agile principles create the same kind of factory for EA if they can do it so successfully for software development in general. The traditional EA has waterfall roots and a strong tendency toward its methods. Barry Boehm described the waterfall pattern[5] as a reversal of the Agile Manifesto (Beck et al., 2001). Malicious tongues could interpret it as a description of contemporary EA:

- *Processes and tools over individuals and interactions*
- *Comprehensive documentation over working software*
- *Contract negotiation over customer collaboration*
- *Following a plan over responding to change*

If lean and agile are the antithesis of a waterfall, they can also be a suitable tool to make EA less waterfall-prone. The ultimate goal of a lean and agile architecture factory is highly skilled and creative yet at the same time industrialized architecture creation. Its processes are streamlined and optimized—but in a pragmatic way, by concentrating on the essential qualities of architectural work, avoiding an overdose of structure and regulations.

---

[4]The noble savage, often wrongly attributed to Jean-Jacques Rousseau (1712–1778), is an idealized pre-society native who has preserved the original human qualities, usually referred to in the context of civilization criticism.

[5]Quoted according to Larman and Vodde, 2009. Boehm gave this statement during a keynote speech at the *Extreme Programming and Agile Processes* 2006 conference in Finland. To be precise, he related it to the way a traditional CMMI auditor would judge a project, but it can be generalized to the waterfall approach in general.

Adepts and critics of lean and agile methods could argue that these methods, or at least their practitioners, often show some fundamentalist, near-religious traits. Can they really be applied in a pragmatic way to an enterprise domain like EA? Indeed, both lean and agile methodologies worship a utopia to some extent.

In agile methods, it is the perfect socialism of a team free of hierarchy and politics. Agility comes from a history of "organizational anarchists" (Beck et al., 2001). This bears the risk of a clash with the rather conservative enterprise culture. And of course, the agile community is not free of self-deception and hypocrisy.[6]

Lean software development, on the other hand, sometimes shows an uncritical worship of the "ideal company," into which Toyota is often superelevated.[7] This surely obscures the reflections how lean methods can be applied to the rather humble and chaotic enterprises that you find in real life.

So, it seems appropriate to take any promises of silver bullets in the lean and agile methodologies with a grain of salt. We will use the ideas from both areas like a toolbox: Not every tool fits everywhere. In the end, stripped from their ideological elements, many lean and agile practices boil down to plain common sense. We will see that they can be applied in a fruitful way to make EA more pragmatic.

Definition of a lean and agile EA

It is now time to define what a lean and agile EA looks like and how the vision of a pragmatic architecture factory can be achieved. Lean and agile concepts overlap to some extent. Therefore, we can cherry-pick the best of both worlds for the EA field.

LEAN AND AGILE ARCHITECTURE FACTORY
Building Blocks for the Lean and Agile Architecture Factory
The following building blocks form a lean and agile architecture factory, as shown here:

No.	Building Block	Goal
1	*Get rid of waste by streamlining architecture processes.*	Values the sparse time of enterprise IT stakeholders by focusing on lean processes with as little management overhead as possible.
2	*Involve all stakeholders by interlocking architecture scrums.*	Makes sure that all stakeholders are involved by focusing on structured human interaction as a main channel of information flow.
3	*Practice iterative architecture through EA Kanban.*	Welcomes change, favors iterative design over large-scale, up-front planning, and supports this approach by tools and methods.

We will describe the lean and agile terms used in this definition (waste, scrum, Kanban) in the subsequent introduction to lean and agile concepts.

---

[6]Philip Kruchten, one of the fathers of the Rational Unified Process and at home in both the enterprise and the agile world, lists 20 "elephants in the room" in a blog post (2011)—issues that are willfully ignored due to ideological reasons.
[7]It is peculiar to note that, in contrast to this popular image, Osono et al. (2008) paints Toyota as a complex and often self-contradictory company.

Building Block 1: Get rid of waste by streamlining architecture processes takes up an essential element of lean methodologies, the elimination of "waste," to analyze the EA processes for unnecessary bureaucracy, overprocessing, delays, and so forth. By removing such wasteful activities, we can streamline EA processes.

Again, the lean quality of adopting a top-down, holistic perspective that is strictly goal oriented helps strip off needless ballast from the EA processes. One example of avoidance of waste is just-in-time modeling (modeling not more than is required at this moment), which is inspired by the lean idea of avoiding in-process inventory.

The lean approach has been tailored toward complex, repeating activities that are to be optimized. EA has a lot of them. Lean principles can be used to streamline top-down decision-making or design processes, such as the creation of an EA vision, an IT strategy, or the design of a complex IT transformation. Rule (2010) describes the effect of lean management in the following way:

> *Being effective is (. . .) achieved by developing your organization's ability to deliver its strategic goals—consistently, repeatably, predictably, efficiently. This requires intelligent and engaged management of the end-to-end value stream.*

Therefore, Building Block 1 combines the essential lean quality of "optimizing the whole," together with its value stream concept, with the scrums and iterations of agile development.

Building Block 2: Involve all stakeholders by interlocking architecture scrums makes sure to include all stakeholders on a regular basis. It forms a kind of "clocked" factory approach to producing EA artifacts. Agile is an iterative way to design a system—whether a house, a production plant, a software system, or a whole enterprise.

Being iterative is the canonical approach for an architect, since architecture is exploratory in nature, especially due to the immature and evolving nature of both business and IT today. This way, the enterprise architect is not overburdened by an up-front mental picture of the complete system in her mind. Instead, she can focus on the structure and problems of the more nearby deliveries and trust in the ability of selective refactoring later on, in the sense of an intentional architecture as coined by Leffingwell (2011). The use of sprints and architecture scrum teams introduces a regular heartbeat to architecture work and allows for a more iterative work mode in which information is shared regularly and early.

In our building blocks, agile principles come into the picture when EA is realized to deliver in a timely way and to get everyone on board. To put it simply, agile methods are good for "doing." They have a strong focus on human interaction, which is a very important part of EA, and provide a number of practices in structuring that interaction. In addition, agile methods have been designed to welcome ad hoc change, helping to make EA more pragmatic and flexible.

Flexibility also plays an important role in *Building Block 3: Practice iterative architecture through EA Kanban*, where architecture backlogs and an EA Kanban board are introduced as a tool for prioritization and focusing on nearby deliveries. We will show that agile concepts for different granularities of requirement definition are well matched to the architecture layering and partitioning defined in EA frameworks.

TOGAF is taken as an example in Building Block 3 to demonstrate how a well-established EA framework can easily be adapted to an iterative work model. This way, the central agile notion of continuous integration is applied to EA. It allows the enterprise architects to deliver intermediate results—strategies, visions, guidelines, and plans—in a flexible and lightweight manner to their recipients. EA work can be tuned to prefer *communication over perfection* when it comes to modeling.

The building blocks are of an exemplary nature. We do not claim to have discovered the silver bullet of wisdom that can save EA once and for all. These are just effective tools that we have used a good deal in our IT careers and that make a lot of sense in architectural processes as well. We will outline them in detail in subsequent sections. For now, let's first take a more detailed look at lean and agile methodologies. The next section will give you a backdrop against which to value our building blocks again. If you are already an adept practitioner of these methods, feel free to skip this discussion and jump directly to the detailed building-block descriptions.

Lean and agile principles

Lean and agile project practices have gained in importance and acceptance over the past decade. They are no longer a playground for innovators and early adopters. When it comes to agility, even conservative organizations express their interest, since there is a solid track record of successful agile projects in the industry. The inherent shortcomings of the waterfall approaches and the accelerated business dynamics simply force IT departments to rethink their traditional ways of software development.

Therefore, agile methods have long left the niche area of garage-based startups and state-of-the-art consultancies and have created a footprint in the traditional world of enterprise IT. Lean software development, on the other hand, has its roots in the Toyota production system. Originally a set of principles designed for optimizing a car-manufacturing process, lean methods have been very successfully applied to general business processes, specifically software development.

Although coming from quite different origins altogether, lean and agile techniques are strongly related. The lean approach, originating from being a simple and consistent rule set for a huge, well-oiled machine (the car factory), borrows many of its practical software development methods from the agile approach.

In contrast, agile methods have their roots in self-organizing teams who designed a pragmatic process that suited their idea of productive software better than the heavyweight waterfall approach did. By simplifying the production environment, agile methods introduced "lean" thinking to software development before the term became a hallmark of its own within the IT community.

In the following sections, we take a closer look at lean and agile methods separately to understand their origins, benefits, and shortcomings. It should be noted that this is not an in-depth description of lean and agile methods; rather, it is an introduction for a reader not accustomed to these methodologies to understand the later discussions, when we apply lean and agile thoughts to EA itself.[8]

We will also analyze the degree of overlap between the two approaches. Finally, we will define our concept of a lean and agile EA, where the lean and agile parts can help make such a waterfall-prone and long-term-oriented area as EA more pragmatic and flexible.

Team-driven and flexible: Agile software development

The traditional waterfall approach in software development assumes that a computer system can be designed and planned in advance, whatever the system's complexity might be—even if the implementation time spans several months or even years. However, the effort to capture all requirements of a

---

[8]You don't need any pre-knowledge of lean and agile to follow the coming sections, just a general familiarity with software development practices. If you would still like a more thorough introduction to the topic, our personal favorite among the many great books on the topic is Mike Cohn's *Succeeding with Agile: Software Development Using Scrum* (2009) and the Poppendiecks' first book of their Lean series, *Lean Software Development: An Agile Toolkit* (2003).

moderately complex application up front, by way of a paperwork exercise, is enormous. Despite all attempts, one usually misses the expectations of the users and stakeholders.

To ask a user to rigidly and exhaustively define how she would like to work with a new application two years from now means asking too much. Something similar can be said about the up-front design of such an application. Everyone in the software business has stories to tell how far the specification can deviate from the executable software system, if the planning lead time is too long. It should be understood that a long planning lead time is not the root cause of the problem, it is just its symptom. Essentially, planning time is an indicator of complexity. The reason for integration failure doesn't lie in the disturbances and changing requirements during that phase. Even without them, it is simply beyond our human capabilities to accurately sketch a complex system with some million lines of code entirely at the drawing board.

The consequence is often a big-bang integration failure when the first end-to-end tests are run. Or, even if the original requirements have actually been met, the business situation has changed, rendering the original design useless. A particularly nice example of this phenomenon is the Safeguard Ballistic Missile Defense System, which was developed for the US army between 1969 and 1975 in an effort of over 5,400 person years. It stayed operational for merely 133 days after six years of development. The system had been overtaken by both political and technical developments: By the time it was finished, the ABM disarmament treaty with the Soviet Union had been signed, and the new Soviet missiles had actually become faster than the anti-missile-missiles (Broad, 2000).

These shortcomings of traditional software development practices triggered the creation of the agile development methodology. As the failure of projects completed using the waterfall approach became commonplace, the frustrations among IT practitioners made them embrace agile practices in their work culture.

Agile methods, in contrast to the waterfall model, accept the limited capability of humans to envision complex systems and their interactions with the environment. Agility continuously delivers working software to users and stakeholders and welcomes them saying, "This is not quite how we want it!" The short delivery and feedback cycle supports an experimental capturing of the user's true requirements.

Agile ideas in software development have been around for longer than one might think (Larman and Basili, 2003). After some theoretical work by Walther Shewhart and W. Edwards Deming in the 1930s and 1940s, NASA (always at the leading edge of innovation in software development) started using an iterative development model in some projects in the 1950s. From 1970 onward, incremental and iterative methods, backed up by the occasional lighthouse project, were discussed among software professionals. Ironically, even the inventor of the waterfall concept, Winston Royce, strongly leaned toward an iterative approach for certain project types.

However, only since the mid-1990s have agile techniques become a force to be reckoned with in software development. They owe a good part of their success to the perception that they are something like an "anti-establishment" approach to software development, going against the traditional waterfall model. As many large IT projects suffer from the inherent shortcomings of the waterfall model, the agile approach received more and more attention.

AGILE MANIFESTO

The Four Values of the Agile Manifesto

- Individuals and interactions over processes and tools
- Working software over comprehensive documentation
- Customer collaboration over contract negotiation
- Responding to change over following a plan

  That is, while there is value in the items on the right, we value the items on the left more. (Quoted from Beck et al., 2001.)

AGILE MANIFESTO

The 12 Principles Behind the Agile Manifesto

1. Our highest priority is to satisfy the customer through early and continuous delivery of valuable software.
2. Welcome changing requirements, even late in development. Agile processes harness change for the customer's competitive advantage.
3. Deliver working software frequently, from a couple of weeks to a couple of months, with preference for the shorter timescale.
4. Businesspeople and developers must work together daily throughout the project.
5. Build projects around motivated individuals. Give them the environment and support they need, and trust them to get the job done.
6. The most efficient and effective method of conveying information to and within a development team is face-to-face conversation.
7. Working software is the primary measure of progress.
8. Agile processes promote sustainable development. The sponsors, developers, and users should be able to maintain a constant pace indefinitely.
9. Continuous attention to technical excellence and good design enhances agility.
10. Simplicity—the art of maximizing the amount of work not done—is essential.
11. The best architectures, requirements, and designs emerge from self-organizing teams.
12. At regular intervals, the team reflects on how to become more effective, then tunes and adjusts its behavior accordingly.

   (Quoted from Beck et al., 2001.)

The term *agile* was coined in the Agile Manifesto (Beck et al., 2001). This set of values and principles was formulated by a group of people who, coming from different backgrounds, had grown tired of ineffective, heavyweight processes. Agile is an umbrella term for various similar development approaches. The Agile Manifesto expresses their essence in four key values and 12 principles.

The 12 principles of the Agile Manifesto outline ways to implement the four key values. There is no such thing as *the* agile practices. Agility comprises many variants: scrum, XP, feature-driven development, and many more. Elaborating on them goes far beyond the scope of this book and is well enough captured in numerous standard works such as Cohn (2009) or Shore and Warden (2008). However, there are common denominators across all agile flavors. In the following subsection, we take a closer look at those practices and attempt an impartial view into their benefits and shortcomings.

AGILE GLOSSARY

A Short List of Core Agile Terms

When you take a closer look at the agile methodology, you are bound to meet the some terms over and over again. Therefore, we list them here (in alphabetical order) as a kind of "agile glossary":

- *Continuous integration.* Continuous integration means a tool-supported automation of software build and test execution, which is repeated in continuous loops. This way, a noncompiling code, or code that causes tests to fail, is noticed with only a minimal delay after checking it into the source code management system.
- *Iteration.* A development cycle, usually between two and four weeks long.
- *Pair programming.* Two developers team up to develop code together in front of only one computer. This practice stems from XP.
- *Product owner.* A role in agile development, acting as a representative of the project customer.
- *Refactoring.* Restructuring the code without changing the system's external behavior.
- *Scrum team.* A team of agile developers, typically between 6 and 10 members.
- *Scrum master.* A team role, responsible for moderating (not managing!) the team and protecting it from outside disturbances.
- *Sprint.* A sprint is one iteration. The precise content of an iteration is planned only at the beginning of the sprint.

What is the agile methodology good for? The main practices, with benefits and shortcomings

The most well-known characteristic of agility is its *iterative, time-boxed approach*. Software is developed in cycles of a fixed length, most often two or three weeks long. It is an iron rule that an iteration is not prolonged. Instead, if a feature cannot be completed in that timeframe, it is dropped and taken up again in the subsequent cycle. The goal of an iteration is always a feature that is completely "done." In development, this means a piece of software that is fully tested and can be shipped.

This iterative approach, on one hand, helps in shaping the users' and stakeholders' requirements. A customer representative is present in all major agile meetings. The customer is not only invited to, but even *responsible* for, giving his input to each iteration planning. On the other hand, the short cycles are a way to respond to the accelerated changes in the business and technology environment. This allows development projects with a time horizon of two or three years to catch up with these changes along the way at much shorter time intervals.

Agile thinking accepts that an application system, designed one or two years ago, no longer matches the actual needs when it is eventually rolled out. The agile approach provides the means for continuous modifications that are necessary because of the way users' work has changed, the company has been reorganized, or the product and service portfolio looks different now.

The short development cycles are accompanied by strict governance on quality. One of the most popular prejudices about agile methods is that "Agile means anarchy." Actually, the opposite is true. Although the agile methodology emphasizes self-organizing teams, it has firm principles in place. Test automation and continuous integration are central concepts in agile projects. The worst blame for an agile developer is that she or he "broke the build." The ultimate goal is to have the software in a fully deployable state after each iteration (ideally, but not always achieved in practice, even throughout the iteration).

This principle—keeping the system always in a deployable state—creates a natural limit on the amount of (temporary) havoc that the developers may wreak on the system between two deliveries. This is sensible, but it also creates a scaling problem for complex features. It is hard to implement a complex feature so that it "fits into one iteration." Complexity comes in three flavors:

1. Systems too huge for one scrum team
2. Features that are too complex in themselves to be implemented in one iteration
3. Features that by their integration into a complex system cause ramifications and ground-level work that do not fit into an iteration

Type 1 complexity can be addressed by decomposing the system into components that are as loosely coupled as possible. Each component is developed by one scrum team. Coordination between the scrum teams is handled by a so-called *scrum of scrums.* This is a coordination board, scheduled usually once a week, where the key representatives of individual scrum teams (for instance, scrum masters and product owners; see the following discussion) meet and discuss integration issues, conflicts, and so forth. This is a standard and proven way to run large agile programs.

Handling complexity of types 2 and 3 is more tricky, since decomposition is not so straightforward if you cannot distribute the problem on several scrum teams. Following the agile paradigm strictly, teams usually solve issue 2 by slicing complex features in such a way that they can be implemented across several iterations. Problem 3 is often addressed by deliberately oversimplistic solutions that fit into one iteration, including all integration work.

Both approaches can have negative consequences with regard to architectural integrity: an unnatural system partitioning in the first case, "refactoring hell" (an endless succession of refactoring operations) in the second. Here, the agile methodology requires deliberate architectural planning to achieve a proper balance between long-term considerations and quick wins.

This is part of the tricky relationship between agile methods and architecture, which we will discuss later in more detail. Another aspect is that the core concept of agile techniques is a cross-functional, self-organized team. The team takes common responsibility for delivering the product. Each team member must fulfill this responsibility in an end-to-end fashion. There are only two predefined, exposed roles:

- The *scrum master*, responsible for moderating (not managing!) the team and protecting it from outside disturbances
- The *product owner*, acting as a representative of that project customer

Beyond these two, specialist roles such as architect are subject to some debate in the agile community. Some authors frown on such dedicated roles in the team, a sign of the tension between the architectural "wisdom of the few" and the agile notion that "the team is everything."

The agile team favors direct communication over written documents. This is in line with common sense: Humans communicate most effectively and efficiently when they come together in a trustful atmosphere, expressing their insights and opinions with words, drawings, symbols, gestures, facial expression, voice modulation, and so forth. Agile has several elements promoting a directly perceivable experience of the development process.

AGILE GLOSSARY
User Stories
User stories are the agile way of formulating requirements. They have a fixed wording:

As a . . ., I want to . . ., so that . . .

This automatically associates them with a specific stakeholder or role and transports the user intention in the *so that* part. A user story describing a book retail website feature might be:

As a book shopper, I can read other customers' reviews of a book online so that I can decide to buy it or not.

A user story normally also contains a *condition of satisfaction*, describing under what circumstances it can be considered "done." Before composing user stories, the team initially compiles a *definition of done*. This is a general declaration applying to all user stories, listing those conditions that always must be met in order for a user story to be "done."

In addition to user stories, *epics* are used for the more coarse-grained agile requirement descriptions. Each epic can be broken down into several user stories.

One is the daily scrum round, another is the wall on which user stories are put as small yellow sticky notes instead of rows in the project manager's Excel sheet. User stories in the Ongoing part of the wall are an ever-present incentive to get the task done. In the same way, moving such a sticky note from Ongoing into the Done quadrant (in front of the team during the scrum meeting) gives a special sense of satisfaction to an agile team member.[9] This way, the entire software development process is implicitly visible and traceable to all the stakeholders.

As sensible as focus on direct communication may be, it also gives rise to some skepticism about agile methods with regard to proper written documentation. Agile proponents seem to hear it frequently—at least that would explain the many voices claiming that the opposite is true (in a more or less unnerved tone[10]) and that being agile doesn't mean writing code without documentation.

The truth is, as we know from our own experience, that in agile methods it is just easier to "forget" documentation than in waterfall methods, where the written document is a mandatory process step. In an agile project, explicit care must be taken to ensure proper documentation—for example, by stating it as part of the condition of satisfaction of a user story or in the definition of done. With an effort, agile projects can produce excellent documentation, as opposed to poorly managed waterfall projects that can come up with hundreds of pages of irrelevant gibberish.

In summary, agile values and principles essentially bring customer centricity, the human touch, professional integrity, and a sense of belongingness into the work culture. At the same time, it demands a high degree of trust and accountability among all team members and stakeholders. It does not suffice to "do" agile methods; the organization must to some extent "be" agile to fully implement this methodology and to benefit from it.

---

[9]To be precise, the procedure described here is part of the so-called *Kanban methodology*, which stems from lean software development but which fits in seamlessly with agile methods and is often used in conjunction with an iterative approach.

[10]For example, take Fitz (2009)—but you can easily find many more statements to the same effect.

Silver bullet, or special tool for the innovator niche? Agile in the enterprise world

Despite the frustration of both IT executives and professionals with the waterfall methodology and its "big bang—big crash" integration shock, it is still the predominant project execution model in the enterprise world.[11] Agile methodology has gained a foothold there, but it still resides in a niche. Common wisdom (outside the agile community) considers it to be mainly suited for innovative projects with limited cost pressure,[12] although there is some indication that adoption of agile methods generally results in a productivity gain.[13] All in all, agile techniques meet several obstacles in the enterprise world:

- *Scaling.* Agile techniques have their roots in rather small-scale projects and have been designed, in their original form, for a developer team with up to roughly 10 members. There are methods for scaling agile methods to larger teams and multisite development (see, for instance, Larman and Vodde, 2009; Cockburn, 2007; or Leffingwell, 2011). But one must be aware that scaling agility is a less well-trodden path than running large programs in waterfall mode and should not be attempted without guidance from process experts. Another challenge lies in the agile methodology's rather hands-on attitude toward software architecture—a topic of special importance for large and complex software systems. We will look at this issue in depth later.
- *Testing.* The agile methodology has a strong affinity for test automation. If the quality assurance of an enterprise mainly relies on managing manually executed test cases, agile concepts are harder to put into practice. In addition, there are areas such as performance tests, load tests, and stability tests where continuous testing work (as preferred by agile methods) is not economically feasible. This requires a reconciliation of the agile testing paradigm with classical waterfall planning and execution of test phases and milestones.
- *Role definitions.* The individual work and its results are frankly exposed to the whole team, in practices like pair programming or by continuous integration, which immediately drags one's contributions and faults onto the stage. Perfectionists have to learn to provide simple solutions and enhance the design only upon stakeholder requests. In addition, agile techniques do not value titles much; instead of being "senior specialist" (or any other shiny job designation), the only honest title for an agile developer can be "team member."
- *Organizational resistance, process incompatibilities, and culture clash.* Introducing agile practices can meet a whole range of defense mechanisms. One can expect a certain clash between the agile activity and the enterprise culture. "To some, this [agile] scenario may appear to be unsupervised, chaotic, and even unprofessional (. . .). [T]he combination of casual dress, pairing, constant communication, and stuff stuck all over the walls does not fly well in some corporate circles," writes Leffingwell (2007, p. 90). The agile methodology's egalitarian spirit is to some extent orthogonal to hierarchical thinking and structures in more conservative enterprises. All of a sudden, the project manager can no longer give commitments without the consent of the team. Agile projects demand constant stakeholder attention and contribution—the good old "create a package and throw it over the fence" mentality doesn't work anymore. Buyers need to give up the

---

[11]There are several surveys indicating this finding (see, e.g., Computer Associates, 2010). It also matches our own experience that usually the larger the project, the more conservative the buyers become in terms of project methodology.

[12]See for instance Keller (2007, p. 94). We have met similar prejudices in our own practice.

[13]In a survey conducted by VersionOne in 2007 (quoted according to Krebs, 2009), 90 percent of companies that have adopted agile practices reported an increase in productivity.

illusion that they can create a requirement specification and get the perfect solution back without any additional contribution. Many more examples can be found. In some cases, the friction results from a "we always did it this way" mentality. In others, agile methods uncover hidden omissions and problems in an organization's processes.

- *Outsourcing*. Outsourcing of agile projects is possible, but it presents considerable obstacles. First, agile methods are easiest to implement in a time-and-material contract model, which often clashes with budgeting and procurement policies. The preferred outsourcing model (fixed-price projects with detailed requirements specified up front) is in conflict with the agile methodology's principle of local planning and welcoming change.[14] Second, especially when it is an offshoring project, agile projects cause a wide range of problems that require a lot of management commitment and process expertise (on both supplier and buyer side) to overcome.[15] However, one should be careful not to condemn agile methods as unsuitable for outsourcing and offshoring. Agile methods are simply less often practiced than waterfall methods. The waterfall methodology is not inherently better; everyone in business knows many stories of failed outsourcing projects.

- *Budget planning*. The budget-planning process of an enterprise typically takes quite some time. In particular, funding for larger projects requires at least a year, and promoters of a project candidate must put a reliable price tag on it in advance and convince the sponsors of its business value. The board will likely reject project proposals, stating, "We'll start off agile with *N* developers, and let's see where we end." An agile project will only have a chance to be approved with a precise effort estimation and a project road map in the granularity of *epics* describing the project's target.

Agile techniques often enter an enterprise through the back door, as a niche methodology used in handpicked innovation or pilot projects. Despite the obstacles, there is a lot of enterprise interest in agile methods, indicating that the adoption rate will further increase beyond that niche.

Agile and architecture: An antagonism?

There is an objection that we should look at in more detail: agility and architecture, does that fit? Doesn't Principle 11 in the Agile Manifesto claim: "The best architectures (. . .) and designs emerge from self-organizing teams" (Beck et al., 2001), declaring something as specialized and top-down as EA obsolete? Does it make sense to apply something to EA that actually despises architectural planning?

Indeed, some authors advocate an architectural practice in Agile projects that can be called lightweight at best, nonexistent at worst. They express a lot of mistrust toward the traditional architecture paradigm. "Software architecture has a history of excesses that in part spurred the reaction called Agile," write Coplien and Bjørnvig (2010, p. 85). Following their concept of design means streamlining architecture to the point of nonexistence: "We will strive for an architecture delivered as

---

[14]There are dedicated Agile contract models (see, for instance, Larman and Vodde, 2009), but they require more trust between the contract partners than other models. In the delicate final phase of closing a software project deal, salespeople are rarely inclined to "rock the boat" and try something out of the ordinary. This, in our experience, makes such models hard to use.

[15]The topic of Agile offshoring would easily fill a dedicated chapter, but it is not the topic of this book. The interested reader should have a look at the respective chapter in Larman's and Vodde's excellent book on agile scaling (2009) or read the article by Fowler (2006).

[application programming interfaces] APIs and code rather than duplicating that information in documents. While the interface is the program, the code is the design" (p. 85).[16] Such a definition of architecture may work for small teams and simple applications, but it doesn't scale up to larger and more complex systems.

With no intention of bashing an otherwise fine book, we believe that Coplien and Bjørnvig is a showcase of the naïve view of EA that some agile apologists seem to have.[17] In contrast, other authors propose a modern, balanced way of thinking about agile architecture. Breivold, Sundmark, Wallin, and Larsson (2010) could not find proof for many of the concerns associated with agile methods and architecture. Leffingwell (2011, p. 386) introduced the phrase *intentional architecture*[18] as an extension of the purely "emergent architecture" from Agile Manifesto Principle 11:

> *Even minor, system-level redesigns can cause substantial rework for large numbers of teams, some of whom would otherwise not have to refactor their module. It is one thing for one team to redesign their code based on lessons they have learned; it's quite another to require ten teams to do so based on another team's lessons learned. (. . .) For developers, architects, and businesspeople who have experience building large-scale systems and portfolios (. . .) a solely emergent architecture is counter to our experience.*

The looming refactoring paralysis as a consequence of a purely emergent architecture is only one side of the coin. Another possible objection against agile methods is that the processes in EA, and in the enterprise generally, are simply not operating with a time window of the typical sprint length of three weeks. This, of course, is true. But it is at closer inspection not a counter-argument against the application of agile principles to EA—just the opposite. The long process cycles add to EA's lack of transparency and promote a silo mentality. Agile techniques can help here.

Having looked at the relationship between agile methods and architecture as a concept, let's also inspect the architect as a person in the agile world. The status of this role is, at first sight, a bit unclear. Agile techniques put emphasis on an empowered team and a spirit to get things done. Therefore, architects are often viewed as notorious residents of the ivory tower. "Things are usually easier said than done, and software architects are notoriously good at coming up with things to say," writes Timothy High (Monson-Haefel, 2009, p. 102).

---

[16]To give another example, Ambler (2006) proposes to "model a bit ahead" or to perform a "model storm," where coding starts after a 30-minute brainstorming session on proper design. More such statements can be found easily.

[17]Their proposal for partitioning large software systems is according to organizational structure, to allow for collocated teams responsible for the parts. In times of outsourcing and highly volatile mergers, acquisitions, and reorganizations, this is certainly not a good way to define a sustainable architecture. In another example, on page 71 they demonstrate a "poor problem statement" in large-scale systems: "We need to increase productivity 40% while cutting costs 40%. This is more like a requirement list than a problem statement. First, it is really two problems, not one. Second, it may be a solution in disguise. Ask why we need to hit these targets. Third, it may set up an over-constrained problem if productivity and cost are linked." Apart from the slightly unrealistic 40% figures: Imagine how in a real IT organization a courageous scrum master would storm into the CIO's office and point out how wrong the directive is from an agile viewpoint. Reality and a purist agile mindset sometimes clash.

[18]He also offers a number of very sound ideas how to deal with large-scale architecture in agile projects, some of which we will take up in the subsequent sections to apply them to EA.

In addition, any specialization is viewed with a certain skepticism. In an ideal agile world, every team member should be involved in every essential development task, especially in the design of the system. This is manifested in the "all hands on deck" paradigm.

An enterprise architect, on the other hand, has a planning horizon of years (instead of just the next two sprints) and performs a highly specialized task that is very far away from designing and coding the end product. That somehow makes her a legal alien in the agile world: eyed with skepticism, tolerated, but not really at home.

The agile architect is therefore a highly adaptable being—responsible for the design but at the same time carefully aware that the true decision power should be in the hands of the team. Johnston (2010) writes:

> In an agile development team many people will contribute to these [architectural] things. The agile architect will help all team members to contribute to the architecture, taking good ideas from everyone and making them part of a coherent whole. The architect may also adapt ideas originating elsewhere, but without losing the team's ownership of the solution.

Kruchten (2004), in an admittedly not completely serious post,[19] formulates:

> The architect doesn't talk, he acts.
> When this is done,
> the team says, "Amazing:
> we did it, all by ourselves!"
> When the architect leads, the team
> is hardly aware that he exists.

Somehow this evokes the notion of a white magician, pulling the strings in the background on behalf of the higher good of architectural order and clarity. This idealized image feels a little bloodless and quixotic. However, the question remains whether this is really a sign for natural antagonism between agile methods and the architect's profession. There is no more consensus and clarity in the image of an architect in EA, either. This role somehow oscillates between the Machiavellian master of political power games (as some enterprise architects would like to see themselves) and the overstrained inhabitants of the EA ivory tower you sometimes meet in real life.

Learning from mass production: Lean software development

The *lean* paradigm stems from the Toyota Production System. At the end of the 1940s, the company faced a challenge to produce inexpensive cars for a striving post-war society. Mass exports were not yet an option (Toyota entered the US market only in 1957, ten years later), and production quantities were low. Therefore, the economies of scale (which Ford achieved by its highly synchronized production system, inspired by Taylor[20]) were not fully available to Toyota.

---

[19]Kruchten used translations of the ancient *Tao Te Ching* to turn it into a statement of his understanding of an architect's "way" (tao).

[20]Frederick Winslow Taylor (1865–1916), often dubbed "the father of scientific management," revolutionized industrial production by decomposing complex workflows into strictly timed, repetitive small tasks that could be executed by a low-skilled workforce.

Henry Ford had managed to produce goods in high quantities and short timeframes but at the price of quite limited flexibility, as expressed by his famous quote, "Any customer can have a car painted any color that he wants so long as it is black" (Ford and Crowther, 1922, p. 71f). This inflexibility could be tolerated when producing for a huge US market, but not in Toyota's case.

Therefore, the Toyota Production System, introduced by Taiichi Ohno (Ohno, 1988), focused on optimizing production efficiency by consistently eliminating "waste," unnecessary or even harmful steps in the design and production processes. At the same time, aspects of human motivation had a much higher importance than in the Taylorian Ford system, adding "respect for humanity" as an explicit value.

In the late 1980s, under the inspiration of the Japanese economic miracle of the past 20 years, Japan was hyped as a role model for industrial efficiency in the Western world. Against this backdrop, lean became a popular buzzword in management theory. The term was coined by John Krafcik (1988) and made popular by the books of James P. Womack (Womack, Jones, and Roos, 1990; Womack and Jones, 1996) and others. They transferred lean management principles to general business organizations. Mary and Tom Poppendieck (Poppendieck and Poppendieck, 2003, 2007) eventually established lean techniques as a software development method by condensing lean thinking into seven principles, adapted to the software creation process.

THE SEVEN LEAN PRINCIPLES

Principle 1: Eliminate waste.
Principle 2: Build quality in.
Principle 3: Create knowledge.
Principle 4: Defer commitment.
Principle 5: Deliver fast.
Principle 6: Respect people.
Principle 7: Optimize the whole.
(Quoted in Poppendieck and Poppendieck, 2007.)

Principle 1: Eliminating waste

Lean thinking starts with the definition of *value* created by the process under consideration, whether industrial production, software development, or architecture creation. This value needs to be defined from a customer viewpoint. Enterprise architecture can be seen as a product; from that perspective, the value of EA lies in the artifacts and services created by the EA group in interaction with other players in the enterprise. We discussed these artifacts and services in Chapter 3, "What Enterprise Architects Do: Core Activities of EA."

Based on this value definition, every step in the product creation process can be divided into two categories: value adding and non value adding. In an ideal lean world, the value stream contains only value-adding steps and therefore would have an efficiency of 100%. The realistically achievable efficiency is much less than that.[21] All non value-adding steps are considered *Muda* (the Japanese term for *waste*) in the lean philosophy. Eliminating waste means working toward an ideal value stream and is therefore the core principle of lean thinking.

---

[21]In manufacturing, as much as 85% of all process steps can be assumed to be waste (Stakutis and Webster, 2005, p. 76). The popular cola-can example (Womack and Jones, 1996, frequently quoted by other authors) has an efficiency of much less than 1%. Although the actual processing steps only total a couple of hours, the total production time (from mining the aluminium to consumption of the can) is nearly one year due to long waiting times in between the processing steps. For software development, the Poppendiecks (2007) describe four case studies with process efficiencies of 1%, 19%, 23–33%, and 33%, respectively. These figures match the personal efficiency of engineers, according to a survey quoted by McManus (2005, p. 14).

Already in the manufacturing-focused Toyota Production System, the interpretation of waste goes way beyond defective pieces and leftover raw material that needs to be discarded. Waste also comprises unnecessary processing steps (i.e., work applied without need), inventory, and waiting. Poppendieck and Poppendieck (2003, 2007) adapted the seven kinds of waste originally described by Ohno (1988) to the software world and provided their interpretation of each waste type for software projects. We have added our interpretation of waste in EA to this compilation, as listed in Table 7-1.[22]

Some authors have added other waste types; Liker (2004), for instance, also lists "unused creativity" of employees as the eighth type of waste. This certainly makes sense, especially when you analyze waste in the IT and architecture field. However, we will cover the broad participation of all EA stakeholders in the architecture decision processes at length in Chapter 8, "Inviting to Participation: EA 2.0." Therefore we will leave it at the original seven types in this chapter.

Some of the waste types are transferable to software creation and EA in a pretty straightforward way (waiting, defects). For others, a bit of creative thinking is needed. The work pieces that are created in manufacturing correspond to the features of a software system. This explains the interpretation of in-process inventory and overproduction to partially done work and extra features in software development. In EA, overproduction can be translated to *over-architecting*. In that case, the architects create more architecture than needed or make it more elaborate and detailed than justified by the need at hand.

Transportation and motion mean, in the production process of tangible goods, a physical movement of half-finished pieces from one plant to another or within a machine tool. In software creation, the "plants" are essentially development teams, and the "machines" are the individual developers. So, waste here means time and traction lost in knowledge transfer and handover procedures between teams and by overloading a developer with too many parallel tasks. This explains the translation for both the software and the EA area to handoffs and task switching.

Extra processing, finally, is interpreted in two different ways in Poppendieck and Poppendieck (2003) and (2007). Both make sense, therefore they are both listed here. Extra processing means applying manufacturing steps to a work piece that are either overdone or not required at all. That matches

Table 7-1 The Seven Types of Waste

Waste in Production	Waste in Software Creation	Waste in EA
In-process inventory	Partially done work	Partially done work
Overproduction	Extra features	Over-architecting
Extra processing	Extra processes, relearning	Redundant processes
Transportation	Handoffs	Handoffs
Motion	Task switching	Task switching
Waiting	Delays	Delays
Defects	Defects	Defects

[22]The two leftmost columns have been compiled based on Poppendieck and Poppendieck (2007, p. 47; 2003, p. 4). The Poppendiecks have varied their terminology slightly between their books and changed the order of waste types. We are using here a hybrid of both quoted books, leaning toward *Implementing Lean Software Development: From Concept to Cash* (2007). The right column is our interpretation of the respective waste types in EA.

a wide range of debatable extra processes in software creation, from the beloved daily status reports in times of crisis, over specifications written but not read, to elaborate QA checklists that are never seriously evaluated. In Poppendieck and Poppendieck (2007), extra processing is translated into relearning, which describes the unnecessary rebuilding of competences and skills not retained in the team from earlier work experience.

For EA, we interpret extra processing as *redundant processes*, which fits better with the procedural character of EA. Other than in the case of over-architecting, the right piece of architecture is created on the proper level of detail—but some steps in the architecture creation process are wasteful, such as performing architecture reviews that are too fine-grained or are done just to demonstrate authority ("I just want to have a say on it") without any value added.

Several tools are used in lean manufacturing for detecting waste in the production processes. The most prominent one is the value stream mapping. The processing steps are noted as a flow diagram, using a dedicated notation that allows us to mark the type of operation, storage, movement, or delay. We will look into waste detection tools for EA more closely in the section "Building Block 1: Get rid of waste by streamlining architecture pocesses."

Principle 2: Build quality in

The statement *Build quality in* expresses a very similar attitude to the agile methodology's emphasis on persistent quality control. The common notion between the two is that quality is not added as an afterthought by a quality assurance phase at the end of the project (with all its undesirable side effects). Instead, quality is ensured on a daily basis as part of the actual software creation. Lean software development draws support from agile techniques with regard to the measures for achieving this daily quality control, such as continuous integration, test-driven development, and refactoring.

The quality of architecture artifacts is usually assured by peer reviews, stakeholder signoffs, and approvals. A mentality to ensure quality during creation, instead of (or in addition to) milestone-based acceptance, requires a continuous and broad participation of all members of the IT community, down to the development teams on the ground. The EA participation concepts described in Chapter 8 can help in dealing with quality assurance.

Principle 3: Create knowledge

The *Create knowledge* principle describes the focus on building and retaining knowledge about the complex processes of software creation and about the domain for which the software is designed. Lean thinking involves constantly monitoring and fine-tuning the production process. Faults are considered a normal part of a lightweight trial-and-error approach and seen as an opportunity to learn, as long as a strict policy for immediate fault correction is in place (see *Principle 2: Build quality in*).

Lean thinking regards the popular myths of *getting things right the first time* and a *zero-defect mentality* as counterproductive, since they tend to create a risk-averse and uncreative atmosphere.[23]

---

[23]Paul Carroll tells in his book *Big Blues* (1993) a famous story attributed to Tom Watson, ex-CEO of IBM. After a middle management decision that resulted in a loss of $10 million for IBM, Watson ordered the responsible manager into his office and asked him if he knew why he had called for him. "I guess you will fire me," said the manager. "Of course not!" said Watson. "I just spent $10 million to educate you." (Quoted by Heath and Heath, 2010, p. 173.)

Instead, lean thinking tries to create an environment that allows a sequence of small decisions that can be easily verified and taken back with little cost if needed.

Principle 4: Defer commitment

Defer commitment means that decisions are taken as late as possible to keep one's options open. This allows being open to change, just like the "welcoming change" attitude in agile thinking. It also induces a simple design (read "as simple as possible"), by avoiding a premature preference for one out of several possibilities for architecting a solution.

The principle also implies using abstraction as a means to switch to a different solution in some modules of the architecture later on. The effect that is perhaps valued most by practitioners is that the architect has more time to learn about the subject and usually has to deal with less uncertainty when she defers commitment to the last responsible moment.

Principle 5: Deliver fast

The principle *Deliver fast* expresses the high value of a quick response to new or changed customer requirements in lean thinking. On one side, the ability of fast delivery is a result of the flexibility created by all lean principles; a lightweight process is easier to set up than a heavyweight one and will therefore create quicker results. On the other hand, this principle specifically expresses that lean thinking regards speed as a value in itself. Not only is IT quick-changing; also outside IT, in the customer's domain, situations change rapidly. An IT department or supplier that is able to react fast to new input simply delivers better value.

It should be noted, however, that *fast* doesn't mean *hacking*. Speed is primarily related to quick decision making and must not conflict with quality; see also *Principle 2: Build quality in*. At face value, deliver fast may also sound contradictory to *Principle 4: Defer commitment*. Again, this is not so. Deferring commitment simply means that decisions should be made as late as needed (to keep all options open) but not so late that they endanger a quick response to customer demands.

An important tool to achieve fast delivery is creation of a seamless flow in the manufacturing process, usually combined with the definition of *takt* time. The German word takt is used throughout the lean literature as a loanword, meaning clock cycle. Each operation should fall into the same beat, guaranteeing a steady manufacturing flow without waste due to waiting or delays.

Another key concept for fast delivery is the *pull* principle. In manufacturing, pulling means to produce goods on demand only, triggered by an order created upstream in the value stream. This is a precondition for the production pipe to have an ideal *flow* (another key lean term) of intermediate work items. The opposite concept is *push*—producing goods based on a forecast of future demands and "pushing" them downstream in the production process in the hope that they are available in sufficient numbers once the need for them arises. Pulling means short lead times and fast order processing in small quantities. Pushing, on the other hands, implies large batch sizes and long storage times. No wonder that lean manufacturing prefers pull over push.

Transferring the pull concept from manufacturing to software development means that features should only be developed (and architecture documents only be written) when a concrete demand exists. The level of detail and refinement should be appropriate to the actual request, avoiding proactive "gold-plating." We will look deeper into the implementation of the pull principle in the section called "Building Block 3: Practice iterative architecture through EA Kanban."[24]

---

[24]The pull concept is a deep-rooted lean idea that can be mapped also to others of the seven main principles. Even the Poppendiecks list it in the same book under different principles (2003, pp. xvii and 49ff).

Principle 6: Respect people

Principle 6: Respect people deals with the human aspects in software creation. The core idea is that decisions should be taken by people who are best qualified to do so. In the agile world this principle is labeled *Empower the team* (Poppendieck and Poppendieck, 2003). It bears a strong resemblance to the agile thought of the team as the primary body of decision making when it comes to operational aspects of software development. Strong entrepreneurial (i.e., focused on team building) leadership, nurturing of technical expertise, and a short decision-making channels characterize a lean organization.

Another aspect of this principle—again a parallel to agile techniques—is the appreciation of stable teams, where knowledge can be built up and cultivated over a long period of time. A self-empowered organization therefore is also the ideal environment in which to implement *Principle 3: Create knowledge*.

Principle 7: Optimize the whole

Optimize the whole emphasizes the holistic approach in lean development. People should see the "big picture" when making decisions instead of considering only their own private silo (team, department, job description, subsystem, application, etc.). A violation of this principle leads to only locally optimized (and therefore suboptimal) solutions.

In software development, optimize the whole primarily means to consider the complete value chain, from gathering requirements down to running the developed software. This requires everyone in the software creation process to step out of the specialization cubicle. A way of thinking that goes like this:

> *I'm an architect, and I do my job well if I produce as many high-quality design documents as possible, and I am measured by the number of features I design.*

is not lean thinking.

Software Kanban

Software Kanban has been derived from the way workflow is organized in lean manufacturing. Its central element is the *Kanban board* (see an example in Figure 7-1).[25] The development tasks flow as *task cards* from left to right. Whenever there is a status change for a task—for instance, the implementation has been finished—the corresponding card is moved one cell to the right.

In Kanban, iterations are optional. The system instead focuses on enforcing the *pull* principle. Each cell (apart from *Backlog* and *Live* in our example) has a *work in progress (WIP)* limit attached to it—a maximum number of tasks that may reside in that cell. When that limit has been reached, no further task card may be moved into it. For instance, if the limit for ongoing development tasks is three, a scrum team already working on three tasks may not accept a further one. The team first must finish at least one of the ongoing tasks. This helps avoid waste from *in-process inventory* and *delays*. A team can easily judge at what time they need new tasks to work on and can pull them from the left of their cell on the board. This effectively promotes the *pull* concept.

When applying Kanban to EA, as we will do later, we will use the term design in progress (DIP), coined by Donald Reinartsen (1997), instead of WIP. DIP describes the maximum number of design tasks currently being worked on.

---

[25]For more details, please refer to the many books on Kanban—for instance, Anderson (2010). Kniberg (2009) provides a concise and amusing comic version of how a Kanban board is used.

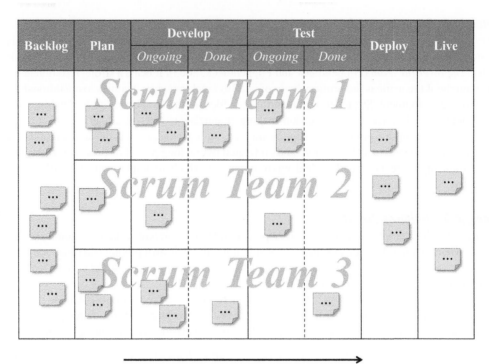

Direction of Progress

FIGURE 7-1

Example of a software Kanban board.

Lean and agile: Parallels and differences

"*Lean is often cited as a foundation of agile, or as a cousin of agile,*" wrote Coplien and Bjørnvig (2010, p. 12). Indeed, there are strong indicators of parallels between the two methodologies. Table 7-2 shows our analysis of their overlap by mapping the four values of the Agile Manifesto against the seven lean principles.[26]

Table 7-2 shows three areas where lean and agile fully match (indicated by the three solid black circles):

1. Empowered, self-organized teams and individuals are the cornerstones of both methodologies.
2. Both approaches value the inseparable coupling of software creation and quality assurance, opposed to the sequential phases in waterfall techniques.
3. Welcoming change and encouragement of a learn-from-your-mistakes attitude, rather than a rigid *a priori* change control, is common to both methodologies.

---

[26]The ratings are based on the authors' subjective evaluation of the respective principles and their meaning. A more detailed mapping of the twelve agile principles against the lean principles, by the way, leads to similar conclusions, not printed here for reasons of space.

Table 7-2 Mapping Between the Seven Lean Principles (Columns) and the Four Elements of the Agile Manifesto (rows). A Solid Black Circle Denotes a Strong Overlap, a White Circle a Partial Overlap

	Eliminate Waste	Build Quality In	Create Knowledge	Defer Commitment	Deliver Fast	Respect (Empower) People	Optimize the Whole
Individuals and interactions over processes and tools	O	O	O			●	
Working software over comprehensive documentation	O	●			O		
Customer collaboration over contract negotiation	O		O	O	O	O	O
Responding to change over following a plan	O		●	O	O	O	

The core lean principle, Eliminate waste, is somewhat ingrained in the agile process, but it's formulated more pointedly in lean techniques. To some extent, this also applies to *Create knowledge, Deliver fast, and Respect people*. All in all, when we compare the wording, we notice that the lean principles describe more the "what" in terms of goals, whereas agile techniques list the "how." In other words, and a little pointed:

> *Lean defines principles, whereas agile describes practices.*

This statement fits with the genesis of both methodologies. Lean thinking, with its origin in large-scale manufacturing business, emphasizes the "big picture" and the governing principles for a lean way of organizing them. The manufacturing world is too large and complex to come up with a uniform set of concrete best practices. Instead, in an ideal lean organization, the individual and the team are provided with an appropriate level of empowerment to develop (and constantly revise) their own practices. One could even say that the lean methodology applies lean thinking to its own implementation. It embodies a belief that complex problems have a simple solution in themselves and can be treated with a fairly limited number of rules.

Agile thinking, in contrast, comes from a relatively narrow field. It is the formalization of the work methods of a small, well-organized, and autonomous software development team. In a way, both methodologies arrive at the same (or at least very similar) conclusions, but they think from different directions—top-down (large to small scale) for lean, bottom-up for agile.

This also explains the two areas in Table 7-2 with a less strong match. Defer commitment and Optimize the whole are seemingly less well covered by agile methodologies. Defer commitment is at least indirectly covered by agile thinking (by the development in iterations and the deliberate renunciation of a big up-front master plan), but Optimize the whole is indeed an aspect missing from the Agile Manifesto. To some extent, this explains the challenges with scaling up agile methods to larger, more complex systems and bigger, distributed teams. We will have a closer look at this aspect in the subsequent section, when we analyze the way lean and agile techniques deal with architecture.

Accepting lean techniques as principle-driven and top-down, as opposed to agile techniques as practice-driven and bottom-up oriented, explains also the close relationship between the two in terms of concrete methods and tools. In many ways, lean software development borrows from agile methods when it comes to concrete practices. Iterations, timeboxing, continuous integration, test-driven development (TDD), and so forth are agile methods that play a strong role in lean development (Poppendieck and Poppendieck, 2003, 2007; Coplien and Bjørnvig, 2010). "Agile practices are manifestations of lean principles," state Shalloway, Beaver, and Trott (2010, p. 6). The notable exception of a thoroughbred lean practice might be software Kanban.

But all in all, the question if a certain method, practice, or tool belongs more to lean or more to agile is only of theoretical interest. Somehow both approaches flow together, with the one contributing more here, the other more there. We can use them side by side for our architecture factory approach to EA.

Building Block 1: Get rid of waste by streamlining architecture processes

The lean methodology is, by origin, an optimization framework for production systems. You can apply it toward two ends:

- *Flow optimization.* Analysis of the process steps in an end-to-end flow that are *pushed* instead of *pulled* (i.e., produced based on forecasts instead of on demand) and redesigning them for a pull-based setup.
- *Waste removal.* Identification and elimination of wasteful steps in the production process.

Classical mass production systems are organized in a batch mode. They produce huge quantities of goods by tightly coupled, fully repeatable processes, based on forecasts rather than actual demand. Here it usually makes sense to tackle flow optimization first. Otherwise there is a risk of neglecting the *big picture* and thus achieving only local optimizations.

However, as outlined earlier, the architecture factory of an EA organization resembles more a "Manufaktur," a highly customized craft shop, than an industrial plant. There is no mass production of architecture work items, and the work processes are highly individualized and loosely coupled. Therefore, in this Building Block 1, we will first analyze wastes for removal. In Building Blocks 2 and 3, we will tackle a big-picture concept for EA processes, using elements from the agile methodology such as architecture scrums and backlogs.

Let's return to our Bank4Us example again. Padma Valluri is an enterprise architect and colleague of Ian Miller, whom we have accompanied in his application rationalization program. Padma's tasks in the EA group comprise responsibility for optimizing the IT and architecture processes at the bank.

Many times Padma has talked with Ian and other architects on the EA team about the efficiency of their IT and EA organization. As an experienced enterprise architect, Padma knows that EA, as practiced today, offers enough possibilities to detect waste. Process bureaucracy, overly strict guidelines, and documents that no one ever reads are just a few prominent examples. All stakeholders in the IT organization struggle with an overload of waste in their daily work, adhering to guidelines that do not provide real value. McManus (2005) puts it this way[27]:

> *Existing process definitions can refer to obsolete practices (. . .). They may also capture practices that once were critically important, but have become irrelevant over time—in lean terms, they may be monuments. Partly as a result, they are often followed only loosely.*

In other words, processes age in the same way as physical hardware does. Its growing inadequacy is a threat to a sound governance system; when rules stop making sense, people don't follow them anymore. Therefore Oscar Salgado, head of the EA team, has given Padma the task of developing a concept for process renewal within the IT and EA organization. It will be aligned with the large-scale *Closer to Customer* IT transformation.

Padma is determined to reduce the amount of processing and control down to the right level needed to leave the EA group operational without stifling creativity. To achieve this goal, she needs to make proposals for removal of unnecessary, or even harmful, steps in design, implementation, test, and management processes, to ensure a pragmatic focus on the really creative activities.

The section "The seven wastes of EA" outlines in detail what the waste types defined in the lean methodology mean in terms of EA. As a second step, in the section "Value stream analysis tools for EA," we will look over Padma's shoulder as she analyzes the EA value stream—the production pipeline for architecture artifacts—and checks it for nonvalue-adding process steps, which should be eliminated as waste.

The seven wastes of EA

In EA, the goods created are less tangible than in the usual industrial manufacturing. Architects are knowledge workers; as a design process, EA has a production pipeline like this:

	organized		*accessed*		*applied*	
data	=====>	information	=====>	knowledge	=====>	wisdom

This model is derived from Millard (2001, p. 26). In his terminology, the end product *wisdom* should be understood in a very broad sense, as a base for further exploitation of the collected body of knowledge.[28]

In the introduction to lean thinking, "Learning from mass production: Lean software development," we have already seen that production waste is not only a phenomenon in manufacturing, but it also occurs in the nonphysical world of software development and IT processes. We will now take one

---

[27]McManus refers to engineering processes in the aerospace industry, which is probably even more process-laden than IT.
[28]We are fully aware that it is quite impossible to find *one* term comprising the full scope of EA.

further step, from the development of software to the development of (enterprise) architecture artifacts. Waste in EA processes can be classified under the following categories[29]:

- *Partially done work.* Information is not available and architectural artifacts are not completed but are stockpiled in a semifinished state.
- *Overarchitecting.* The wrong architectural issues are tackled, or the right ones are covered in too much detail.
- *Redundant processes.* Essentially, the right things are done but with too much effort; inadequate, unnecessary, or duplicate processes render the overall process inefficient.
- *Handoffs.* Friction occurs in the interaction of different actors in the EA processes, due to task handovers or communication problems.
- *Task switching.* Enterprise architects and other participants in the EA process lose time and energy as they switch between many concurrent tasks.
- *Delays.* People wait for information, feedback, or approvals.
- *Defects.* EA strategy, models, and documents contain flaws, or participants in the EA processes display erratic behavior.

Let's look at all of these waste areas in detail. You will find many concrete examples in the subsequent subsections, which you can use as a blueprint for your own organization's analysis.

Partially done work

Partially done work, together with *Overarchitecting* (covered in the next subsection), is the most obvious waste area in the life of any architect. The manufacturing counterpart is *In-Process Inventory*: A heap of work pieces stored between two processing steps. *Partially done work* means that architectural artifacts—specification, models, documentation—are not completed and closed but are left in a semifinished state and stockpiled for later use.

This can be the result of narrow-minded thinking. A customer business representative once told us:

> *Well, our enterprise architects are usually happy when they have some Web service available in the ESB; that's where they stop thinking. I have to convince them that their job is not done unless the service has reached the consumer on a mobile app or through some other channel.*

Probably you know this lack of end-to-end consideration from your own experience (of yourself and others).

In other cases, the architecture concepts are sound but are just put on the shelf in an unfinished state because a more important issue came up. As often as not, these half-ready specifications will never be touched again. That turns them into waste via *Overarchitecting*.

Navigating between these two waste types—*Partially done work* and *Overarchitecting*—is the tightrope walk an architect must perform as part of her daily business. It is basically the chasm between too little and too much elaboration and attention to detail (or the detail work being done at the wrong time). A common sense approach to priorities, combined with solid time management, is the architect's main tool to make the proper decision in each particular case.

---

[29]The EA waste interpretation as outlined in this section is mainly derived from Womack and Jones (1996), Poppendieck and Poppendieck (2003, 2007), and McManus (2005). These authors describe waste in lean manufacturing and product design. We have adapted their terminology and ideas to EA processes.

It may sound curious, but partially done work can also manifest itself as *too much* information. An unstructured clutter of data, concepts, and ideas is of no use to the reader. In a similar way, a model without a view appropriate for the target audience—one that the reader is used to and can understand—is not ready to be used.

Another aspect of this waste type is the possible lack of a clear information owner. If many actors work on the same piece of information and no crystal-clear rules on document storage and archiving are in place, a plethora of parallel document versions exists—scattered across multiple inboxes and C: drives, many of them with minor changes and additions.

Table 7-3 lists the interpretation of this waste type in manufacturing, software development in general, and architecture in general as well as examples for wasteful activities in the main EA activities EA-1 to EA-8, as introduced in Chapter 3. As can be seen from these examples, waste due to partially done work is often associated with doing things halfheartedly. It can be the result of an underempowered or understaffed EA group, but it might just as well indicate some suboptimal EA processes that put too little stress on completion and results.

Table 7-3 Waste Due to Partially Done Work

Area	Waste Due to *Partially Done Work*
Manufacturing	In-process inventory
Software development	Partially done work
Software architecture in general	Business knowledge known but not yet captured in feature specifications No or insufficiently reviewed specifications Finalized, mature architecture concepts not yet implemented Omissions of important aspects in specifications—for example, forgetting about deployment and distribution issues Permanent makeshift solutions
EA-1 Defining the IT Strategy	No or insufficiently reviewed strategies
EA-2 Modeling the Architectures	Too much unstructured information No view on the model that the target audience can understand Lack of document repository and clear storage rules, everybody storing files locally No rules or best practices in place how to deal with outdated information (when to purge and archive)
EA-3 Evolving the IT Landscape	Outdated and/or incomplete documentation and specification of the business, application, or technology architecture Systems not on the EA radar, or systems with no future road map Systems in transition to a EA-compliant status *(unavoidable to some extent)*
EA-4 Assessing and Developing Capabilities	No (real) EA organization Architectural skill gaps identified but not acted upon
EA-5 Developing and Enforcing Standards and Guidelines	Immature EA standards, policies, and guidelines (incompletely elaborated, discussed with stakeholders, and documented) Insufficient backing for EA by higher management, leading to lack of support for implementing EA standards, policies, and guidelines Standards not considering business requirements Standards and guidelines exist but are not available to the public

Continued

Table 7-3 Waste Due to Partially Done Work—Cont'd

Area	Waste Due to *Partially Done Work*
EA-6 Monitoring the Project Portfolio	Shadow IT (parts of IT projects are run outside the control of enterprise architects and thereby leave some work to make them EA compliant) Ineffectual monitoring (violations of EA principles have no consequence; no sanctions imposed on non-EA-compliant projects)
EA-7 Leading or Coaching Projects	Project architects are left alone Enterprise architects are involved in IT projects but only requested as technology consultants
EA-8 Managing Risks Involved in IT	Too IT-centric view on risks, neglecting business consequences

Overarchitecting

As indicated, the waste types *Partially done work* and *Overarchitecting* are to some extent two sides of the same coin (the attention to detail is in some way mismatched). The manufacturing counterpart to *Overarchitecting* is *Overproduction*. Transferred to EA, this means that an enterprise architect performs activities and produces documents that no one needs. Or, if the EA's work actually meets a demand, the documents' level of detail is such that no one will read them. Sending out all information to everyone (i.e., *pushing* instead of *pulling* information) also is a flavor of overarchitecting. Essentially, the EA effort is invested into the wrong activities and initiatives. Table 7-4 lists examples of this waste type.

Table 7-4 Waste Due to Overarchitecting

Area	Waste Due to *Overarchitecting*
Manufacturing	Overproduction
Software development	Extra features
Software architecture in general	Stockpiling specifications for future applications Specifying extra features Specifications or concepts with no business need Model overcomplexity in anticipation of future features Technology/platform choice in anticipation of future needs
EA-1 Defining the IT Strategy	IT strategy derived from industry hype (SOA, WOA, Cloud, . . .) rather than business maxims Vendor-driven, technology-focused, or product-centric IT strategy with no correlation to what the business is asking for Overly complex solutions for simple problems (for example, "Do everything with SAP")
EA-2 Modeling the Architectures	Modeling too detailed (e.g., for a mere strategy option where a superficial model would suffice) Architecture view too formalized for an audience of nonarchitects Uncontrolled flow of information; forwarding too much information to too many recipients

Continued

Table 7-4 Waste Due to Overarchitecting—Cont'd	
Area	**Waste Due to *Overarchitecting***
EA-3 Evolving the IT Landscape	IT transformations not justified by business needs or IT strategy Up-front investments in technologies and platforms in anticipation of future needs Planning horizon reaching too far into the future
EA-4 Assessing and Developing Capabilities	Bloated EA organization
EA-5 Developing and Enforcing Standards and Guidelines	Transition to EA standards, policies, principles, and guidelines that later turn out to be irrelevant, abandoned, replaced, rejected, or ignored Overspecification of corporate standards and guidelines
EA-6 Monitoring the Project Portfolio	Too much involvement of enterprise architects in the nitty-gritty details of IT projects
EA-7 Leading or Coaching Projects	Enterprise architects de facto working only as project architects Key architecture concepts (adaptation, mediation, transformation) introduced on project level only because EA compliance requires it, not because they are suitable for the project
EA-8 Managing Risks Involved in IT	Listing risks that that are improbable, too far in the future, or have already materialized Architecture as an overreaction to never-to-recur problems of the past

The strong presence of overarchitecting can indicate the control freak mindset of the *Guardians of Wisdom* type of EA organization, which we portrayed in the EA caricatures in Chapter 1. In any case, overdoing architecture efforts will create waste and can even have harmful consequences.

Redundant processes

Waste due to *Redundant processes* means that, although the architectural work may have the proper focus, it requires too much effort. The manufacturing counterpart is *Extra processing*—the right work piece is being worked on at the right time, but too many processing steps are used on it. As Table 7-5 outlines, this type of waste can manifest itself as too much bureaucracy or in general as an ineffective EA or IT organization.

Meetings (if not properly moderated) or excessive reviews are a relatively harmless nuisance but can pile up into a veritable time sink. A more serious source of waste is a strictly hierarchical chain of command in which technical decisions are by principle made on a high management level, where the technical implications are no longer understood. Such an organization requires a lot of communication across the ranks to properly brief the decision makers. Another very frequent case of unnecessary effort by *Redundant processes* is the creation of proprietary technology platforms, where slightly customized standard frameworks would suffice.

Handoffs

Waste due to *Handoffs* is the counterpart to transporting a work piece between different machines in manufacturing. Passing on partially completed tasks to someone else will always create friction. But even communication (or the lack of it) between stakeholders in the EA process is a potential source of

Table 7-5 Waste Due to Redundant Processes

Area	Waste Due to *Redundant Processes*
Manufacturing	Extra processing
Software development	Extra processes Relearning
Software architecture in general	Reinventing the wheel Reviews with the wrong circle of people Unnecessary bureaucracy, such as tiring signoff procedures
EA-1 Defining the IT Strategy	Creation of an IT strategy from scratch instead of deriving it from business maxims
EA-2 Modeling the Architectures	Reviews with the wrong circle of people Too many review iterations Gold-plating of architecture models
EA-3 Evolving the IT Landscape	Too detailed capturing of the as-is architecture as a common trap in application rationalization (delving too deeply into the current state and getting lost) Too many meetings with too many participants Too-long approval chains Strictly hierarchical chain of command so that decisions are made on too high a level, where the technical implications are no longer understood and a lot of communication is needed
EA-4 Assessing and Developing Capabilities	Ignoring the industry-specific architecture blueprints and EA capabilities models and instead creating frameworks from scratch
EA-5 Developing and Enforcing Standards and Guidelines	Proprietary technology platforms where slightly customized standard frameworks would suffice (e.g., for user interfaces) Too much compliance bureaucracy (potentially from both the project architect's and the enterprise architect's points of view)
EA-6 Monitoring the Project Portfolio	Too many meetings with too many participants
EA-7 Leading or Coaching Projects	Micro-management of project architects
EA-8 Managing Risks Involved in IT	Too much risk management on the project level (perspective too low)

waste by handoff. If the dialogue between enterprise architects, business managers, management boards, IT management, IT development teams, and implementation partners is disrupted, the EA process will not work properly.

Table 7-6 lists several examples of the *Handoffs* waste type. Many of them are, in some way or another, associated with a silo attitude. The chief mechanic mindset described the EA caricatures in Chapter 1 is one example of a lack of proper communication between stakeholders. The "over-the-fence" mentality of passing implementation projects over to partners without proper interaction along the way is another.

Waste due to Handoffs is also created if the EA organization gives up too much responsibility to partners. In general, partnering and outsourcing can have critical side effects. In one of our projects, a mobile network operator had outsourced its network. As a consequence, it had problems accessing

Table 7-6 Waste Due to Handoffs

Area	Waste Due to *Handoffs*
Manufacturing	Transportation
Software development	Handoffs
Software architecture in general	"Fire and forget" mentality in software development, especially when writing requirement and design specifications for software projects Huge number of software systems involved in implementing business processes Incompatible applications and system components Silo design
EA-1 Defining the IT Strategy	"Chief mechanic" mindset in the IT organization, waiting for precise requirements from the business side instead of proactively position IT as a business enabler
EA-2 Modeling the Architectures	Lack of information access due to IT system limitations, overly strict security guidelines, or legal constraints in partner agreements Incompatible information formats
EA-3 Evolving the IT Landscape	Too much organizational specialization among members of the IT organization; no end-to-end responsibility for IT systems Only rudimentary written documentation on existing systems, unclear "who knows what" Fragmented knowledge on the overall IT system so that no single person has the "big picture" EA stakeholders (business and IT) globally distributed, making meeting arrangements difficult Leaving EA core activities, such as application portfolio planning, to implementation partners
EA-4 Assessing and Developing Capabilities	Completely leaving the development of architectural skills in the IT organization to HR or external consultants EA organization has no control over its own processes
EA-5 Developing and Enforcing Standards and Guidelines	Creation of standards and guidelines without properly involving the IT ground workers who have to implement them Project architects not properly informed about EA rules and responsibilities, leading to an excessive search for the proper contact for approving a technical solution
EA-6 Monitoring the Project Portfolio	Outsourcing, at least when approached with an "over-the-fence" mentality Lack of proper reporting on key indicators for project health status
EA-7 Leading or Coaching Projects	Enterprise architects not communicating enough with project architects No enterprise-wide system for effective knowledge management
EA-8 Managing Risks Involved in IT	Enterprise architects not communicating enough with the business so that the business impact of IT decisions is not properly understood (and vice versa)

key data about network failures, which the operator needed for enhancement planning. The problem was that, by accessing the failure data, the operator also would have gained insight into the individual fault resolution performance of the partners' monitoring personnel. The network operator was not in the least interested in this information but was not allowed to have access for data privacy reasons.

But even a less drastic way of collaborating with partners can cause serious extra effort due to handoffs. When consultancy companies perform application modernization initiatives on behalf of their client's IT organizations, they often own the architecture of the whole solution. After finishing, they leave the scene—with the client's architects scratching their heads because they do not understand the architecture decisions that have been made.

Task switching

In manufacturing, *motion* means the movement of a work piece within one machine (as opposed to *transportation*, where it is moved between different machines or production sites). Transferred to the abstract principles of software architecture, an overly layered system exhibits too much motion.[30]

In terms of software and architecture processes, motion means *Task switching*. A human brain is by nature ill suited for parallel processing. The damaging effect of information overload and too many concurrent activities on organizational effectiveness is well known (see, for instance, Spiro, 2011). Enterprise architects are no exceptions to this rule. Table 7-7 lists many examples in which the architect can be overloaded by a multitude of parallel tasks in her daily work.

Sometimes task switching can grow out of control if one of the manifold side activities of an enterprise architect prevails to an extent that it doesn't leave room for much else. In that case, there is actually not much task switching anymore (apart from the one big switch to the predominant side activity). However, the enterprise architect is prone to deteriorate to a program or project manager or to a universal Mr. Fix-It for technology issues no one else can solve.

Table 7-7 Waste Due to Task Switching

Area	Waste Due to *Task Switching*
Manufacturing	Motion
Software development	Task switching
Software architecture in general	Overly layered architecture Work overload for architects; too many specifications to be worked on in parallel Too many meetings on various topics Reworking specifications over and over again
EA-1 Defining the IT Strategy	Permanently reworking IT strategies and concepts; trying to follow volatile or self-contradictory business strategies
EA-2 Modeling the Architectures	Enterprise architect working on too many architectures in parallel due to understaffing of the EA group or to a misjudgment of the appropriate level of detail Modeling tools with poor usability, or no tools whatsoever Information overload with irrelevant details
EA-3 Evolving the IT Landscape	Too many unproductive meetings Enterprise architect responsible for too many applications
EA-4 Assessing and Developing Capabilities	EA organization understaffed

Continued

---

[30]See, for instance, Eric Dörnenburg's blog post, "Making ESB Pain Visible" (2009), where he outlines how many implementation layers a (seemingly simple) connection of service provider and consumer via an ESB can actually produce.

Table 7-7 Waste Due to Task Switching—Cont'd

Area	Waste Due to *Task Switching*
EA-5 Developing and Enforcing Standards and Guidelines	Too little understanding of the nature and importance of EA, resulting in many occasions where the enterprise architect needs to explain the basic concepts and goals
EA-6 Monitoring the Project Portfolio	Enterprise architect acting effectively as a program manager for IT projects
EA-7 Leading or Coaching Projects	Enterprise architect involved too deeply in running IT projects—possibly even by acting as project manager, not only project architect In an underskilled IT organization, the enterprise architect is pushed into a "Mr. Fix-It" role, being the best available expert on certain technology areas Too much time spent on insufficient communication environment for multisite projects
EA-8 Managing Risks Involved in IT	Purely reactive (instead of proactive) risk management, EA jumping from one operational outage to the next

Delays

Other than in manufacturing, the intermediate products of information design processes—specifications, concepts, models—are nearly always perishable goods. They lose their value when kept on the shelf too long. Therefore, *Delays* are always harmful in EA. Unfortunately, they are also a very common waste. All stakeholders in the EA process (with the exception of the enterprise architects themselves) do have other main priorities than the creation of EA. In addition, these stakeholders mostly belong to the ranks of middle and higher managers, whose schedules are always packed. This makes the EA processes prone to holdups.

Table 7-8 lists some examples, such as waiting for appointments, information, review feedback, or approvals. In some cases, it is not the EA organization that has to wait: When a project wants to use a certain technology but the EA group has not made up its mind yet, another delay is created.

Defects

Defects in general are considered waste in lean thinking. The *Build quality in* principle demands that production processes should be set up in a way that no defects occur in the first place. Lean software development proponents even go so far to claim that if you detect faults in final testing, something is wrong.[31]

For architecture, this principle is hard to implement. It can be as flawed as any other human product or service—maybe even more so due to its fuzzy and forward-pointing nature, which makes verification difficult. Architectural defects in general, as listed in Table 7-9, comprise all kinds of misguided design, from a plain misunderstanding of the business requirements to more sophisticated flaws such as resume-driven design.[32]

---

[31]"The goal is that the final test should not find defects; they should have been found earlier. If you routinely find defects at final testing, then you are testing too late" (Poppendieck and Poppendieck, 2007, p. 56).

[32]*Resume-driven design* means that a particular technology platform or framework is selected only because it belongs to the set of currently hyped technologies and makes a good entry on the architect's CV (see, for instance, Shah, 2004).

Table 7-8 Waste Due to Delays

Area	Waste Due to *Delays*
Manufacturing	Waiting
Software development	Delays
Software architecture in general	Performance problems due to increased execution time in layered middleware and business process orchestrations Developers cannot start since specification is not ready Developers waiting for time slot in architect's busy schedule to clarify specification issues
EA-1 Defining the IT Strategy	Waiting for board-level decisions on business strategy Business representatives not available for giving input to strategy discussions Waiting for approval by CIO
EA-2 Modeling the Architectures	Waiting for information from business side or from the IT departments
EA-3 Evolving the IT Landscape	Waiting for information or feedback input from business experts or IT representatives
EA-4 Assessing and Developing Capabilities	Delays in hiring process due to missing HR approvals or EA budgets Architects with the right skills cannot be internally transferred to the EA group due to political or budget issues
EA-5 Developing and Enforcing Standards and Guidelines	Feedback from various stakeholders is missing Waiting for approval for IT guidelines and standards
EA-6 Monitoring the Project Portfolio	Waiting for information on IT projects
EA-7 Leading or Coaching Projects	Projects are delayed and cannot take design decisions since the EA point of view has not yet been decided
EA-8 Managing Risks Involved in IT	No reaction from business side when approached for risk assessment feedback

Table 7-9 Waste Due to Defects

Area	Waste Due to *Defects*
Manufacturing	Defects
Software development	Defects
Software architecture in general	Architect ignores or misunderstands business requirements Specification cannot be implemented, since it conflicts with technology capabilities Specification has grown so much over time that it has become self-contradictory Resume-driven design
EA-1 Defining the IT Strategy	IT transformations justified by only ostensible business needs that are actually not in line with business strategy Basing the IT strategy on wrong assumptions

Continued

Table 7-9 Waste Due to Defects—Cont'd

Area	Waste Due to *Defects*
EA-2 Modeling the Architectures	Models that appropriately reflect neither the current nor the future state of IT Forgoing (or choosing unsuitable) model languages and notations Presenting formalized models to a nontechnical audience (confusing model and view)
EA-3 Evolving the IT Landscape	Clinging to bespoke systems for political reasons, against better judgment Changes to the IT landscape that are rejected by affected business stakeholders Introducing changes without fully understanding the impact on business operations Biased assessment of applications, when technology freaks believe that an application needs to be retired because they dislike the technology, although it supports business operations well
EA-4 Assessing and Developing Capabilities	Building an EA practice without proper planning and preparation—for example, without the help of a standardized EA framework
EA-5 Developing and Enforcing Standards and Guidelines	Wrong platform, technology, or vendor decisions taken for political reasons EA standards, policies, and guidelines are self-contradictory
EA-6 Monitoring the Project Portfolio	Pet projects
EA-7 Leading or Coaching Projects	Disconnect between project and enterprise architecture
EA-8 Managing Risks Involved in IT	Ignoring or underestimating IT-related risks

Enterprise architecture in particular offers a rich choice of options for building in flaws and defects—from politically motivated technology decisions and pet projects down to inappropriate modeling languages. Every enterprise architect will have her own set of tales in this department; therefore, the list in Table 7-9 (like any of the other waste tables) does not claim to be comprehensive. It merely outlines some frequently occurring EA defects.

Value stream analysis tools for EA

The process of waste detection in EA should start (as trivial as this may sound) with an analysis of *where* to look. It is essential to concentrate on low-hanging fruit. The EA organization is usually understaffed and already fully loaded with its day-to-day tasks. Any additional activities, such as an initiative to look for efficiency gains in the EA practice, need to take that fact into account. The creation of an *EA Waste Matrix* is therefore the first step on the way to a lean and agile EA.

The EA Waste Matrix (see next section) sums up the waste potential. It combines the contents of Tables 7-3 through 7-9, which list the waste types per EA activity, into one overview matrix. The matrix should be compiled as a group exercise in a workshop with just a little preparation and post-processing. This makes it a low-effort tool for identifying those parts of the EA processes that promise quick wins by waste removal.

Once the areas for closer inspection have been selected, other tools come into play. Taking up the notion of an architecture factory as outlined in the beginning of this chapter, EA can be seen as a product with associated services. In the lean methodology, the production steps of a product are described and analyzed by a set of tools usually summed up as value stream mapping. Some of them, in an adapted form, make sense to use in the quite specific "production process" of EA artifacts and services.[33]

Process activity mapping (to be discussed in detail in the coming sections) is the central tool to describe the process flow in creation of an EA artifact. It denotes the transformation of initial information over intermediate work products to the final document or model. The diagram nodes carry special tags such as processing, review, waiting, or storage. In addition, a timeline at the bottom of the figure visualizes value-adding and nonvalue-adding phases so that it becomes immediately apparent where the process has potential for waste removal.

A useful complement to process activity mapping is the design structure matrix (DSM), which focuses on the uncovering of time-consuming iterations and loops. It uses a very simple format, a square matrix, making it easy to use and understand in interactive workshops.

The pipeline response matrix is another addition. Like the DSM, this tool focuses on one particular aspect of the EA process flow: the relationship between in-process time and inventory size. Each processing node is simply drawn as a stacked box, where the edge lengths relate to the times mentioned earlier. This makes it easy to identify a bottleneck in the EA process, since it shows up as particular thick box.

The EA waste matrix

Padma Valluri, Bank4Us enterprise architect with a mission of purging the EA processes of bureaucratic ballast, has been allocated a small budget for an external consultant. She decides to contact Sandro Poggi, an expert in lean and agile architecture. Padma has worked with Sandro in earlier projects and knows that he is the right person to support her efforts.

On Sandro's advice, Padma organizes a workshop to jointly compile an EA waste matrix. Most of her colleagues on the EA team can free up time to participate. To get an outside view of the EA work, Padma also approaches those key IT and business representatives with whom the enterprise architects interact most. She has good standing with them. In addition, there is a mutual feeling that the interaction of business, IT, and EA has room for improvement. Therefore many of the stakeholders promise to take part in the workshop, too.

For the meeting, Sandro paints the matrix in Table 7-10, with the cells left empty, onto large sheets of paper he hangs on the meeting room walls. After a brief introduction to the lean concepts and the meaning of the seven waste types, he asks each workshop participant to write her or his personal ideas for waste removal on sticky notes. The notes should be marked with ● or ○ as a priority indicator and then be pinned to the appropriate cell in the matrix. Afterward, Sandro moderates the group's joint

---

[33]Hines and Rich (1996), Millard (2001), and McManus (2005) give the most comprehensive description of value stream mapping tools. The tools not considered here are the production variety funnel, quality filter mapping, demand-amplifying mapping, decision point analysis, physical structure mapping, Gantt charts, and Ward/LEI maps. These tools mostly focus on aspects of mass production. Since EA artifacts are all "custom-built," we have not presented them here.

Table 7-10 Example of an EA Waste Matrix (● = High Potential for Waste Removal, ○ = Medium Potential)

EA Activity	Potential for Waste Removal (● = High, ○ = Medium)						
	Partially Done Work	Overarchitecting	Redundant Processes	Handoffs	Task Switching	Delays	Defects
EA-1 Defining the IT Strategy				○			○
EA-2 Modeling the Architectures	○	○	○			○	○
EA-3 Evolving the IT Landscape	●	○	○	○		●	○
EA-4 Assessing and Developing Capabilities						○	
EA-5 Developing and Enforcing Standards and Guidelines	●	○	●	●	○	●	○
EA-6 Monitoring the Project Portfolio	○	○		○			○
EA-7 Leading or Coaching Projects	○	○		○	●	○	○
EA-8 Managing Risks Involved in IT			○	○		○	

review of all sticky notes. The notes are reallocated to other cells if needed, duplicates removed, and the final priorities per table cell agreed on.

The outcome of the workshop is a filled-in matrix, as shown in Table 7-10. In addition, Sandro and Padma compile the notes for the detailed waste tables we saw in Tables 7-3 through 7-9. Before Padma can write a business case for a dedicated lean and agile EA project, she wants to perform one exemplary deep dive to ensure that the lean approach is indeed the right way for her EA organization. Table 7-10 helps her select the area to look at first. It seems that EA-3 (Evolving the IT Landscape) and EA-5 (Developing and Enforcing Standards and Guidelines) offer the most potential for waste removal.

After some discussion with her teammates and with Sandro, Padma picks one particular, slightly infamous project from EA-5 that ran under the name of *MobileDevGuide*. This exploration of mobile technologies and platforms, targeted at creating an enterprise-wide technology and development guideline for Bank4Us mobile applications, was not a badge of honor for the EA team. The project took much longer to complete than anticipated, yet none of the stakeholders was really happy with the result. Padma reasons that if the lean and agile EA approach reveals how this project would have run better, it should as well be able to help her improve the more frequently occurring EA processes.

The EA value stream

The removal of waste is, in lean methodology, inseparably linked to the analysis where value is generated. In other words, the *EA value stream* needs to be analyzed. Trivial as it might sound, the first step in value stream analysis is always a clear definition of the term *value*. Any process step either adds value or it does not. In mass production, a step is value-adding if it directly contributes to manufacturing of a work piece.

Painting a car body is value-adding; storing it to dry is not. The latter might be an example of a step that does not have a value in itself but is required by the process. Therefore, lean experts usually use the three-fold classification scheme that follows.[34] The goal of value stream optimization is to eliminate the NVA and minimize the R-NVA process steps.

- *Value-adding (VA)*. Directly contributing to the outcome of the process.
- *Required but nonvalue-adding (R-NVA)*. No direct value contribution but required due to the technical nature of the production process—for instance, coordination of meetings.
- *Nonvalue-adding (NVA)*. Process steps that are not required by the process and do not add value.

What is now value-adding in terms of EA activities? There is no general answer to this question. The creation of architecture documents and models can be value-adding—or not, depending on whether there is a true demand for them (as opposed to the documents that are produced but never read). The same applies to the definition of architecture processes and the creation of architecture views (such as executive summaries or presentation slides). Communication, learning, or measures to improve employee satisfaction are usually not directly value-adding but can fall into either the R-NVA or the NVA category.

As a conclusion, the definition of EA value depends on the context of the creation process and on the specific goal defined for it. Therefore the first step should always be the precise definition of a process goal. The sidebar contains a useful template for goal definition.

PROCESS GOALS

A Template for EA Process Goals

The following template[35] can be used to phrase the goal for a specific EA process:

Produce the <required outputs> *in an efficient way and without defects and* <at the right time>.

The process outputs should adhere to the *FFFT* criteria (McManus, 1999, quoted from Millard, 2001, p. 25):

- *Form.* Information must be in concrete form, explicitly stored.
- *Fit.* Information must be in a form that is useful to downstream processes and provided seamlessly.
- *Function.* Information (in the form of a design) must satisfy end-user and downstream process needs and communicate an acceptable amount of risk.
- *Timeliness.* The right information at the right time.

---

[34]We use the definitions by McManus (2005). Sometimes R-NVA is also abbreviated as NNVA (*necessary but nonvalue-adding*). Other authors—for instance, Urdhwareshe (2011, p. 290)—make an additional difference between customer value-added (CVA), for features immediately useful to customers, and business value-added (BVA) for activities required by law, regulations, and business needs.

[35]The template is taken from McManus (2005, p. 28). We replaced the original wording *as efficiently as possible* with *in an efficient way*, to avoid the slightly nebulous "as possible"—someone could always claim that it was not possible to be more efficient, which would be hard to negate.

In the goal template, the parts in pointed brackets should be replaced by a specific work result and the appropriate time constraints. The fragments without defects and in an efficient way are not negotiable; they should, without exception, always be part of the goal. The timeliness criterion means "at the right time" and not necessarily "as fast as possible." As we saw in the "Seven Wastes of EA" subsection, information is a perishable good that should not be stockpiled.

Padma and Sandro now ponder how they can analyze the MobileDevGuide value stream. Sandro points out that the initial EA value stream analysis should be performed again as a group exercise. All major stakeholders in the process need to be present. Padma should consider upstream and downstream actors as well—representatives from the business lines who gave the requirements for MobileDevGuide but also the guideline consumers, such as project managers and architects from the IT department. This might even involve implementation partners from different companies.

In the workshop itself, Sandro prefers using wallpaper, pens, and sticky notes instead of drawing tools. The market offers a rich set of flowcharting tools as well as dedicated lean value stream mapping editors, which can be used to capture and refine the workshop results afterward. When moderating the value stream analysis workshop, Sandro plans to use the process activity mapping, design structure matrix, and pipeline response matrix tools.

Process activity mapping

Lean process experts use *process activity mapping* to analyze the concrete process flow and search for improvement potential. There is no fully standardized terminology and notation for it. We lean toward the version by McManus (2005),[36] with slight adaptations to the specific situation in EA processes.

A value stream map is created by "put[ting] yourself in the position of a design as it progresses from concept to launch" (Womack and Jones, 1996, p. 16). The map depicts the flow of an EA document or model through different kinds of processing steps. The notation is listed in Figure 7-2. Broad arrows symbolize major flow of information or intermediate work products; the fine arrow stands for contributing information, such as review feedback. The process nodes can be:

- Starting or end points
- Operations (such as *Generalize Requirements*)
- Other activities such as review, approval, and handover between different actors[37]
- Temporary inventories where intermediate products wait for further processing

---

[36]McManus uses Rother and Shook's *Learning to See* method (2003) and adapts it to engineering and product design processes, where the flow of intermediate physical work items has already been replaced by the handling of data, information, and half-finished design artifacts. This is much closer to architecture creation in EA than the "classic" lean focus on mass production of physical goods.

[37]The *Approval* and the *Handover* nodes are not part of the notation as described by McManus and other authors but have been added specifically for EA processes.

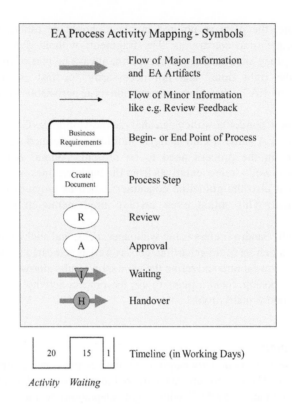

FIGURE 7-2

Process activity map notation, as used in this book.

This list is not comprehensive. An exhaustive best-practice guide for process activity mapping could easily fill a book of its own.[38] The lack of standardization leaves room for individual customizing of the notation if it makes sense for a specific process. One sensible enhancement, for instance, is to use *swim lanes* to correlate process nodes with actors.

Below the process activity diagram, a *timeline* can be added. It denotes phases of activity (line at bottom) versus waiting (line at top).[39] The timeline is usually annotated with the lengths of the respective phases. Further key performance indicators (KPIs), such as lead time or in-process time, can be added to the process nodes. However, this makes more sense for the analysis of frequently repeated tasks, where exact measurements count. In EA, the value stream map is more useful as a tool to detect potential for optimization and design improvements. A precise quantification of the improvement

---

[38]There are many books available on the topic of process activity maps. Sometimes the terms *process activity map* and *value stream map* are used as synonyms. Probably the most concise guide for using this technique can be found in McManus (2005, pp. 24–55).

[39]This is the way that timelines are shown throughout the literature on lean concepts. Just to avoid confusion: The Poppendiecks' influential adaptors of lean ideas in the IT world denote timelines the other way around (activity is depicted by the top line, waiting by the bottom line).

potential is usually neither needed nor possible, at least not without introducing additional monitoring as the first step.

Back at Bank4Us, Padma Valluri has organized a lean deep-dive workshop, moderated by Sandro Poggi, to analyze the MobileDevGuide project. The project is notorious among the Bank4Us IT crowd, which makes it a good showcase for Padma to explore the capabilities of lean EA. How could this project have been executed in a better way?

MobileDevGuide was started in the context of the *Closer to Customer* strategy assigned by the Bank4Us CIO (see Chapter 1). One IT maxim in this strategy was *Full Multichannel Capability*, but at first the company had absolutely no standards in place that covered mobile technology. Oscar Salgado, chief architect, dealt with the topic of mobility support already in our discussion of EA activity, "Monitoring the project portfolio (EA-6)," in Chapter 3.

Therefore, the EA team proposed a thorough technology and platform evaluation, targeting the creation of compulsory standards and development guidelines. Not much mobile know-how was available in the bank's IT organization. For that reason, the allocated budget for MobileDevGuide included an unprecedented luxury: the creation of a small prototype by an offshore team of one of Bank4Us' preferred implementation partners, managed by the bank's IT organization.

Much to everybody's dismay, the project turned out to be a failure. It took a full year instead of the planned six months, overrunning schedule and budget by 100%. Yet after all this effort, no one was really happy with the result. The IT crowd claimed that the guidelines were impractical and overly rigid; the business crowd was disappointed with the prototype's capabilities. Worst of all, due to the delay several development projects could not wait for the guidelines to be finalized (or claimed they couldn't) and started with the implementation of their mobile applications—each using a different technology, of course.

MobileDevGuide is still a bit of a political minefield. So Sandro, moderating the process activity mapping workshop, uses all his professional experience to avoid finger-pointing. As a first task, he discusses with the workshop participants which goal statement would have been appropriate for the project. They come up with the following:

> *Produce the mobile application development guidelines for Bank4Us in compliance with both the business and the IT requirements and validated by a working prototype, in an efficient way and without defects, within six months.*

He guides the group to map out the process on whiteboard and flipchart. The final result is shown in Figure 7-3, with the process steps numbered 1 to 9. This drawing is pretty revealing to the workshop participants. It shows that most of the project's difficulties did not stem from personal failure but from the intrinsic waste in the creation process. In the evaluation phase of the workshop, Sandro and Padma note down the following insights:

- *Long lead time before reviews.* The unwritten rules of the Bank4Us IT culture demand that reviews need a lead time of roughly three weeks.
- *Each review triggered extensive rework.* The project had three formal reviews (two with business, one with IT). Each of them caused rework. In the second review (no. 6), where the finished prototype was inspected, gaps in the initial specification were detected. The third review (8) with IT architects and project managers was even worse: One requirement was discovered to

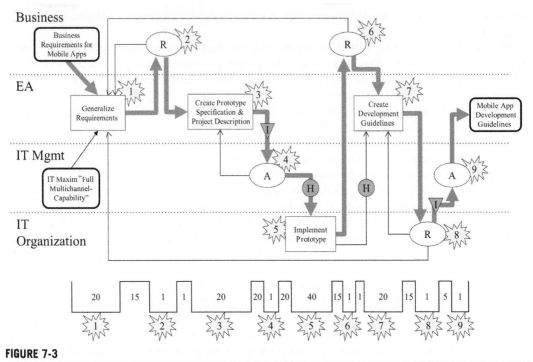

FIGURE 7-3

Process activity map for the MobileDevGuide project (times given in working days).

be incompatible with the bank's security guidelines and had to be changed in the initial specification.

- *Long waiting time before the prototype implementation.* Although the budget for the prototype implementation had already been approved, the interaction with procurement, which had to approve the project order and select the implementation partner (3–4), cost a full four weeks.
- *Difficult handover to the offshore prototype team.* Another four weeks passed with the ramp-up of the prototype implementation team offshore and the knowledge transfer to this team via teleconference (4–5).
- *Poor knowledge transfer from the prototype team to the enterprise architect.* The architect in charge of the project had only limited access to the experience of the prototype implementation team when he wrote the final guideline document (7). The employees of the partner company had already been allocated to other projects and were only available for a relatively short phone conference.
- *No requirements input from the IT organization.* Requirements were only discussed with the business departments, not with the project managers, architects, and developers who would eventually implement mobile applications.

All in all, the findings indicate a fair amount of waste—at least delays, redundant processes, partially done work, and handover (with a potential for the other waste types as well). Padma and Sandro decide to evaluate the results from the other analysis tools first before drawing final conclusions.

The Design Structure Matrix (DSM)

In addition to the process activity map, Sandro introduces a second tool in the MobileDevGuide workshop. The design structure matrix (DSM) uses a very simple tabular format[40] to specifically highlight iterations and rework in the process. Figure 7-4 shows the DSM table that the participants created in the workshop.

If step k provides input to step n, the intersection of column k and row n is marked with an x. All dots below the diagonal line in the lower half of the matrix represent forward flow—intermediate work products proceeding from one processing step to the next. This is unproblematic. Dots *above* the line, however, denote *iterations* and *backward flow*. They are a strong indicator of waste due to redundant processes or overarchitecting.

Not surprisingly, the culprits in MobileDevGuide are Steps 2, 4, 6, and 8—the review and approval steps (and their iterations) that were the source of some rework in the project. Had the process activity map been more complex, this might have been overlooked but made visible by the DSM.

The pipeline response matrix

Sandro asks the workshop participants to create, as a third tool, a *pipeline response matrix*[41] for the MobileDevGuide project. This is a specific view of the process activities, focusing on the ratio between the *in-process time* (the number of working days really spent on the task at hand) and the *task inventory* (the time needed to work on unrelated, parallel tasks). Each task is visualized as a square, with the horizontal edge denoting cumulative in-process time and the vertical one indicating cumulative task inventory time. The total duration is the sum of horizontal and vertical edge length. An "ideal" task in the diagram is as flat as possible to avoid waste due to delays.

Figure 7-5 shows the MobileDevGuide matrix. Let's take a closer look at Task 1, *Generalize requirements*. Its overall duration was 20 working days. During that period, the enterprise architect was able to work roughly 50% of his available working time on this task (*in-process time* = 10 d); the second half he had to dedicate to unrelated, parallel activities (*task inventory* = 10 d). The underlying thought model originates from manufacturing, assuming a first-in, first-out (FIFO) processing of incoming tasks—therefore the term *inventory* for the architect's other activities.

The pipeline response matrix is a good way to analyze waste due to *task switching* and *delays*. In Figure 7-5, the total in-process time is 79 days—less than half the total duration of 197 days. The rest is waiting. In other words, it might have been possible to finish the project in the planned six months if the internal processes had been better organized and less riddled with parallel processing and waiting. As a consequence, Padma and Sandro formulate the following additional findings for MobileDevGuide:

---

[40]The tool has been proposed by McManus (2005). Other than in the case of process activity mapping, there is not much more to it than is covered in this subsection. It is a complementing tool that focuses on a certain aspect of the value stream, no more and no less.

[41]In the lean literature this tool is referred to as a *supply chain response* (or *responsiveness*) *matrix*; see, for instance, Hines and Rich (1996). We have slightly adapted the terminology to make it more intuitive to understand for EA processes.

	A	B	1	2	3	4	5	6	7	8	9	C
A Business requirements on Mobile Apps												
B IT Maxim "Full Multi-Channel Capabilities"												
1 Generalize requirements	x	x										
2 Review by business			x									
3 Create prototype specification and project description				x								
4 Approval by IT management & procurement					x							
5 Implement prototype						x						
6 Review by business							x					
7 Create development guidelines							x	x				
8 Review by IT organization									x			
9 Approval of guidelines by IT management										x		
C Mobile app development guidelines ready											x	

FIGURE 7-4

DSM for the MobileDevGuide Project at Bank4Us.

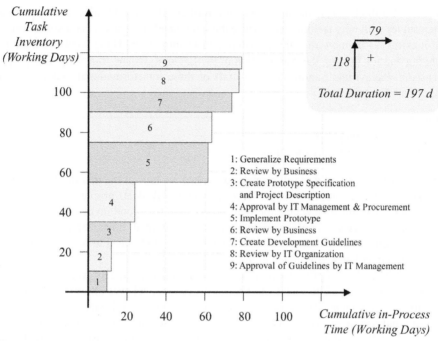

FIGURE 7-5

The pipeline response matrix for the MobileDevGuide project.

- *The enterprise architects might have to reconsider their work planning.* Steps 1, 3, and 7 were executed by an enterprise architect. In each of the steps, he could not spend more than roughly half his working time on his main activity.
- *Until the EA processes will have changed, a buffer for internal delays should be added to the planning process.* In Figure 7-5, the actual operations (specification and implementation) are displayed in a darker gray, the inspection tasks (review and approval) in a lighter shade. Surprisingly, the delays in both types of activities are roughly the same. If MobileDevGuide is indeed a typical EA activity, the planning buffer size should be at least 100%.[42]

Transition to a lean and agile EA organization

The lean approach has convinced Padma. She feels that this is the right way forward for her EA organization. She meets again with Sandro to plot the strategy for her next moves in the internal process transformation. Sandro recommends developing a systematic *waste catalogue*—a list of minor and major process improvement proposals. The waste identified by the MobileDevGuide analysis will be the base stock, to be enhanced and verified by further analysis of other EA projects and activities. This can be done via interviews. This way the planners avoid a dedicated workshop, which is always hard to organize.

---

[42]No one in a sane mind will actually propose a 100% buffer without keeping her resignation letter ready in her pocket. Therefore, this is a more a "political" conclusion. The real conclusion is of course to change the process so that it becomes more effective.

But Sandro also thinks they should go one step further. They might miss the big picture if they content themselves with only tackling the waste catalogue. Sandro proposes that Padma derive a small number of maxims[43]—no more than three—from their results so far. These would be material for internal lobbying and for funding the continuation of the EA analysis and transformation project. After some discussion, Padma and Sandro create a draft of three transformational maxims (to be tested against other past EA projects):

- Speed up EA.
- Bring more transparency to EA.
- Move EA closer to the IT organization.

The direction of *Speed up EA* is self-explanatory when we look at the manifold delays in Mobile-DevGuide. The second maxim, *Bring more transparency to EA*, deals primarily with the evident ineffectiveness of the current review and approval processes. "Everyone involved must be able to see and must understand every aspect of the operation and its status at all times," state Womack and Jones (1996, p. 61). It seems clear that the stakeholders (business and IT) need to be involved much earlier and on a more frequent basis. But how can that be done?

Sandro thinks that the overall way in which the enterprise architects work together with their stakeholders should change. The architects need a process model that allows them to focus more on the essential EA activities. The stakeholders should be an integral part of the process, not just bystanders who have to be drawn in case by case. He proposes that Padma venture into agile architecture ideas. We will accompany the two on their journey in "Building Block 2: Involve all stakeholders by interlocking architecture scrums" and "Building Block 3: Practice iterative architecture through EA Kanban."

The third maxim, *Move EA closer to the IT organization*, takes up the friction between EA on one side and IT plus implementation partner on the other. Padma is convinced that she and her fellow enterprise architects need access to a pool of local IT resources. If a pilot or prototype is to be implemented, it should be done by a collocated team, with the enterprise architect directly involved in the implementation.

With regard to *Move EA closer to the IT organization*, Sandro recounts an experience from a consulting engagement at Boeing. "Boeing adopted ruggedized tablets for shop floor employees on the Dreamliner 787 program. This allowed mechanics to collaborate with engineering and visualize work instructions with 3D models in real-time as work was actually being done," he tells Padma. In addition, the engineers' desks were physically moved from their offices to the shop floor in order to bring the airplane's designers closer to its builders.[44] So, if it worked for Boeing, why not try it at the bank in the collaboration of EA and IT ground workers? The agile methodology has ideas here as well. We will look over Padma's and Sandro's shoulders as they implement Building Block 2: Involve all stakeholders by interlocking architecture scrums.

---

[43]The rules of lean consumption by Womack and Jones (2005, quoted by Schmidt and Lyle, 2010, p. 139f) can be a yardstick for finding such maxims: 1. Solve my problem completely. 2. Don't waste my time. 3. Provide exactly what I want. 4. Deliver value where I want it. 5. Supply value when I want it. 6. Reduce the number of decisions I must make to solve my problems.

[44]Both Boeing stories are true. The quotation about the ruggedized tablets is from a blog post, www.apriso.com/blog/2011/10/the-mobility-movement-is-well-underway/. The story about moving the design engineers to the shop floor was told by a tour guide when Stefan visited a Boeing plant in Everett, Washington, in 2010.

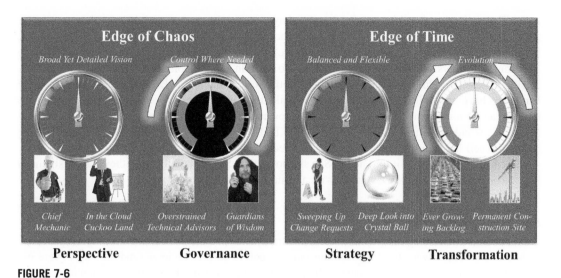

FIGURE 7-6

The EA Dashboard for Building Block 1: Get rid of waste by streamlining architecture processes.

Summing it up: Assessment by the EA dashboard

As we saw in the Bank4Us example, Building Block 1: Get rid of waste by streamlining architecture processes is in any case a good starting point for analysis of EA processes. Not all of the findings, though, can be tackled by eliminating waste. Trivially enough, this kind of lean optimization works best if there are *processes in place* that you can optimize. Figure 7-6 summarizes, in a somewhat pointed way, where the lean approach can be helpful beyond its role as a general analysis tool. Taking the EA Dashboard that we introduced in Chapter 6 as a base, we see that lean concepts can work well in the *Governance* and the *Transformation* dimensions—every time "doing less" makes the EA work more effective.

Waste removal can be a good cure for overly strong governance, or it can be a stimulator for an EA organization suffocating from overload and its own ineffectiveness. A too-strong governance is likely to be rightsized by waste removal. The situation with a too-weak governance may be similar, but it also might first require additional empowerment of the EA group—something that the lean approach (at least in the flavor we present here) does not provide.

The situation in the *Transformation* dimension is the other way round. One can imagine that an overly slow speed can be increased by offloading waste. On the other extreme, in the case of the *Frequent Revolution*, waste removal might or might not help. The effects in the *Perspective* and the *Strategy* dimensions are too indirect to be considered here.

Building Block 2: Involve all stakeholders by interlocking architecture scrums

Padma Valluri, the enterprise architect in charge of streamlining the Bank4Us EA processes, has arranged another full-day meeting with her external consultant, Sandro Poggi. Jointly they want to develop a concept to make EA faster, more efficient, and positioned closer to the stakeholders, especially to the IT organization. Sandro proposes that they look again at the process activity map they created for the MobileDevGuide project. If this is the as-is process, says Sandro, how could a *target* process look, taking MobileDevGuide as their concrete example?

Padma considers this idea. Of course, there is no value in itself to optimizing a one-off pilot project. Their real target should be numerous, repetitive activities that eat up the EA team's time. On the other hand, they have now collected a lot of data on MobileDevGuide, which makes it a natural candidate for testing Sandro's concept. Even more important, everyone in the Bank4Us IT world knows it. That makes it a wonderful showcase if Padma decides that she wants to pursue this new line of thinking and has to sell the idea to management and her peers to gain acceptance and funds.

That last thought settles it for Padma. She sits down with Sandro and together they start designing a hypothetical rerun of MobileDevGuide with an improved process model.

An agile EA project

First, Sandro reasons, they should introduce a *takt* time, as in lean manufacturing. Among the problems in MobileDevGuide were the long waiting periods before formal reviews (and still they were not effective in involving the stakeholders). The perfect countermeasure is to structure such a project in iterations, or *sprints*, of a fixed length, as in agile software development. At the end of each iteration, results from the sprint are demonstrated to the stakeholders. They provide feedback and input for the next sprint planning. The demo dates are known well beforehand. No extra lead time is necessary.

The next idea Sandro brings to the table is to give up the dedicated prototype implementation. Instead he proposes to join forces with one of the mobile application development projects. They were supposed to wait for the mobile guidelines, but in reality they started on their own, since the guidelines were delayed. Wouldn't it make sense if one of these projects would perform a dual role: pilot for this new technology at first and then implementer of a specific business application? As a precondition, the EA would need to convince the leader of one of these projects to start earlier than planned and to broaden its scope.

Padma likes the idea. The extra burden for the project is limited. It would not have to implement a complete and reusable mobile platform; that was not the original goal of MobileDevGuide. It just would have to "behave well" to serve as a technology pilot, meaning:

- Architectural issues need to be handled with care.
- Ad hoc solutions must be strictly avoided.
- Stakeholder feedback is to be meticulously tracked.

In return, the project would be provided with extra developers (those budgeted for the original prototype), and an enterprise architect would be available to oversee the project architecture. In other words, the risk of project failure is much lower in return for a bit of organizational overhead. Padma is pretty sure that she would have been able to strike such a deal with the business sponsors she knows.

The other precondition is a bit harder to swallow. Since Sandro has proposed agile techniques as the process paradigm for MobileDevGuide, the development project needs to switch to agile methods as well. Otherwise the close interlocking of EA activity and pilot implementation cannot be realized.

Padma knows that the agile concept enjoys some sympathy across the Bank4Us IT and business community. The process guidelines allow agile projects under certain circumstances, but the default approach is still the good old waterfall. For the particular example of MobileDevGuide, Padma thinks she could have convinced one of the business sponsors to use agile. But any general role model for collaboration between EA and IT must be applicable to waterfall projects as well. Padma makes a mental note to raise the issue with Sandro again at a later time.

Figure 7-7 shows the idealized *target* process activity map for the MobileDevGuide project, drafted by Padma and Sandra using agile elements. It looks radically different from the real scenario depicted in Figure 7-6. With this process model, it would be possible to finish in time. Padma's and Sandro's plan foresees six sprints of three weeks each and a little more than a week for the final approval. This means a total duration of less than five months.

By introducing sprints, the review lead times are eliminated. There is no real waiting time in the process anymore, only the demo day is not directly productive (therefore a sprint is denoted as 14 + 1 days). Architecture and pilot implementation are handled within *one* project but not merged up to a point where the architecture work is in danger of becoming swallowed up by many implementation tasks. Both are handled in separated tracks according to the general pattern depicted in Figure 7-8.

The generic word *track* has been used deliberately. There are several ways to implement this pattern. The simplest option is to handle architectural work items in the same way as implementation features and to simply tag them differently in the requirements management system. This might be sufficient in the MobileDevGuide example. In larger programs or IT transformations, EA work should be handled by a dedicated architecture scrum team; we will describe possible setups for such a situation later in this section.

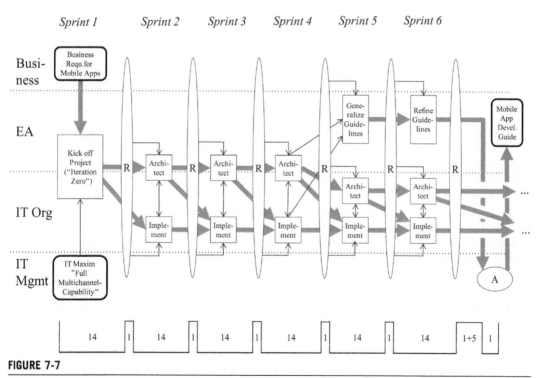

FIGURE 7-7

Process activity map for a lean and agile version of the MobileDevGuide project (times in working days).

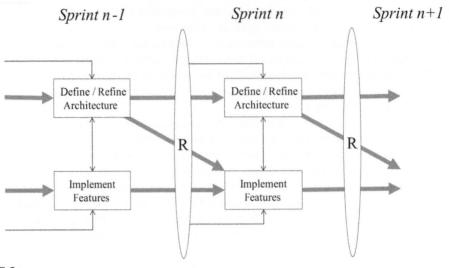

FIGURE 7-8

Pattern for combining architecture and implementation track.

In the process redesign for MobileDevGuide, the important issue for Padma and Sandro is the elimination of uncontrolled rework of architecture specifications. The stress in this statement is on the word *uncontrolled:* Of course, the frequent reviews will provide feedback and cause changes. But these changes are routinely incorporated into the next sprint planning; they are expected as a natural part of the process. There is constant interchange between those project members working on architecture and those implementing features.

However, major input from the architecture track is translated into implementation features only at the *beginning* of a sprint. There is a strict rule in the agile methodology not to accept additional requirements in the middle of a sprint. In case of a major change in the project requirements or constraints, when immediate action is necessary, the sprint can be *terminated*. Only after new planning and prioritization can it be restarted. This approach protects both architects and developers from uncontrolled ad hoc changes and half-baked architecture decisions.

In sprints 2 to 4, the enterprise architect works as part of the project's architecture group. This allows the EA to learn and teach at the same time. She gathers first hand knowledge on the technology and can in parallel coach the project architects in their design decisions. It allows her to keep the option open to generalize certain features into an enterprise platform later.

From sprint 5 onward, architecture is handled exclusively by the project architects. The enterprise architect uses her knowledge from the pilot phase of the project to write the guidelines document. That work is still handled as part of the project, and its result is presented in the demos. This ensures that experience, concerns, and ideas from the IT crowd are sufficiently embodied in the development guideline document.

Each sprint in Figure 7-7 is structured in the same way. A sprint ends with the customer demo, and the next one starts with a planning phase. There are no hard rules as to how sprint planning should be done. Figure 7-9 shows a setup that has been proven to work well in practice. In the *scoping workshop* the priority order for the next requirements is identified, and the sprint content is defined.

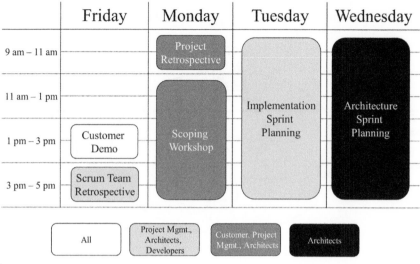

FIGURE 7-9

A proven pattern for organizing the planning phase of a sprint.

It should be noted that if there is a dedicated architecture track, the scoping workshop has a double role. For the implementation track, it selects the user stories for the upcoming sprint N. However, the architecture track focuses on the *future* items. Therefore, the scoping workshop also needs to determine the user stories for the $N + 1$ sprint as well—at least on a coarse level. This principle applies to the sprint demos as well: The architecture track's demo result refers to user stories of the *future* sprint.

In a project with both architecture and implementation tracks, the scoping is followed first by *implementation sprint planning*. Participants are developers and architects who break down the high-level requirements to the task level and provide effort estimation and commitment. Subsequently, the architects do the same in *architecture sprint planning*.

All sprints are usually performed following this pattern, with the exception of the first sprint of the project, in agile terminology often called *iteration zero*. Here the project has room to define itself, from setting up the development environment and project infrastructure to becoming familiar with new domains or technologies.

Scrum patterns for EA

The MobileDevGuide project setup as drafted by Padma and Sandro is depicted in Figure 7-11. For better understanding, Figure 7-10 shows the notation we use here for organizational patterns using agile elements. The scrum master, the product owner, the scrum team members, and the outside stakeholders are marked by different shades.

A setup like the one shown in Figure 7-11 can be used for running any key IT project that is considered strategically critical and therefore should be run under the technical guidance of an enterprise architect. If the project is set up using agile processes, the enterprise architect would simply join the

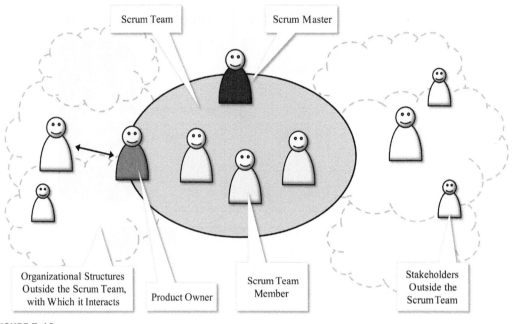

FIGURE 7-10

Notation used for depicting scrum patterns in agile EA.

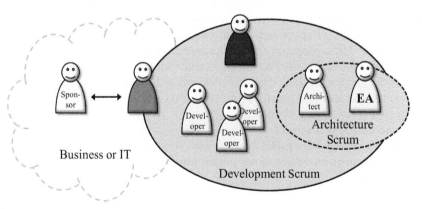

FIGURE 7-11

Pattern 1: An enterprise architect involved in an agile project—for instance, as a technical lead.

architecture team and fulfill her leading, coaching, and supervising role there. If the project contains a large amount of architectural work and has more than one architect, the introduction of a dedicated architecture scrum (indicated by a dotted line) might be advisable.

If the project is entirely dedicated to developing EA artifacts—for instance, a proof of concept for a new technology or development of an enterprise-wide platform component—an agile setup like the one

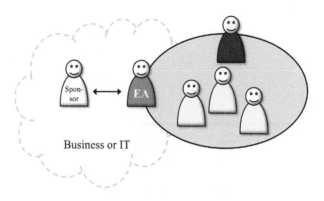

FIGURE 7-12

Pattern 2: A dedicated agile EA project.

shown in Figure 7-12 is a useful option. The enterprise architect takes over the role of the product owner in this case, since she is the primary recipient of the project deliverable.

The agile scrum patterns outlined so far work for a collaboration of enterprise architects with agile IT projects. But what about EA work in general, especially the steering and monitoring of IT projects and programs that use the classical waterfall model?

The solution for the latter issue is an *architecture scrum of scrums,* as depicted in Figure 7-13. This tool can be used for a variety of situations, from supervising an IT transformation consisting of several

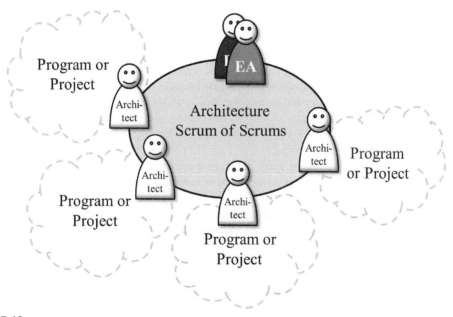

FIGURE 7-13

Pattern 3: An architecture scrum of scrums.

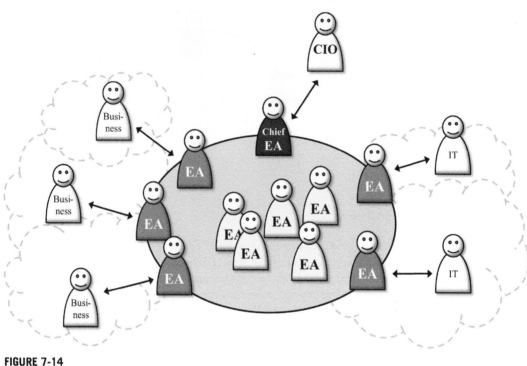

FIGURE 7-14

Pattern 4: The EA group as scrum team.

loosely related programs to developing EA guidelines with an early buy-in from the IT community. This pattern does not require the projects or programs to be agile. The lead architects from each project or program join a regular scrum-of-scrum meeting (for instance, on a weekly basis). The enterprise architect takes either the scrum master or the product owner role, or a combination of both.

Last but not least, Pattern 4 in Figure 7-14 depicts a model for the EA team itself. The chief enterprise architect (or whoever heads the EA team) should take the scrum master role. Unlike in agile software development, the EA scrum team develops more than one product and pursues multiple activities at the same time. This means addressing a variety of stakeholders on both the business and IT sides.

Therefore it makes sense to have *several* product owners on the team. Each product owner should have a deep expertise of the enterprise areas(s) and stakeholder(s) he represents, whether on the business side or the IT side. This should not be a problem on a well-composed EA team, which should be a mix of members originating from both business and IT backgrounds.

In such a setup, the EA team should subscribe to a regular sprint and demo rhythm. This way, the main stakeholders for various EA tasks can become used to the enduring existence of an EA group (whether they like it or not). Strict adherence to a *takt* time for EA-related review and demo meetings helps establish EA as a reliable key player in IT decision processes. In addition, the quality will improve due to the necessity to demonstrate the results.

Table 7-11 Suitability of the EA Scrum Patterns per EA Area

Area	Pattern 1: EA Involved in Agile Project	Pattern 2: Dedicated Agile EA Project	Pattern 3: Architecture Scrum of Scrums	Pattern 4: EA Group as Scrum Team
EA-1 Defining the IT Strategy				●
EA-2 Modeling the Architectures	*Modeling is always an integral part of other EA activities in EA-1 and EA-3 … EA-8*			
EA-3 Evolving the IT Landscape				●
EA-4 Assessing and Developing Capabilities			●	●
EA-5 Developing and Enforcing Standards and Guidelines	●	●	●	●
EA-6 Monitoring the Project Portfolio			●	
EA-7 Leading or Coaching Projects	●	●	●	
EA-8 Managing Risks Involved in IT				●

In summary, Table 7-11 maps the proposed four scrum patterns to the EA areas EA-1 to EA-8, as introduced in Chapter 3. A marker in a table cell means that the particular scrum pattern is well suited to supporting this type of activity.

Setting up the EA group as a scrum team (Pattern 4) helps steady the flow of EA work and decrease wait time. In addition, it ensures effective information flow by the regular stand-up scrum meetings within the team. Such setup is especially helpful in areas such as *Defining the IT strategy* (EA-1), *Evolving the IT landscape* (EA-3), and *Managing risks involved in IT* (EA-8), which are prone to the "ivory tower effect" if the constant interaction with the stakeholders is neglected.

Pattern 3, the architecture scrum of scrums, helps in all areas where EA has a supervising, monitoring, or evangelizing function. It can also be used as a way to organize an architecture board for technical approvals. Patterns 1 and 2, with the direct involvement of enterprise architects in the practical development work, are a proper antidote against IT anarchy on one side and EA detachment from reality on the other. With joint scrums, IT and EA are at least sitting in the same boat (even if they still might not row in the same direction all the time). That makes it harder to simply ignore each other.

A pilot project at Bank4Us

Padma has now seen enough to consider piloting the lean and agile approach with a real EA project. She discusses with her boss, Oscar, which activity would be suitable to test the idea. Her own proposal to Oscar is to approach Ian Miller and his team of enterprise architects, who work on the application rationalization program in the *Closer to Customer* initiative. (We accompanied Ian and his team in describing the typical EA activities in Chapter 3.)

From the occasional meeting in the coffee kitchen, Padma knows that Ian is inundated with work. She reckons that he will gratefully accept any support that might help him better organize his project. In addition, she has a trustful relationship with Ian; she knows him as a critical yet open-minded person. If the concept works for Ian, Padma feels, she can convince her other peers as well.

In an initial meeting with Ian, Padma and Sandro establish the basic facts about the application rationalization program. Ian leads a project team of five other people who all work (more or less full-time) on the application rationalization program: two further enterprise architects from Oscar Salgado's EA group, two dedicated business process experts, and someone from the IT organization who is focused on planning and coordinating implementation projects.

In addition, Ian's list of key people who need to be kept informed, interviewed, or monitored for progress runs into the several of dozens: business heads who want to know what's going on, key users who understand the crucial and undocumented traits of business processes and applications, IT program managers like Sarah Taylor (whom we met in Chapter 1), architects and managers from projects implementing parts of the transformation—the list could be continued seemingly endlessly.

So far, Ian struggles with organizing his project. The governance boards of the EA and IT organizations are not much help. They are useful in monitoring the project milestones, but they do not offer much help in steering the architecture work for a complex IT transformation program. Office space is scarce at Bank4Us; therefore Ian was not even able to seize a permanent "war room" for his team. Luckily, at least two of his team members reside on the same floor as Ian himself. But the coordination of meetings with the larger team and the main stakeholders alone takes up a substantial amount of Ian's time.

After the meeting with Ian, Sandro and Padma design a possible architecture scrum setup for the application rationalization program, as shown in Figure 7-15. Ian acts as scrum master. Chief architect Oscar Salgado takes the role of the product owner, representing the sponsor's intentions for the program. The team will meet every morning in Ian's office for 15 minutes in a daily face-to-face scrum meeting, standing up in order to keep it brief and concise. Team members who are traveling participate via phone. Each participant in the scrum round answers the three typical scrum questions:

- What did you do yesterday?
- What will you do today?
- What is blocking progress?

Oscar Salgado is invited to participate in the *chicken* role, meaning that he is allowed to listen in but should not ask questions or give comments. Any in-depth discussion is postponed to after the scrum.

In addition to the core scrum team, Sandro has designed two scrum of scrums, which will meet once a week in a fixed timeslot. The *IT Project Portfolio Scrum of Scrums* gathers the program managers of the IT organization involved in the program implementation. The meeting will make sure that everyone is on the same page with regard to the implementation progress, planning, and showstoppers.

The *Architecture Scrum of Scrums* helps supervise the architecture implementation. It provides a platform for regular exchange between the EA team and the project architects. Both scrums are coordinated by one member of Ian's team. As the overall project manager, Ian is also invited to both meetings.

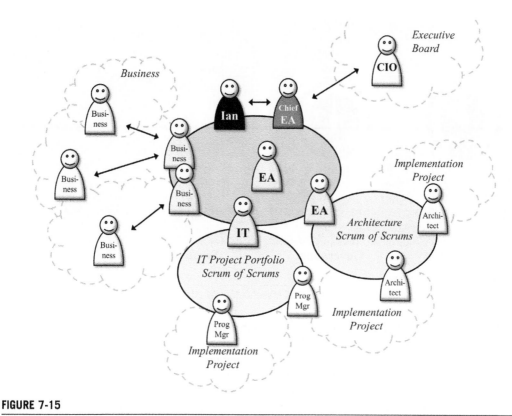

FIGURE 7-15

Architecture scrum setup for the *Closer to Customer* application rationalization program at Bank4Us.

Padma likes the concept. She decides to present it to Ian and his team once she has better understood how the actors in this organization structure will interact in practice. She tells Sandro that she will require more of his time.

Summing it up: Assessment by the EA Dashboard

As depicted in Figure 7-16, the introduction of architecture scrums can help adjust the perspective of an EA organization. The information flow is strengthened between enterprise architects and their stakeholders in business and IT as well as within the EA team itself. This helps in overcoming silo thinking, regardless of whether the particular silo is located in a strategic utopia or in the IT repairmen's shop on the ground.

As a side effect, the enterprise architects will know better the consequences of their guidelines on IT projects. In the case of overly strict EA governance, it could encourage them to think in more pragmatic ways. In a similar manner, it can be expected that distortions in the Strategy and the Transformation dimensions may be alleviated by the regular contact between EA and its stakeholders. Frequent exposure to a situation makes you see it more realistically. However, this effect is only an indirect one; therefore we did not list it in Figure 7-16.

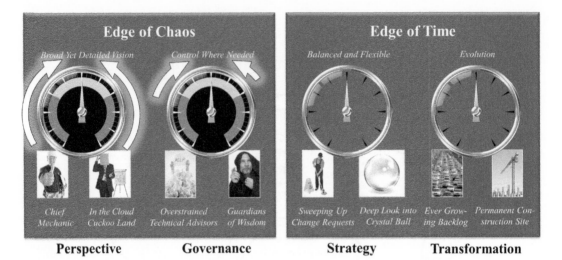

FIGURE 7-16

The EA Dashboard for Building Block 2: Involve all stakeholders by interlocking architecture scrums.

The other main effect of the scrum approach, together with an iteration structure and regular result reviews, is to increase the EA organization's visibility. This can help an overstrained enterprise architect to get her foot in the door in certain decision making processes. As trivial as this may sound, it makes the business and IT key persons realize that there *is* an EA team, and that it cannot be ignored easily. The first step in the long path of building mutual trust is *acknowledgement*.

At Bank4Us, Padma Valluri writes an intermediate report for her boss, Oscar Salgado. She has now some models for reorganizing the EA processes on the table. Padma is convinced that the agile approach works fine for smaller projects with EA participation—Patterns 1 and 2. Sandro Poggi has even addressed her concern about the collaboration with waterfall projects and programs in Pattern 3. By and large, she knows she can use agile methods as a niche process where appropriate and that she would not have a hard time convincing others of that.

Still, Padma has some concerns as to whether agile techniques are a suitable model for an activity so long-term oriented, so riddled with signoffs and approval chains as EA. Could Ian Miller benefit from the lean and agile EA approach in his application rationalization program, fighting with the organization's bureaucracy on one hand and the executive board's expectations on the other? Can the EA processes and frameworks that Bank4Us uses really be reconciled with an agile approach?

Padma sighs and checks her calendar to schedule some more meetings. Together with Sandro, she will dig through the existing process material and perform a sound sanity check. Let's stay with them into the next section.

Building Block 3: Practice iterative architecture through EA Kanban

Enterprise architects are involved in a large number of different activities in IT, business, and board-level management. As Figure 7-17 shows, these tasks have very different time horizons. Operational aspects of IT are planned with a granularity of months. This can go down to weeks and even days

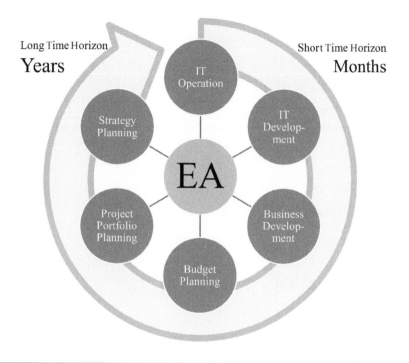

FIGURE 7-17

Different time horizons for the activities in which EA is involved.

when they're reacting to an emergency. Other activities—such as enterprise strategy or project portfolio management—are so long-term in nature that they are planned with a lead time of several years.

One of the biggest challenges for EA is to handle each activity with the proper time granularity. If the enterprise architect fails to do so, she is prone to finding her in either one of the Chapter 1 caricatures, *A Deep Look into the Crystal Ball* (ignoring the present) or *Sweeping Up the Change Requests* (ignoring the future). EA needs a planning and managing system for architecture tasks that is flexible enough to handle short *and* long time horizons simultaneously. Agile development provides such a system, and we will see that it fits EA very well.

Agile EA requirements management

Enterprise-level planning can be categorized in the following horizons, with each step adding more details:

> *Vision – Roadmap – Release – Project Milestone* or *Iteration*

Requirements exist on parallel granularity levels, from the enterprise vision down to the program and project level:

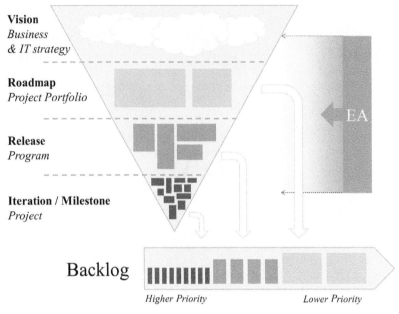

FIGURE 7-18

Translation of different levels of detail and time horizons into a backlog.

- Creating the enterprise business and IT vision is a strategic activity, as summed up in EA-1 in Chapter 3. Its output is a set of concise maxims intended for a time horizon measured in years.
- Project portfolio management and budgeting are done based on road maps that usually cover 12 to 24 months.
- The release planning for programs and projects is already fairly concrete, with a time span of normally three to six months.
- The most detailed level consists of project milestones and (in case the project is executed in agile mode) iterations. They are part of the day-to-day project planning and usually cover two to eight weeks.

One of the key strengths of the agile approach is to handle requirements from such different layers of detail very well. This especially includes the transformation of maxims from the vision level down to the concrete implementation. As depicted in Figure 7-18, two agile traits specifically support this:

- The agile backlog manages elements of *different granularity side by side*, distinguished by priority. Only the items high on the priority list need to be provided at the implementation level of detail. Detail planning is done only when the work item is actually tackled, not up front as in a waterfall approach. This way not much planning work is wasted in case items are dropped due to reprioritization.

- Changing priorities, even altering or adding requirements, is controlled by a lightweight process. It is easy to keep the overall planning and design flexible.

While a project architect primarily provides architecture for the lowest two levels (release and iteration), an enterprise architect is regularly involved in all four levels.[45] EA frameworks take this fact into account by providing means for classifying and structuring the architectures according to the layers of detail. TOGAF[46] proposes three levels of granularity for architecture work, as depicted in Figure 7-19[47] (left side). In comparison, agile requirement levels are shown in the right side of this figure. There is an evident match between the two worlds.

Enterprise strategic architecture deals with the overall IT landscape. When Bank4Us CIO Dave Callaghan announces 20% savings in the IT budget, transformations are first tackled on the enterprise strategic architecture level. One measure is the global application rationalization program that Ian Miller drives. To *implement* transformations, their architecture needs to be specified on *segment* levels.

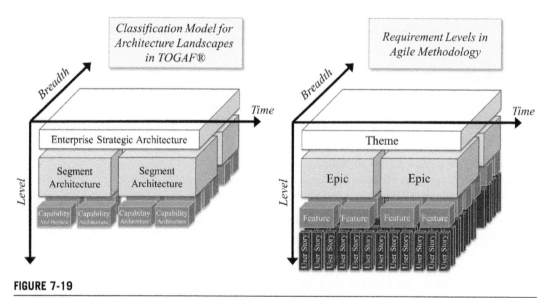

FIGURE 7-19

Classification for the architecture landscape in TOGAF (*left*); levels of requirement specifications in agile techniques (*right*).

---

[45]Her main focus is in the middle two layers (roadmap and release; see activities EA-3, *Evolving the IT Landscape*, and EA-6, *Monitoring the Project Portfolio*). However, EA also contributes to the vision (see EA-1, *Defining the IT Strategy*) and the iteration and project level (see EA-5, *Developing and Enforcing Standards and Guidelines*, and EA-7, *Leading or Coaching Projects*).

[46]The FEA framework provides a partially similar structure; see Chapter 4.

[47]The Open Group (2011), used with kind permission.

Table 7-12 Mapping of Planning Horizons, Architecture Levels, and Means of Agile Requirement Description

Enterprise Level	Planning Horizon	Architecture Level According to TOGAF	Requirement Level in Agile
Business and IT strategy	Vision	Enterprise strategic architecture	Theme
Project portfolio	Road map	Segment architecture	Epic
Program	Release	Capability architecture	Feature
Project	Milestone/ iteration		User story

The partitioning for the segment architecture can vary from case to case. In the application rationalization case, it is a division by business lines and application groups, such as human resources, customer relationship management, trading, and so forth. The *capability architecture*, one level down, describes the design of a particular solution, such as the consolidation of one specific application. Table 7-12 sums up the mapping between the enterprise planning horizons and the agile requirement types.

Levels of agile requirements

The basic building block of agile requirements management is the *user story*. It follows a fixed wording pattern: *As a ..., I want ..., so that ...*, which associates it with a specific stakeholder or role. The *so that* part transports the user intention. A typical user story for a reporting system in the Bank4Us IT landscape reads like this:

> **As** *head of compliance for the US/West region,*
> **I want** *a daily report on the main SOX compliance indicators*
> **so that** *I can report the compliance level to my regional board.*

A user story is sized so that it can be implemented within one iteration (usually two to four weeks). For requirements that need more effort, agile techniques provide the more coarse-grained terms *feature, epic,* and *theme*.

These terms are not standardized, though. When you use agile methods for small or midsize software projects, *epics* are just a kind of large user stories.[48] In the same context, themes denote a related group of user stories. For an online job placement portal, the themes *job search*, *CV database*, and *job application* comprise all stories describing these particular aspects of the portal.

For use in an enterprise context, we are at liberty to interpret these terms in a broader sense so that we can apply them to the whole IT landscape instead of just one project. Some authors[49] have provided their interpretation of these agile terms for the enterprise.

---

[48]Mike Cohn, one of the agile gurus, puts it this way: "Although there is no magic size at which we start calling a user story an epic, generally an epic is a user story that will take more than one or two sprints to develop and test" (Cohn, 2009, p. 246).
[49]In this building block, we essentially follow the agile terminology and its interpretation as provided by Leffingwell and Widrig (2003), Leffingwell (2007, 2011), and Shalloway, Beaver, and Trott (2010).

- As the level immediately above a user story, Leffingwell and Widrig introduce the *feature*. "Features are services provided by the system that fulfill stakeholder needs," they write (2003, p. 70). The feature level is suitable to describe requirements on program and release levels, which in turn correspond to the capability architecture in TOGAF.
- The next level, suitable for roadmap content, is *epic*. Leffingwell describes *epics* as "large-scale development initiatives that realize the value of investment themes" (2011, p. 83). "[Their] objective is strategic intent, not specificity. In other words, the Epic need only be described in detail sufficient to initiate a further discussion about what types of features an Epic implies" (2011, p. 44). This matches TOGAF's *segment architecture*.
- On top of all this resides the *theme*. It is coarse-grained enough to be derived from an *IT maxim*, the expression of strategic intents introduced in activity EA-1 in Chapter 3. Ian Miller's application rationalization program can be described by a theme, derived from the CIO's statement announcing global savings. In TOGAF, the counterpart is *enterprise strategic architecture*.

Leffingwell (2011) sees an effort factor of roughly 50 between the different granularities.[50] This fits well into usual dimensions encountered in different planning horizons, as shown Figure 7-18 and Table 7-12.

It is worth noting that there is *no fixed format* for the higher abstraction levels described here. "Epics may be expressed in bullet form, as a sentence or two, in video, as a prototype, in a short business case, or indeed in any form of expression suitable," writes Leffingwell (2011, p. 453), but that applies to the other levels as well. One can use the user story format if this adds value.

But it is also suitable to use any particular domain-specific format—for example, in our case, the taxonomy that EA uses to describe transformations of the IT landscape. It is even advisable to keep the descriptions concise and domain-specific. "I was once at a meeting where an (otherwise) clever agilist, pushing back on what he considered to be delaying and excessive epic-level documentation requirements, told his PMO management, 'You can even tell us in interpretive dance; we'll take it from there,'" writes Leffingwell (2011, p. 453)—not entirely seriously, though.

Iterations in EA

Padma Valluri has scheduled another series of meetings with Sandro Poggi, her agile architecture consultant. Together they analyze the parallels between the TOGAF framework, which the Bank4Us EA team is using, and the agile methodology. After Sandro has given her a quick introduction to agile requirements management, Padma sees the match. The main question for her is how iterations, as promoted by the agile methodology, fit TOGAF.

As already outlined in Chapter 4, TOGAF does allow, and even explicitly recommends, the use of iterations in its ADM part. Figure 7-20 displays some proposed iteration cycles. In addition, ADM users can define their own cycles without losing the TOGAF-compliancy seal. Nonetheless, the *architecture development iteration* will be the most common iteration type, covering phases A–F.

As Figure 7-21 shows, the iterations can be used to connect the various levels of architecture detail with each other. The ADM phases A–F on the enterprise strategic architecture level prepare and kick off architecture work on the next lower level of detail, in this case the segment architecture level, and from there down to capability (or capability increment) architecture.

---

[50]See Leffingwell (2011, p. 440, in Figure 22-4).

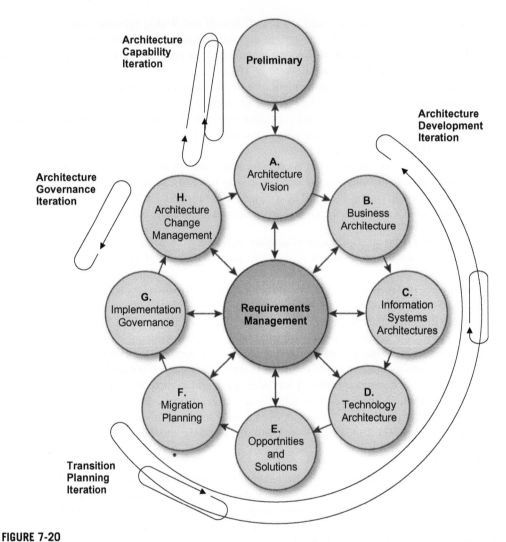

FIGURE 7-20

Recommended iteration cycles in TOGAF ADM (The Open Group, 2011, used with kind permission).

TOGAF supports iterative work very well. We can nicely reconcile the ADM phases with lean and agile's lightweight control mechanisms.

An EA Kanban board using TOGAF ADM

Padma now feels she has enough information to turn back to Ian Miller's application rationalization program. She wants to understand if it might support Ian's work to run the program in an agile mode. To answer this question, Sandro and Padma have to analyze the process part of Ian's application rationalization program.

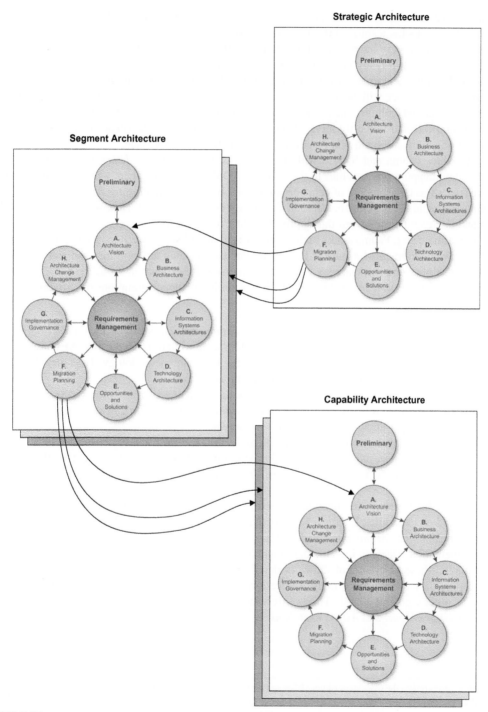

FIGURE 7-21

Interweaved TOGAF ADM iterations on different architecture levels (The Open Group, 2011, used with permission).

Another brief meeting with Ian and one of his team members produces the required data. At the moment, Ian tracks his team's work via entries in an Excel spreadsheet that he distributes regularly via email. He is not very happy with this solution. Not even he himself, let alone his team members and stakeholders, has a really good overview of where they stand.

So far, the implementation work has not yet started. But the sponsors start growing restless. The first implementation project will be kicked off soon. Ian awaits this further explosion of coordination activities with mixed feelings. The use of fancier project management tools might be inevitable by then, but Ian is afraid that it will only increase the amount of time he has to spend on management tools instead of on architecture and that it will not solve the transparency issue.

Ian provides Padma and Sandro with access to his work item lists. Using this material, Padma spends a day mapping the activities to the TOGAF ADM framework. Then, with the help of Sandro, she condenses this large amount of data into a very simplified list of requirements and tasks. Her goal is to emulate an agile EA backlog that she can use in presenting the concept. How would that have looked if Ian and his team had followed this approach right from the start?

For the time being, Padma sticks to the simple Excel-style list format. It is just a first step to prove that the agile requirements format fits to the way Ian and his team are working. She and Sandro will tackle the visibility and transparency issue later. Their result is shown in Table 7-13.[51]

All in all, Ian's team made full use of TOGAF's ability to support iterations on different levels of architectural detail:

- The theme *Achieve 20% savings by application rationalization* is part of the CIO's original statement, which we quoted in Chapter 1. Ian and his team went through the TOGAF phases A–F on *Enterprise Strategic Architecture* level to define the KPIs and methodology. Then they defined the segmentation, and created Epics to work on in the next level.
- The assessment of the trading application landscape on *Segment Architecture* level required two loops.
  - In the first, defined by the Epic *Assess the trading applications segment for rationalizations,* the initial target application landscape was drawn.
  - Then Ian and his team discovered the possible shift in functionality between TAR and TR2. As a consequence, they went a second time through phases A–F on segment level, and re-modeled the target architectures. This is labeled *Assess TAR extension to make TR2 obsolete.*
- Following this Segment Architecture, a deep dive will soon be started. At least two Features have to be worked on in parallel: *Enhance TAR application* and *Ramp-down TR2 application.* These loops through *Capability Architecture* will now cover the full cycle A–H, including the actual implementation. One can imagine how much complexity this will involve. For the sake of simplicity, these tasks are not shown in detail in Table 7-13.
- In parallel to assessing the trading application landscape, Ian and his team need to go through several other segments as well. This is only hinted at in Table 7-13, by the Epics *Assess the customer relationship systems* and *Assess core banking systems.*

---

[51]The table entries reflect the work steps of Ian Miller and his team in the course of the program. We described these activities in detail as an example for activity *EA-3, Evolving the IT Landscape,* in Chapter 3.

Table 7-13 Hypothetical Backlog for Ian Miller's Application Rationalization Program

Theme/Epic/Feature	TOGAF Phase(s)			Architectural Task
	ESA	SA	CA	
Theme: Achieve 20% savings by application rationalization	A			Define KPIs for application rationalization
				Specify assessment methodology
	B			Define segmentation for segment architecture
	C			Revise application catalogue
				Revise data structure catalogue
	D			Analyze technologies due for retirement
	E			Create work packages (*epics* for Segment level)
	F			Estimate effort
	F			Prioritize epics
. . .	. . .			. . .
Epic: Assess the trading applications segment for rationalizations		B		Model business processes
		C		Assess application landscape using Ward-Peppard classification
		. . .		. . .
. . .	. . .			. . .
Epic: Assess TAR extension to make TR2 obsolete		B		Remodel business architecture with hindsight to possible TAR extension
		C		Remodel application architecture with TAR extension and TR2 ramp-down
		. . .		. . .
		E		Create work packages (features for Capability level)
		F		Estimate efforts
		F		Prioritize features
. . .			A	. . .
Feature: Enhance TAR application			. . .	. . .
			H	. . .
. . .			A	. . .
Feature: Ramp down TR2 application			. . .	. . .
			H	. . .
. . .		A		. . .
Epic: Assess the customer relationship systems		. . .		. . .
		F		. . .
. . .		A		. . .
Epic: Assess core banking systems		. . .		. . .
		F		. . .
. . .				

ESA = enterprise strategic architecture, SA = segment architecture, CA = capability architecture

TOGAF as blueprint for EA Kanban

Padma and Sandro discuss what kind of lean and agile process would be able to organize the tasks for Ian's team in a flexible, efficient, and TOGAF-compliant way. Sandro proposes a *Kanban* approach.

We have introduced software Kanban in the section "*Learning from mass production: Lean software development.*" The principle of Kanban is that task cards flow through a series of process steps. In software development, these steps typically form a sequence like *Plan – Implementation Ongoing – Testing Ongoing – Waiting for Deployment – Live.*

For EA tasks, there is a perfect match in TOGAF ADM, which already provides a detailed process model for EA activities with standardized phases. Instead of the above steps for software development, Ian and his team can use the TOGAF phases A–H (plus Preliminary phase). The rich set of predefined activities within each phase provides a blueprint for possible EA tasks.

Figure 7-22 shows the principle of an EA Kanban Board using TOGAF ADM. Requirements such as *Assess TAR extension to make TR2 obsolete* flow clockwise through the ADM phases (instead of from left to right, as in software Kanban), triggering phase-specific tasks (for example, *Model business processes* in Phase B) along the way. The *Requirements Management* phase in the middle is replaced by a joint backlog for all phases, marked "To be done."

Rules for the EA Kanban board

When entering a phase, the Kanban cards are first placed in the corresponding "To be done" sector. As Figure 7-23 shows, cards in progress are placed inside the circular shape denoting a TOGAF phase, and

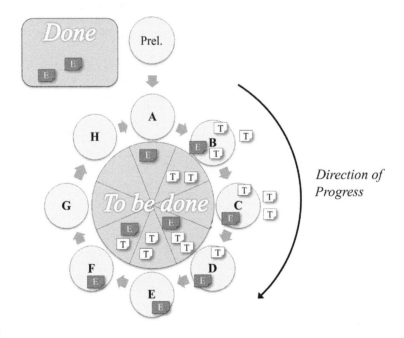

FIGURE 7-22

EA Kanban board using TOGAF ADM.

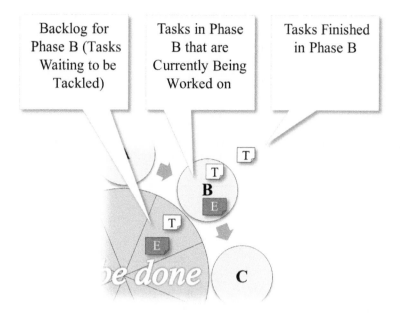

Backlog for Phase B (Tasks Waiting to be Tackled)

Tasks in Phase B that are Currently Being Worked on

Tasks Finished in Phase B

FIGURE 7-23

Locations for Kanban cards on the EA Kanban board.

finished tasks are placed outside the phase. After all applicable phases are completed, the cards are either moved into the top left box marked "Done" or else iterated again.

Two types of cards should be used on the Kanban board:

- *Requirement cards* denoting (architectural) themes, *epics*, features, and user stories. (For the sake of simplicity, we have only pictured *epics* in our examples, marked by an *E* on a gray background.) These are the main requirement items that flow through the EA Kanban board.
- *Task cards* denote EA tasks within one phase (colored in white and labeled with a *T* for *task* in our examples).

The following nine steps explain in detail how the Kanban cards are handled. The step descriptions are supported by Figures 7-24 through 7-26. We focus on only one TOGAF phase (B in our example) of the segment architecture. A typical epic might be *Assess TAR extension to make TR2 obsolete*, as handled by Ian Miller and his team. Epics and tasks are denoted by *E* and *T*, respectively.

1. Once the epic is finished in Phase A, it is moved into the backlog of Phase B.
2. When the enterprise architects start working on the epic, they first plan what they intend to do in this phase. They create a number of new task cards in the process, which describe in detail which models need to be updated, which business scenarios need to be written, and so forth.

   This approach gives the architects quite some flexibility. They can choose between a *breadth-first* or a *depth-first* strategy for tackling the architecture.
   - In the breadth-first approach, the EA team opts for faster, more superficial iterations through the TOGAF cycle (with fewer tasks per phase). This makes sense in the early

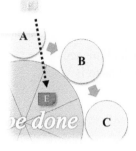 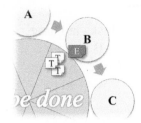 

1. Move Epic to Backlog of Phase B

2. Start Working on Epic by Splitting into Tasks

3. Start Working on Task

FIGURE 7-24

Rules for the EA Kanban board (Steps 1–3).

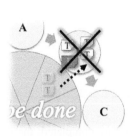 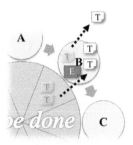 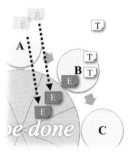

4. Too Many Tasks Worked on in Parallel (DIP Limit Exceeded)

5. One Task Finished, OK to Start Work on New Tasks (DIP Limit Kept)

6. Two More Epics in Backlog, OK (No Limit on Backlog)

FIGURE 7-25

Rules for the EA Kanban board (Steps 4–6).

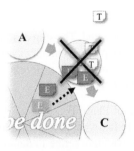 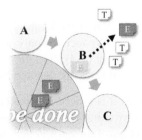 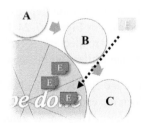

7. Too Many Epics Worked on in Parallel (DIP Limit Exceeded)

8. All Tasks Done → Epic Done

9. Continue with Epic in Next Phase

FIGURE 7-26

Rules for the EA Kanban board (Steps 7–9).

stage of a program or when we're facing a highly complex landscape. More and shorter iterations allow for quick feedback to sponsors and a flexible prioritization of which segment needs to be handled first.

- In the depth-first approach, the enterprise architects can plan more tasks and attempt to finish the TOGAF phase for good, without reiterations. This makes sense in case the path ahead is already pretty clear and the most important goal is delivery of the first tangible results.

3. The new tasks are placed in the "To be done" area. They are moved into the TOGAF phase only once someone starts working on it.

4. In TOGAF Phase A, when methodology is discussed, the EA team also decides on a practical *design in progress (DIP)* limit. This figure denotes the maximum number of Kanban cards (tasks, *epics*, themes, etc.) that the team is allowed to work on in parallel. The DIP limit prevents one TOGAF phase from becoming a bottleneck in which the tasks are delayed too long.

   It is advisable to treat the DIP maximum as a "soft" limit, not as a hard constraint. This means that the maximum DIP *should not* be exceeded, instead of *must not* be exceeded. The number of work packages flowing through the ADM is quite low, and the variability is very high—at least in comparison to manufacturing or even software development. According to lean theory, these limits should be adjusted in a trial-and-error approach. This requires several TOGAF cycles and fast feedback—not always easy to achieve in practice.

   It is also quite likely that the optimal DIP limits will be different in each release: A migration from IBM mainframes is essentially different from introducing a multichanneling platform. The optimal DIP limits for crafting a target architecture in the A–H phases will be quite different, too. Therefore, it makes sense to treat the DIP limits as an indicator of a wasteful situation rather than a hard rule to be obeyed in each and every situation. Nonetheless, for the sake of our example, we will assume a strict DIP limit of two to demonstrate the principle. The team is advised not to start work on the remaining two tasks in the backlog at the same time; that would mean three ongoing tasks in Phase B.

5. The DIP limit indicates that the team should first finish one task; then they are allowed to start working on the remaining ones. The finished task card is placed outside the phase circle.

6. Two more *epics* have passed through Phase A and are ready to be handled in Phase B. They are placed in the "To be done" area. It may contain an arbitrary number of cards; there is no DIP limit on the backlog (the "To be done" area).

7. There are separate DIP limits for tasks and *epics* (as well as themes, features, and user stories). For *epics*, we assume a DIP limit of 1 in this example. Therefore, the team should not start planning for a second epic in Phase B before the first one has been done.

8. When all tasks are done and the corresponding epic is finished, it is moved outside the Phase B circle.

9. The epic can then be placed in the backlog of the next phase, or the "Done" area of the board.

The targets of this process are to produce a constant flow through Phases A–H to reduce the overall cycle time, increase visibility, and allow for flexible task planning. All tasks of a theme, epic, or feature must be completed before it can be moved into the next phase. However, it is possible to drop a task, just as in lean and agile software development. In that case, it is a deliberate decision to speed up cycle time instead of completing the architecture within one TOGAF phase. The whole TOGAF cycle will have to be iterated again.

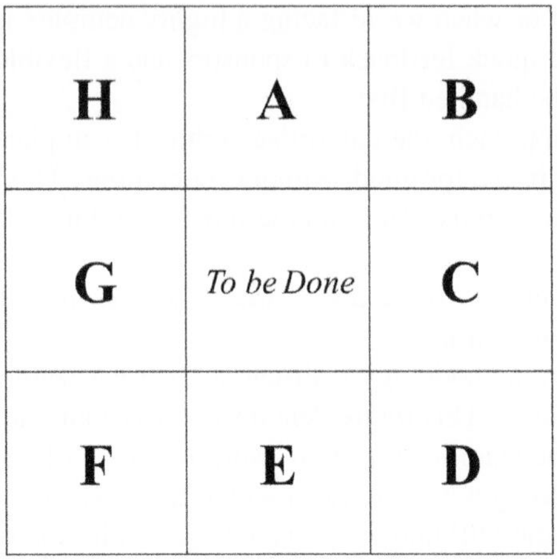

FIGURE 7-27

Rectangular EA Kanban board for practical use.

This rule, together with a consequent observation of DIP limits, will prevent the EA Kanban board from overflowing with piles and piles of cards. However, the Kanban approach is not a silver bullet that solves work overload problems. It simply makes that overload plainly visible and offers a structured approach to process the card piles by and by and to avoid them in the future.

A final note on the design of the EA Kanban board: We have reused the circular shapes of the TOGAF ADM visualization for the sake of better recognition. When Kanban is used as a tool in the daily EA business, it makes sense to hang the Kanban board physically on the wall and use sticky notes for task cards. In that case, it will be more practical and space-efficient to use a rectangular design like the one depicted in Figure 7-27.

The process we have sketched here applies to a collocated EA team that can have its regular stand-up scrum meetings in front of a physical board. For distributed teams, there are manifold commercial or open-source Web-based Kanban tools that can be used as a base for a distributed EA Kanban.

Synchronization with implementation projects

Padma and Sandro decide to invite Ian and his team for a workshop to present their ideas. Despite their workload, Ian accommodates a three-hour timeslot in their schedule to discuss the concept.

In the introductory round, Ian's team members voice their desire for more structure and regular communication in their work. They perceive TOGAF as a mixture of treasure trove and attic storeroom—very useful as a reference of what activity is to be done at what time, when you dig into it, but a bit too bulky to carry along as a lightweight travel guide. Therefore, when Sandro shows them the architecture scrum structure and the EA Kanban board and explains the high-level principles, their reaction is carefully positive.

Sandro has designed the board in a threefold version for the different levels of detail in the architecture, as shown in Figure 7-28. Together they simulate the application rationalization project so far,

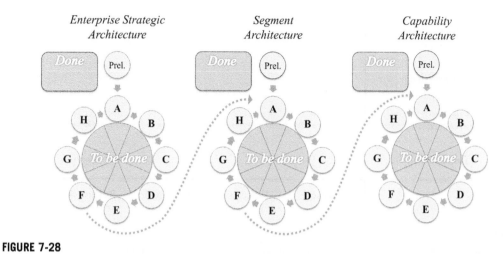

FIGURE 7-28

EA Kanban board with three corresponding levels of granularity.

based on Padma's data collection (see Table 7-13). As an alternative to the sticky-notes-on-the-wall version, Sandro also gives them a quick demonstration of his favorite Web-based agile requirements management system.[52]

When one of the enterprise architects brings up how to coordinate the upcoming implementation projects for their application rationalization program, the discussion becomes more lively. Most members of Ian's team share the concern that they will sink into chaos if they continue with the current way of organizing their work.

They draw their worst-case scenario on the whiteboard. The information flow between EA team and implementation projects (within the different levels of architecture) looks like the drawing in Figure 7-29. At worst, a change in the high-level architecture would need nine months to be passed down to the implementation level! Although in practice the lead time will be less than that, all participants in the room agree that this scenario is not altogether unrealistic and that it poses a real threat to their program's success.

As a contrast, the group assembles again in front of the whiteboard and jointly designs a more suitable model. The outcome is depicted in Figure 7-30. They use the EA Kanban approach, which allows them more lightweight loops through the TOGAF cycle. Loops on different levels of granularity—strategic, segment, and capability—can run in parallel.

Combined with three-week iterations and Sandro's scrum setup, work results can be forwarded to the next level much faster. This is because of the cadence of stakeholder reviews at the end of each sprint. This way, all actors in the process have a clear synchronization point for handovers between

---

[52]The market offers a number of mature and highly customizable systems, such as JIRA (www.atlassian.com/en/software/jira/).

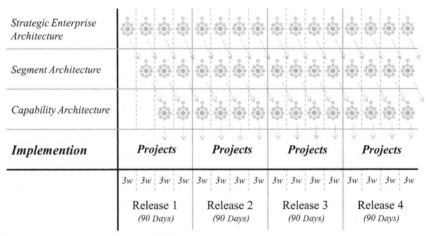

Strategic Enterprise Architecture				
Segment Architecture				
Capability Architecture				
Implemention				*Projects*
	Release 1 *(90 Days)*	Release 2 *(90 Days)*	Release 3 *(90 Days)*	Release 4 *(90 Days)*

FIGURE 7-29

Information flow between EA and implementation projects in a "classical" work mode.

Strategic Enterprise Architecture				
Segment Architecture				
Capability Architecture				
Implemention	*Projects*	*Projects*	*Projects*	*Projects*
	3w 3w 3w 3w	3w 3w 3w 3w	3w 3w 3w 3w	3w 3w 3w 3w
	Release 1 *(90 Days)*	Release 2 *(90 Days)*	Release 3 *(90 Days)*	Release 4 *(90 Days)*

FIGURE 7-30

Information flow between EA and implementation projects using EA Kanban and iterations.

the different roles (enterprise and project architects, business, project managers, etc.) and the parallel TOGAF cycles on the Enterprise Strategy, Segment, and Capability levels.

The Kanban approach specifically helps maintaining a clear overview at all times. The Kanban board visualizes clogging of the task flow at process bottlenecks, making it easier to resolve them or even avoid them altogether.

At the end of the meeting, the team discusses the next steps. Ian is not one to be convinced easily, but he admits that the approach might work with his application rationalization program. He likes that it is lightweight and does not require more tools than posters on the wall and sticky notes for a start.

Padma proposes to allocate Sandro to their team as a scrum coach for a period of three months. Ian quickly warms to the idea; all process concepts aside, it means that he will have to spend less time compiling Excel task lists and can dedicate himself more to the true EA work. Padma and Ian decide to approach their boss, Oscar Salgado, for an additional budget for Sandro. Both are confident that Oscar will agree to it; Ian's program has high visibility among the sponsors.

Padma is quite happy with the outcome of this meeting. Still, she feels that they will need some mindset switch to make the idea fly. Shorter and parallelized TOGAF loops require change in the way architecture is documented, too. The classical *I-write-a-200-page-Word-document-and-release-it-to-peer-review* approach will be too heavyweight for this. Maybe, she thinks, *just-in-time modeling* describes it properly. The architecture documents will have to become iterative in nature—for instance, by introducing collaborative tools such as wikis and forums.

In addition, the review process needs to become more transparent by allowing the stakeholders more participation in the architectural design process. Padma sighs. It looks like a whole new field of activities is still ahead for them. Nonetheless, she makes a note to follow up this approach, too. We will accompany her and her peers on that journey in the next chapter, "Inviting to Participation: EAM 2.0."

Summing it up: Assessment by the EA Dashboard

In the first two building blocks of this chapter, we have laid the foundation to effectively combine EA with lean and agile methods:

- Lean process analysis, as outlined in Building Block 1, helps us understand waste in EA and provides guidance in the transition process toward lean and agile EA.
- The architecture scrums introduced in Building Block 2 provide the team structure for implementing lean and agile EA methodology.

This last block, *Building Block 3: Practice iterative architecture through EA Kanban,* provides the capstone to finish the building. It adds the following aspects:

- An *agile backlog*, mapped to the different levels of architecture granularity as defined in TOGAF, allows flexible and lightweight planning of EA activities.
- The *concept of iterative refinement of architecture* is ingrained in both the lean and agile approach and in an EA framework like TOGAF.
- The *EA Kanban board* provides a flexible, lightweight, and efficient planning instrument for architectural tasks.

Looking at the EA Dashboard for Building Block 3 (see Figure 7-31), as we did for the other two building blocks, reveals that we can expect an improvement on the *Edge of time* side through a more steady flow of architectural work. *Strategic directives* will arrive on the shop floor earlier, which helps both sides; the strategy will be more connected to reality, and the people on the ground can more effectively use strategic maxims as guidance for their work.

Furthermore, the *transformation pace* can be expected to be better calibrated to the actual needs of the enterprise. At least there are now efficient tools available to avoid the clogging of the architecture

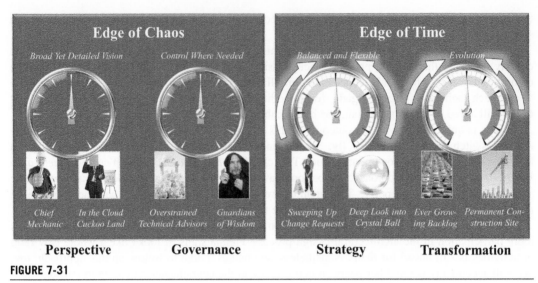

FIGURE 7-31

The EA Dashboard for *Building Block 3: Practice iterative architecture through EA Kanban.*

backlog. In the same way, too much change at a time will be visible on the EA Kanban board. It is easy to detect bottlenecks and slack periods.

However, the EA organization is not the driver for transformation; it is just one of several controllers. The effect of the building block on the transformation pace depends on how much influence the EA team has in the overall IT organization.

Inviting to Participation: EAM 2.0

CONTENT

A Primer on Enterprise 2.0 237
Building Block 4: Participation in Knowledge 246
    The Strategy Blog 247
    Collaborative Data Modeling: The ObjectPedia 249
    Weak Ties and a Self-Organizing Application Landscape 251
    Summing It Up: Assessment by the EA Dashboard 256
Building Block 5: Participation in Decisions 258
    The Diagnostic Process Landscape 259
    The Bazaar of IT Opportunities 261
    Summing It Up: Assessment by the EA Dashboard 264
Building Block 6: Participation in Transformation 265
    Mashing Up the Architecture Continuum 265
    The Change Management Microblog 270
    Summing It Up: Assessment by the EA Dashboard 277
The Bottom Line: Inviting to Explore 278

The Western intellectual tradition shows a certain bias against crowds. The ancient Greek philosopher Plato (424–348 BC), for instance, conceptualized the idea of a *sophocracy* in his classic *The Republic* (in Greek: *Politeia*). The essence of this government is that the most knowledgeable and wisest—the philosophers—should rule. The German poet Goethe made the point clear in 1833:

> *Nothing is more repugnant than the majority; it consists of a few strong trailblazers, rogues and weak characters that assimilate, and the crowd that trolls after them without a clue what it wants.*[1]

What contributions can be expected from those trolling behind, as Goethe puts it? Throughout the centuries, one can spot a conviction among Western thinkers that a crowd is never wiser than its most capable members. It is accompanied by the misanthropic belief that individuals even become "dumbed

---

[1]Cited in (1958), translated by the authors.

down" in a crowd; they *vulgarize*: laugh at insipid jokes, applaud harebrained slogans, or lower their ethical standards to a degree they otherwise would feel ashamed of. The television entertainment of our time indeed gives some evidence for such opinions.

Nevertheless, as *general* statements about the capabilities of crowds, these convictions are wrong. James Surowiecki has gathered an abundance of research results from social sciences and economy that prove the sometimes fabulous capabilities of crowds in his bestseller *The Wisdom of Crowds* (2005). The title of this booklet has become a headline for the intellectual capabilities that show up when individuals are networking: The crowd often is smarter than the plain addition of its members' capabilities. The economist and Nobel laureate Friedrich August von Hayek wrote (1979, p. 54):

> [...] *the only possibility of transcending the capacity of individual minds is to rely on those super-personal, self-organizing forces which create spontaneous orders.*

What von Hayek had in mind were the self-organizing forces of market economies. These economies are not planned or controlled by a mastermind; nevertheless they are unbeatably efficient in producing and distributing the goods in response to actual needs. The "super-personal" forces at work, for instance, condense the whole knowledge about the production and distribution circumstances and the criticality of a demand in a single number, the price—something individual minds generally fall short off. But von Hayek's tenet goes beyond economy and is today also proven by spectacular crowd achievements such as Wikipedia or Linux.

Turning to IT architecture, we find that the traits of sophocracy are still carved into IT architecture as a discipline: Here's the brain with the blueprint, the architect; and there are the hands implementing the plan accordingly. These traits are particularly visible in enterprise architecture, maybe due to the proximity to the illustrious CxO level, maybe because it sometimes is considered the peak of the IT architecture profession. Yet we know that wisdom is not just with a few and that modern IT has grown to a challenge where enterprise architects cannot afford to lock out insights and ideas from whomever.

This chapter is centered on building blocks accounting for the wisdom of crowds—proposals for ways to implement the third of the central maxims set out in Chapter 6, "Foundations of Collaborative EA":

> Foster and moderate open participation instead of relying *only on experts and top-down wisdom*

The turn we're taking for putting this maxim into practice is EA 2.0—the application of Enterprise 2.0 to EA. From the public space we know that social software platforms and other Web 2.0 techniques elicit collaboration, knowledge sharing, and the super-personal spontaneous orders that von Hayek wrote about. Enterprise 2.0 for good reason backs on the hope of utilizing this momentum in a general enterprise context and for general enterprise ends. What is more compelling than pursuing this ideal for the sake of EA, too?

The following sections exemplify the EA 2.0 vision using concrete Enterprise 2.0 tools in the context of our Bank4Us case. We're not saying that these are the only or the best tools. Instead, they should convey an idea of how to give birth to a viable EA 2.0 culture. We have arranged them into three major building blocks:

- Building Block 4: Participation in knowledge
- Building Block 5: Participation in decisions
- Building Block 6: Participation in transformation

Building Block 4 pursues new traits of sharing and combining knowledge. *ObjectPedia* will be one of the examples demonstrating this aspect—a self-organizing, company-wide data dictionary of business objects that is roughly built along the lines of the famous archetype, Wikipedia.

Building Block 5 is about collaborative decision making. The *diagnostic process landscape* demonstrates how decisions can be *prepared* on the ground using crowd input, whereas our second example, the *ITO bazaar,* even shows how *common decisions* can be moderated in an Enterprise 2.0 fashion.

Finally, Building Block 6 exemplifies how the transformation that eventually changes the IT landscape can be fostered by participation.

But before we come to the building blocks, we start the EA 2.0 journey with a recap of the basic ingredients of Web 2.0 and Enterprise 2.0. We must come to a clear understanding of these somewhat fuzzy subjects and discuss their general benefits and pitfalls in a wider scope.

A primer on Enterprise 2.0

The term *Enterprise 2.0* was coined by Andrew McAfee, professor at the MIT Sloan School of Management at Harvard. In 2006, McAfee published a paper, *Enterprise 2.0: The Dawn of Emergent Collaboration* (McAfee, 2006a), in which he described social software as a means of collaboration in an enterprise context. The paper gained a great deal of attention. Social software had always been regarded as a playground for leisure time or private activities; that it could also add value to the grave, professional world of modern enterprises was a new idea.

McAfee took up two trains of thought that were widely discussed and applied them to his research topic: the "impact of IT on how businesses perform and how they compete" (McAfee, 2009, p. 3). One train of thought is Web 2.0. The other is a series of related research about collective intelligence—the way communities collaborate, coordinate their activities, manage knowledge, and come to new insights.

Let's first take a look at Web 2.0.[2] There is no straightforward definition of this term. An authority like Sir Timothy Berners-Lee, inventor of HTML, professor at the Massachusetts Institute of Technology (MIT), and director of the World Wide Web Consortium (W3C) even regarded it as "[...] a piece of jargon, nobody even knows what it means" and claimed that it actually adds nothing that wasn't there in the good old Web 1.0 (Berners-Lee, 2006). The "tag cloud" of notions people associate with Web 2.0 is indeed diverse and full of concepts lacking a reliable definition.

The most important description of Web 2.0 goes back to Tim O'Reilly, founder and CEO of O'Reilly Media, in 2005. In his much-quoted article "What Is Web 2.0?" he defends the term against the criticism of fuzziness: "Like many important concepts, Web 2.0 doesn't have a hard boundary, but rather, a gravitational core" (O'Reilly, 2005). In other words, just as there is no hard boundary between jazz and pure noise, there's no hard boundary between things that are Web 2.0-like and things that are not—but that doesn't render the concept meaningless.

---

[2]Composed by Markus Angermeier and used with his kind permission.

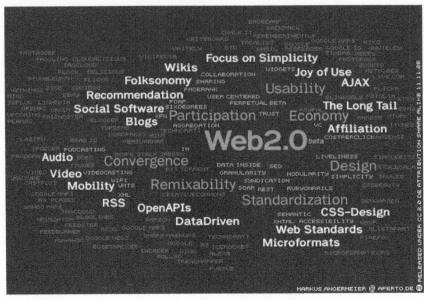

FIGURE 8-1

Web 2.0 tag cloud.

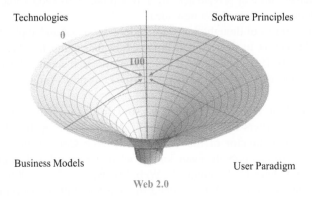

FIGURE 8-2

Aspects and the gravitational core of Web 2.0.

Web 2.0 is a conglomerate of technologies, software principles, business models, and, most important, a different user paradigm of the Internet as a social medium. Web things scoring 100% in all these aspects clearly are at the gravitational core of Web 2.0, as shown in Figure 8-2.

Take, for instance, a Web application built on specific technologies according to specific software principles, distributed according to new business models, *and* addressing the user as a social being; this application would beyond doubt deserve the label "Web 2.0." On the other side, if we stepwise subtract these properties, we more and more move toward the boundary until it eventually becomes dubious whether it still is Web 2.0 or not.

We do not want to go deeper into the *characteristic technologies*, since there is a broad literature available on this topic. Nevertheless, to indicate what we mean by Web 2.0 technologies, here's a short and certainly not exhaustive list:

- Feeds (RSS or Atom), permalinks, and trackbacks
- Web-services (REST or SOAP WS-*)
- Server-side component frameworks such as Java Server Faces or Microsoft ASP.NET
- Full-stack-frameworks for rapid development such as Ruby on Rails or Grails
- Client-side technologies such as AJAX, JavaScript, Adobe Flex, or Microsoft Silverlight
- Content and application integration technologies, namely portals and in particular mashups such as IBM Mashup Center or Software AG MashZone

These technologies are the enablers for the new Web 2.0 game. Feeds, permalinks, and trackbacks, to explore some examples, are the foundation of the *blogosphere*, the social ecosystem of cross-connected Web blogs.

The *software principles* outlined here as a second characteristic of Web 2.0 guide the way software is designed and developed on the new Web. The most eye-catching principle is the design for a richer user experience, or, in more glowing words, for joy of use. It is the quality leap from the stubborn, form-based request-response behavior of classical Web applications to the handsome comfort we've gotten used to with desktop applications. Modern Web applications offer fluid navigation, context-aware menus and help, visual effects and multimedia, and a look that doesn't feel like something out of a bureaucrat's cabinet.

Another principle is the so-called *perpetual beta*. Contrary to traditional software products that are released as ready-made, compact feature packs in relatively long-lasting release cycles, Web 2.0 software is typically in a state of continuous improvement. It is released frequently in short cycles,[3] and upgrades happen seamlessly, without the blare of trumpets that announce traditional software releases.

The perpetual beta also invites users to be development partners. It is a trial-and-error approach to guessing what the user wants. Features are tentatively placed on a Website, but if users do not embrace them, the provider removes them. Both the "release soon and often" factor and the unresisting adaptation to user behavior also characterize lean and agile development approaches, as we know from Chapter 7. These approaches therefore are natural complements to Web 2.0.

The last principle we want to outline here is the design for remixability. This means that data and functionality are delivered to the client in the form of extensible services, as opposed to the closure of functions traditional applications offer. The services are intended to be remixed by the service consumer, even in a way that the provider has not got the faintest idea about. Their design therefore strives for lightweight APIs, versioning, and other ingredients of loose coupling.

Remixability brings us to the *business models* characterizing Web 2.0. The business models of Web 2.0 are no longer centered on competition between applications. Internet users today simply expect reasonable user interfaces, but it is nothing they get excited about. What separates the wheat from the chaff are the services, in particular the data offered by a competitor. Companies that provide highly valuable data in a remixable way and that demonstrate operational excellence in ensuring performance, security, and other nonfunctional properties are gaining market share.

---

[3]The media-hosting Website Flickr releases new software every 30 minutes, which is a rather extreme case.

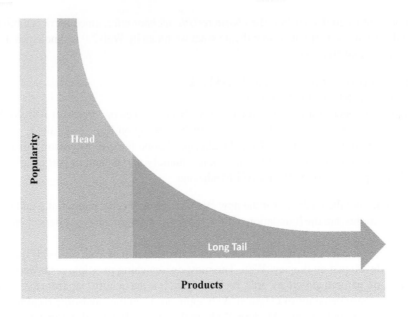

FIGURE 8-3

Long tail of product distribution.

Another feature of Web 2.0 business models is that they serve the *long tail*. The long tail (see Figure 8-3)[4] is a metaphor the journalist Chris Anderson (2006) applied to the large market segment of diversified low-volume offerings.

Internet marketplaces such as Amazon demonstrate strong support of the long tail. Bookworms find rare bibliophilic editions there because Amazon remixes the services offered by smaller or specialized booksellers and creates a seamless link between seller and bookworm. This is a nice example of how the openness and remixability of Web 2.0 services enable providers to meet individualized, uncommon requirements.

A third feature of Web 2.0 business models is that they turn the formerly passive role of the consumer into active participation. Consumers act, for example, as marketing agents: They spread the news and—consciously or not—recommend products. Marketing folks use the (slightly insane) term *viral marketing* for the methodology to influence this genuinely autonomous consumer activity.

Tim O'Reilly finds this kind of marketing so characteristic that he writes: "You can almost make the case that if a site or product relies on advertising to get the word out, it isn't Web 2.0" (O'Reilly, 2005). Consumers have an important say in the public appearance of a product. They evaluate products, write critiques and user guides, publish hints and tricks, relate products to each other, and so forth. In contrast to pre-Web 2.0 times, it is now much more difficult for a company to control the public image of their offerings.

The last feature of Web 2.0 business models we'd like to mention here is that services get better the more people use them. Examples of this characteristic are public spam filters or file distribution models

---

[4]Used with Chris Anderson's kind permission.

such as BitTorrent. Such services functionally depend on being used, and the more users there are, the better the services work.

The features of business models already indicate what can be regarded as a *litmus test for Web 2.0*. It is the question whether the Internet is utilized as just a rather one-directional publication channel or as a platform that addresses users as social beings and invites them to participation and exchange. Figure 8-4 nicely illustrates this distinction in paradigms.

The social momentum of Web 2.0 is particularly visible in social software, which is an important subcategory of Web 2.0 applications. The most prominent examples of social software such as Wikipedia, Facebook, or Twitter are ubiquitous and known to everyone. Tom Coates defines social software as "software which supports, extends, or derives added value from human social behavior" (Coates, 2005).

Though the definition is crisp and nicely emphasizes the value lying in IT-enabled social behavior, it is slightly too general. Email, for example, would fall under Coates's definition, but email is generally not regarded as social software. Social software offers a *platform*, a space where actions are publicly visible and persistent. A platform invites an indeterminate cloud of people to react, whether sooner or later; that's up to them. Email, on the contrary, opens a channel visible to a small group only and imposes an obligation to reply soon. Thus, email is ruled out of the social software equation.

But what about company portals—are they social software? According to McAfee (2009), this depends on how much structure they impose. Most portals we have seen are intended to support a tightly coupled working group in predefined tasks. They show a rich and somewhat rigid structure in terms of workflows, data and document types that can be published, permissions, and roles. This is not social software. Social software minimizes the pre-given structures and leaves the rest to self-organization. This doesn't mean it is unstructured, but the pre-given landmarks are reduced to a few condensation-points where content can accumulate.

FIGURE 8-4

Information source versus platform of participation.

McAfee (2009) uses the term *emergent* to characterize structure that is not preplanned by a mastermind but emerges out of local activities in a community. The structure is, as McAfee puts it, *irreducible:* It results from network effects and economies of scale but cannot be deduced from the contributions of individual actors.

The tag clouds of the Yahoo! bookmarking service Delicious are an example of an emergent structure. Internet users make their bookmarks publicly available and assign tags to the bookmarks that, in their very subjective view, describe the contents of the bookmarked page. The aggregation of individual tags yields a tag cloud that puts Web content into categories with amazing accuracy and facilitates catchword-based searching. Such categorizations are called *folksonomies*—taxonomies created by a large crowd of folks.

A common way to systematize the manifold social software applications is by means of a social software triangle, as shown in Figure 8-5. This triangle arranges application types according to their contribution to the three fundamental use cases of social software:

- *Information management.* Creating, aggregating, finding, evaluating, and maintaining information.
- *Identity and network management.* Shaping and presenting their own personal profiles, building and cultivating social ties.
- *Interaction and communication.* Direct and indirect communication, conversations, correspondence, information exchange, quotations, and comments.

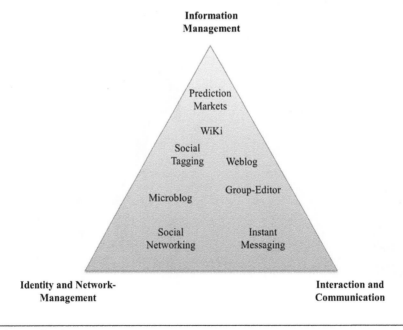

FIGURE 8-5

The social software triangle.

Another well-established characterization of an information platform as social software is formulated by McAfee (2009, p. 3) and condensed into the acronym SLATES, which stands for:

- *Search*. Users must be able to find what they are looking for.
- *Links*. Users must be able to link content. Links structure the content in an emergent way and rate the relevance of some content by counting the links referring to it (which is Google's page-rank algorithm).
- *Authoring*. Users must be able to contribute their knowledge, experience, insights, facts, opinions, and so on.
- *Tags*. Users must be able to apply tags to categorize content in an emergent way.
- *Extensions*. Users get automatic hints on content that might be interesting to them based on user behavior and preferences ("If you like this, you might like . . .")
- *Signals*. Users can subscribe to alerts or feeds so that they are continuously informed about new or updated contents. By using feed aggregators, they also can choose to automatically incorporate the most recent content into their own content.

But let's conclude here. We hope that the reader by now has a good grasp of what Web 2.0 is about, given that this notion cannot be defined with ultimate sharpness. At this point, we also have collected all ingredients to state McAfee's famous definition of Enterprise 2.0. It reads (McAfee, 2006b):

> *Enterprise 2.0 is the use of emergent social software platforms within companies, or between companies and their partners or customers.*

Today, many organizations in which knowledge work is an essential part of the business have adopted social software in some way. Wikis, blogs, and Facebook-like social networks can be found in many companies or institutions. The momentum such tools have is not caused by technology but rather by the social dynamics they elicit. They fill what the sociologist Ronald Burt denotes as *structural holes* in a knowledge network (Burt, 1995)—missing links between people that otherwise would provide some information benefits.

The observation goes back to Mark Granovetter, who in 1973 published his influential paper *The Strength of Weak Ties* (Granovetter, 1973). Prior to this landmark paper, studies of social dynamics always emphasized the importance of the closely related group. This is a group of peers, friends, relatives, colleagues, and other people who have strong ties.

But Granovetter argued that for gathering information, solving problems, and inspiration from unfamiliar ideas, the weak ties are at least as important. Strongly tied groups are in a sense islands of static knowledge. The members more or less share the same experiences, convictions, and tenets. Even if there are different opinions or backgrounds, exchange must usually come to a "we agree to disagree" arrangement. Weak ties, on the other hand—relationships to people you know only superficially or by name—are bridges to other knowledge islands and can therefore be strong in acquiring new insights.

Andrew McAfee adopted Granovetter's idea and extended it based on the potential of the new Web 2.0 technologies to what he calls the "bull's eye" (Figure 8-6).[5]

At the center of the bull's eye are strongly tied people. In the working world, these are the people you work with on a regular basis—people who belong to your *community of practice*. This is the inner circle

---

[5]Adapted from (McAfee 2009) and used with kind permission.

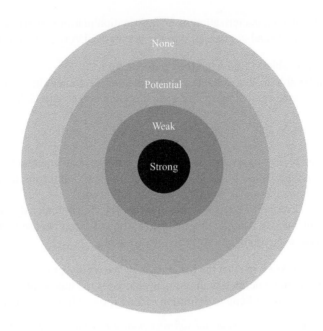

FIGURE 8-6

The bull's eye.

that has been addressed by traditional IT tools for collaboration by so-called groupware. Web 2.0 does not revolutionize this circle except that it provides lighter accessibility and a less rigorous structure.

The social net grows to the second circle of the bull's eye if you take in people you worked with on a project long time ago, people you just met once on a conference, or people who happen to be in your address book for some other reason— in short, people to whom you have weak ties. These are the ties that become important when you want to know something off the beaten track of your daily routine. They are the people you want to contact when all your buddies are shrugging their shoulders.

Maybe your concern is to introduce an orchestration engine into your ESB[6] and use BPEL[7] as a means to implement business processes, but nobody in your company has any experience with the pros and cons of doing such a task. Today this might be the point at which you turn to professional networks such as LinkedIn or even Facebook. These tools not only provide an address book and lightweight connectivity; they also make you aware of what your weakly tied counterparts are doing and knowing— they provide what Enterprise 2.0 apologists call *network awareness*.

But the potential of Web 2.0 goes beyond people's weak ties. The characteristic trait that people contribute content to platforms on a broad basis spawns potential ties between them. If you find something relevant in the blog of some author or a comment or backtrack in your own blog left by some person, it can be the starting point of a conversation or even a collaboration.

The outermost circle labeled "None" on the bull's eye is not there in all versions of this diagram. It denotes the kind of social dynamic that is not centered on ties but rather on an anonymous

---

[6]Enterprise service bus, a middleware and communication infrastructure for enterprise-wide application integration.

[7]Business Process Execution Language, a fourth-generation programming language for orchestrating business processes.

aggregation of information contributed by people who have no intention of getting in contact with each other. Examples of such dynamics are tagging, rating, and prediction markets.

It is a remarkable feature of the bull's eye that it has backtracks from the outer circles to the inner ones. Since the communities of practice at the inner circle also place their content on public platforms, they become more open to comments or opinions from the outer space, which is one of the major advantages of Web 2.0 with regard to the inner circle.

The public space offers convincing examples of how the means of Web 2.0, which look inconsiderable at first sight, can change the rules of the game. Take, for instance, the way we consume products today—aided by ratings, consumer forums, links to similar products, and so forth. *Don't we have reason to suspect that there is some potential to Enterprise 2.0—that it implies a major shift in the way people are doing knowledge-intensive work?* This is the reason we analyze it here for its applicability to EA.

The introduction of Enterprise 2.0 into an organization is, on the other hand, not a straightforward thing. It is in no case sufficient to install a wiki, some social networking tool, a blogging platform, or other Web 2.0 software, then leave the rest to emergence. The hope that tools alone will make knowledge and communication flourish like a tropical rainforest is illusory. The introduction is to a large extent a question of organizational measures, and we list here just the ones we find most critical:

- *Enterprise 2.0 platforms must be put into "the flow."* They should not come as an additional burden apart from the daily work processes. This might imply a clear-cut replacement of existing tools.
- *Enterprise 2.0 platforms must be governed by carefully defined rules and norms.* The authoring rules of Wikipedia are a good example of how this guides the direction, contents, and etiquette of such a system.
- *Enterprise 2.0 platforms should come with a skeleton of predefined structure.* This structure provides crystallization points at which contributions of the user community can sediment. A *tabula rasa* leaves too many contextual considerations to users and is perceived as an obstacle for starting to use the platform.
- *Contributions to Enterprise 2.0 platforms must be valued.* There's a wide range of options here, from somewhat childish goodies[8] to incentive-related goal agreements. But the most convincing signs of appreciation are that (a) that authorities or highly respected persons start using the platform and (b) important content is published and discussed there. If the CEO writes a blog but the staff finds nothing more important there than her impressions of the New York marathon, the platform is not earnestly valued.

A thorough discussion of the weaknesses and threats of Enterprise 2.0 is beyond the scope of this book, so we refer the interested reader to Chapter 6 of McAfee (2009) for such a discussion. There is in fact a broad variety of pernicious things that can show up in a social platform—for example:

- *Inappropriate content.* Pictures of doggies and kittens, conversations about cycling training methods, off-topic discussions, and the like.
- *Flame wars.* Discussions for the sake of discussion, insults, airing of dirty laundry, mobbing, troll behavior, etc.

---

[8]McAfee (2009) reports that the US intelligence agencies reward contributors to their cross-agency wiki *Intellipedia* with a little plastic shovel bearing the slogan, "I dig Intellipedia! It's wiki, wiki, Baby!" printed on the handle. Well, it probably is a matter of taste.

- *Wrong content.* Self-proclaimed experts giving wrong advice, employees uttering opinions that are contradictory to the company position, etc.

We tend to agree with Andrew McAfee that these downsides are, as he puts it, "red herrings"—threats that can be overcome by suitable norms, corrective actions of authorities, or role models. The self-healing capabilities of social platforms may also auto-correct them to some extent.

But the loss of confidentiality and the danger of security leaks are, in our view, more serious concerns than McAfee thinks. Envision a company that has outsourced a large part of its IT function to service providers, business partners, or freelancers. This typically results in a politically delicate conglomerate of conflicting interests. Making the IT strategy, the map of the IT landscape, product decisions, or other highly interesting topics public to all involved parties changes the game between service provider and buyer.

From the buyer's perspective it gets more difficult to pull the wool over the provider's eyes, and from the provider's point of view it is simpler exploit weak spots as cash cows. One might ask in such a constellation whether it is the new openness or the game of "partners" itself that smells fishy, but such shifts in the political equilibrium caused by Enterprise 2.0 must be given due consideration.

The most serious threat about Enterprise 2.0 certainly is that it simply doesn't work due to a lack of participation. By April 2011, there were 3,649,867 English articles in Wikipedia,[9] a tremendous number that outreaches other encyclopedias by magnitudes. At the same time, the number of contributors, who are the users with at least 10 edits since their arrival, counts up to 684,737.[10] This is an impressive absolute number, but given that there are more than one billion English-speaking Wikipedia users, the number melts down to a tiny relative percentage of about 0.068% of the whole.

If the same percentage applied to an Enterprise 2.0 platform featuring topics regarding the IT function of an enterprise, a theme that does not reach more than 1,000 addressees, the whole idea would collapse to a homepage and publication channel of a handful of expert authors. Thus, countermeasures must be taken to raise the percentage of contributors to a viable level. Some of these measures have been outlined previously—for instance, the advice to put Enterprise 2.0 tools into the flow—but we must have an eye on this aspect in the following sections, where we ponder Enterprise 2.0 as an enabler for EA.

Building Block 4: Participation in knowledge

Our first building block primarily invites the IT staff in participation. According to the British sitcom "The IT Crowd,"[11] these folks lead a despised, nerdish life in the untidy, shabby basement of a company, in dazzling contrast to the glamorous marble and glass architecture the rest of the company enjoys. How can enterprise architects fight against a technophile subculture that rules the basement? How can they excavate the treasure of knowledge buried in the cellar?

---

[9] http://stats.wikimedia.org/EN/Sitemap.htm.

[10] http://stats.wikimedia.org/EN/TablesWikipediansContributors.htm.

[11] http://en.wikipedia.org/wiki/The_IT_Crowd.

The Strategy blog

Oscar Salgado, the chief architect of our Bank4Us EA case, has recently participated in the maxim workshop spelling out the CIO's *Closer to Customer* mission statement set out in Chapter 3, activity EA-1, Defining the IT strategy. The outcome has now been published as a slideshow to the employee portal. But Oscar knows his IT crowd inside out: They will play a round of buzzword bingo[12] with it and turn to something "more substantial."

During the workshop, Oscar learned a lot about the business concerns, the market conditions, and the financial figures that are causing a headache for higher management. He understood that *customer empowerment*, one of the strategic goals of Bank4Us, is more than a marketing label. Many of the services still offered at the bank's branch offices are too expensive and simply must be replaced with Internet-based self-services. This is not a matter of value-adds but of financial survival.

Oscar has also started to believe that the initiatives subsumed under customer empowerment can really make a difference to the consumer. The idea of a financial dashboard, for instance, that transparently shows the customer's financial health state at any time and on any device—desktop, smartphone, or tablet—is something Oscar would actually like to have for himself. One workshop participant brought this example up, but such details didn't make it to the strategy slides.

After some hesitation, Oscar decides to publish his insights regarding the strategy in some blog posts. He feels a bit uneasy about it because it is a different kind of writing than the impersonal, matter-of-fact stuff he usually authors. On the other side, he is a seasoned consultant and knows that showing some passion about the strategic goals helps win over the people in the company. Therefore, he decides to make himself a spokesman of the strategy and utter some personal views at the risk that technocratic mockers among the IT crowd might enjoy tearing them apart. But he is convinced that a deeper understanding of the strategy's motivation, a clearer view of what it means in practice and a closer identification with the goals, will help kick off the mission. Dave Callaghan, his boss and CIO, embraces the idea and encourages Oscar to do so.

The EA group has long played with the idea of utilizing a social software platform (SSP) for the sake of architecture management. Leon Campista, a peer of Padma Valluri on the EA team focusing on processes and methods, is acting as an evangelist for Enterprise 2.0 and has set up an SSP on the corporate intranet to invite participation. Hence Oscar decides to volunteer as a trailblazer and posts his first blog to Leon's SSP, as shown in Figure 8-7.

Oscar's blog post addresses the economic reasons behind customer empowerment, the opportunities it offers, and the implications for the technical landscape. Nevertheless, the major part is less concrete and analytical; it is about finding the right slogans, scenarios, metaphors, and comparisons. Two Japanese founders of modern knowledge management, Ikujiro Nonaka and Hirotaka Takeuchi, would applaud this approach. Their classic *The Knowledge Creating Company* (1995) furnishes evidence of the importance of nonanalytical knowledge in giving organizations a common direction.

Oscar, for instance, compares messages that Bank4Us currently provides to its customers about their savings with the information parents receive from their teenage kids on a school trip to Paris. Every now and then, you get some difficult-to-decipher messages on how they're doing, but all in

---

[12]Write a certain number of buzzwords on a card before a presentation starts—for example, *agility, multichanneling,* or *modular enterprise*. If your buzzword is selected first, you win—"Bingo!"

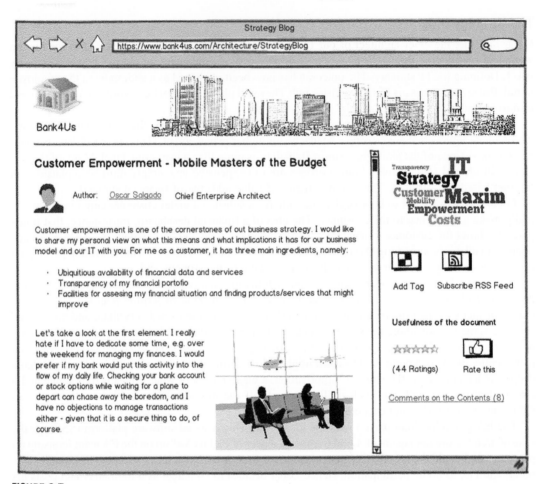

FIGURE 8-7

Oscar's first post to the Strategy blog.

all your insight and influence are rather limited. This resembles Oscar's impression when he receives monthly account statements about his equity fund.

After publishing his post, Oscar remembers Leon's advice that *Enterprise 2.0 platforms must be valued* (as explained in "A Primer on Enterprise 2.0"), and he asks some peers to read his blog. They in fact take up the blog as a means of spreading the word and add comments contributing their own notes and points of view.

All in all, the majority of the IT crowd welcomes the blog posts because they add some beef to the meager maxims of the strategy slides. Leon, acting as the technician behind the SSP, has added a widget to the blog whereby readers can assess the usefulness of the document. The enterprise architecture group wants to use this as a criterion for a regular clean sweep of the SSP to avoid the proverbial document graveyard.

Yet blogs are still rather unidirectional and similar to the bulletin-like publications found in most employee portals. Blogs elicit comments but do not invite participation in the full sense. There is another example at Bank4Us that goes one step further: the ObjectPedia.

Collaborative data modeling: The objectPedia

Data modeling always has been a headache at Bank4Us. Until a few years ago, the company did not have an explicit, enterprise-wide data model. Some units had a detailed, rigid model—in particular those dealing with accounts and money transfers—but others, such as marketing and sales, were drowned in an unconsidered proliferation of concepts and database entities. However, with the advent of more and more cross-unit business processes and the struggle for a unified, seamless customer interface, the absence of an enterprise data model grew into an obstruction. This problem became particularly visible with the introduction of an enterprise service bus (ESB) as a data exchange platform.

Steve Pread, the enterprise architect in charge of the data architecture, has sent a cry for help to Padma Valluri, who maintains the EA processes at Bank4Us. The process for bringing business objects (BOs) into the ESB draws heavy criticism. To ensure the interoperability of services, Steve's team had been entitled to be the only authorities defining BOs that are admissible as service parameters in the ESB.

The objective was a unified data model shared among all service providers and consumers in the ESB. But that turned out to be overambitious. Steve's team was soon overloaded with requests from projects. Furthermore, his architects did not understand the semantics of the hundreds of BOs well enough. Finally, they also had to acknowledge that the dozen interpretations of a central BO like "customer" all had good reasons: The marketing view of a customer is essentially different from what bank transactions attribute to this entity. Hence, Steve asks Padma for a pitiless inspection of his approach.

Padma, seeing this as an opportunity to show the benefits of the recently developed lean toolkit, invites Steve to a process activity mapping of the BO definition, review, and approval process (see Building Block 1 in Chapter 7). They soon agree that more autonomy must be given to projects and that central control of data definition must be given up in favor of a federated, self-organizing approach.

After some days of self-critical musing, Steve comes up with the idea of an *ObjectPedia*, a social software data dictionary along the same lines as Wikipedia. Padma immediately embraces this suggestion because it points to the direction of the just-in-time modeling and iterative design she regards as a prerequisite for the EA Kanban idea (see Building Block 3). Together Steve and Padma draft a first sketch of this platform, as shown in Figure 8-8.

The page has some standard SSP functions that Padma and Steve find promising:

- Steve hopes that the tag cloud makes the search for architecture information more efficient. The company portal the enterprise architecture group used in the past to publish documents (Microsoft Office) eventually felt like searching for a needle in a haystack.
- Users can subscribe to feeds so that they are notified of changes on a page. Padma wants to raise common awareness of changes and automatically synch up all stakeholders as soon as an author publishes modifications.

But a Website is just a start and is not sufficient for self-organization. Leon Campista, the EA 2.0 evangelist, reminds Padma and Steve of the advice that *Enterprise 2.0 platforms must be governed by*

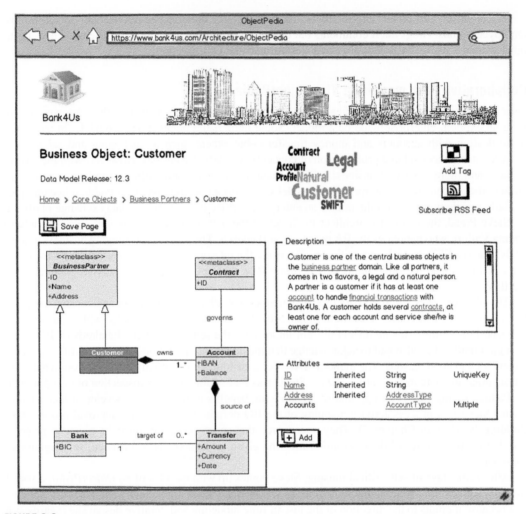

FIGURE 8-8

Collaborative modeling: A sketch of ObjectPedia.

carefully defined rules and norms (see "A Primer on Enterprise 2.0"), and together they constitute the following *ObjectPedia Charter*:

- ObjectPedia shall follow the same code of conduct as Wikipedia, which lives on a respectful and forgiving *netiquette*.
- Authors must not create redundant concepts. If there is some potential to reuse an existing business object, it should be exploited.
- Authors must integrate new concepts into the existing model. Semantic relationships to existing entities must be explicated.

The charter also lists some rules governing the integration with the overall software development process:

- ObjectPedia is open to data architects from each project. The projects nominate their data architects, who then work on the BO model in a fully authorized, self-responsible way. There's no authority from above reviewing the contents or moderating in case of conflicting views.
- The data model has several releases per year. At the end of such a cycle, a snapshot of the most recent data model is frozen, labeled with the release number, and activated in the service repository of the ESB.
- Before a project deploys a service provider implementation into production, it has to decide what data model release it adheres to. This decision is part of the service-level agreement (SLA).

The charter gives wide autonomy to the projects and downsizes the role of Steve's team to consultancy and moderation. ObjectPedia will have a version and change history as well as discussion pages, like Wikipedia. But with these facilities, projects are left to their own responsibility for resolving conflicts. They can approach Steve's modeling gurus for advice but shouldn't expect that they'll get an authoritative model from the top down.

Padma, Steve, and Leon are convinced that this scheme might work. They present the idea to Oscar, the chief enterprise architect, on the next possible occasion and win him over to fight for a prototyping budget. But they also know that efforts go beyond planned SSP implementation: Weakening the grip in favor of self-organization is a brave step and needs some coaching during ramp-up. It is a long haul, as Andrew McAfee puts it (2009).

The Bank4Us example is a case where the designing capabilities of a central authority did not suffice to tame the complexity of an enterprise data model. Way back in our *Reflections on Complexity,* we gave some reasons that a network of autonomous designers has the potential to do better: It gets more hands on board and benefits from a diversity of knowledge. ObjectPedia shows how this can be achieved in an EA context.

Weak ties and a self-organizing application landscape

Ian Miller, the Bank4Us enterprise architect whom we already encountered on several occasions, has recently drafted a landscape map of the Internet portal applications in the online banking and trading business domains. An excerpt of this map is shown in Figure 8-9. The map is a view of the as-is architecture and addresses several stakeholders: developers, operational staff, and planners.

It was a strenuous effort to draw the full map consisting of 46 applications and 129 application interfaces. But Ian is an old hand and knows the fate of such architecture views: They are inaccurate from the first day onward, and their reliability melts like ice in summer with each release of an application. Developers and operational staff start ignoring the map as soon as they discover major inaccuracies, and planners will blame Ian if they base erroneous decisions on faults in the map. It has happened more than once that the credibility and reputation of the enterprise architecture group was damaged by such blaming that eventually escalated to the CIO.

The enterprise architecture group had pursued various approaches to ensure the accuracy and timeliness of models. They mandated that development projects had to submit their architecture input at defined milestones, and they monitored the projects by architecture compliance reviews as described in Chapter 3, "Monitoring the project portfolio (EA-6)."

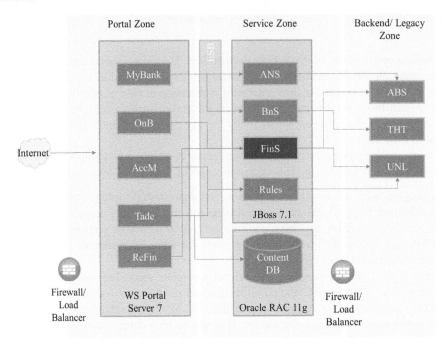

FIGURE 8-9

Ian's landscape map of portal applications.

But the results of these governance mechanisms were disappointing for various reasons: The projects unwillingly submitted just a minimum of information "to make the EAs happy," or the project architect did not have sufficient insight into the de facto implementation, or the delivered input was already outdated when the release went into production. In many cases, models were simply abandoned or kept alive at high cost by frequent and laborious software archeology. The run for up-to-date models felt like an inverse "hare and hedgehog" race: Whenever the modeler was under the happy impression he had captured reality, the de facto implementation had already moved on to a different place.

To escape this dilemma, and with growing support for ObjectPedia in the offing, Ian decides to publish the landscape map to the SSP and open it for comments, corrections, amendments, and evaluations by the IT crowd. A realization of this idea is sketched in Figure 8-10.

The site has some standard functions of an SSP: tag clouds to facilitate searching, feeds to raise the awareness of changes, and usefulness ratings to alleviate cleansing. But the treasure is in the content-related comments that Ian harvests in a corresponding subpage (see Figure 8-11).

The inaccuracy pointed out by software engineer Harriet and the service-level concern discovered by system operator Carl are exactly the fallacies that would probably have not been discovered without the SSP. Ian knew Carl, and maybe he would have stated his concern in an ordinary review of the architecture specification. But Ian had no relation to Harriet; she was one of the so-called *potential ties* connected by the SSP.

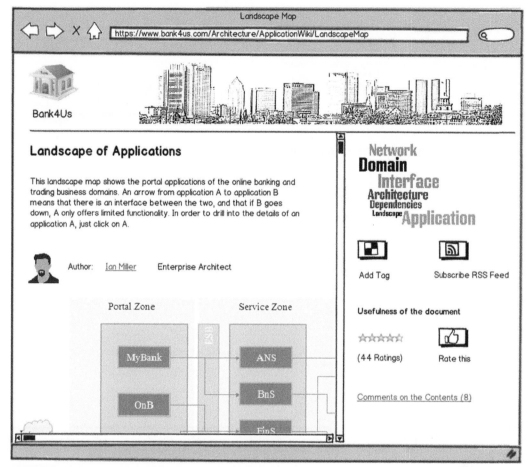

FIGURE 8-10

Ian's landscape map in the architecture SSP.

So far, so good—but this site has shortcomings:

- The drafting of the landscape map still remains a solitary effort and invites participation only with hindsight.
- The review of the map is an additional burden to the project teams. In addition to the documents they have to provide for an architecture conformance review (ACR), they are now called to find flaws in Ian's filings. This breaks the maxim that *Enterprise 2.0 platforms must be put "into the flow."*
- Because the development process does not mandate review of the landscape map, the finding of fallacies is a matter of luck.

Hence, Ian would like to take one step further in the direction of a self-organizing application catalogue. The project teams are currently submitting their input to the ACR on Excel sheets. They could as well use an SSP site like the one shown in Figure 8-12.

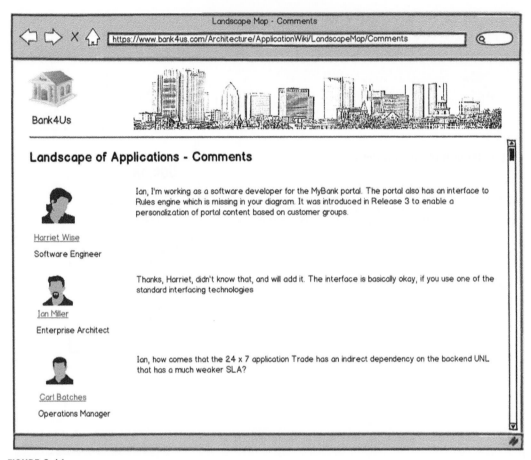

FIGURE 8-11

Comments on Ian's landscape map.

The site provides a template in which project architects can fill in the details about their applications. The landscape map is then generated from this input without further manual work.

Meanwhile, Ian starts appreciating emergent models and wonders whether self-organization could not also answer a notorious meta-problem involved in templates, as shown in Figure 8-12. Templates like this one incorporate the taxonomy of enterprise architecture—for example, the EA understanding of the concept "application." But the application domains are different and the technologies widespread, so a template that makes sense to all is a least common denominator conveying just meager information.

Ian started his career as a software developer in the data warehouse (DW) domain, and he implemented ETL[13] flows by means of Perl and Structured Query Language (SQL). At that time, Common

---

[13]Extraction, transformation, and loading (ETL) is the first DW stage, which gathers information from operational systems and loads it into the DW database.

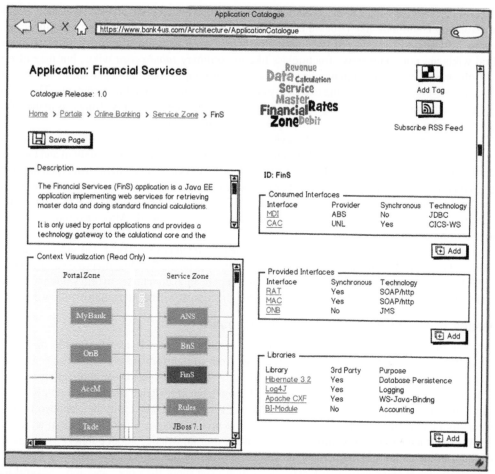

FIGURE 8-12

The application catalogue site.

Object Request Broker Architecture (CORBA) was the ruling hype technology, and all architecture documentation standards at Bank4Us were targeted at CORBA applications. The templates were all about components, implementation-independent interfaces, IDLs,[14] stubs, skeletons, and interface operations. Ian remembers how awkward it was to express his file- and database-centric mass data flows in these terms. It also felt as though his well-thought-out, useful flows were something dirty or half-legal.

From reviewing the input the project teams submit to the ACR, Ian got the impression that many project architects are scratching their heads as they fill in the templates. They do not feel at home in the taxonomy designed by the EA team. What if this taxonomy could also be emergent and he could invite the project architects to shape it according to their views on the subject?

---

[14]Interface Definition Language, the CORBA standard format for defining interfaces.

Recent research conducted at the Technical University of Munich gives an idea what such an emergent taxonomy could look like (Buckle et al., 2010).[15] The research group Software Engineering for Business Information Systems (SEBIS) promotes *hybrid wikis* as a tool for emergent meta-models. Hybrid wikis are not completely structureless like the ordinary *tabula rasa* wikis, but they also are not rigidly prestructured by templates, as in the case of Ian's application catalogue site. Their structure is given to self-organization, and the taxonomy emerges while users are editing contents. The method of choice to achieve this functionality are *typed tags*. These tags are not simply strings, as in the case of ordinary tags, but key-value pairs. An example is shown in Figure 8-13.

The application FinS is tagged with several typed tags—for example, with *CatalogueItem* and *JavaEE*. Therefore, FinS inherits the simple attributes *ID* and *Name* from CatalogueItem and the multi-valued attribute *Libraries* from JavaEE. As usual with tags, users can create their own typed tags while editing contents in the HybridWiki. An author in charge of some ETL flow would not pick the JavaEE tag but could annotate the flow with a new typed tag. This tag would be specific to ETL flows and list the target database tables and shared stored procedures being accessed. After creation, it would be available to other authors, too.

The SEBIS research group distributes an open source hybrid wiki called Tricia. The video recording at (SEBIS, 2012) nicely demonstrates how a meta-model emerges on the fly while users are editing contents with this SSP. The researchers also discovered EA as an application domain for hybrid wikis and founded the industry collaboration Wiki4EAM to proceed in this direction. It will be interesting to follow their work.

Summing it up: Assessment by the EA Dashboard

Throughout this section we've come across blueprint examples of how Bank4Us embarks on Building Block 4, Participation in knowledge. The tools range from straightforward ones, like Oscar Salgado's Strategy blog, to rather futuristic means, like Ian Miller's vision of a hybrid wiki application catalogue.

The addressees of the given examples are the IT crowd, but knowledge sharing is certainly not confined to this target group. Ian's application landscape, for example, can easily be extended by forum elements to a collaboratively written user manual that invites users to share their best practices and tricks. We don't have to dwell on this; today half of the user knowledge about publicly available software is not in the authoritative manuals but instead written by the users themselves.

The examples support various EA activities (often even more than one) and apply several techniques of social software platforms (SSPs); Table 8-1[16] summarizes these.

In this table, a solid bullet marks the most crucial techniques, whereas a hollow bullet denotes a feature that plays a role but is not key. Nevertheless, the general, ubiquitous functions of an SSP should not be underestimated. The ability to connect people and make the network participants aware of what others are thinking and doing is presumably a paramount benefit of an SSP. Only the landscape map explicitly highlighted this benefit, but it is implicit in the other examples, too.

What more specific benefits can we expect for EA? Figure 8-14 measures the expected value of Building Block 4 on our EA Dashboard.

Since Building Block 4 is about knowledge but not about taking action, the expected impact is on the order-chaos dichotomy but not on the timeline.

---

[15]Available at http://wwwmatthes.in.tum.de/wikis/sebis/bu10w-a-lightweight-approach-to-enterpris.

[16]EA-7. Leading or coaching projects fits, too, but we picked one best fit here that also formed the background of our Bank4Us case.

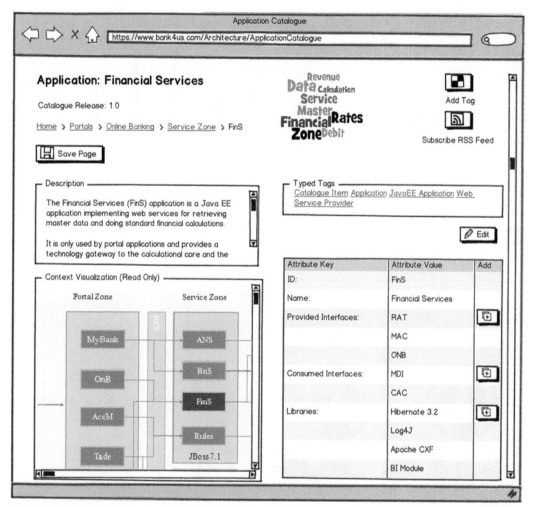

FIGURE 8-13

The application catalogue as a hybrid wiki.

Tools like ObjectPedia and the landscape map are dedicated to guiding EA out of "Cloud Cuckoo Land." Their very essence is to meet implementation realities and local knowledge on the ground. The Strategy blog, on the other hand, demonstrates that EA 2.0 tools can also help propagate business concerns and visions among the IT crowd. The Perspective gauge therefore deserves arrows in both directions but with a stronger emphasis on getting our feet back on the ground.

ObjectPedia was initially designed to overcome a governance bottleneck: the solitary top-down definition of a data model by EA. The application catalogue and its futuristic twin, the hybrid wiki, exemplify how the mode of documentation obligations can change from top-down examinations to a more self-responsible authorship of projects. Hence, we expect that Building Block 4 can help the guardians of wisdom weaken the grip.

Table 8-1 Building Block 4: Supported Activities and Employed Techniques

Tool	EA Activity	Search	Links	Tags	Coll. Authoring	Comments	Ratings	Extensions	Signals
Strategy blog	Defining the IT Strategy (EA-1)	○	○	○		●	○		○
ObjectPedia	Modeling the Architectures (EA-2)	○	○	○	●				○
Landscape map	Modeling the Architectures (EA-2)	○	○	○		●	○		○
Application catalogue	Monitoring the Project Portfolio (EA-6)	○	○	○	●				○
Hybrid wiki	Monitoring the Project Portfolio (EA-6)	○	○	●	●				○

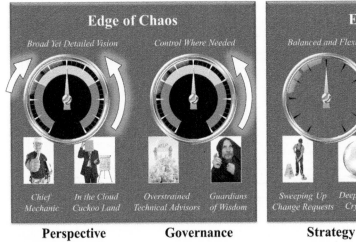
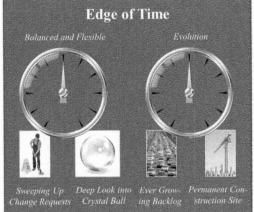

Edge of Chaos

Broad Yet Detailed Vision   *Control Where Needed*

Chief Mechanic   *In the Cloud Cuckoo Land*   *Overstrained Technical Advisors*   *Guardians of Wisdom*

Perspective   Governance

Edge of Time

Balanced and Flexible   *Evolution*

Sweeping Up Change Requests   *Deep Look into Crystal Ball*   *Ever Growing Backlog*   *Permanent Construction Site*

Strategy   Transformation

FIGURE 8-14

The EA Dashboard for Building Block 4, Participation in knowledge.

Building Block 5: Participation in decisions

The crucial question in this section is, how can enterprise architecture benefit from broader participation in finding future directions and taking decisions? Can the wisdom of crowds also improve decision making in EA?

In thinking about this question, one can easily lose footing. What we're after is a realistic answer against the background of today's enterprise constitutions. There's no use in chasing butterflies in utopia: Grassroots democracy is not a model for companies. Which application server software we choose to use will not be a subject of general elections. Enterprise architects won't form political parties and fight to win the votes for a particular target IT landscape.

Sometimes it is striking how close the work of an enterprise architect in a federated, "political" enterprise can come to such a mode. Nevertheless, it is more a fight for the consent and support of those with budget and influence; applause from the ground workers is neither necessary nor sufficient.

Democracy is marvelous because it respects the autonomy of the individual, not because it is particularly effective in making the right decisions. Unlike society as a whole, an enterprise is, as the name indicates, an organization pursuing particular business goals, and the autonomy of the employees is not its primary concern. Unless this changes, democracy also is not the only rational choice for enterprise constitutions. Hence, we're not calling for democratic subversion with Building Block 5. Rather, our focus is on providing *more and broader input* into the decision-making process.

Today we are used to basing our decisions on the opinions and knowledge of Internet social networks. The orientation in terms of what friends, colleagues, neighbors, or relatives do and cherish has always been a trait in decision making, but the advent of social software platforms broadened the scope beyond the strong ties we formerly took into account. The decision to buy a book or a car or even to look for a new job is influenced by the comments, ratings, and cross-links we search for on the Internet. And usually we're better off with it than with only reading one article written by a profound expert. Why should this day-to-day experience be wrong in enterprise architecture?

The diagnostic process landscape

Bank4Us in the meantime has taken further steps toward Enterprise 2.0. The social software platform (SSP) launched by the EA group is now applied beyond the bounds of the IT crowd, too. The extensive office manuals giving instructions on how to perform activity X of process Y have been accompanied by a forum, as shown in Figure 8-15.

The forum is gathering best practices from daily work; it is a self-written user manual. The user contributions arrange themselves around the process landscape model of EA, which works as a crystallization point for this knowledge. All users directly or indirectly involved in a process can post advice. The motives for authoring are widespread: Some authors just want to help other poor strugglers, some recognize the SSP as a valuable source of information and want to pass knowledge back in return, whereas others enjoy being regarded as old hands and advisors in their specific areas.

Furthermore, it feels good that the SSP to some extent makes the practitioners owners of the process. This in particular holds true for the rating widget, which is also the interesting part with regard to choosing future directions and making decisions. It collects the pain points from those who feel the pain.

Franca Bertapelle, for example, a local advisor at the branch office in Pittsburgh, rates the business case evaluation process step (a customer applies for a loan, and Franca needs to qualify his case) quite low. She complains that she has to apply several heuristics to assess the profitability of a credit application, but there are no means to transfer data from one heuristics to the next, which implies that she has to type the same data again.

The idea for this rating and the "Have your say" box did not come from the EA group but from the users. Nevertheless, it has become an important diagnostic tool in activity EA-3, "Evolving the IT landscape." In assessing the sanity of processes or applications, the EA group still collects input from

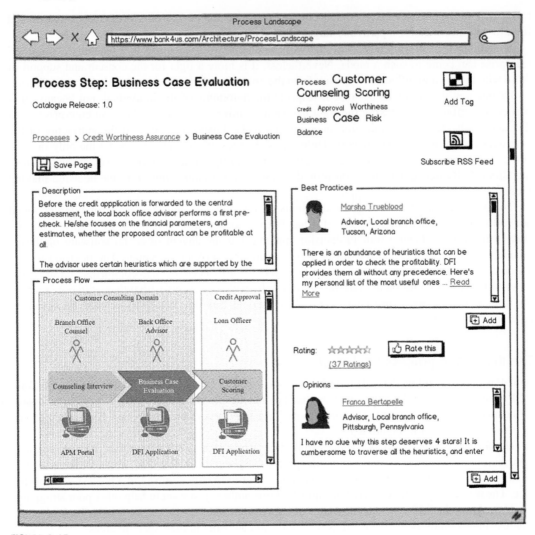

FIGURE 8-15

The process landscape forum.

experts, but they never draw conclusions without taking a look at what the users report. If the user ratings suggest that a process is cumbersome and poorly supported by IT, an expert's praise for it will be taken with a grain of salt.

The diagnostic process landscape is a straightforward quick win with Enterprise 2.0. The next example, however, is more subtle and not only prepares decisions by gathering information but drives them to a result.

The bazaar of IT opportunities

Given the right circumstances, crowds are not only good at assessing present things but also at prognosticating the future. One of the most famous research projects in this direction is the Iowa Electronic Market (IEM) project conducted by the Henry B. Tippie College of Business at Iowa University (Surowiecki, 2005, p. 40). The project started in 1988 but is still under way. IEM is an online, not-for-profit trading market where traders can trade prospects with real (but relatively small amounts) of money.[17] Prospects are statements about a future course of issues—for example:

- P1: The current German chancellor will be reelected next year: US$1
- P2: The Democrats win the US presidential elections next year

Traders can buy, for example, shares of P1, and if the German chancellor in fact wins the elections one year later, they receive US$1 as revenue per share. The price of the shares depends on the market supply and demand: If the price of a P1 share is 52 cents, IEM prognosticates a 52% probability that the current chancellor will win. The second prospect, P2, is more fine-grained: The revenue depends on the percentage of votes the Democrats win. Assume they attain 56%; then the owner of a P2 share receives 56 cents in return. A price of 48 cents per share is therefore interpreted as a prognosis that the Democrats will win 48% of the votes.

The IEM frequently outperforms the survey-based prognosis of accredited statistical institutes—presumably because the traders pay more attention to it than to a nonbinding survey and the market mechanism has more self-correction capabilities than the plain summation of polled opinions.

Two items that frequently need to be prognosticated in IT are effort and business value of a solution alternative. Effort estimation finds support in a rich toolbox of techniques,[18] but business value estimation is still in its infancy. Big strategic IT initiatives usually undergo a business case assessment that somehow numbers their expected value. But for so-called *IT opportunities*, such an approach causes too much effort or is principally impossible due to a lack of predictability.

The term *IT opportunity* (ITO) was coined by Broadbent and Kitzis (2005) and denotes the bag of ideas and bleeding-edge innovations complementing the big strategic initiatives. IT opportunities are typically perilous, in regard to the expected outcome or technology. They are the wildest among the Wild Cats in the Ward-Peppard square (see the section "Assessing Applications").

Broadbent and Kitzis recommend designing a management process for the highly volatile bag of ITOs in parallel with strategic planning. The process should be shaped like a funnel with a broad entry for gathering the rich plenty of ideas but an early and rigid cutting down to the really smart ones. What would be more suitable than a marketplace for implementing this funnel? Folks can easily place an offer, but if it doesn't sell, it's out.

Padma Valluri, the enterprise architect at Bank4Us who focuses on EA processes, finds marketplaces like IEM highly inspiring. Together with Leon Campista, the Enterprise 2.0 evangelist, she proposes the idea of an *ITO bazaar* and eventually convinces the EA group and management to

---

[17]Refer to the IEM home page, http://tippie.uiowa.edu/iem/, for more information. You can also register there, become a trader, and invest $5–500 to gamble. The IEM is (with a few exceptions) open to interested people worldwide.

[18]Function point analysis, cost constructive model (COCOMO), or agile story point estimation, just to name a few prominent techniques. Steve McConnell's book, *Software Estimation: Demystifiying the Black Art,* provides a nicely readable introduction to this topic (McConnell, 2006).

furnish it in the EA social software platform (SSP). The prototype Leon helped her set up is shown in Figure 8-16.

The site again shows many basic functions of an SSP: tags, RSS feeds, links to people and further assets, and the possibility of leaving suggestions. But its most remarkable feature is the bidding widget on the right side. There people can bet how much effort is involved in the realization of the ITO and, as an option, can also offer a certain amount of person days they are willing to contribute to the solution.

Betting on the effort is just a game. People who came close to the de facto effort (determined after the implementation) are rewarded with a corresponding number of scores that can be converted into money in an online store.

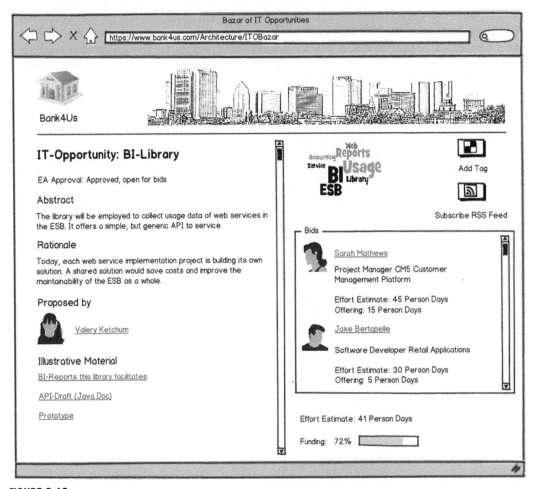

FIGURE 8-16

First bids in the ITO bazaar.

Offering a certain amount of work time, however, is more serious. Bidders are responsible for ensuring that, if the ITO indeed becomes a project, they can fulfill their offering. Project managers like Sarah Mathews should ensure that her team has the needed capacity, and individual software developers like Jake Bertapelle should agree with their supervisors to be exempt from other duties to the extent needed.

There is no automation behind the ITO bazaar that kicks off projects. If an ITO gains sufficient interest—meaning that the ratio of available offerings and estimated effort exceeds 100%—bidders are invited to a meeting with the project portfolio management. This is to check that the preconditions for a kickoff are given and in particular that all bidders can fulfill their shares.

This bidding mechanism helps estimate the true business value of an ITO: Only if there is a need for the proposed solution, and sufficient faith in the success of the idea, does the ITO get funded. Furthermore, the mechanism mitigates a chicken-race problem related to the funding of shared, cross-unit software components: In the past, the first unit to jump on such a component had to pay the price all alone.

There was a saying in Bank4Us that "The first guy who wants to swim has to pay for the swimming pool," which is a break for both innovation and cross-unit collaboration. The bidding mechanism puts an end to this idea by bargaining a fair sharing of the efforts.

The ITO bazaar is open to the IT crowd but also to others with sparkling ideas about the profitable exploitation of information technology. The filings therefore range from rather down-to-earth, technology-driven submissions like the one shown in Figure 8-8 to high-flying exciters. But this variety is put under EA governance: Each ITO needs approval from the EA group before it is open for trading. The reasons for erecting such a quality gate are:

- Filings contradicting strategic maxims, the future application landscape, or the technology reference model are likely to be rejected. This is to ensure that the ITOs do not head in a different direction from the non-ITO initiatives planned by the strategy board.
- Filings that are sheer nonsense or rather naïve with regard to technical feasibility are sifted out. Insignificant ideas are also sieved so that the bazaar does not dissipate energies in tiny code writings here and there.

Whether such a quality gate should be erected was the subject of fierce discussion at Bank4Us. Some opponents believed it endangers the free development of the market (the discussions showed the usual traits of debates about market regulation). The convincing argument in favor of such a gate was a look at the governance of open source software programs: They also employ quality sieves to prevent the essence of the program from being eroded by nonfitting projects or the grooming of hobbyhorses.[19]

Experience will show whether the previous "business model" for the ITO bazaar will work out. This model is the essence of the ITO bazaar, and its functionality needs more attention and care than mere tooling. The responsible parties at Bank4Us therefore decided to set up frequent monitoring and optimization of the trading rules.

---

[19]A case study from a large IT organization supports the necessity of quality gates. The organization set up a marketplace for innovative ideas and was choked with more than 15,000 proposals, most of them of poor quality.

Summing it up: Assessment by the EA Dashboard

Building Block 5, Participation in decisions, applies the principles and techniques of Enterprise 2.0 to choosing future directions and making decisions in connection with EA. We have seen two examples from Bank4Us of how this looks in practice:

- The rather straightforward *diagnostic process map* exemplified how key performance indicators regarding IT can be polled from a wider crowd of IT stakeholders. The diversity of viewpoints caught up by such a poll can counterbalance the tunnel view experts sometimes fall victim to.
- The more subtle *ITO bazaar* provides an innovative answer to how IT opportunities should be managed. The trading mechanism on one hand prognosticates the business value of solutions and on the other solves a problem with the funding of shared software components.

The EA activities and SSP techniques of these examples are summarized in Table 8-2.[20]

In summary, what do we expect from Building Block 5 for EA? Figure 8-17 measures the expected impact by the EA Dashboard.

The essence of participating in decisions is giving a voice to the crowd with respect to identifying where there is need for action and exploring alternatives. We can therefore expect it to set the perspective right if this has lost contact with the ground-level realities (Cloud Cuckoo Land). Furthermore, the building block is an antidote against a tunnel view in strategy, a single faraway vision that is mostly based on the beliefs and wishes of the top brass. The reality check ventilated by the SSP may draw EA away from its hypnotic fixation on the crystal ball and uncover additional tracks worth following. Furthermore, participating in decisions establishes a funnel for ideas and innovations, as the ITO bazaar demonstrates. It therefore can help us escape from congealing that anxiously focuses on keeping the existing system running; hence, the transformation gauge is rising, too.

Table 8-2 Building Block 5: Supported Activities and Employed Techniques

Tool	EA Activity	Search	Links	Tags	Coll. Authoring	Comments	Ratings	Extensions	Signals
Diagnostic process map	Evolving the IT Landscape (EA-3)	○	○	○	●	○	●		○
ITO bazaar	Monitoring the Project Portfolio (EA-6)	○	○	○		●	●		○

[20]The legend is the same as with Table 8-1 and Table 8-2: A solid bullet marks the most crucial techniques.

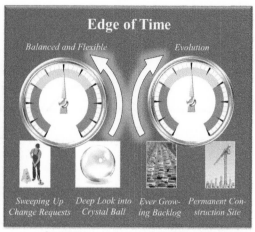

FIGURE 8-17

The EA Dashboard for Building Block 5, Participation in decisions.

Building Block 6: Participation in transformation

The previous two building blocks provided good reason to assert that EA 2.0 techniques spur on knowledge sharing and organizational learning and are valuable tools in preparing to make and actually making decisions. But how can they help when you eventually go hands-on?

Building Block 6 addresses transformation: implementing change up to deploying and operating the next release of the IT landscape. Transformation in a sense is an ultimate practical test of EA: How well EA guides projects and eventually realizes the target landscape is one of its most important success criteria. What can Enterprise 2.0 contribute to the effectiveness of EA in the transformation phase? This is the question we explore in the following section.

Mashing up the architecture continuum

Enterprise architectures are not monoliths, they are mosaics composed of architectures designed by different owners. In Chapter 7 we came across a classification of architecture types by granularity into strategic, segment, and capability architectures. The architectures of this classification are nested according to the dimensions of time horizon, subject matter, and level of detail. They range from long-term, far-reaching, and high-level strategic architectures to short-term, special, and detailed capability architectures. Furthermore, these architectures are usually crafted by different teams of architects.

Beneath the capability architectures, we even find another layer of architectures made up of the daily design decisions of development teams and therefore yet another team contributing to the overall picture. This daily hands-on layer is not irrelevant. During the 2010 conference of The Open Group in Amsterdam, Len Fehskens, vice president of this organization, asked where the borderline between architectural Design (with a capital *D*) and design (with a small *d*) actually is. This line is indeed difficult to draw when adopting a definition of Design such as Booch's explanation of architecture, "[. . .] *the significant design*

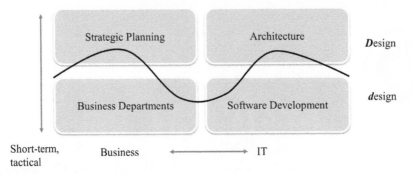

FIGURE 8-18

The borderline between Design and design.

decisions that shape a system, where significant is measured by cost of change" (Booch, 2006). On this ground, the borderline presumably meanders across the teams, as shown in Figure 8-18

The assumption that design decisions on a lower layer can be revised at low cost turns out to be wrong in practice: The innocent decision for a certain primary key in some database table design can freeze change in some wider application domain for years.[21]

Another rationale for continuity is reuse. The Open Group has conceptualized the vision of what they call the *architecture continuum*. It is a subdivision of the enterprise architecture according to generality. Figure 8-19[22] depicts the four divisional classes.

The flow from left to right goes from general to special, from technology focused to business focused, and from logical to physical.

- *Foundation architectures* are the most generic type of architecture. They typically consist of a general taxonomy and a frame of functional domains. The TOGAF Technical Reference Model (TRM) is an example of foundation architecture (The Open Group, 2009, p. 575 ff).
- *Common system architectures* are one step more specific and typically specify building blocks for particular aspects—for instance, security, system management, or networking services. The TOGAF Integrated Information Infrastructure Reference Model (III-RM) is an example of a common system architecture that addresses several aspects centered on the vision of a boundary-less, enterprise-wide information flow (The Open Group, 2009, p. 607 ff).

---

[21]This statement refers to a story from our own experience as developers: The development team of a data warehouse system reporting on telecom network performance decided for a primary key in the measurement fact tables that reflected the hierarchical relationships of network elements. Each fact table contained an identifier for the measured network element but also identifiers of the managing parent network element, of the parent's parent, and so on up to the root element. These hierarchical relations were the most widely used reporting dimension, and the rationale behind the decision was to avoid joins with a separate dimension table for performance reasons. The team wasn't aware that the hierarchical structure of network elements is subject to frequent change, and they had to struggle with such changes over subsequent years because it was a nightmare to modify the primary keys of hundreds of fact tables containing gigabytes of data.

[22]Adapted from The Open Group (2009), used with kind permission.

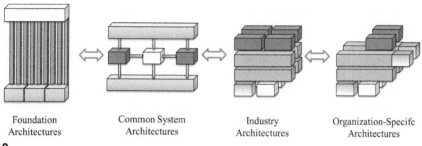

| Foundation Architectures | Common System Architectures | Industry Architectures | Organization-Specifc Architectures |

FIGURE 8-19

The Open Group's architecture continuum.

- *Industry architectures* specify building blocks for particular verticals. They add branch specifics on top of the two previous architectures. Examples are the telecom NGOSS[23] architecture and the finance BIAN.[24]
- *Organization-specific architectures* are the most specific architectures that structure the IT landscape of an individual enterprise.

The more specific architectures on the right reuse the more generic ones on the left. They use the capabilities of general building blocks—for instance, the functionality of a general single sign-on security solution, or are embedded in a more general frame, for instance as concrete SOA service providers in the service landscape of BIAN.

The two architecture classifications—by generality and granularity—are different but not entirely orthogonal: The foundational architectures typically belong to the strategic class, just to name one correlation. Nevertheless, there are strategic elements in the organization-specific architectures as well as quite detailed capability architectures among the common system architectures, so the two classifications are founded on widely independent dimensions.

Common to both classifications is a rich network of links that exist between the different architectures—and this eventually is where Web 2.0 comes into play. The design principle of remixability and the focus on linking and backtracking content provide the ideal ground for mashing up a true architecture continuum. Web 2.0 renders possible an architecture knowledge repository that is consistently navigable across multiple dimensions, integrates data and models from various sources, and facilitates a continuous flow from high-level strategic plans to code design or from standards to custom solutions.

Padma Valluri, the lean evangelist among the enterprise architects, is excited by this vision set forth by her EA 2.0 counterpart, Leon Campista. She is convinced that a continuous flow of architecture design across strategic, segment, and capability teams down to code design (with a small *d*) cannot be achieved with plain old paper documentation. But this flow is at the heart of the EA Kanban and is a prerequisite for a continuous integration of designs. Padma therefore supports Leon's struggle

---

[23]New Generation Operating Support Systems (NGOSS), a framework developed by the Tele Management Forum (TMF) consisting mainly of a standard data model (SID), a process catalogue (eTOM), and some minor building blocks.
[24]Banking Industry Architecture Network (BIAN) is a not-for-profit organization defining a generic SOA service landscape for finance.

for some time and budget that would allow Leon and his helping hands to prototype the idea sketched in Figures 8-20 and 8-21.

The prototype's first page shows a map of the application landscape mashed up with information stemming from various sources. The map serves as a navigational component—a mouse click on an application rectangle, an interface bubble, or a dependency arrow brings up related information in the other widgets of the page. The information these widgets display depends on the selected item and whether it is an application, an interface, or a dependency. For an application, the linked-in information is about system management, operating environments, the BIAN service area the application is mapped to, and other items worth knowing. An interface, on the other hand, is displayed with a different set of items.

The links highlighted in Figure 8-20 are pointers to more generic architectures. They either point to entire pages—the System Management link to the Tivoli Monitoring common system architecture is such a case—or to data items provided by the higher-level architectures, as in the case of the BIAN combo box that displays the service areas available in this industry-specific architecture.

While these navigation links are paths from specific to more general architectures, a different kind of magic happens when we double-click on the FinS application rectangle: The SSP drills into a deeper

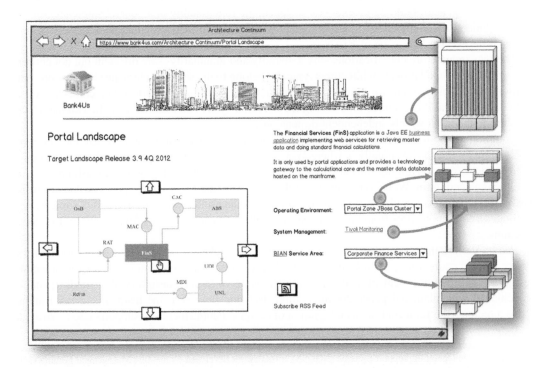

FIGURE 8-20

The application landscape mashup.

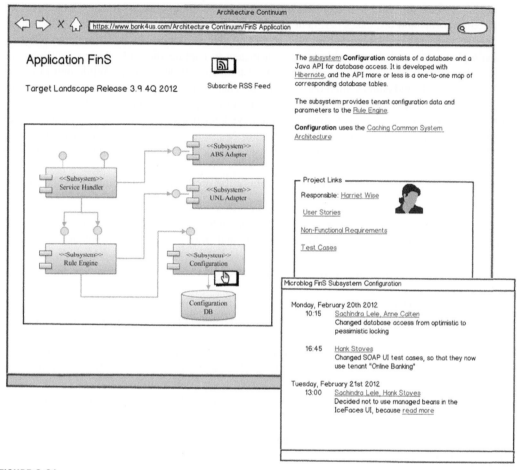

FIGURE 8-21

The application-level mashup and microblog.

level of detail. Figure 8-21 shows the target page, the decomposition of FinS into subsystems, which is the highest application-internal part of Kruchten's Logical View[25] on the software architecture.

The logical view is mashed up with links to more generic architecture building blocks—for instance, with a link to a common database caching architecture. Double-clicking on the subsystem rectangle, on the other hand, zooms deeper into the inner structure, eventually down to class diagrams, scenarios, pages with HTML-formatted code headers, and so on.

---

[25]The logical view is one of the views Philippe Kruchten proposed (1995) to document software architectures. His so-called 4+1 view model underlies the Rational Unified Process. The other 3+1 views are process, development, and physical + use case (scenario) views.

In addition, there are links into requirements management and quality assurance. They direct the user to requirements and test cases pertinent to the subsystem that is currently in focus. These navigation paths connect the architecture SSP with other knowledge islands of a transformation program.

Leon's plans also include microblogging as a means to capture the daily design decisions and changes. The postings are grouped by software subsystem. Here is an example: While pair programming, Sachindra Lele and Anne Calten (two developers) decide to switch database access from an optimistic to a pessimistic transactional locking and report this decision to the microblog.

This can be a useful piece of information some days later if a sudden database deadlock or lock timeout problem occurs in the next round of load testing. Multiple channels are open to this micro-blog: the SCM[26]-system, a standalone desktop or Web user interface, an SMS, a mobile app, or whatever else is used in daily work.

The benefits that Leon and Padma list to promote the architecture continuum mashup (ACM) idea are:

- The ACM enforces referential integrity between the architectures and therefore a stringent modeling of architectures from top down to coding and from generic building blocks to highly specific ones.
- The ACM makes people aware of what architecture building blocks there already are and therefore fosters reuse.
- The ACM is a knowledge repository that makes the transformational paths visible and navigable and therefore is a means to monitor and control the transformation. Wrong directions and frictions can be spotted more easily.
- The ACM is a tool for collaborating on working copies of architectures and therefore makes possible the EA Kanban vision of just-in-time (JIT) modeling and of a steady flow of design from top to bottom.
- The ACM closes gaps between knowledge islands of a transformation program and therefore helps in making the left hand know what the right hand is doing.

Leon's microblog is a ground-level example illustrating the last bullet quite well. The next section's Bank4Us case, however, comes up with an even more thrilling story of how Enterprise 2.0 can bridge gaps between knowledge islands.

The change management microblog

Knowledge islands can be fatal. One of the most well-known examples is the failure of the US intelligence community to spot the 9/11 attacks in advance. "In the months preceding 9/11 troubling signs were apparent to intelligence agents and analysts throughout the world," writes McAfee (2006b, p. 31). But there were 16 agencies making up the US intelligence community, and they shared information reluctantly (if at all) and ineffectively. Furthermore, the prevalent safety culture in these agencies was "need-to-know"—do not let people know more than what they absolutely need to do their duties. Hence, all the knowledge was there, but no one was able to piece the jigsaw together.

---

[26]Software configuration management (SCM) is a system primarily used to manage versions of software source code and other assets. Coders typically add notes about their changes while committing new versions of their code to the SCM system. The microblog will take these notes up, too.

In 2011, 10 years after 9/11, a similar case was discovered in Germany. A small group of extremists had committed acts of terror and murdered a still undetermined number of people over a period of 10 years. In retrospect, the units of the highly federated law enforcement agencies had all bits of information they needed to arrest the group years previously, but the bits were "safely" isolated and locked away.

Enterprises are not doing better than governmental agencies in this respect: They also fall victim to knowledge islands. The consequences may not be as deathly—in particular, when thinking of the comparably harmless failures in IT—but they nevertheless do harm. When a consultant is helping companies in matters of IT problems, the value the consultant adds often is not in the additional knowledge she brings but in the fact that she *listens* to stakeholders from *all* parties. It sometimes is stunning: All the knowledge is already there, but it needs an external player to put the puzzle together.

Likewise, when tracking an IT failure back to its root causes, one often discovers that the problem could have been avoided if only two or three people had shared their knowledge. A test engineer, under full steam to get a release out the door, manually changes the JVM heap size[27] of an application server to get rid of out-of-memory exceptions and kick off functional integration testing.

One week later, the same lack of memory rocks the boat when the tested release is being deployed in production, this time with a customer-facing outage that is brought to the attention of the CIO. The information about the change simply got lost in the chain from test engineer over project manager to release coordinator and eventually to the administrator of the production server.

The causal chain often is much more intricate than in the previous example. Sarah Taylor, program manager at Bank4Us, feels like yelling at someone. One of the critical applications she is accountable for suddenly crashes without apparent reason during the early morning hours and even brings the whole server down. Restarting the server helps, but the outage inevitably happens again the next morning. The affair is a red flag to senior management boards, and Sarah has to defend herself each morning in a telephone conference with Dave Callaghan, the CIO. Her team is working overtime on troubleshooting but feels a bit lost, in particular because the failure cannot be reproduced in the quality assurance environments.

During an ad hoc brainstorming session with administrators, they learn that the number of CPUs of a client system had been doubled, which caused a higher number of requests to the critical application. But the upgrade happened one week before the first outage, and the system supervision logs prove that Sarah's application handled the change smoothly, according to the service-level agreements. What else could it be?

An operator tells Sarah that he had shifted the file backup of the critical application to morning hours. This time coincidence is suspicious, yet the shift is a proven, ordinary procedure, and it was applied three days prior to the first disaster. The days pass and the outages constantly recur each morning. Dave is getting more and more impatient when finally the crucial bit of information is revealed in a cross-departmental emergency meeting: The backend system Sarah's application is relying on for calculating interest rates had reverted to an older set of business rules just one day before the nuisance started.

Financial analysts had discovered that the new calculation rules for one of the financial products were disadvantageous. But the older set of rules, though long proven under earlier circumstances, had some more complicated calculation algorithms, and that was the last straw. With the increased volume of requests, the resource consumption of the file backup, and the slightly longer response times from the rate calculation, threats were queuing in Sarah's application and eventually choked the whole application server.

---

[27]JVM stands for Java Virtual Machine, and the heap size determines how much RAM Java programs can use.

IT "thrillers" like Sarah's hot-headed days of haunting outages happen all the time. In the end there also is no one to arrest, since all actors did perfectly reasonable, admissible things. The mutual impact of well-thought changes to the IT landscape accumulates to a failure for which no one is to blame.

This is one of the traits of a complex system that we highlighted in "Reflections on Complexity": The addition of linear changes such as the increase of requests or the longer response times of rate calculations suddenly pile up to an exponential growth of threats destabilizing the whole system. In addition, the failure pops up at a spot that's at first sight rather unrelated to the changes: It hits the innocent stranger, so to speak. Figure 8-22 shows the pattern.

There are failures that happen simply because somebody did something wrong, but the pattern shown in Figure 8-22 is usually more difficult to hunt down. It also poses the more severe organizational challenge: Preventing wrong acts is one thing, but coordinating best practices of several actors so that they do not collide is a more intricate matter. How can we avoid incidents like the one we've described? Furthermore, presuming that we never will be able to completely ban them, how can we at least shorten troubleshooting times? In Sarah's case, it took more than a week before the team eventually understood what was going on.

One countermeasure is to rely on tools like change and incident management applications or a configuration management database (CMDB). This is perfectly valid, even recommendable, but a closer inspection of the two cases shows that it is not a panacea. These tools are confined to a narrow group of users such as administrators, release coordinators, or operational staff. The test engineer has no access to these tools for reporting the JVM parameter change, and the business analyst does not even know what a CMDB is, not to speak of logging changes to calculation formulae with it.

Another countermeasure is to fine-tune processes and information flows. This again is reasonable, even a mandate. But constructing a channel of information obligations in a way such that those who need to know will know is like solving the traveling salesman problem: The effort grows exponentially with the number of people who need to know.

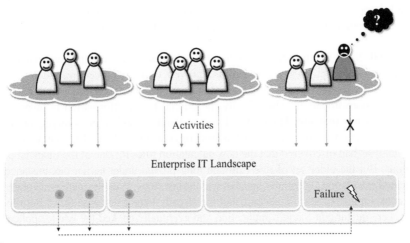

FIGURE 8-22

Cumulative side effects of admissible activities.

Figure 8-22 shows that activities and effects cross the boundaries of organizational units. The financial analyst who reverted back to the older calculation formulas, the administrator who upgraded the client system with new CPUs, and Sarah belong to different communities of practice. In 99% of their activities, it is all right that they are not aware of what the others are doing; their respective knowledge islands provide sufficient information. However, there might be this 1% residuum that no one can guess in advance.

But this is where Enterprise 2.0 can come to the rescue—not as a replacement for the traditional countermeasures explained previously but as a complement. The general accessibility, the enhanced search capabilities, and the ease of use of Web 2.0 can help to bridge the gaps between the knowledge islands and convert potential ties into actual ones as needed.

What if all people who performed changes to the IT landscape would send notice of their activities to a microblog? After pausing for a breath, Sarah decides to do something about the ineffective troubleshooting she experienced. She schedules a meeting with all involved colleagues for a retrospective analysis. Ian Miller, the enterprise architect looking after Sarah's applications, attends as a matter of course and brings Leon Campista with him. Leon has circulated the idea of using microblogging as a means to manage changes of the IT landscape. What he impassionedly explains to Sarah and the other listeners is sketched in Figure 8-23.[28]

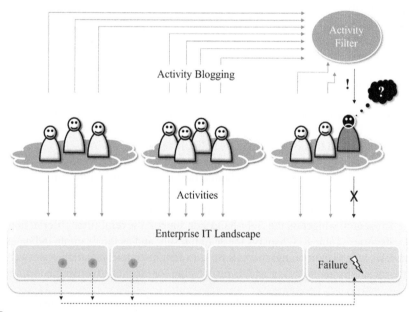

FIGURE 8-23

Microblogging change activities.

---

[28]The general idea is taken from a conference paper by Stefan Bente and Jürgen Karla (2009). The paper applies the idea to the management of telecom networks as one example of a complex technical system. We transcribe this idea here to the context of an IT landscape. Figure 8-22 is adapted from Bente and Karla (2009) and used with permission.

The starting point of Leon's idea is that all IT transformers notify their activities to a microblog. This group of transformers includes administrators, operators, installation engineers, release coordinators, testers, project managers, software developers, and content editors (like the financial analyst in our example)—basically all actors who directly change the IT landscape.

The number of actors will be roughly 800 in the case of Bank4Us. Leon estimates that if blog posts are kept at a reasonable level of interest, the average number would be one or two blog posts per actor per day. Administrators presumably post their hands-on screwing and installations more often, maybe on an hourly basis, whereas project managers or software developers would stick to more infrequent summaries of their day-to-day activities.

Nevertheless, the numbers indicate that some intelligent filtering must be applied to the stream of blog posts to give those who are seeking help a chance to discover the relevant bits. The filtering that does the job in public microblogs like Twitter is based on personal relations: You receive posts only from those you want to follow—your friends, relatives, colleagues, role models, or whomever you are interested in. But this is insufficient, even counterproductive, in the case of a change management microblog: The essence of the idea is to transcend awareness beyond the boundaries of those you are following anyway. There's a wide range of filter criteria, including:

- Date and time when the activity was performed
- The user who acted
- The application domain or application the user acted on
- The technology the user primarily worked on (for instance, Oracle RDBMS)
- The ITIL process or activity category the act is an instance of

The last bullet deserves a broader explanation: The IT Infrastructure Library (ITIL) is a de facto standard for planning, building, and running IT services. It evolved out of the operational side of IT but has expanded to a full-fledged framework of good practices for providing IT services to an organization. One of its assets is a catalogue of change processes and activities at the operational level (Cabinet Office, 2007), and this is what the last bullet is referring to.

Leon has no time to prototype the idea of a change management microblog. Nevertheless, he presents the simple draft shown in Figure 8-24 to Sarah, Ian, and the other brainstorm attendants to sketch the idea.

Small stickers position the activities on an application landscape; their color code marks how recent the activity is. The search widget on the right-hand side supports several filter criteria, in particular the ITIL activity categories. Table 8-3 displays the search result, and as the example indicates, users with quite different roles logged their doings there: Ralph, an administrator; Saptarshi, a software developer; and Scott, an associate from marketing who is responsible for placing advertisements on the company portals.

Leon's audience immediately comes up with a wish list of enhancements and changes to this sketch. Nevertheless, they strongly agree that a tool like this provides the cross-departmental visibility that avoids taking a stab in the dark for days. But how can such a tool be built? Furthermore, would it be yet another tool the actors have to feed with data? Administrators, for example, are already logging most of their activities to a CMDB and do not want to be burdened with yet another logbook.

Leon draws three possible integration scenarios on a whiteboard, as shown in Figure 8-25. They adhere to the general Enterprise 2.0 rule that tools must be put into the flow of daily working practices.

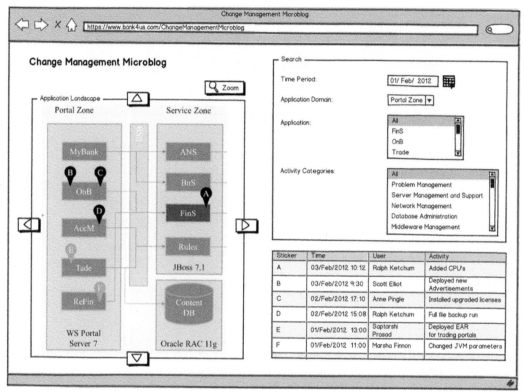

FIGURE 8-24

Sketch of the change management microblog.

Table 8-3 Building Block 6: Supported Activities and Employed Techniques

Tool	EA Activity	Search	Links	Tags	Coll. Authoring	Comments	Ratings	Extensions	Signals
ACM	Leading or Coaching Projects (EA-7)	○	●		○	○		●	○
CMM	Managing Risks Involved in IT (EA-8)	●	○		●	○			○

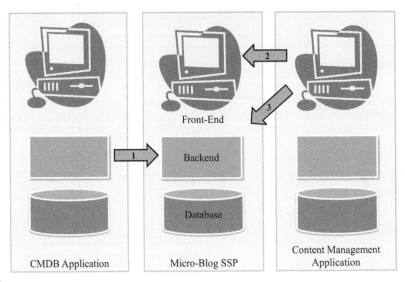

FIGURE 8-25

Integration scenarios.

The intention for the change management microblog is certainly to implement a dedicated application with a database holding all the posts and a front end for submitting blogs and searching. This application is the middle pillar in Figure 8-24. Then there are three options for integration:

- *Back end to back end.* The CMDB, for example, is integrated by a service exporting activity logs entered to this application into the CM microblog. Database triggers would be one way to implement this service. As a result, CMDB users work with their familiar tools as usual.
- *Front end to front end.* The content management application is a portal application and can be mashed up with the microblog Web user interface at the presentation layer. When a user pushes a Commit button to deploy advertisements to the system, for example, the microblog opens and asks for a log entry.
- *Front end to back end.* The content management application could also be extended by a browser plugin or some JavaScript add-ons that automatically post certain activities on the Web UI to the back end of the microblog.

In addition, it might be possible to pick some low-hanging fruit. Bank4Us had to invest heavily in features that serve regulatory compliance. Some of those regulations impose the requirement to capture each change, including what was changed, who did it, and when. These data are already collected in certain areas; they could be reused for the microblog.

Sarah finds Leon's answers quite convincing and suggests seizing the opportunity. Dave Callaghan's anger about the recurring troubleshooting marathons has not yet evaporated. Maybe he is in the mood to spend some money for a proof of concept?

Summing it up: Assessment by the EA Dashboard

"Never touch a running system" is a valuable piece of advice, and most people feel uncomfortable intruding into such a system; they are afraid of opening a Pandora's box. But changes, both structural transformations as well as tunings of the status quo, are a mandate to keep the system viable in an environment with varying demands.

Enterprise architecture wants to be a scout and companion in touching a running system, and Building Block 6, Participation in transformation, shows how Enterprise 2.0 can be an ally in fulfilling this role more effectively.

- The *architecture continuum mashup* (ACM) gives an idea of how the vision of a continuous EA is realized on the basis of Web 2.0. Continuity here means a frictionless tracing of designs from high-level models down to code and from generic foundational architectures to organization-specific ones. Furthermore, the ACM links architecture to requirements and project work, thereby fostering integrity and traceability in this dimension, too.
- The *change management microblog* (CMM) goes beyond enterprise architecture in its vision of how social software platforms can help manage a huge technical system like the enterprise IT landscape on an operational level. But EA is the landscape map to position and find activities on and therefore is context for understanding and coordinating activities.

Table 8-3 lists the EA activities with the closest relationship to the application examples of ACM and CMM. It also marks the social software functionality the examples rely on, with a solid bullet highlighting the most crucial ones.

The benefit of EA 2.0 in guiding transformation is summed up in the Dashboard assessment in Figure 8-26.

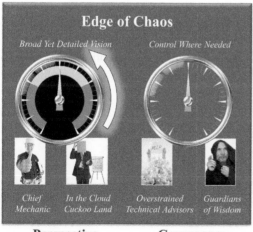
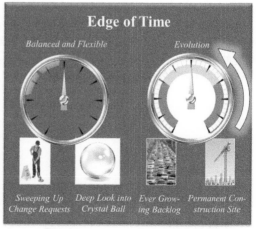

FIGURE 8-26

The EA Dashboard for Building Block 6, Participation in transformation.

The major benefit of the ACM is to enforce that the big picture Design (with an uppercase *D*) is consistently implemented in the nitty-gritty design (with a small-case *d*). It therefore helps avoid the notorious friction between what is written in the high-level specifications and code-level reality and draws the Perspective gauge away from Cloud Cuckoo Land.

The CMM effect is more on the Transformation gauge. It does not change the pace of change, but it helps that the organization actually can manage this pace. Therefore, it takes away some negative side effects and risks that people experience on a permanent construction site.

The bottom line: Inviting to explore

The various examples given in this chapter demonstrate well how Enterprise 2.0 can make a difference in enterprise architecture management. As stated in the introduction, the examples are not the only ones, and Leon Campista and his EA 2.0 peers will soon find further and maybe even better ways of inviting members to participation.

The Bank4Us stories that served as a kind of thought experiment, along with the Dashboard assessments, make clear that there is much we can expect from a more participatory enterprise architecture culture. Furthermore, EA 2.0 does not stand by itself; it is in a sense the natural organizational counterpart for the lean and agile enterprise architecture of Chapter 7.

On the other hand, EA 2.0 is not a quick win. One has to invest in tools and probably also some custom software. Furthermore, the rules and "business models" of the social software platforms need to develop in iterations in a trial-and-error approach. The implementation motto cannot be "Right the first time." Lean and agile techniques, as described in Chapter 7, can be used to gradually develop and improve platforms. This is just another reason that EA 2.0 is tightly connected with lean and agile EA concepts in Building Blocks 1 through 3.

But even more, the organizational culture needs to change. The crucial thing for success with EA 2.0 is that people accept the invitation to participate, and the incentives for such participation must be carefully chosen.

We hope that you accept this and the previous chapter's invitation to go for a collaborative enterprise architecture—lean, agile and participative; a new paradigm of EA 2.0 in one way or another. We will gather some advice on how to push such EA 2.0 changes through your enterprise in the closing of this book, "The Next Steps: Taking Collaborative EA Forward."

The Next Steps: Taking Collaborative EA Forward

CONTENT

A Summary 279
Getting Started with Collaborative EA 283
    Interpreting the Organizational Attitude Toward Change 283
    Motivate the Elephant 286
    Direct the Rider 288
    Shape the Path 290
Looking Ahead 293

A summary

In the wake of the rise of IT in our globalized business world, enterprise architecture has reached the mainstream. There is hardly any large company in the world that does not have an EA team, whatever it is called in the respective organization. The primary task of EA is to align the IT landscape to the business needs while at the same time keeping its ever-growing complexity under control. The enterprise architect is like the driver of a cart drawn by a wild horse: She needs to keep the cart on track and tame the horse at the same time.

This can be a Herculean assignment at times. In Chapter 3, we categorized the manifold tasks of an enterprise architect into eight main activities. They range from contributing to the high-level IT strategy over designing the large-scale IT landscapes down to supervising the concrete implementation projects. In addition, the EA organization is responsible for defining the "how-to" of IT implementation and architecture by providing guidelines and standards.

There is no doubt that EA is a useful, even necessary, function in today's enterprise. Yet in many organizations its impact is not living up to the sustainable and sweeping effect that it promises. Our caricatures way back in Chapter 1 outlined to what extremes EA can deteriorate in practice. As matters stand, EA is too often not realizing the full potential of its core concept.

Why is that so? EA is still a maturing discipline. In some areas its development has come a long way already if you consider, for instance, the rich offering of formal EA frameworks and maturity models that we described in Chapters 4 and 5. But the spirit of EA, as practiced today, is often still marked by a top-down, elitist approach that was characteristic of the IT management style of the 1960s to 1980s. In EA frameworks and literature, enterprise architects ever so slightly resemble a group of enlightened high priests. They receive their wisdom from above in the shape of the strategic maxims decided by the board. Then they hand it down, neatly packaged, to the common IT folks on the ground.

This is not always true, of course. And not that this approach is entirely wrong; it just ignores two major trends that have made the IT industry and user community a more effective and creative place. We have summed them up under the label *Collaborative*:

- *Lean and agile* development methods have made IT projects more flexible, given more responsibility to individuals, and made processes more lightweight.
- *Web 2.0 and Enterprise 2.0* participation concepts have given more influence to IT users, boosted the creation of a true IT ecosystem, and added the wisdom of the many to the findings of the few.

The two concepts have not replaced the traditional way of doing things. Waterfall projects, release dates, and milestones are still in use, and editorially managed content without user participation still has its place. Sometimes the new style and the traditional style compete, sometimes they exist side by side. In any case, lean, agile, and participation concepts have proven to be an enrichment for IT and software development. They have rendered this area more flexible and effective. Why not try that for EA, too?

In this book, we have applied lean, agile, and participation concepts to EA and called it *collaborative EA*. These ideas refresh EA in much the same way they did for IT and software development in general. Our guidelines for collaborative EA sum up how this works in practice:

- *Establish a lean set of processes and rules* instead of overloading the stakeholders with bureaucratic processes and unsolicited artifacts.
- *Adopt evolutionary problem solving* instead of blueprinting the whole future rigidly on a drawing board.
- *Foster and moderate open participation* instead of relying only on experts and top-down wisdom.

Each EA organization can profit from collaborative EA. In Chapter 6, we outlined the nature of complexity that an EA group faces within the enterprise. Based on findings from management theory and cybernetics, we have drawn conclusions about what strategy is most effective in dealing with it. In essence, it boils down to accepting the limits of management in these kinds of ultra-complex systems. Management on a detail level is bound to fail. Instead it is better to steer by simple but clear rules and strengthen the organization's ability to change by introducing flexible process frameworks.

As a consequence, we introduced the term *edge of chaos*, with the underlying finding that a system works in the most effective way when kept in the narrow ridge between too much and too little structure. The EA Dashboard, introduced in Chapter 6, takes up the concept and visualizes it by four gauges. You can use this tool to assess the state of your own EA as well as taking it as a yardstick to gauge the effectiveness of changes to the EA processes.

We have enhanced the edge-of-chaos idea with the notion of the *edge of time* to assess the pacing of change processes. In all, there are four dimensions: Perspective, Governance, Strategy, and Transformation. In each of these dimensions, an effective EA should aim at a good balance. It is at its optimal point (the edge of chaos and time) when it is poised between anarchy and overstructuring, short-sightedness and tunnel vision, standstill and revolution.

Lean, agile, and participation concepts provide tools that can help achieve this balance. In Chapters 7 and 8 we outlined a set of six building blocks that transfer these ideas to the EA domain. Table 9-1 sums them up again.

In mapping out the impact of each building block on EA effectiveness, you get a summarized EA Dashboard, as shown in Figure 9-1. This tool allows you to focus on those building blocks that specifically tackle the issues you found in your own organization.

In addition, Table 9-2 sums up which building block has a potential effect on which of the main EA activities, EA-1 to EA-8, that we outlined in Chapter 3.

Table 9-1 The Six Building Blocks of Collaborative EA

	No.	Building Block	Goal
Lean and Agile	1	*Get Rid of Waste by Streamlining Architecture Processes*	Values the sparse time of enterprise IT stakeholders by focusing on lean processes with as little management overhead as possible
	2	*Involve All Stakeholders by Interlocking Architecture Scrums*	Makes sure that all stakeholders are involved by focusing on structured human interaction as a main channel of information flow
	#3	*Practice Iterative Architecture Through EA Kanban*	Welcomes change, favors iterative design over large-scale, up-front planning, and supports this approach by tools and methods
Participation	#4	*Participation in Knowledge*	Pursues new traits of sharing and combining knowledge by building self-organizing, company-wide information repositories
	#5	*Participation in Decisions*	Allows collaborative decision making by the relevant stakeholders on the ground
	#6	*Participation in Transformation*	Fosters transformation (that eventually changes the IT landscape) by participation

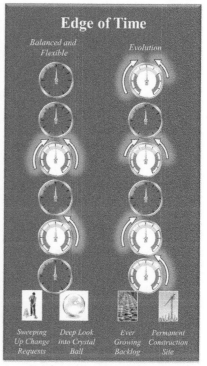

FIGURE 9-1

EA Dashboard summary of the potential impacts of our six building blocks.

Table 9-2 Mapping Activities EA-1 to EA-8 to the Six Building Blocks of Collaborative EA

EA Activity	Impact of Collaborative EA Building Block (● = high, ○ = medium)					
	1 Get Rid of Waste by Streamlining Architecture Processes	2 Involve All Stakeholders by Interlocking Architecture Scrums	3 Practice Iterative Architecture Through EA Kanban	4 Participation in Knowledge	5 Participation in Decisions	6 Participation in Transformation
EA-1 Defining the IT Strategy	●	○	○	●		○
EA-2 Modeling the Architectures	●	●	●	●		○
EA-3 Evolving the IT Landscape	●	○	●	○	●	
EA-4 Assessing and Developing Capabilities	○	○	●			
EA-5 Developing and Enforcing Standards and Guidelines	●	●	●		●	
EA-6 Monitoring the Project Portfolio	●	○	○	●	●	○
EA-7 Leading or Coaching Projects	●	●	●			●
EA-8 Managing Risks Involved in IT	●	○	○	○		●

You can judge for yourself what building blocks might fit your particular way of practicing EA. Figure 9-1 and Table 9-2 can help in this assessment. You are invited to treat collaborative EA as a *toolbox*. You can select and pick from it what you find useful in your daily work.

Getting started with collaborative EA

I don't know what I'll be working on. I expect it'll be a bit of everything, seasoned with a large dose of grumpy curmudgeon.

—James Gosling[1]

Let's assume that we convinced you to take up some ideas from this book in your own architecture practice. If we did, you will have to change something. (If everything is brilliant already and there is no need for change, why did you read this book?) You might have to influence the attitude of business and IT management toward EA. You might want to correct the positioning of the enterprise architects within your organization. And almost certainly you will have to change something in the way you, *yourself*, and your stakeholders, peers, and managers, work and collaborate.

No one ever implements change by simply giving an order. Not even the CEO or the CIO can do that. Backing from the authorities is a necessary but not sufficient precondition for change. You need to win over the people who have to adhere to a different process in the future. In other words, you need to start thinking about *change management*.

Change management, as meant in this section, is a systematic approach to bringing persons, organizations, and processes from the current to a targeted future state.[2] In our case, the *current state is the traditional way of running the EA practice, and the target state is collaborative EA*. We would like to provide some cues as to how you can use concepts and tools from change management in your own journey toward collaborative EA. Take this section as a first rough set of directions. From here onward, you must draw your own map.

Interpreting the organizational attitude toward change

Chip and Dan Heath, in their highly recommendable book *Switch: How to Change Things When Change Is Hard* (2010), sum up three surprising insights about people's attitude toward change.[3] We will use them as a guiding theme in this section. They are not meant to be generally applicable theorems about human behavior; rather, they are fresh, unconventional ways to look at human behavior in the face of organizational transformation.

---

[1]James Gosling (known as the father of the Java programming language), on his reasons to start working for Google. Retrieved on February 13, 2012, from his blog entry http://nighthacks.com/roller/jag/entry/next_step_on_the_road, dated March 28, 2011.

[2]EA and its surrounding areas are riddled with different interpretations of the term *change management*. To name only a few: Managing change as part of a business transformation program is change management. The handling of scope changes in project management is also called change management. The same term is used in ITIL as part of changing the operational infrastructure that belongs to the service transition phase. There are probably more meanings to it. Just to avoid confusion: *None* of these interpretations are meant here.

[3]Heath and Heath (2010); quoted from pages 3, 15, and 12, respectively.

Insight #1: What looks like a people problem is often a situation problem.

"People" factors (personality, culture, and so forth) and situational constraints both influence human behavior. Their respective impact is as difficult to tell apart as, for instance, the influence of genes and upbringing on character development.

However, a key learning from numerous experiments in behavioral psychology is that we tend to *over*estimate the influence of personality on other people's behavior and we *under*estimate situational factors. This phenomenon is called *fundamental attribution error*, a term coined by Lee Ross (1977). We intuitively tend to file someone's negative attitude as hostile or rude—and leave it at that instead of reflecting on what situational factors may have contributed to it.

This does *not* mean that there is no such thing as a people problem. It only means that if you want to implement change and meet resistance, *there might be hope*. People may react reluctantly not because they hate you, despise your ideas, or are in general a bunch of stubborn imbeciles. If you manage to change the circumstances for launching your ideas, people might be more open to them.

When you speak to a group and feel resistance, it might indeed be that some members of the group *do not understand what you expect from them*—however clear the message might sound to yourself. Interpreting this lack of clarity as a sign of resistance would be, again, a symptom of fundamental attribution error. It is better to give people the benefit of the doubt if you cannot tell confusion and resistance apart. This brings us to the second insight:

Insight #2: What looks like resistance is often lack of clarity.

Probably all of us would subscribe to the opposite wording of this statement: "What looks like lack of clarity is often resistance." Indeed, claiming not to understand a speaker's message is a well-proven path of resistance. But this is not the point of this insight.

Maybe you have tried to convey this clarity already many times, in earlier situations, but to no avail. Perhaps you lack the authority to give direct orders to people—or, if you *do* have that authority, people still find ways to dodge your requests. Well, it might be that you simply *did not use the right means* to motivate people. This brings us to insight number three.

Insight #3: What looks like laziness is often exhaustion.

We probably all know this: Even if everyone agrees that your ideas make sense, change still might not happen. You can talk until you are blue in the face, but people pay only lip service to change; instead, they quickly abandon the new approach and return to the old habits. In moments of gloom, it seems to you that most people are just too lazy to really care. A colleague of ours, an IT consultant who often works for in-house IT departments, told us:

> *You often meet people whose brain fell asleep some years ago. They don't want to change, and they have "oh so many things to do." But they are just lazy. Or exhausted. Or both. Who can tell? Who cares?*

Yet there *is* a difference between laziness and exhaustion. Both hinder change, but they require a different approach from you as a person trying to instigate change. In brief: Ignore the lazy ones (for the time being) and focus on the exhausted ones. If you cannot tell who is what, assume that people are exhausted, not lazy.

The truth is that change is tiring. It requires a lot of self-control to do things differently. Just think of the last time you tried to cut down on coffee, went on a diet, or resolved on more frequent visits to the gym. Habits are the well-trodden paths of life, broad and easy to walk on; new ways have to be cut out of the jungle with a mental machete. So, people are not lazy by nature; often they are simply worn out.

The elephant and rider metaphor

Jonathan Haidt (2006) has coined the *elephant and rider* metaphor for the human mind. It has been taken up by many other authors on change management. According to Haidt, the *emotional, habitual side* of a person is like an elephant, and the *rational, willful* side is its rider.[4] The rider plots the path ahead and tries to make the elephant walk it. The elephant, however, is a strong and stubborn animal. It does not like unfamiliar situations, it hates being bossed around, and it needs an immediate reward to get going. The rider is our self-control, trying to steer an animal 20 times heavier and stronger than himself. No wonder the rider is exhausted at times.

So, to commit the *whole* person to change—the odd pairing of rider and elephant—it is necessary to address the elephant, too. In other words, if you appeal only to the intellect in your plea for change, you are only appealing to the rider and hence are bound to fail. One long and comprehensive PowerPoint presentation listing all the benefits of your ideas will get people nodding, but it is their riders who do the nodding. You need to make people *feel* the need for change. You have to *motivate the elephant*, too. We will explore in the next section how you can do that.

But of course we do need to address the rider, the rational and planning minds of our audience. More specifically, *helping the rider steer the elephant* is essential in implementing change. It is not only the elephant that has problems with unfamiliar situations (which change brings by definition). The rider is in acute danger of losing overview. Our rational side is used to analyze situations, draw conclusions, and implement them. In circumstances not encountered before, there is not enough data to do that.

When you propose a new process to your team members or stakeholders, your own rider perhaps has a vision of the path ahead, because you have thought about it for months. The riders—the people you address—lack that clarity. For them, the situation is unfamiliar and new. They are prone to fall into *analysis paralysis*. This is why you have to direct the rider, and give him crystal-clear instructions where to go. We will discuss means to do that, too.

The whole change process can be condensed into three simple maxims[5] that Chip and Dan Heath have compiled, based on a lot of psychological research. We will use their framework as a blueprint for the implementation of collaborative EA in your organization.

1. *Motivate the elephant.* You need to address the emotions, imagination, and creativity of your colleagues or employees, not only their rational minds. It is vital to create identification with your ideas; people should accept them as something they feel is necessary. In that way, you have to overcome the elephant's despondence by shrinking the size of the change.
2. *Direct the rider.* Draw a mental map for the rider and spell out crystal-clear instructions. In addition, you should provide a long-term vision as a beacon for the rider to follow.

---

[4]The elephant-rider metaphor should be taken for what it is: an image of human nature, narrowed down to its attitude toward change. It is not adequate (and not intended) as a comprehensive model of our conscious and subconscious minds.
[5]Heath and Heath cover these steps in a different order. However, the steps are not sequential; they rather represent different aspects that all have to be taken care of.

3. *Shape the path.* It is not enough to simply throw your ideas on the ground and assume that they will bear fruit. You need to transform them into habits for people. On that path, make sure to build political alliances.

We will now analyze each of these steps in detail and make proposals as to how to cover the particular aspect on the path to collaborative EA.

Motivate the elephant

Are you one of the people in your organization who have some influence on decision making but no (or little) direct authority? If you are a project manager, software architect, middle-level manager, or subject-matter expert, you will probably find the following situation familiar.

You have analyzed a certain issue—technical, architectural, procedural, or organizational— in depth and you are deeply convinced that things are not the way they should be. You even have an idea how it could be done better. Many of your peers with whom you discussed the matter agree with you. You have made several proposals about the issue to the powers that be. And what has happened as a result? Nothing.

Yet in some cases, all of a sudden something *does* happen. Perhaps the issue has caught top-level management's attention and the whole organization springs into action. Or for whatever reason, people start behaving differently and things are changing—not necessarily in the way you envisioned, and not always for the better. You feel a little bypassed, maybe even left open to ridicule.

What we see here is a classical misconception by people with an analytical mindset. You would assume that a decision-making process works in the sequence *Analyze, Think, Change*. You provide a thorough analysis, the management thinks about it, and change is triggered. Indeed, this is the kind of rational reasoning incorporated in numerous engineering disciplines and process frameworks.

The catch is, as Kotter and Cohen (2002) point out, things do not work exactly that way. Change processes follow the pattern *See, Feel, Change*. The issue needs to raise people's attention (*see*). If they develop a sense of urgency and importance about the topic (*feel*), they are likely to trigger action (*change*).

If you follow the *Analyze, Think, Change* pattern, you will appeal to the rider only by rational arguments. But if you neglect the elephant, the rider alone will not move anywhere. You will earn many understanding and sympathetic nods with your analytic research, but these are not sufficient to get people moving. You need to make them *feel* the need for change.

Kotter and Cohen recount one impressive example of appealing to the elephant.[6] Jon Stegner worked for a large manufacturing company. He had the notion that procurement processes were suboptimal since every plant handled its own purchasing. To prove this, he selected a single work item— protective gloves for the workers—and compiled a detailed list how many different gloves his company bought and for what price. He ended up with the incredible number of 424 kinds of gloves, with pricing ranging between $5 and $17 for the same glove type in two plants.

When presenting his research to the decision makers and asking for a change in the purchasing procedures, Stegner could simply have created and shown an Excel sheet. The numbers were indeed impressive enough. However, the independence of the business lines was deeply ingrained in the

---

[6]See Kotter and Cohen (2002, p. 29ff.).

organizational structure. Stegner was asking for deep shift in the organization's mindset. The risk of the plain Excel method was that the managers would simply think, "Well, gloves ... who cares?"

Instead Stegner chose a different approach. He asked an intern to purchase one pair of each of the 424 gloves, put a price tag on it, and pile the gloves on the conference room table before calling in the managers. The managers, seeing a huge heap of gloves instead of the usual strategy proposals on the shiny table, were taken aback. Stegner led them around and showed them the vastly different price tags on the same kinds of gloves. The managers were stunned. Stegner immediately received the mandate for change that he had hoped for.

Convincing people of a need for change in EA

What can be *your* pile of gloves? When you organize a workshop with enterprise architects, IT people, and business stakeholders, you could replicate the previous example. You could print out *all* the specifications that were written during the past year and pile them up on the conference table. Maybe you can stack those specifications that actually ended up in running software systems into a second pile and compare the sizes of the two piles.

You can also use tools from this book to have the people *feel* the need for change. For instance, create cardboard badges with large icons of the eight EA caricatures from Chapter 1 printed on them. Each workshop participant can pick a badge and wear it, denoting which particular floor of the madhouse he or she inhabits. This might help the participants identify with the need for change; at the very least, it creates a good visual impression of the majority opinion in the room.

In a similar fashion, you could create a cardboard edition of the EA Dashboard from Chapter 6 with moveable scales. Each workshop participant can come to the front of the room, adjust the scales according to his or her own judgment, and give reasons for that choice.

The *EA value stream analysis* tools, described in Building Block 1 in Chapter 7, also provide a good impression of ineffectiveness and waste within the EA processes. Especially the *EA waste matrix* (see Table 7-10) and the *process activity map* (see Figure 7-2) are a powerful visualization of the damage done to an organization by suboptimal processes.

Another way of stimulating the readiness for change is the *creation of empathy*. If you have the impression that your EA organization matches the *Living in Cloud Cuckoo Land* or the *Guardians of Wisdom* caricature, invite the EA team and management to an experience-sharing session with people from selected IT projects. This can take the form of a joint "lessons learned" workshop. You can also use the participation concepts from *Building Block 6: Participation in transformation* in Chapter 8. If you do not have any Enterprise 2.0 tools available, you can at least emulate the concepts as a preparation for this workshop—for instance, by conducting an online survey.[7]

Lower the bar: Create an entry level

Let's assume that you gained a mandate for your mission from management and an initial buy-in from peers and stakeholders. Next you need to create an appropriate first step—an *entry level* to collaborative EA.

Changing existing habits is like embarking on a journey into uncharted land. This confuses the rider and scares the elephant. The elephant does not care about long-term visions; it needs immediate

---

[7]Commercial online survey platforms are available from many providers for a small fee. In addition, Microsoft SharePoint, used in many enterprise intranets, has a useful online survey feature.

rewards for each little step it takes. Therefore, opposed to the old management cliché of "raising the bar," you need to *lower the bar* for the elephant. It must be capable of stepping over the bar without much ado; otherwise it will shy at the challenge.

The entry level to collaborative EA needs to be an *achievable goal* in order to satisfy the elephant. "You want to select small wins that have two traits: (1) They're meaningful. (2) They're in immediate reach," write Heath and Heath (p. 145). "And if you can't achieve both traits, choose the latter!" With such a quick win identified, you have a good chance that the ponderous machinery of change can start rolling. Success creates hope, and hope fuels progress.

A good tool for identifying that small win is the so-called *miracle question* (Shazer, Dolan, and Korman, 2007). It is a question-and-answer technique usually used in therapy to find starting points for long and hard personal transformations, such as fighting a drinking problem or saving a failing marriage. The starting point is the assumption that a miracle has happened and the problem has disappeared overnight. How would we notice? What is the first thing that is different in the morning, now that our problem has gone? The first indicator that comes to mind is often a pointer to a possible *small win*.

If you have a small group of people in a workshop or you are in a one-on-one situation with a member of the EA team, you can try a dialogue like the following[8]:

Q: Please let me ask a very weird-sounding question. Let's assume one night a miracle happens and all the problems we have identified in your EA processes have gone overnight. Now you come to work in the morning. What would be the very first, small sign that something has changed and all problems have gone?

A: Well, I don't know. Suddenly things would move in a smoother way.

Q: How would you notice?

A: Well, I would have time to work on my project.

Q: What would make you think that?

A: Let me think ... No interruptions all morning. No emails about emergencies and board-level escalations that came up overnight and need to be tackled first. Things like that. If that would go on all day, I'd know something is different ... And if then the business sponsor of my project would return my call within the hour, I would indeed start believing in miracles.

The miracle question gets people emotionally involved and commits them to the change process. It may not be an all-encompassing analytical tool, but it helps identifying the true pain points—in our example case they are permanent interruptions and reprioritization of tasks and some disconnect with the enterprise architect's business counterpart. Having a list of these concrete hints will help us select the first concrete change measures.

Direct the rider

In the rider-and-elephant metaphor, the rider's task is to guide the way (as shown in Figure 9.2). We have seen above, in Insight 2, that what appears to be resistance is often lack of clarity. This means you have to guide the rider to enable him to guide the elephant. The rider needs a set of crystal-clear directions; otherwise he will lose overview, sink into analysis paralysis, and surrender to a hesitant and grumbling elephant.

---

[8]Heath and Heath provide an elaborate example for this technique in a therapeutic context (marriage counseling) on page 36ff.

Find the bright spots

The first step in guiding the rider is to *find the bright spots*. This means identifying those areas where the EA organization works really well. This may sound like a paradox; is this whole section not about identifying weaknesses and obtaining buy-in for tackling them? Surprisingly, looking at positive (counter-) examples actually helps us understand *why something in general does not work well*. Why is that so?

We have a natural tendency to focus on the negative side of things. However, in analyzing the root cause of people resisting rules and processes, focusing too much on "why not?" often leads you into the dead end of the aforementioned *fundamental attribution error*. Frequently, you hear statements like "People are just lazy" or "People do not have enough discipline." By looking at the positive counter-examples, you are more likely to identify the situational constraints that make it hard for others to change.

Let's assume that the activity area *EA-5: Developing and Enforcing Standards and Guidelines* has been identified as generally problematic. Are there standards that are considered reasonable by both IT and business and that are followed without discussions or many exceptions? If so, what was done differently in creating and enforcing these standards?

As a side effect, starting from positive examples promotes identification with your chosen approach. It supports the impression that your approach is built on something people have achieved themselves (before you showed up with your new ideas). If you play this well the perception is that the new practices actually came from within the team or the organization, and you simply help bring them out.

That way, you also avoid the *Not Invented Here* trap, with its deep-rooted resistance to solutions from outside. For that matter, it might help to downplay the term *agile* in the collaborative EA definition, if your organization is rather conservative; the iterations and sprint demos can be dubbed *iterative milestones* and *regular revisions*, or whatever fits the organization's terminology. It lowers the risk that the agile concepts are perceived as some fancy outsider concept "that will never work around here."

Set a collaborative EA vision

Appropriate directions for the rider include a *collaborative EA vision*—a guiding light, a beacon for the rider. It is a focus point in the (not too distant) future and helps the rider obtain his bearings when he is disoriented. The process to define the vision is essentially the "management by maxim" technique described by Broadbent and Weill (1997), which we introduced at length in the discussion of EA-1 in Chapter 3.

The collaborative EA vision for your organization needs to be aligned with the IT maxims as described in EA-1. You can use the waste analysis techniques from Chapter 7 and the recommendations from this chapter to identify the weak points, then formulate the vision describing a target state. As an inspiration for wording your visions, consider the building block statements in this book.

COLLABORATIVE EA VISION

Black-and-White Goals

The most extreme form of a vision is the *black-and-white goal*. It can be an effective tool for overcoming strong resistance and breaking die-hard habits. A black-and-white goal does not leave room for *any* kind of interpretation, nor does it allow any rationalization as to why "just this time" we could not follow it. For example, the SOA directive

---

Continued

COLLABORATIVE EA VISION—CONT'D

that Jeff Bezos gave out for Amazon, backed by the "Anyone who doesn't do this will be fired" sideline (see Chapter 3, activity EA-5), is an example of a black-and-white goal.[9]

A vision of that kind is a double-edged sword. If not properly analyzed or not fiercely implemented, it entails the risk of being ridiculed. Or if enforced in an overly strict manner, it could destroy proactive, creative, and risk-taking behavior. It is an extreme tool that is good to employ in extreme circumstances—for instance, in the case of a very strong resistance to really important change. Still, one should not actually attempt to achieve a 100% implementation. The main goal is to *eliminate the cases where people act against better judgment* just because "they always did it that way."

So, let's assume that, instead of a collaborative EA vision that is just a paraphrasing of *Let's All Be Nice to Each Other*, a vision like *No Failed EA Initiatives* or (even more unthinkable) *No Failed IT Projects* is chosen. It can be considered a success if projects and initiatives will no longer be pushed through against the better judgment of the ground workers. It will actually force management to take workers' concerns seriously. The knowledge about project risks often remains unspoken—for instance, when everyone but the decision makers knows that the schedules are overambitious, the technology platforms immature, and the implementation partner incapable of delivering. With such a black-and-white vision in place, no one dares to start an initiative many people are warning against.

Specify concrete directives

Besides vision, you need a set of *easy-to-remember and easy-to-follow directives*. Again, you can use the maxim technique described in EA-1 in Chapter 3. The directives help plot the next step on the road for the rider. The directives need to be very clear instructions—for instance, in the form of a checklist. Here are some examples (in this case, from Building Block 2):

- Always form an architecture scrum when you as an enterprise architect supervise a large program with multiple project architects.
- If you work on a larger EA initiative, form a scrum team, report your work in a daily standup round, and plan for regular result demos every three weeks.

Again, remember Insight 2: The clearer your instructions, the less room for interpretation they leave, the more you can hope that they will be followed. And note that *clearer* does not mean *more elaborate*; collaborative EA is set to reduce bureaucracy in EA, not to add to it.

Shape the path

Any transformation is a journey over a bumpy road. You should plan for a good start and provide a strong vision for the destination. But planning all the steps in between does not help much; too many unforeseeable events can happen. As Heath and Heath put it (p. 144f.):

> *Any important change is not going to feel like a steady, inevitable march toward victory. [...] More typically, you take one step forward and 1.3 steps back and 2.7 forward and then 6 steps to the side, and at that moment, a new CEO will come and declare a new destination.*

---

[9]Chip Heath and Dan Heath describe another example. The oil company BP, in an attempt to reduce its exploration costs for new oil fields, gave out the vision *No Dry Holes* (Heath and Heath, p. 86ff.). Before drilling, the explorers try to spot the oil fields by remote sensing. The real costs are then caused by drilling an oil well. Before the maxim, BP had a success rate of 20% with its wells; only in 20% of the cases they actually did find oil—the other 80% produced dry holes. The new maxim required a 100% success rate. BP at least came close to fulfilling it: The company's hit rate climbed to 65%, three times the industry average (*Slogans That Work*, 2007).

FIGURE 9-2

"Guide the rider and motivate the elephant."[10]

The crucial issue is to keep going in the difficult middle part. Figure 9-3[11] sums up the typical development of the mood in any complex undertaking. Let's assume that you managed to motivate your coworkers' elephants well; that means that you have started off in hope-fueled good spirit. What follows is a long slump, where *insight* takes the better of your illusions. The team doubts its capability to implement the change. This may end in a long death march toward failure. But if you are successful, the initiative will end on a positive note with a strong feeling of confidence in the chosen approach.

Note that this is a statement about *mood and confidence* in the ability to deliver, not about risks. Normally, you run out of time toward the end in any initiative, which puts the delivery result at risk. But in a successful project you manage this challenge because your confidence in your own capability has grown again.

Once you're started, you need to deal with skepticism and doubt in the middle part—of those you want to lead to change as well as your own. You, as an enterprise architect, also do not know the exact

---

[10]The picture shows how one of the authors, Uwe, applies this section's motto in practice. It was taken during a writing workshop for our book in Goa, India, in November 2011.

[11]Heath and Heath describe the *project mood chart* verbally on page 168 of their book. We added the success and failure markers and the possible death-march outcome.

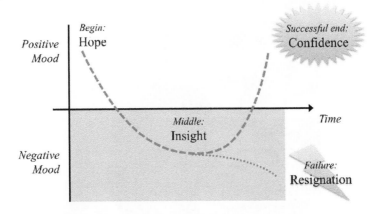

FIGURE 9-3

Project mood chart.

path, but you will act as the pathfinder. For that matter, you need to continue looking out for a series of quick and small wins, as described in the "Motivate the elephant" section.

Build alliances

It is of equal importance to *build and maintain alliances*. Broadbent and Kitzis (2005) recommend classifying your surrounding key players into strong and weak supporters as well as strong and weak opponents.[12] They recommend the following priorities when dealing with alliances:

1. *Convert influential opponents to the cause.* Strong opponents are the most likely people to hinder you as you try to reach your change targets. Focus on their arguments and pain points as you look for small wins. If they can gain by using your approach, you have a chance to win them over.
2. *Restrict influential opponents you can't convert.* If your efforts to convert your strong opponents fail, you need to restrict their influence. It is advisable to use governance mechanisms of your IT organizations (boards and councils) to distribute opinion formation onto many shoulders.
3. *Retain your influential supporters.* The best way to keep your supporters motivated regarding your cause is to deal with them directly rather than through the typical group situations offered by meetings or decision boards. Asking for suggestions and regular feedback is a good way to retain bonding and to hear about complaints early on. The regular stakeholder interaction induced by architecture scrums is a natural step in this direction (see the description of *Building Block 2* in Chapter 7).
4. *Recognize your weak supporters.* You should keep track of those stakeholders who sympathize with your approach so that you can use their group influence in decision making and budgeting.
5. *Keep track of your weak opponents.* Just make sure the weak opponents do not turn into strong ones.

---

[12]Broadbent and Kitzis (2005) describe a Boston square for the opponent and supporter classification and recommend a priority order to deal with them (p. 52ff.). Strictly speaking, their advice is targeted at a CIO dealing with her peers in top management. However, as for nearly all other parts of this extraordinary book, it applies also to initiatives driven by less influential members of the organization, such as enterprise architects or middle managers.

Build habits

In the long run, the best way to ensure that processes are followed is to *build habits*. Many psychological experiments have shown that humans have a strong tendency to watch their peers out of the corner of their eyes in unfamiliar situations. When you observe the majority around you acting in a certain fashion, you will likely act the same way.

The agile techniques, as described in our *Building Blocks 2* and *3* in Chapter 7, are great for creating habits. They are repeated in a strict clock cycle. Each cycle follows the same sequence of kickoff and planning at the beginning, with results demonstrated at the end of an iteration.

Looking ahead

The need for enterprise architecture management will grow because the complexity of IT is growing and because business success in more and more verticals is depending on IT. *Good* enterprise architecture management will evolve from a basic tool for managing the complexity of an IT landscape to a strategic instrument used to create new business opportunities from technology advancements.

There is a broad range of methods and frameworks for the practicalities of EA in place. It also is widely acknowledged that EA cannot successfully be implemented without top management commitment. But we believe that the core success factor is collaboration—not only with top managers and business sponsors but also with software developers, operational staff, and users; in other words, with those who are directly exposed to IT.

Collaboration basically means making use of the diversity of knowledge and opinions in an organization and responding to changes that are brought in by stakeholders—not because they are evil-minded destroyers of road maps but because they have some concern.

In this book, we have suggested methods and tools for putting collaboration into practice. Some of them are well known and have been proven in several contexts. Others are rather innovative and still need to undergo a practical test. They all are assembled in a toolbox, and you may pick from it what you need. It is still up to you to combine them into a recipe for your own enterprise. If you want to share your experience in finding such a recipe, you can provide feedback on our book at the following Website: www.collaborative-ea.org.

Your enterprise needs EA, and EA needs more collaboration. We wish you good luck in the journey ahead.

Appendix: The Bank4Us staff

Throughout this book, we accompanied employees of the global bank Bank4Us on their way toward a collaborative EA. In the following table they are listed for easy reference (in order of their appearance).

Board	
Dave Callaghan	CIO

EA Team and Externals	
Oscar Salgado	Chief architect and head of the EA team
Ian Miller	Enterprise architect responsible for an application rationalization program
Shashi Malhotra	Enterprise architect, expert on service-oriented architecture (SOA)
Padma Valluri	Enterprise architect responsible for optimizing the EA processes
Sandro Poggi	Freelancing consultant to Padma, expert in lean and agile architecture
Leon Campista	Enterprise architect, evangelist for Enterprise 2.0
Steve Pread	Enterprise architect in charge of data architecture

IT Organization	
Sarah Taylor	IT program manager, responsible for 62 IT applications
Harriet Wise	Software engineer
Jake Bertapelle	Software engineer
Carl Batches	Operations manager
Sarah Matthews	Project manager
Sachindra Lele	Software developer
Anne Calten	Software developer

Business Departments	
Franca Bertapelle	Local advisor at the Pittsburgh branch office

References

Allega, P., 2010. Defining EA: Low Barriers to Entry (My Mother Has an EA Definition, too). Gartner.com, a Weblog by Philip Allega. Retrieved December 17, 2011, from http://blogs.gartner.com/philip-allega/2010/08/11/defining-ea-low-barriers-to-entry-my-mother-has-an-ea-definition-too/.

Ambler, S., 2006, January 1. Agile Best Practice: Model a Bit Ahead. Agile Modeling (AM) homepage: Effective Practices for Modeling and Documentation. Retrieved April 15, 2011, from www.agilemodeling.com/essays/modelAhead.htm.

Anderson, C., 2006. The long tail: why the future of business is selling less of more. Hyperion, New York.

Anderson, D.J., 2010. Kanban: successful evolutionary change for your technology business. Blue Hole Press, Sequim, Washington.

Bak, P., 1996. How nature works: the science of self-organized criticality. Copernicus, New York.

Beck, K., Beedle, M., Cockburn, A., Cunningham, W., Fowler, M., Grenning, J., et al., 2001, February 1. Manifesto for Agile Software Development. Retrieved April 6, 2011, from http://agilemanifesto.org/.

Bemer, R., 1968. Machine-controlled production environment. In: Software engineering: report of a conference sponsored by the NATO Science Committee, Garmisch, Germany, 7th to 11th October, 1968. NATO Science Committee, Brussels, pp. 94–95.

Bente, S., Karla, J., 2009. Enterprise Social Network Platforms as a Management Tool in Complex Technical Systems. In: Proceedings of the Fifteenth Americas Conference on Information Systems. San Francisco, California.

Berners-Lee, T., 2006. DeveloperWorks Interviews: Tim Berners-Lee. IBM developerWorks. Retrieved March 4, 2011, from www.ibm.com/developerworks/podcast/dwi/cm-int082206.txt.

Booch, G., 2006, March 3. On design. Software architecture, software engineering, and Renaissance Jazz. Retrieved November 15, 2011, from https://www.ibm.com/developerworks/mydeveloperworks/blogs/gradybooch/entry/on_design?lang=en.

Brisco, B., Odlyzko, A., Tilly, B., 2006. Matcalfe's Law Is Wrong. IEEE Spectrum. Retrieved February 16, 2012, from http://spectrum.ieee.org/computing/networks/metcalfes-law-is-wrong/1.

Breivold, H.P., Sundmark, D., Wallin, P., Larsson, S., 2010. What Does Research Say About Agile and Architecture? Proceedings of the Fifth International Conference on Software Engineering Advances 1 (1), 32–37. Retrieved August 21, 2011, from www.computer.org/portal/web/csdl/doi/10.1109/ICSEA.2010.12.

Broad, W.J., 2000, June 30. A Missile Defense With Limits. New York Times p. A10. Retrieved February 13, 2012, from www.nytimes.com/2000/06/30/world/nuclear-shield-repelling-attack-missile-defense-with-limits-abc-s-clinton-plan.html?pagewanted=5.

Brown, S.L., Eisenhardt, K.M., 1998. Competing on the edge strategy as structured chaos. Harvard Business School Press, Boston, Mass.

Burt, R., 1995. Structural Holes: The Social Structure of Competition. Harvard University Press, Cambridge, Massachusetts.

Burton, B., 2010. Best and worst enterprise architecture practices: Delivering value. Gartner Webinars. Retrieved February 20, 2011, from http://my.gartner.com/portal/server.pt?open=512&objID=202&mode=2&PageID=5553&ref=webinar-rss&resId=1525314.

Broadbent, M., Kitzis, E., 2005. The new CIO leader: setting the agenda and delivering results. Harvard Business School Press, Boston.

Broadbent, M., Weill, P., 1997. Management by Maxims: How Business and IT Managers Can Create IT Infrastructures. Sloan Management 38 (3), 77–92.

Buckl, S., et al., 2010. A Lightweight Approach to Enterprise Architecture Modeling and Documentation. In: Soffer, P., Proper, E. (Eds.), Information Systems Evolution, CAiSE Forum 2010, Hammamet, Springer, Lecture Notes in Business Information Processing (LNBIP), vol. 72, pp. 136–149.

Cabinet Office, 2007. ITIL Service Operation. TSO Publisher, London.

Carroll, P., 1993. Big blues: the unmaking of IBM. Crown Publishers, New York.

Coates, T., 2005. An addendum to a definition of Social Software. Plasticbag.org, a Weblog by Tom Coates. Retrieved March 21, 2011, from www.plasticbag.org/archives/2.

Cockburn, A., 2007. Agile software development: the cooperative game, second ed. Addison-Wesley, Upper Saddle River, NJ.

Cohn, M., 2009. Succeeding with agile: Software development using Scrum. Addison-Wesley, Upper Saddle River, NJ.

Coplien, J., Bjørnvig, G., 2010. Lean architecture for Agile software development. Wiley, Hoboken, N.J.

Daft, R.L., 2010. The executive and the elephant: a leader's guide for building inner excellence. Jossey-Bass, San Francisco, CA.

Dörnenburg, E., 2009, July 1. Making ESB pain visible. Erik Dörnenburg Articles. Retrieved March 7, 2011, from http://erik.doernenburg.com/2009/07/making-esb-pain-visible/.

Eckerson, W., 2011. Personal communication with the authors.

Ford, H., Crowther, S., 1922. My life and work. Doubleday, Page & Co, Garden City, N.Y.

Fowler, M., 2006, July 18. Using an Agile Software Process with Offshore Development. Martin Fowler. Retrieved April 15, 2011, from http://martinfowler.com/articles/agileOffshore.html.

GAO, 2004, May 19. Information technology: the federal enterprise architecture and agencies' enterprise architectures are still maturing. U.S. Government Accountability Office (U.S. GAO). Retrieved July 27, 2011, from www.gao.gov/products/GAO-04-798T.

Goethe, J.W., 1953. Maximen und Reflexionen. Dieterich'schen, Leipzig.

Gharajedaghi, J., 2011. Systems Thinking, Managing Chaos and Complexity: A Platform for Designing Business Architecture, third ed. Morgan Kaufmann, Burlington, MA.

Granovetter, M.S., 1973. The Strength of Weak Ties. Am. J. Sociol. 78 (6), 1360–1380.

Haidt, J., 2006. The happiness hypothesis: finding modern truth in ancient wisdom. Basic Books, New York.

Hanschke, I., 2010. Strategic IT management: a toolkit for enterprise architecture management. Springer, Heidelberg.

Henry, S., Kafura, D., September 1981. Software Structure Metrics Based on Information Flow. IEEE Transactions on Software Engineering SE-7 (5), 1981.

Hines, P., Rich, N., 1997. The seven value stream-mapping tools. International Journal of Physical Distribution & Logistics Management 17 (1), 46–64.

IEEE Computer Society, 2000. IEEE Recommended Practice for Architecture Description of Software-Intensive Systems. In: IEEE Std. IEEE, New York, pp. 1472–2000.

ISACA, 2009. The Risk IT Framework. ISACA Association. Retrieved February 12, 2012, from www.isaca.org/Knowledge-Center/Risk-IT-IT-Risk-Management/Pages/Risk-IT1.aspx.

ISACA, 2007. COBIT 4.1: Framework, Control Objectives, Management Guidelines, Maturity Models. Retrieved February 12, 2012, from www.isaca.org/Knowledge-Center/cobit/Documents/CobiT_4.1.pdf.

Johnston, A., 2010. Role of the Agile Architect. Welcome to the Agile Architect Website. Retrieved April 16, 2011, from www.agilearchitect.org/agile/role.htm.

Jones, J.A., 2005. An Introduction to Factor Analysis of Information Risk (FAIR). Risk Management Insight. Retrieved February 13, 2012, from www.riskmanagementinsight.com/media/docs/FAIR_introduction.pdf.

Kauffman, S.A., 1993. The origins of order: self-organization and selection in evolution. Oxford University Press, London.

Kauffman, S.A., 1995. At home in the universe: the search for laws of self-organization and complexity. Oxford University Press, New York.

Keller, W., 2007. IT-Unternehmensarchitektur. Von der Geschäftsstrategie zur optimalen IT-Unterstützung. dpunkt.verlag, Heidelberg.

Kniberg, H., 2009, June 26. One day in Kanban land. Crisp's Blog. Retrieved February 7, 2012, from http://blog .crisp.se/2009/06/26/henrikkniberg/1246053060000.

Koch, M., 2009. Enterprise 2.0 Planung, Einführung und erfolgreicher Einsatz von Social-Software in Unternehmen. (2., aktualisierte und erw. Aufl. ed.). Oldenbourg, München.

Kotter, J.P., Cohen, D.S., 2002. The heart of change: real-life stories of how people change their organizations. Harvard Business School Press, Boston, Mass.

Krafcik, J., 1988. Triumph of the Lean Production System. Sloan. Manage. Rev. 30 (1), 41–52.

Krafzig, D., Banke, K., Slama, D., 2006. Enterprise SOA: service-oriented architecture best practices. (6 print. ed.) Prentice-Hall, Upper Saddle River, NJ.

Krebs, J., 2009. Agile portfolio management. Microsoft, Redmond, Wash.

Kruchten, P., 1995. Architectural Blueprints: The "4+1" ViewModel of Software Architecture. IEEE Software 12 (6), 42–50.

Kruchten, P., 2004, February 5. The Tao of the Software Architect. Enterprise Architecture, Software Architecture, Architects, and Architecting. Retrieved April 16, 2011, from www.bredemeyer.com/tao_by_Kruchten.htm.

Kruchten, P., 2011, February 11. The Elephants in the Agile Room. Philippe Kruchten. Retrieved April 6, 2011, from http://pkruchten.wordpress.com/2011/02/13/the-elephants-in-the-agile-room/.

Kruchten, P., 2008. What do software architects really do? The Journal of Systems and Software 81, 2413–2416.

Lankhorst, M., 2009. Enterprise architecture at work: modelling, communication and analysis, second ed. Springer, Berlin.

Larman, C., Basili, V.R., 2003. Iterative and Incremental Development: A Brief History. IEEE Computer 36 (6), 47–56.

Larman, C., Vodde, B., 2009. Scaling lean & agile development: thinking and organizational tools for large-scale Scrum. Addison-Wesley, Upper Saddle River, NJ.

Leffingwell, D., Widrig, D., 2003. Managing software requirements: a use case approach, second ed. Addison-Wesley, Boston.

Leffingwell, D., 2007. Scaling software agility: best practices for large enterprises. Addison-Wesley, Upper Saddle River, NJ.

Leffingwell, D., 2011. Agile software requirements: lean requirements practices for teams, programs, and the enterprise. Addison-Wesley, Upper Saddle River, NJ.

Liker, J.K., 2004. The Toyota way: 14 management principles from the world's greatest manufacturer. McGraw-Hill, New York.

Linowski, B., 2011, June. Schlanke Modellgetriebene Entwicklung in Agilen Projekten. Java Magazin 1, 1.

Lucas, C., 2005. Self-Organization and Human Robots. International Journal of Advanced Robotic Systems 2 (1). Retrieved September 28, 2011, from www.ars-journal.com/ars/Free_Articles/Chris_Lucas.htm.

Mack, R., 2003a. Real IT Strategies: Steps 1 to 4—Laying a Foundation. Gartner Group, Report R-21-4950.

Mack, R., 2003b. Real IT Strategies: Steps 5 to 8—Creating the Strategy. Gartner Group, Report R-21-4074.

Mack, R., Frey, N., 2002. Six Building Blocks for Creating Real IT Strategies. Gartner Group, Report R 17-3607.

Manes, A.T., 2009. SOA is Dead; Long Live Services. Application Platform Strategies Blog. Retrieved January 23, 2012, from http://apsblog.burtongroup.com/2009/01/soa-is-dead-long-live-services.html.

Mar, A., Spacey, J., 2011, January 7. Enterprise Architecture Anti Patterns. Simplicable.com. Retrieved July 27, 2011, from http://simplicable.com/new/enterprise-architecture-anti-patterns.

March, J., Simon, H., 1958. Organizations. John Wiley, New York.

McAfee, A., 2006a. Enterprise 2.0: The Dawn of Emergent Collaboration. MIT Sloan Review 47 (3), 21.

McAfee, A., 2006b. Enterprise 2.0, version 2.0. Andrew McAfee's Blog—The Business Impact of IT. Retrieved April 8, 2011, from http://andrewmcafee.org/2006/05/enterprise_20_version_20/.

McAfee, A., 2009. Enterprise 2.0: new collaborative tools for your organization's toughest challenges. Harvard Business Press, Boston, Mass.

McManus, H., 1999. A Framework for Lean Engineering. MIT Lean Aerospace Initiative Product Development Focus Team, Boston.

McManus, H., 2005. Product Development Value Stream Mapping (PDVSM) Manual 1.0. The Lean Aerospace Initiative, Boston.

McConnell, S., 2006. Software estimation: demystifying the black art. Microsoft Press, Redmond, Wash.

Merriam-Webster, (n.d.). Dictionary and Thesaurus: Merriam-Webster Online. Retrieved June 29, 2011, from www.merriam-webster.com/.

Millard, R.L., 2001. Value Stream Analysis and Mapping for Product Development. Department of Aeronautics and Astronautics, Massachusetts Institute of Technology, Boston.

Monson-Haefel, R., 2009. 97 things every software architect should know: collective wisdom from the experts. O'Reilly Media, Sebastopol, Calif.

Nonaka, I., Takeuchi, H., 1995. The knowledge-creating company: how Japanese companies create the dynamics of innovation. Oxford University Press, New York.

O'Reilly, T., 2005. What Is Web 2.0? O'Reilly Media. Retrieved March 6, 2011, from http://oreilly.com/pub/a/web2/archive/what-is-web-20.html?page=1.

OECD, 1999. OECD Principles of Corporate Governance. Directorate for Financial, Fiscal and Enterprise Affairs, SG/CG(99) 5 and 219, April 1999.

Ohno, T., 1988. Toyota production system: beyond large-scale production. Productivity Press, Cambridge, Mass.

OMB, 2009. Improving Agency Performance Using Information and Information Technology (Enterprise Architecture Assessment Framework v3.1). Office of Management and Budget. Retrieved December 17, 2011, from www.whitehouse.gov/sites/default/files/omb/assets/fea_docs/OMB_EA_Assessment_Framework_v3_1_June_2009.pdf.

Osono, E., Shimizu, N., Takeuchi, H., 2008. Extreme Toyota: radical contradictions that drive success at the world's best manufacturer. John Wiley & Sons, Hoboken, N.J.

Poppendieck, M., Poppendieck, T.D., 2003. Lean software development: an agile toolkit. Addison-Wesley, Boston.

Poppendieck, M., Poppendieck, T.D., 2007. Implementing lean software development: from concept to cash. Addison-Wesley, Upper Saddle River, NJ.

Porter, M.E., 1998. Competitive strategy: techniques for analyzing industries and competitors: with a new introduction. Free Press, New York City.

Reinertsen, D.G., 1997. Managing the design factory: a product developer's toolkit. Free Press, New York.

Ross, J., 2005. Forget Strategy: Focus IT on Your Operating Model. MIT CISR Research Briefing V (3 C).

Ross, J., 2006. Maturity Matters: How Firms Generate Value from Enterprise Architecture. MIT CISR Research Briefing IV (2 B).

Ross, J., Woerner, S., Scantlebury, S., Beath, C., 2010. The IT Organization of the Future: Driving Business Change. In: IT Advantage, Spring 2010. The Boston Consulting Group. Retrieved December 17, 2011, from www.bcg.com/documents/file40521.pdf.

Ross, L., 1977. The intuitive psychologist and his shortcomings: distortions in the attribution process. Advances in Experimental Social Psychology 10, 173–220.

Rother, M., Shook, J., 2003. Learning to see: value stream mapping to create value and eliminate muda. (Version 1.3 ed.). Lean Enterprise Institute, Brookline, MA.

Rule, G., 2010, January 31. Lean enterprise architecture: how to achieve better business performance from soft systems. SMS Exemplar White Papers. Retrieved March 8, 2011, from www.smsexemplar.com/wp-content/uploads/15PGRLeanEntArchitecture_v1g1.pdf.

Saha, P., 2011, May 18. Six reasons why EA should not be assigned to the IT department. LinkedIn, The Enterprise Architecture Network. Retrieved August 18, 2011, from www.linkedin.com/groups/Six-Reasons-Why-EA-Should-36781.S.52757710?view=&srchtype=discussedNews&gid=36781&item=52757710&type=member&trk=eml-anet_dig-b_pd-ttl-cn.

Schekkerman, J., 2008. Enterprise architecture good practices guide: how to manage the enterprise architecture practice. Trafford, Victoria, BC.

Schekkermann, J., 2011. Enterprise Architecture Tool Selection Guide. Institute for Enterprise Architecture Development, Jaap Schekkermann. Retrieved December 9, 2011, from www.enterprise-architecture.info/Images/EA%20Tools/Enterprise%20Architecture%20Tool%20Selection%20Guide%20v6.3.pdf.

Schmidt, J.G., Lyle, D., 2010. Lean integration: an integration factory approach to business agility. Addison-Wesley, Boston, Mass.

Schwarzer, B., 2009. Einführung in das Enterprise Architecture Management: Verstehen, Planen, Umsetzen. Books on Demand, Norderstedt.

Sessions, R., 2007. A Comparison of the Top Four Enterprise-Architecture Methodologies. Microsoft Development Network (MSDN). Retrieved December 17, 2011, from http://msdn.microsoft.com/en-us/library/bb466232.aspx.

Shah, S., 2004, April 29. Resume-Driven Development (RDD). Shahid's Perspectives. Retrieved December 30, 2011, from http://shahid.shah.org/?p=15.

Shalloway, A., Beaver, G., Trott, J., 2010. Lean-agile software development: achieving enterprise agility. Addison-Wesley, Upper Saddle River, N.J.

Shazer, S., Dolan, Y.M., Korman, H., 2007. More than miracles: the state of the art of solution-focused brief therapy. Haworth Press, New York.

Shore, J., Warden, S., 2008. The art of agile development. O'Reilly Media, Inc, Beijing.

Slogans That Work, 2007, December 13. Forbes.com. Retrieved January 27, 2012, from www.forbes.com/forbes/2008/0107/099.html.

Spacey, J., (n.d.). Survey: Success of EA Programs. Simplicable.com. Retrieved November 12, 2011, from http://simplicable.com/survey1/enterprise-architecture-success-survey.html.

Stakutis, C., Webster, J., 2005. Inescapable data: harnessing the power of convergence. IBM Press, Upper Saddle River, NJ.

Surowiecki, J., 2005. The wisdom of crowds. Anchor Books, New York.

The Open Group, 2009b. Risk Taxonomy Technical Standard.

The Open Group, 2008. The Open Group ArchiMate(R) 1.0 Technical Standard. The Open Group. Retrieved January 4, 2012, from www.opengroup.org/archimate/doc/ts_archimate/.

The Open Group, 2009. TOGAF™ Version 9. Van Haren Publishing, Zaltbommel, Netherlands.

The Open Group, 2011. TOGAF™ Version 9.1. Document Number: G116, ISBN: 9789087536794. Retrieved December 16, 2011, from http://pubs.opengroup.org/architecture/togaf9-doc/arch/.

Urdhwareshe, H., 2011. Six Sigma for business excellence approach, tools and applications. Dorling Kindersley (India), New Delhi.

US Department of Commerce, 2007. Enterprise Architecture Capability Maturity Model Version: 1.2. Office of the Chief Information Office, US Department of Commerce. Retrieved December 16, 2011, from http://ocio.os.doc.gov/ITPolicyandPrograms/Enterprise_Architecture/PROD01_004935.

Ward, J.M., Peppard, J., 2003. Strategic planning for information systems, third ed. J. Wiley, Chichester etc.

Wikipedia, 2011. Strategy (Game Theory). Retrieved September 10, 2011, from http://en.wikipedia.org/wiki/Strategy_%28game_theory%29.

Weill, P., Ross, J., 2004. IT Governance: How Top Performers Manage IT Decision Rights for Superior Results. Harvard Business School Press, Boston, MA.

Winter, R., 2006. Ein Modell zur Visualisierung der Anwendungslandschaft als Grundlage der Informationssystem-Architekturplanung. In: Schelp, J., Winter, R. (Eds.), Integrationsmanagement: Planung, Bewertung und Steuerung von Applikationslandschaften. Springer, Berlin, pp. 1–30.

Womack, J.P., Jones, D.T., Roos, D., 1990. The machine that changed the world: based on the Massachusetts Institute of Technology 5-million dollar, 5-year study on the future of the automobile. Rawson Associates, New York.

Womack, J.P., Jones, D.T., 1996. Lean thinking: banish waste and create wealth in your corporation. Simon & Schuster, New York, NY.

Womack, J.P., Jones, D.T., 2005. Lean solutions: how companies and customers can create value and wealth together. Simon & Schuster, London.

Valen, L.V., 1973. A New Evolutionary Law. Evolutionary Theory 1, 1–30.

Yegge, S., 2011. Stevey's Google Platforms Rant. Plus.google.com: an internal memo on Google + that mistakenly leaked into the public domain. Retrieved January 9, 2012, from https://plus.google.com/112678702228711889851/posts/eVeouesvaVX.

Zachman, J., 1987. A Framework for Information Systems Architecture. IBM Systems Journal 26.

Zachman, J., 2008. John Zachman's Concise Definition of The Zachman Framework™. Zachman International, Inc. Retrieved December 17, 2011, from www.zachman.com/about-the-zachman-framework.

Index

Note: Page numbers followed by *b* indeicate boxes, *f* indicate figures and *t* indicate tables.

A

ACMM. *See* Architecture Capability Maturity Model (ACMM)

ADM. *See* Architecture development methodology (ADM)

Agile methodology
  architectural practice in, 172–174
  architecture scrums interlocking
    architecture and implementation track, 208*f*
    Bank4Us, pilot project, 213–215
    EA dashboard, 215–216
    future sprint, 209
    implementation and architecture sprint planning, 209
    iteration zero, 209
    MobileDevGuide, 206–207, 207*f*
    scrum patterns for, 209–215
    sprint 5, 208
    sprint planning phase, 208, 209*f*
    sprints 2 to 4, 208
  definition, 163–165
  development methods, 280
  EA Kanban board, TOGAF ADM
    architectural levels, 224–226
    breadth-first approach, 227
    card location, 227*f*
    depth-first approach, 229
    design in progress (DIP) limit, 229
    EA team and implementation projects, 231, 232*f*
    levels of granularity, 230–231, 231*f*
    Miller's Application Rationalization Program, 225*t*
    principle, 226, 226*f*
    rectangular, 230, 230*f*
    requirement cards, 227
    rules for, 226–230
    task cards, 227
  EA transition, 203–204
  foundations, collaborative EA, 138
  principles, 162–163
  requirements management
    architecture landscape, TOGAF, 218–219, 219*f*
    capability architecture, 220
    detail and time horizons translation, 218–219, 218*f*
    enterprise strategic architecture, 219
    levels of, 220–221
    TOGAF ADM iterations, 221–222
  software development
    Agile Manifesto, 167–168, 167*b*
    "anti-establishment" approach, 166–167
    complexity, 169
    Safeguard Ballistic Missile Defense System, 166
    short development cycles, 168
    traditional waterfall approach, 165–166
  technical obstacles
    budget-planning process, 172
    organizational resistance, 171
    outsourcing, 172
    process incompatibilities and culture clash, 171
    role definitions, 171
    scaling agile methods, 171
    test automation, 171

ArchiMate modeling standard
  description, 54
  design, 54
  disadvantages, 55
  pickup and delivery process, 54, 55*f*
  taxonomy, 54–55, 56*t*

Architectural conformance review (ACR), 85

Architecture
  applications, 33–34
  architectural thinking
    communication, 33
    modeling, 32
    relevance of, 32, 33*f*
    visualization, 33
  blueprint, 35
  business-IT management, 35*b*
  definition of, 32
  software-intensive systems, 31
  stakeholders, 32

Architecture capability framework
  aspects of, 118
  concepts
    board, 116
    compliance, 117
    contract, 117
    maturity model, 118
    skills framework, 118
  description, 115–118

Architecture capability maturity model (ACMM)
  capability areas, 131
  criteria, 131, 131*t*
  description, 130
  maturity levels, 130–131

Architecture content framework
  content meta model
    categories, 114–115
    description, 114
    entity-relationship diagram, 114, 116*f*
    representation, 114, 115*f*
    viewpoints, 115, 117*f*
  description, 114
Architecture continuum mashup (ACM), 265–270, 277
  application landscape mashup and microblog, 268*f*, 269*f*
  benefits, 270, 278
  common system architectures, 266
  Design and design, boderline, 266*f*
  foundation architectures, 266
  industry architectures, 267
  microblogging, 270
  Open Group, 267*f*
  organization-specific architectures, 267
Architecture development methodology (ADM)
  description, 111
  iterations, 111, 113*f*
  module, 113
  phases of, 110, 112*f*
  requirements management, 111, 112*f*
  waterfall software development life cycle, 111, 111*f*
Ashby's law, 143–144, 146

C

Capability maturity model (CMM), 123
Change management microblog, 270–276, 277
  change activities, 273*f*
  collaborative EA, 283
  cumulative side effects, 272*f*
  filter criteria, 274
  fine-tune processes and information flows, 272
  integration scenarios, 274, 276, 276*f*
  IT Infrastructure Library, 274
Cluster diagram, 51, 52*f*
Collaborative EA, 283–293
  building blocks, 281*t*
  change management, 283
  elephant and rider metaphor, 285–286
  foundations (*see also* Foundations, collaborative EA)
    EA dashboard, 152–157
    reflections on complexity, 139–151
  fundamental attribution error, 284
  guidelines, 138*f*, 280
    agile, 138
    Enterprise 2.0, 138
    lean, 137
  lack of clarity, 284

  laziness and exhaustion, 284
  mapping activities EA-1 to EA-8, 282*t*
  people factors and situational constraints, 284
  success factor, 137
Common requirements vision (CRV), 120
Complexity
  complex systems
    Ashby's law, 145
    coevolution, 143
    cybernetic control system, 144, 144*f*
    edge of chaos, 146
    Law of Requisite Variety, 143–144
    management, 145
    vs. simple system, 141*t*, 143–144
    structure and behavior, 140–141
  management capabilities
    balanced hierarchy, 147, 148*f*
    connectivity, 151
    degree of autonomy, 147–148
    exponential growth, 148, 149*f*
    hierarchical organizations, 146, 151
    Law of Requisite Variety, 146
    manager illustration, 147, 147*f*
    managers network, 149, 149*f*, 150
    Metcalfe's law, 150
    network organizations, 146
    system adaptability factors, 151
    Zipf's law, 150
  management principles, 141–146
  structure and behavior, complex phenomena, 140–141
  threshing machine
    description, 139
    Laplace demon, 140
    model of, 139, 139*f*
Complex systems
  Ashby's law, 145
  coevolution, 143
  cybernetic control system, 144, 144*f*
  edge of chaos, 146
  Law of Requisite Variety, 143–144
  management, 145
  vs. simple system, 141*t*, 143–144
  structure and behavior, 140–141
Content framework. *See* Architecture content framework
Content meta model
  categories, 114–115
  description, 114
  entity-relationship diagram, 114, 116*f*
  representation, 114, 115*f*
  viewpoints, 115, 117*f*

D

Design structure matrix (DSM), 201
Dilbert Test, 42, 42*f*

E

EA dashboard
  cardboard edition, 287
  foundations
    edge of chaos, 152, 152*f*
    governance dimension criteria, 155*t*
    perspective dimension criteria, 154*t*
    representation, 153, 153*f*
    strategy dimension criteria, 156*t*
    transformation dimension criteria, 157*t*
  potential impacts, 281*f*
EA Kanban board, TOGAF ADM
  architectural levels, 224–226
  breadth-first approach, 227
  card location, 227*f*
  depth-first approach, 229
  design in progress (DIP) limit, 229
  EA team and implementation projects, 231, 232*f*
  levels of granularity, 230–231, 231*f*
  Miller's Application Rationalization Program, 225*t*
  principle, 226, 226*f*
  rectangular, 230, 230*f*
  requirement cards, 227
  rules for, 226–230
  task cards, 227
EAM. *See* Enterprise architecture management (EAM)
Edge of chaos
  complex systems, 146
  EA dashboard, 152, 152*f*, 280
Elephant and rider metaphor
  analysis paralysis, 285
  direct the rider, 285
    collaborative EA vision, 289–290
    concrete directives, 290
    find the bright spots, 289
  motivate the elephant, 285
    achievable goal, 288
    Analyze, Think, Change pattern, 286
    EA value stream analysis tools, 287
    EA waste matrix, 287
    entry level, collaborative EA, 287–288
    miracle question, 288
    See, Feel, Change pattern, 286
  shape the path, 286
    build and maintain alliances, 292
    build habits, 293

    issues, 291
    mood and confidence, 291, 292*f*
Enterprise 2.0
  McAfee's definition, 243
  participation in decisions, 258–264
    diagnostic process landscape, 259–260
    EA dashboard, 264
    ITO bazaar, 261–263
  participation in knowledge
    collaborative data modeling, 249–251
    EA dashboard, 256–257
    landscape map, 251–256
    strategy blog, 247–249
  participation in transformation
    architecture continuum mashup, 265–270
    change management microblog, 270–276
    EA dashboard, 277–278
  practices, EA activities, 27–28
  weaknesses and threats, 245–246
    flame wars, 245
    inappropriate content, 245
    wrong content, 246
  Web 2.0, 237
    advantages, 245
    aspects and gravitational core, 238*f*
    blogosphere, 239
    bull's eye, 243, 244*f*
    description of, 237
    folksonomies, 242
    long tail, 240*f*
    perpetual beta, 239
    remixability, 239
    SLATES, 243
    social software, 241, 242–243
    software principles, 239
    tag cloud, 238*f*
    viral marketing, 240
Enterprise architecture (EA)
  agile EA (*see* Agile methodology)
  applicability and use, 36–38
  application rationalization
    constraints, 64
    description, 58–59
    KPIs, 58–61
    reassessment of transformation, 64, 64*f*
    treatment strategies, 63*f*
    Ward-Peppard classification, 61–62, 62*f*
  architecture blueprint, 35
  Bank4Us technology products and standards list, 81, 82*t*
  collaborative
    Enterprise 2.0 practices, 28, 28*t*
    guidelines, 27*b*

Enterprise architecture (EA) *(Continued)*
  lean and agile practices, 28, 28*t*
  community of practices, 73–74
  competence development, 69–74
  competency area
    business acumen, 70
    capability streams, 70–71
    description, 70–71
    evaluation criteria, 71
    job rotation, 73
    organizational leadership, 71
    process excellence, 70
    skill profile, Ian Miller, 71, 71*t*
    technical expertise, 70
  complexity, 280
  core concept, 34–35, 34*f*
  definition, 34–35
  description, 1
  design structure matrix, 201
  EA dashboard, 281*f*
  EA value stream, 196–197
  EA waste matrix, 193–195, 195*t*
  failures
    analysis paralysis phenomenon, 21
    caricatures, 14, 15*t*
    change requests, 22
    chief technology mechanic, 17
    Cloud Cuckoo Land, 16
    commodities, 18
    decision-making body, 19
    Ever-Growing Backlog, 25
    Global Spark program, 23–24
    governance, 19–21
    in organizational units, 11–12
    over-ambition, 24
    overstrained technical advisors, 20
    perspective, 14–18
    pet programs, 24
    poor program management, 24
    short-term strategies, 22
    strategy, 21–22
    between success and disappointment, 12–14
    technology risks, 24
    transformation, 23–25
  formalization
    team composition, 75
    team organization, 74–75
  functional roles and responsibilities, 76*t*
  goals and benefits
    aligning business and IT, 9–11
    controlling IT complexity, 6–9
  integrated tool, 57, 57*f*

interim project reviews, 85
IT management, 35, 36*f*
IT risks
  business objectives, 101, 102*f*
  categories, 100, 101*f*
  FAIR's taxonomy, 104
  response types, 103–104
  roles, 103
  subdomains, 103
IT strategy
  business goal, 42–43
  business maxims, definition of, 43
  competitive strategy, 45
  cost efficiency, 45
  differentiation, 45
  focus strategies, 45
  fundamental business outlooks, 44–45
  Gartner grid, 46–48
  governance, 45
  initiatives, identification of, 48–49
  IT maxims, 43–44
  management by maxims process, 43
  operating models, 44, 44*f*
  role of, 49
  TOGAFT framework, 46
IT transformations, 66–67
leading/coaching projects, 98–100
lean, agile and Enterprise 2.0 practices
  activities, 27–28
  challenges, 26–27
  chaos and order, 25
  EA dashboard, 26, 26*f*
  guidelines, 27*b*, 28
lean and agile
  development methods, 280
  EA transition, 203–204
lean software development *(see* Lean software development*)*
models
  application roadmap, 51–52, 53*f*
  cluster diagram, 51, 52*f*
  description, 49–50
  flip-book visualization, 52, 53*f*
  modeling standards, 52–58
  process map, 51, 51*f*
  vs. views, 50
  visualization, 51–52
need for, 2
Open Certified Architect (Open CA) program,
    72–73
orange-squeezing effect, 18
organization structure, team position, 76–77
pipeline response matrix, 201–203

primary task, 279
process activity mapping, 197–201
  key performance indicators, 198–199
  MobileDevGuide, 199–201, 200*f*
  notation, 198*f*
  timeline, 198–199
project portfolio management
  auditing, 93–98
  description, 86
  IT-focused effort, 89–90
  IT management, 87, 87*t*
  planning process, 87–92, 88*f*
  portfolio governance process, 93, 93*f*
  project prioritization, 90–92, 91*t*
seven wastes
  defects, 191–193, 192*t*
  delays, 191, 192*t*
  handoffs, 187–190, 189*t*
  overarchitecting, 186–187, 186*t*
  partially done work, 184–185, 185*t*
  redundant processes, 187, 188*t*
  task switching, 190, 190*t*
single point of contact (SPOC), 81
SOA transformations, 67–69
socio-technical system, 35
standards and guidelines
  bottom-up approach, 79
  enforcement, 83–86
  new architectural paradigms, 83
  organizational dynamics, 84–85
  outright denial, 84
  subsurface resistance, 84
  technology classification, 79, 80*f*
  top-down approach, 78, 79
streamlining architecture process, 182–205
techniques, 3
top-down approach, 14, 17
Web 2.0 and Enterprise 2.0 participation concepts, 280
widespread acceptance scenario, 84
Enterprise architecture management (EAM)
  complexity of IT, 293
  core activities, 39–40, 40*t*
  definition, 35
  OMB EAAF, 127
  TOGAF, 110–118
Enterprise governance, 45
Enterprise service bus (ESB), 249

F

Federal Enterprise Architecture (FEA), 107, 127
Flip-book visualization, 52, 53*f*
Folksonomies, 242

Foundations, collaborative EA
  complexity management principles, 141–146
  complex systems
    Ashby's law, 145
    coevolution, 143
    cybernetic control system, 144, 144*f*
    edge of chaos, 146
    Law of Requisite Variety, 143–144
    management, 145
    vs. simple system, 141*t*, 143–144
    structure and behavior, 140–141
  EA dashboard
    edge of chaos, 152, 152*f*
    governance dimension criteria, 155*t*
    perspective dimension criteria, 154*t*
    representation, 153, 153*f*
    strategy dimension criteria, 156*t*
    transformation dimension criteria, 157*t*
  management capabilities
    balanced hierarchy, 147, 148*f*
    connectivity, 151
    degree of autonomy, 147–148
    exponential growth, 148, 149*f*
    hierarchical organizations, 146, 151
    Law of Requisite Variety, 146
    manager illustration, 147, 147*f*
    managers network, 149, 149*f*, 150
    Metcalfe's law, 150
    network organizations, 146
    system adaptability factors, 151
    Zipf's law, 150
  structure and behavior, complex phenomena, 140–141
  threshing machine
    description, 139
    Laplace demon, 140
    model of, 139, 139*f*
Frameworks
  description, 106
  FEA, 107
  future specifications, 107–108
  Gartner methodology
    CRV, 120
    description, 119
    effort in EA, 120
    top-down approach, 119
  methods, 106–107
  role and use, 121
  TOGAF
    ADM, 111–114
    architecture capability framework, 115–118
    architecture content framework, 114–115
    basic parts, 110

Frameworks *(Continued)*
description, 110
Zachman framework
classification schema, 110
composite model, 110
description, 108
representation, 108, 109*f*
rules, 109–110
Fundamental attribution error, 284

G

Gartner methodology
common requirements vision (CRV), 120
description, 119
effort in EA, 120
Gartner grid, 46–48
top-down approach, 119

I

Ian's landscape map
application catalogue site, 255*f*
in architecture SSP, 253*f*
comments, 254*f*
FinS application, 256
hybrid wikis, 256
portal applications, 252*f*
Information technology (IT)
aligning business
benefits, 9–10
customer-facing business processes, 10
description, 9
goal, 9
hygiene factor, 11
controlling IT complexity
benefits, 8
complexities, 6–7
goals, 6
immature software engineering practices, 7
system redundancy, 8
infrastructure portfolio quality, 129
investment patterns, maturity models, 132–133
project portfolio management
IT-focused effort, 89–90
IT management, 87, 87*t*
risks
business objectives, 101, 102*f*
categories, 100, 101*f*
FAIR's taxonomy, 104
response types, 103–104
roles, 103
subdomains, 103
strategy

business goal, 42–43
business maxims, definition of, 43
competitive strategy, 45
cost efficiency, 45
differentiation, 45
focus strategies, 45
fundamental business outlooks, 44–45
Gartner grid, 46–48
governance, 45
initiatives, identification of, 48–49
IT maxims, 43–44
management by maxims process, 43
operating models, 44, 44*f*
role of, 49
TOGAF framework, 46
transformations, 66–67
Internet protocol version 6 (IPv6), 128
IT Infrastructure Library (ITIL), 274
IT opportunity (ITO), 261

K

Key performance indicators (KPIs)
fan-in and fan-out, 60
formulation, 67
strategic fit (SF), 59
total cost of ownership (TCO), 59
value contribution (VC), 59

L

Law of Requisite Variety, 143–144, 146
Lean, agile and Enterprise 2.0 practices, EA
activities, 27–28
challenges, 26–27
chaos and order, 25
Dashboard, 26, 26*f*
guidelines, 27*b*, 28
Lean methodology
development methods, 280
EA transition, 203–204
optimization framework, 182
production steps, 194
removal of waste, 196
waste types, 183
Lean software development
vs. agile
dissimilarities, 181, 182
similarities, 180–181, 181*t*
definition, 163–165
principles, 162–163
seven principles, 175*b*, 176*t*
build quality in statement, 177
create knowledge principle, 177–178

defer commitment, 178
deliver fast principle, 178
Optimize the whole approach, 179
Respect People principle, 179
Software Kanban, 179, 180*f*
waste elimination, 175–177
Toyota production system, 174, 175
Long tail, Web 2.0, 240, 240*f*
Loss event frequency (LEF), 104

M
Maturity models
ACMM
capability areas, 131
criteria, 131, 131*t*
description, 130
maturity levels, 130–131
assessment result, 124, 125*t*
CMM, 123
collaboration and reuse, 128
continuous maturity approach, 125
cost savings and cost avoidance, 129
CPIC integration, 128
description, 124
EA program value measurement, 129
IPv6, 128
IT infrastructure portfolio quality, 129
limitations, 134–135
maturity assessment
acedemic, 134
bureaucratic, 134
manipulative, 134
misleading, 135
subjective, 134
superfluous, 135
Maturity Grid, 124, 124*t*
mission performance, 129
MIT Center for Information System Research
IT investment patterns, 132–133
management practices, 133, 133*t*
notional state, 127
OMB EAAF
assessment criteria, 129, 129*t*
categories, 127
completion capability area, 128
description, 127
results capability area, 129
use capability area, 128–129
order taker, 127
performance improvement integration, 128
rule of thumb, 126–127
scorecard, 124

staged maturity approach, 125
US Department of Commerce, ACMM, 130–131
uses, 126
Metcalfe's law, 150
MIT Center for Information System Research
IT investment patterns, 132–133
management practices, 133, 133*t*
MobileDevGuide, 200*f*

O
ObjectPedia, 249–251
charter, 249–251
objectives, 249
SSP functions, 249
OMB Enterprise Architecture Assessment Framework (OMB EAAF)
assessment criteria, 129, 129*t*
categories, 127
completion capability area, 128
description, 127
results capability area, 129
use capability area, 128–129
Open Certified Architect (Open CA) program, 72–73

P
Participation
in decisions, 258–264
diagnostic process landscape, 259–260
EA dashboard, 264
ITO bazaar, 261–263
in knowledge
collaborative data modeling, 249–251
EA dashboard, 256–257
landscape map, 251–256
strategy blog, 247–249
in transformation
architecture continuum mashup, 265–270
change management microblog, 270–276
EA dashboard, 277–278
Perpetual beta, Web 2.0, 239
Pipeline response matrix, 201–203
Post-implementation review (PIR), 85–86
Probable loss magnitude (PLM), 104
Process activity mapping, 197–201
key performance indicators, 198–199
MobileDevGuide, 199–201, 200*f*
notation, 198*f*
timeline, 198–199
Process map, 51, 51*f*
Project portfolio management
auditing, 93–98
description, 86

Project portfolio management *(Continued)*
    IT-focused effort, 89–90
    IT management, 87, 87*t*
    planning process, 87–92, 88*f*
    portfolio governance process, 93, 93*f*
    project prioritization, 90–92, 91*t*

R
Remixability, Web 2.0, 239
Rule of thumb, 126–127

S
Safeguard Ballistic Missile Defense System, 166
Service-oriented architecture (SOA) transformations
    advantages, 68
    architecture paradigm, 67–68
SLATES, 243
Software development life cycle (SDLC), waterfall, 111, 111*f*
Strategy blog, 247–249
    customer empowerment, 247
    Oscar's blog post, 247, 248*f*

T
The open group architecture framework (TOGAF)
    ADM
        description, 111
        iterations, 111, 113*f*
        module, 113
        phases of, 110, 112*f*
        requirements management, 111, 112*f*
        waterfall software development life cycle, 111,
            111*f*
    architecture capability framework
        aspects, 118
        description, 115–118
    architecture content framework
        content meta model, 114, 115*f*, 116*f*, 117*f*
        description, 114
    basic parts, 110
    description, 110
    framework, 46
Threshing machine
    description, 139

Laplace demon, 140
    model of, 139, 139*f*

U
Unified Modeling Language (UML), 52–54

V
Viral marketing, Web 2.0, 240

W
Ward-Peppard classification of applications, 61–62, 62*f*
Waste matrix, EA, 193–194
Waterfall software development life cycle (SDLC), 111, 111*f*
Web 2.0, 237
    advantages, 245
    aspects and gravitational core, 238*f*
    blogosphere, 239
    bull's eye, 243, 244*f*
    description of, 237
    folksonomies, 242
    long tail, 240*f*
    perpetual beta, 239
    remixability, 239
    social software
        company portals, 241
        identity and network management, 242
        information management, 242
        interaction and communication, 242
        platform, 241
        SLATES, 243
        Tom Coates definition, 241
    software principles, 239
    tag cloud, 238*f*
    viral marketing, 240

Z
Zachman framework
    classification schema, 110
    composite model, 110
    description, 108
    representation, 108, 109*f*
    rules, 109–110
Zipf's law, 150

Printed and bound by CPI Group (UK) Ltd, Croydon, CR0 4YY

03/10/2024

01040322-0001